Grief and the Shaping of Muslim Communities in North India, c. 1857–1940s

Drawing on approaches from the history of emotions, Eve Tignol investigates how they were collectively cultivated and debated for the shaping of Muslim community identity and for political mobilisation in north India in the wake of the Uprising of 1857 until the 1940s. Utilising a rich corpus of Urdu sources evoking the past, including newspapers, colonial records, pamphlets, novels, letters, essays, and poetry, she explores the ways in which writing took on a particular significance for Muslim elites in north India during this period. Uncovering different episodes in the history of British India as vignettes, she highlights a multiplicity of emotional styles and of memory works, and their controversial nature. The book demonstrates the significance of grief as a proactive tool in creating solidarities and deepens our understanding of the dynamics behind collective action in colonial north India.

EVE TIGNOL is CNRS Research Fellow at the Institute of Asian Studies in Marseilles.

Grief and the Shaping of Muslim Communities in North India, c. 1857–1940s

EVE TIGNOL
French National Centre for Scientific Research

CAMBRIDGE
UNIVERSITY PRESS

CAMBRIDGE
UNIVERSITY PRESS

Shaftesbury Road, Cambridge CB2 8EA, United Kingdom

One Liberty Plaza, 20th Floor, New York, NY 10006, USA

477 Williamstown Road, Port Melbourne, VIC 3207, Australia

314–321, 3rd Floor, Plot 3, Splendor Forum, Jasola District Centre, New Delhi – 110025, India

103 Penang Road, #05–06/07, Visioncrest Commercial, Singapore 238467

Cambridge University Press is part of Cambridge University Press & Assessment, a department of the University of Cambridge.

We share the University's mission to contribute to society through the pursuit of education, learning and research at the highest international levels of excellence.

www.cambridge.org
Information on this title: www.cambridge.org/9781009297653

DOI: 10.1017/9781009297684

First published 2023

A catalogue record for this publication is available from the British Library.

Library of Congress Cataloging-in-Publication Data
Names: Tignol, Eve, 1986– author.
Title: Grief and the shaping of Muslim communities in north India, c. 1857–1940s / Eve Tignol, Le Centre national de la recherche scientifique, Irasia, Marseille.
Description: Cambridge ; New York : Cambridge University Press, 2023. | Includes bibliographical references and index.
Identifiers: LCCN 2022039234 | ISBN 9781009297653 (hardback) | ISBN 9781009297684 (ebook)
Subjects: LCSH: Muslims – India, North – Social conditions. | Muslims – India, North – Ethnic identity. | Collective memory – India, North. | Emotions – Political aspects – India, North. | India, North – Politics and government. | India – History – Sepoy Rebellion, 1857–1858.
Classification: LCC DS432.M84 T54 2023 | DDC 305.6/97054–dc23/eng/20220920
LC record available at https://lccn.loc.gov/2022039234

ISBN 978-1-009-29765-3 Hardback

Contents

Figures

Acknowledgements

This book is a significantly revised version of my doctoral thesis in history written at Royal Holloway University of London between late 2012 and early summer 2016. Since 2011, when this project first started taking shape, my thesis supervisor, Francis Robinson, has remained a continuous and inestimable source of guidance, support, and inspiration. I could not have wished for a better mentor and I will be forever grateful. Faisal Devji and Francesca Orsini, my examiners, provided the decisive encouragement and essential feedback to start the long process of transforming the thesis into a book. Its final completion owes much to the friendly and supportive research environments provided by Fonds Wetenschappelijk Onderzoek (Research Foundation, Flanders) at the Languages and Cultures Department at the University of Ghent in 2019–2021, and by the Centre National de la Recherche Scientifique at the Institute of Asian Studies (IrAsia) in 2022. Research was also supported by a Reid scholarship from Royal Holloway, the Friendly Hand Trust, Royal Holloway Postgraduate Funds, the History Department at Aligarh Muslim University, and the Institute of Asian Studies at Aix-Marseille.

I consider myself blessed to have so many kind and encouraging colleagues. Frances Pritchett, Margrit Pernau, and Pasha M. Khan in particular have generously read and commented on drafts. Parts of my research were published in the *Journal of the Royal Asiatic Society* and presented at conferences. I am grateful to the editors and to the colleagues who invited me to give talks on my work at Oxford (Elizabeth Chatterjee, Sneha Krishnan, and Megan Robb), Chicago (Daniel Morgan and Faridah Zaman), Paris (Anne Castaing, Nicolas Dejenne, and Claudine Le Blanc; Julien Levesque and Laurence Gautier), Marseilles (Nguyen Thi Phuong Ngoc), and Ghent (Eva De Clercq). In the last push, I was especially indebted to Margrit Pernau and the 'South Asia and Beyond' colloquium participants at the Max-Planck Institute Berlin, to Markus Daechsel and the Frontier Urbanism project at Royal Holloway, and to the directors and researchers of the Centre d'Etudes de l'Inde et de l'Asie du Sud, Paris. In India, I wholeheartedly thank Abdur Rasheed, Kamal Abdul Nasir, Waseem Raja, Ashraf Rafi, the late Asghar Abbas, Chander Shekhar, Karen Leonard, Hilal Ahmed, Ali Nadeem Rezavi, and Mohammad Khalid, who all have been incredibly welcoming and generous with their time and resources. Over the course of this research, many other colleagues and friends offered me assistance, helped me refine my ideas and correct many mistakes or simply supported me. Special thanks to Alain Désoulières, Megan Robb, Layli Uddin, Laurence Gautier, Anne Castaing, Soheb Niazi, Julien Columeau, Hamid Moein, Javed Wani, Hur Hassnain, Sumbul Jamal, Richard Williams, Maryam Sikander, and Sanjeev Nagpal.

The British Library kindly granted me copyright permission for the pictures reproduced in Chapter 3. I much appreciated Aliki-Anastasia Arkomani's painstaking search for material at the British Library, and the help of librarians and archivists in Delhi, Aligarh, Hyderabad, Oxford, London, Cambridge, Marseilles, and Chicago. Without the *rekhta.org* digitising project this research would have been near impossible, especially in the last two years. I further thank the two anonymous press reviewers and the editors at Cambridge University Press for guiding me through the last stages of this book.

For almost a decade now, Nuzhat Farzana has patiently corrected my *talaffuz*, read with me through volumes of depressing Urdu poetry, and opened her home and heart: *dil se shukriyah*. Any errors in translation or interpretation are of course my own. Finally, my deepest thanks go to my family: my parents for everything; Céline and Jean for thought-provoking discussions; Martin and Thomas for their contagious joyfulness and Matthieu for his patience, constructive criticism, and love.

Note on Transliteration

This book mainly uses textual sources in Urdu. All translations are mine unless otherwise stated. A glossary of useful and recurrent terms is found at the end.

Proper names appear un-transliterated, according to their common usage in English, for example Mohamed Ali rather than Muḥammad ʻAli. In case the English transliteration of proper names is not known, a simplified transliteration without diacritics is applied. Place names are either spelled according to their common modern English usage or according to the predominant form used in the sources. All other words from Urdu (or Persian and Arabic) are transliterated with diacritical markings as described below and italicised, except for the terms that are widely used in English scholarship and are included in the *Oxford English Dictionary* (e.g. ulama, haveli, Nawab).

Rendering the Urdu through roman transliteration is a nightmare, especially for poetry, because it does not always accurately replicate pronunciation. I have tried to be as consistent as possible but in some instances I have taken liberties with short vowels, especially before a *chhoṭī he*, to reflect pronunciation better, as with *Dehlī* instead of *Dihlī*. I have transliterated according to the spelling of the original Urdu material: for instance only the nun ġhunnahs noted in my sources are transliterated.

ا	a/i/u	ڑ	ṛ	م	m
آ (and medial and final ا)	ā	ز	z	ن	n
ب	b	ژ	zh	و	au/ū/o/w
پ	p	س	s	ہ	h
ت	t	ش	sh	ی	ī/y
ٹ	ṭ	ص	ṣ	ے	ai/e
ث	ṡ	ض	ẓ	ء	ʼ
ج	j	ط	t̤	ں	ṇ
چ	ch	ظ	z̤	ھ	h
ح	ḥ	ع	ʻ		
خ	k͟h	غ	ġh	izāfat	-e
د	d	ف	f	zer	i
ڈ	ḍ	ق	q	zabar	a
ذ	ż	ک	k	pesh	u
ر	r	ل	l		

Abbreviations

AIG	*Aligarh Institute Gazette*
AMU	Aligarh Muslim University, Aligarh
BL	British Library, London
DSA	Delhi State Archives, New Delhi
INC	Indian National Congress
IOR	India Office Records, London
JMI	Jamia Millia Islamia, New Delhi
NAI	National Archives of India, New Delhi
NMML	Nehru Museum and Memorial Library, New Delhi
NNRNWP&O	Native Newspapers Reports for the North-Western Provinces and Oudh
SJM	Salar Jung Museum Library, Hyderabad
UP	United Provinces

Introduction

In the 1890s, Muhammad Husain Azad (1830–1910), a famous Urdu writer, rushed to Muslim reformer Syed Ahmed Khan's house in Aligarh in a fit of madness and confessed that he was hearing the voices of ancient masters dictating a book (*Darbār-e Akbarī*, published in 1898).[1] The fact that the past haunted Indian elites after the establishment of British rule in northern India was not only anecdotal. After 1857, writing about the past emerged as a prime concern, as the 'enormous public "enthusiasm for history"'[2] led local communities to engage with the writing of their genealogies, newspaper editors to report on failures to preserve the built heritage, and Urdu poets to romantically recall pre-colonial times. Deep changes in ways of living, being informed, and consuming – as social scientists have argued – gave rise to gradual and profound feelings of rupture and disconnectedness in modern, and certainly even more so in colonised, societies.[3] In order to face and adapt to new circumstances, memory has often been considered a way of maintaining or reconstructing identity continuity. As Wulf Kansteiner has argued: 'memory is valorized where identity is problematized'.[4]

In 1983, Benedict Anderson underlined the importance of the past for the articulation of national identities, with the significant play between memory and forgetting, and its role in the elaboration of a narrative of 'imagined' communities.[5] The 'ideologisation' of memory driven by collective identity politics indeed usually takes the form of narratives of reconfiguration through changes in emphasis,

[1] A. Farrukhi, *Muḥammad Ḥusain Āzād*, vol. 1, pp. 362–3 quoted in F. W. Pritchett, *Ab-e Hayat*, p. 6.
[2] D. Chakrabarty, 'The Public Life of History', p. 170.
[3] P. Connerton, *How Modernity Forgets*, p. 143. See also S. Boym, *The Future of Nostalgia*.
[4] W. Kansteiner, 'Finding Meaning in Memory', p. 184.
[5] B. Anderson, *Imagined Communities*, p. 205.

erasing, and retellings,which can lead to the development of what Eric Hobsbawm called 'invented traditions'.[6] As has been emphasised in recent decades, the past in contemporary South Asia is often claimed to create identity by a variety of actors, even when it is 'historically invalid'.[7] Before the 'history wars', the 'partisan passions', or the 'veritable festival of tradition invention' of the 1930–1940s, writings about the past had played a crucial role in the creation of collective identities since the late nineteenth century.[8] While many studies on South Asia have focused on 'official' memory politics – how colonial memory was imposed upon Indian minds,[9] or how monuments or school textbooks have shaped particular visions of nationality[10] – scholars have also interrogated memory narratives in the vernacular.

Partha Chatterjee was one of the first to respond to Anderson's study from a South Asian perspective. Against the latter's suggestion that non-Western countries developed nationalism as a derivation from Western forms of nationality, Chatterjee argued for South Asia's alternative construction of the concept of the nation in the spiritual domain, notably through analyses of historical narratives.[11] In his steps, Sudhir Chandra explored nineteenth-century literature to recover 'the vernacular mind',[12] Sudipta Kaviraj researched the emergence of nationalist discourse in Bankim Chandra Chattopadhyay's late nineteenth-century writings,[13] and Vasudhia Dalmia undertook a similar task for the Hindi literary figure of Bharatendu Harishchandra (1850–1885).[14] Francesca Orsini carried on Dalmia's work by studying

[6] See E. Hobsbawm 'The Invention of Tradition'; see also P. Ricoeur, *La mémoire, l'histoire, l'oubli*, pp. 579–80.

[7] R. Thapar, 'Somnatha: Narratives of History', p. 49 quoted in D. Chakrabarty, 'The Public Life of History', p. 169.

[8] D. Chakrabarty, 'The Public Life of History', p. 180.

[9] See, for instance, G. Chakravarty, *The Indian Mutiny and the British Imagination*; I. Sengupta (ed.), *Memory, History, and colonialism*; S. Kavuri-Bauer, *Monumental Matters*; H. Ahmed, *Muslim political discourse*.

[10] In South Asia, textbook studies have particularly emerged after the rise of the Janata Party coalition in India and Zia ul-Haq's regime in Pakistan in the late 1980s. For example, V. C. P. Chaudhary, *Secularism versus Communalism*; K. K. Aziz, *The Murder of History*; S. Guichard, *The Construction of History*.

[11] P. Chatterjee, *The Nation and Its Fragments*. See also P. Chatterjee, *Nationalist Thought and the Colonial World*.

[12] S. Chandra, *The Oppressive Present*, p. 12.

[13] S. Kaviraj, *The Unhappy Consciousness*.

[14] V. Dalmia, *The Nationalization of Hindu Traditions*.

the role of history in inspiring a collective sense of belonging in the early twentieth-century Hindi public sphere.[15] Representations of the past by important nineteenth- and twentieth-century Muslim figures such as Syed Ahmed Khan (1817–1898), Altaf Husain Hali (1837–1914), and Muhammad Iqbal (1877–1938) have also been considered the 'foundational' textual basis for a distinct Muslim national identity, and symptoms of the so-called two-nation theory that would divide nations on the basis of religion in 1947.[16] More recently, scholars have, however, emphasised the plurality of vernacular imaginings of the past and their much-debated nature in order to complicate the history of Muslim nationalism in the Urdu-speaking public sphere.[17]

My work initially aimed at addressing the role of memory among the Indo-Persian elites who used to revolve around the Mughal court – the Urdu-speaking *ashrāf*, or the 'respectable' (the nobility, and then middle classes) – as they negotiated the loss of secular power, and colonial rule.[18] The project started with the identification of a corpus of primary source material produced by those elites that engaged with the past. Besides searching through secondary sources and archival catalogues, I systematically read the *Native Newspapers Reports for the North Western Provinces* (and then *United Provinces*) *and Oudh* to identify significant episodes, and actors, in the region from 1864 to 1937. I simultaneously skimmed through volumes of prominent vernacular periodicals (*Aligarh Institute Gazette*, *Tahẕib ul-Ak̲h̲lāq*, *Hamdard*, *The Comrade*, and *Al-Hilāl*) and Urdu literary sources. Paying attention to Muslim *ashrāf* as well as to the Hindu Urdu-speaking scribal castes who used to work in Mughal administration (the Kayasths, Khatris, and Kashmiri Brahmins), I also read through

15 F. Orsini, *The Hindi Public Sphere*.

16 See, for instance, M. A. Raja, *Constructing Pakistan: Foundational Texts*. For critical studies on Muslim separatism: P. Brass, *Language, Religion and Politics*; F. Robinson, *Separatism among Indian Muslims*; F. Shaikh, *Community and Consensus*; M. Hasan, *Nationalism and Communal Politics*; A. Jalal and S. Bose (eds.), *Nationalism, Democracy and Development*; A. Jalal, *Self and Sovereignty*; F. Shaikh, *Making Sense of Pakistan*; M. Hasan, *From Pluralism to Separatism*.

17 See recently J. Dubrow, *Cosmopolitan Dreams*; M. Robb, *Print and the Urdu Public*; S. A. Zaidi, *Making a Muslim*; A. Khan Mahmudabad, *Poetry of Belonging*.

18 For more on the category of the *ashrāf* during that period, see M. Pernau, *Ashraf into Middle Classes*.

as many issues of *Zamānah*, *Awadh Punch*, and *Kayastha Samachar and Hindustan Review*, whose editors and/or contributors were usually non-Muslims.

Through this varied corpus, I address the ways in which the past was imagined and written in Urdu, focusing on different episodes – as vignettes – of the history of British north India from 1857 to the late 1930s. Although I foresee the important developments of the 1930s–1940s, I do not delve into the Pakistan movement or into the complex memory narratives that fed communal politics around the Partition of 1947. If, as Congino argued, one of the main contributions of memory studies has consisted in shedding light on 'politics of memory',[19] I do not use memory or emotions to 'explain' the ultimate success of communal politics in British India. As scholars have indeed warned, memory should not be considered an outcome but a complex social process of cultural production and consumption. It should take into account the intellectual and cultural traditions which fashion representations, 'memory makers' (those who produce works of memory), and audiences that respond to those productions.[20] By considering both well-known and less researched sources and actors, and by including the rich and dynamic periodical archive, I emphasise the multiplicity and heterogeneous character of Urdu writings on the past. Works of memory are manifold, lively, and debated, and their significance transforms according to the historical context and to who reads them too.[21]

In many aspects, this book is like a *dvija* (twice-born), as Mohamed Ali characterised his Urdu daily *Hamdard* in 1913: while the doctoral dissertation that gave birth to this book engaged more with the argument of memory in 2016, it gradually refocused less on how the past was represented and more on how it was invested with feelings. I soon measured the powerful affective dimension of my material. One typical vernacular (and emotional) way of remembering the past, which cut through much of the corpus, is the Urdu poetic genre of *shahr āshob* (literally 'the devastation of the city'). While the genre first served to lament

[19] A. Congino, 'Collective Memory and Cultural History: Problems of Method', p. 1393.

[20] W. Kansteiner, 'Finding Meaning in Memory', p. 179.

[21] For instance, Avril Powell and Seema Alavi have emphasised the controversies that historical representations of the past triggered in relation to textbooks or stories of 1857: A. Powell, 'History Textbooks and the Transmission of the Pre-colonial Past'; S. Alavi, 'Rethinking Religion and Politics'.

the ruin of north Indian cities (sometimes with a typical satiric tone), it became increasingly associated with the elegy (*marṡiyah*) after 1857. It continues to be practised today. The special status of poetry in South Asia and in Urdu especially is well known: poems regularly appeared in letters, essays, periodicals, and political gatherings.[22] This justified taking it into account thoughtfully. My exploration into memory works was thus complemented by an analysis of the evolution of the *shahr āshob* genre. Nevertheless, I am not interested in writing a literary history as such, rather a cultural history of emotion for which poetry is a major source. This allows me to reassess the history of British north India in seriously taking into account sources that are sometimes dismissed or neglected by historians, but which nonetheless provide important insights into Urdu culture, representations, and emotions.

I argue that the emotional dimension of memory is precisely what gave power to it. I hence concentrate on the emotion that most powerfully emerged in relation to the past in Urdu-speaking colonial north India: *ġham* (grief). Whether it was pre-1857 Mughal rule, the time of the Prophet, or the glorious Muslim kingdoms of Andalusia, the past was usually described within a semantic web of pain, nostalgia, and regret in Urdu sources. Characterising that grief and showing how diverse actors engaged with it, transformed it, and used it in a variety of contexts, this book explores how grief acted in turn as a driving force in the history of British India. Without minimising the impact of British epistemologies, and, in fact, sometimes hinting at intersecting considerations of collective feelings, I explore how grief and memory provided 'new frames of action'.[23] As Rana Iqbal argued about the force of contemporary Pakistani *marṡiyah*-poetess Taswir Fatima: 'When something is written under the influence of sorrow, it's definitely effective'.[24] How emotions can be 'effective', however, is a relatively recent question of historians.

1 Emotions and Memory in History

Memory and emotions emerged as objects of history around the same time, with the development of *new history* by the Annales School and of Cultural Studies, which opened the fields of 'mentalities',

[22] About Urdu poetry and political mobilisation, see C. Petievich, 'From Court to Public Sphere'.
[23] A. Assmann (ed.), *Memory and Political Change*, p. 4.
[24] A. Bard, 'Value and Vitality in a Literary Tradition', p. 332.

representations, and 'sensibility'.[25] Until the beginning of the twentieth century, as Damien Boquet and Piroska Nagy have explained, the urge to 'rationalise' history as a scientific discipline led historians to focus mainly on economic and political history – the history of 'facts'.[26] In the 1950s, the discipline benefited from the development of social constructionism and of disciplines that questioned the traditional opposition between heart and reason (cognitive psychology, neurosciences, philosophy of mind). This provided new ground for historical research.[27] Until then, and Norbert Elias' work on the 'civilising process' provides good evidence, emotions were usually seen as primitive, human instincts that needed to be both controlled and rationalised in order to bring about an advanced modern civilisation.[28] Feelings were 'considered to be part of a universal, natural, heritage, beyond the cultural, and thus unhistoricisable'.[29]

With theories of social constructionism, individual cognitive processes like memory and emotions were to be understood as being developed and maintained by social interactions. Maurice Halbwachs first described memory as a social construct in his two main works, *The Social Frameworks of Memory* (1925) and *On Collective Memory* (published posthumously in 1950), since 'in reality we are never alone'.[30] In *The Social Frameworks of Memory*, Halbwachs took the example of his visit to London. He walked by himself only in appearance: while passing by Westminster, he thought about what he had read in a travel guide; looking at St Paul's Cathedral, he remembered some novel read in his childhood; admiring the view on the Thames, he thought of what a friend once told him; and so on. Eventually, his own recollections of London were the shared memories of the groups to which he belonged.[31] While he maintained that it is the work of individuals to remember, the process of remembering itself relies on

[25] L. Febvre, 'La sensibilité et l'histoire'. Johan Huizinga's *Herfsttij der Middeleeuwen* was published in 1921.

[26] D. Boquet and P. Nagy, *Politiques des émotions au Moyen Âge*, p. 10.

[27] D. Boquet and P. Nagy, *Le Sujet des émotions au Moyen Âge*, pp. 16 and 19–20. See also the introduction to D. Boquet and P. Nagy, *La Chair des émotions*.

[28] For an excellent critique of Elias' work, see H. P. Duerr, *Nudité et Pudeur* and the introduction by André Burguière.

[29] D. Boquet and P. Nagy, *Le Sujet des émotions au Moyen Âge*, p. 18.

[30] M. Halbwachs, *La mémoire collective*, p. 2. [31] Ibid., pp. 2–3.

the sole condition of possibility of the existence of social groups, and also works at binding society together. Emotions too, while felt in the body, are modelled by society as 'communicative practices'[32] and 'instruments of sociability'.[33]

As is still the case today, the definition of emotions is an object of debate. Psychologists such as Paul Ekman have argued for the universality of 'basic' emotions – anger, disgust, fear, happiness, sadness, and surprise – and, on the other side of the spectrum, social constructionists have claimed that 'emotional experience is not pre-cultural but *pre-eminently* cultural'.[34] With varying degrees of adherence to social constructionism,[35] scholars of many disciplines now aim at bridging the nature–nurture divide and at understanding the relationship between 'feeling', that is, the capacity of experiencing emotion, and 'emotion', that is, the conscious act of 'translating' the emotion – what Abdul Majid Daryabadi respectively termed *ehsās* and *jazbah* in Urdu in his *Falsafah-e jazbāt* ('Philosophy of Emotions', 1914).[36]

Scholars have generally remarked that the 'material reality' of feelings cannot be easily disentangled from their interpretation, and that they 'co-produce each other in an endless loop'.[37] In *The Navigation of Feeling*, historian William Reddy suggested a dynamic relationship between emotional experience and emotional expression.[38] He criticised the social constructionists' denial of inner emotional residuum. 'No meaningful history of emotions is possible from a strong constructionist position',[39] he claimed, since it hardly allows for agency and change, but he emphasised the importance of language in the 'naming' process of emotional expression.[40] He consequently elaborated

[32] M. Scheer, 'Are Emotions a Kind of Practice?'
[33] B. Rosenwein, 'Problems and Methods', p. 19.
[34] C. A. Lutz, *Unnatural Emotions*, p. 5. See also Jean Briggs' study of the Utku Inuits, *Never in Anger*, p. 6.
[35] B. Rosenwein, 'Problems and Methods', pp. 8–10; R. Harré (ed.), *The Social Construction of Emotions*; D. Boquet and P. Nagy, *La Chair des émotions*, pp. 8–15.
[36] See C. Traïni, 'Des sentiments aux émotions (et vice-versa)'; A. Blom, 'Emotions and the Micro-foundations of Religious Activism'. About Abdul Majid Daryabadi, see M. Pernau, *Emotions and Modernity*, Chapter 8.
[37] M. Pernau, 'Introduction', p. 25
[38] W. Reddy, 'Against Constructionism', p. 329.
[39] Ibid., p. 331. [40] Ibid., p. 329.

the theory of 'emotives' to characterise the way feelings are translated into expressions that are, in turn, performative.[41] Emotives, he argued, 'do things to the world' and 'are themselves instruments for directly changing, building, hiding, intensifying emotions'.[42] It is in this capacity that emotions (or rather, for Reddy, emotives) can drive historical change.

Historians have taken on-board the theory that – at least in part – 'emotions depend on language, cultural practices, expectations, and moral beliefs. This means that *every* culture has its rules for feelings and behavior; *every* culture thus exerts certain restraints while favoring certain forms of expressivity'.[43] Even though historical sources give access only to already interpreted and mediated emotions, studying them across time provides valuable information on past and present societies. In recent decades, historians have explored how emotional norms are implemented, maintained, or refashioned through the concepts of 'emotionology',[44] 'emotional styles and regimes',[45] or 'emotional communities'.[46]

Since Lucien Febvre (1878–1956) at least, emotions have indeed been said to play an important role as social glue that, like rituals, 'cement community consciousness'.[47] The fact that adherence 'to the same valuations of emotions and their expression'[48] helps create community is essential – although the exact type of community that is thus created is debated: while Barbara Rosenwein argued that emotional communities are based on pre-existing social groups, Margrit Pernau suggested that emotions themselves have the power to create community.[49] Scholars have further argued, and this is addressed briefly in Chapter 3, that the (emotional) productions of elites and middle classes sometimes possess or have the purpose to

[41] Ibdi., p. 331. [42] Ibid., p. 332.
[43] B. Rosenwein, 'Worrying about Emotions in History', p. 837.
[44] P. Stearns, *American Cool.*
[45] W. Reddy, *The Navigation of Feeling.*
[46] B. Rosenwein, *Emotional Communities.*
[47] L. Febvre, 'La sensibilité et l'histoire' and P. Gay, *Education of the Senses: The Bourgeois Experience* quoted in E. Chatterjee, S. Krishnan, and M. Robb, 'Feeling Modern', p. 540.
[48] B. Rosenwein, 'Problems and Methods', p. 1.
[49] See Barbara Rosenwein, *Emotional Communities* and M. Pernau, 'Feeling Communities: Introduction'. I use 'emotional communities' for convenience, but I do not agree with the fact that they necessarily correspond to social groups.

cut across classes,[50] and sometimes borrow from subaltern aesthetics. Simultaneously, the pursuit of upward social mobility – or 'ashraf-isation' in Muslim South Asia – also leads lower caste groups to embrace practices and values of higher castes to improve their own social status. Regardless of the type of interactions (face-to-face, textual, imagined) in which they find expression,[51] shared emotions 'frequently spill over into feelings for those who feel (or do not feel) the same way, leading to more or less intense emotions within the community and the demarcation of its boundaries'.[52] Emotions indeed perform 'boundary work', marking identity and belonging (sometimes enabling social mobility), as well as marking distinction.[53]

Historians of South Asia are, of course, already contributing to this expanding field, exploring the way emotions can create and sustain a sense of collective belonging, feed political mobilisations, or exclude. Friendship and love in pre-modern and colonial India have received special attention,[54] along with the relation between emotion and place.[55] For colonial north India, Akbar Zaidi has recently argued for the agentive role of *żillat* (humiliation) in 'encouraging [Indian] Muslims to redefine who they were'.[56] The power of emotions, such as anger, nostalgia, or hope, in initiating political mobilisation and collective action in South Asia has also been queried.[57] Emotions have further been investigated in their capacity to differentiate groups: Joel Lee, for instance, has recently studied *ghr̥ṇā* (disgust) as a way to mark hierarchies of caste.[58]

[50] D. Boquet and P. Nagy, *Le Sujet des émotions au Moyen-Âge*, pp. 38–9.

[51] Despite the fact that Benedict Anderson, as Margrit Pernau noted, did not consider emotions in his study of national identities; M. Pernau, 'Feeling Communities: Introduction', p. 5.

[52] Ibid., p. 11. [53] L. Mitchell, 'Whose Emotions?'

[54] See, among others, F. Orsini, *Love in South Asia*; D. Ali and E. Flatt, *Friendship in Pre-Modern South Asia.*

[55] For emotions and place in particular, see the special issue of *The Journal of the Economic and Social History of the Orient* devoted to the topic (vol. 58): M. Pernau, 'Mapping Emotions, Constructing Feelings'; R. Khan, 'The Social Production of Space and Emotions'; R. Khan, 'Local Pasts: Space, Emotions and Identities'; E. Chatterjee, S. Krishnan, and M. Robb, *Feeling Modern*; and D. Bredi, 'Nostalgia in the Re-construction of Muslim Identity'.

[56] A. Zaidi, *Making a Muslim*, p. 7.

[57] A. Blom and N. Jaoul, *The Moral and Affectual Dimension of Collective Action*; A. Blom and S. Tawa Lama-Rewal, *Emotions, Mobilisations and South Asian Politics.*

[58] J. Lee, 'Disgust and Untouchability'.

Due to Margrit Pernau's impulse and to the fact that language and conceptual studies have been considered valuable methodological entry points into emotions, Urdu emotional concepts have received special consideration.[59] Pernau's recent work on the transformation of emotion in colonial South Asia is outstanding: analysing the development of emotion concepts and practices in Urdu sources in the late nineteenth and early twentieth centuries, she argued that while modernity has often been associated with the disciplining of emotions, the history of colonial north India was marked by a transformation of the ideal of emotional balance into the exaltation of emotional fervour.[60]

In many ways, my understanding of grief across a similar period corroborates these findings. It also aims to complement them by exploring how 'one' emotion reflected a multiplicity of voices and practices that do not point to a linear development but to the co-existence of different emotional communities. Historians of emotions have often emphasised the importance of language, of not transposing modern Western concepts to non-European phenomena, and of exploring the evolution of concepts as an evolution of modes of thinking.[61] My close reading of a variety of sources with a special attention to their emotional vocabulary and its transformation sheds light on the evolution of emotional styles and communities. At the intersection between the intimate and the cultural and political, I argue that emotions were not just the expressions of particular communities, but proactive tools used to form a basis for solidarity and for discrimination, to shape communities, and to motivate collective action.

2 Poetry, Emotions, and Sincerity

This book relies on a variety of textual sources: colonial reports and records, conference proceedings, (banned) pamphlets, English- and Urdu-language periodicals, edited letters, essays, ethical treatises, and poetry – all of which are compared and contextualised. The reason this book draws much from the Urdu poetic genre of *shahr āshob* is

[59] C. Oesterheld, 'Changing Landscapes of Love and Passion'; C. Oesterheld, 'Campaigning for a Community'; M. Pernau, H. Jordheim, E. Saada, et al. (eds.), *Civilizing Emotions: Concepts*; M. Pernau, 'Introduction'; M. Pernau, 'Feeling Communities'; M. Pernau, 'From Morality to Psychology: Emotion Concepts'.
[60] M. Pernau, *Emotions and Modernity*.
[61] Y. Robreau, *L'honneur et la honte*, p. 7.

not merely due to my own conscious selection, but to the fact that the practice of the genre was popular across the period and spontaneously appeared in the corpus. As Barbara Rosenwein has discussed:

> The constraints of genre admittedly pose a problem. Might not the well-meaning historian mistake a particular genre, with its rules of expression, for an 'emotional community'? [...] The rules of genre were not, however, ironclad. They themselves were 'social products'—elaborated by people under certain conditions and with certain goals in mind – and they could be drawn upon and manipulated with some freedom.[62]

The codes of the *shahr āshob* genre were indeed mobile and blurry, and studying their transformation and adjustment – sometimes confrontation – by different writers highlights important changes in the way grief operated from 1857 to the 1930s.

Cultural historians have increasingly considered popular literature as a legitimate source to understand concepts, representations, and emotions, underlining deep connections between texts and contexts.[63] The debate around the relevance of poetry as a historical source has crystallised in Urdu scholarship with the dispute between Frances W. Pritchett and Ralph Russell in the 1990s. In her 1994 *Nets of Awareness*, Frances Pritchett claimed 'any attempt to move from poetic imagery to social reality [...] is destined to break down'.[64] Ralph Russell challenged this view, emphasising the historical embeddedness of Urdu poetry. He himself used the Urdu *ġhazal* (a highly conventional form of poetry) to shed light on elements of poets' biographies.[65] I do not resort to poetry to explain any specific aspect of its composers' lives, and indeed it might be difficult to do so compellingly, as Frances Pritchett highlighted. But I support the view that poetry – however conventional – is a reflection of the society that produces it. As Laurel Steele argued about Altaf Husain Hali's famous poem (1879), which will be examined in Chapter 2, 'conditions in the society created a place for the *Musaddas* – it could not have been written in Lucknow in 1840, for Indian Muslims as a group had not undergone

[62] B. Rosenwein, *Emotional Communities*, p. 27.
[63] For instance, the literary current of *new historicism*, since Stephen Greenblatt, has emphasised the need to extent 'attention to the historical contexts in which literary texts originate.' H. White, 'New Historicism: A Comment', p. 293.
[64] F. W. Pritchett, *Nets of Awareness*, p. 176.
[65] For instance, R. Russell and Kh. Islam, *Three Mughal Poets.*

the traumatic change which created the need for a unity to be made out of the fragmented parts of a destroyed culture'.[66] It is not in my capacity to provide an appreciation of the literary value of poetry, or 'to discover why Mir and Ghalib tower above their contemporaries', as Pritchett does admirably.[67] The poetry presented in this book was not selected according to such criteria, but according to popularity, and political or cultural relevance. I am not a translator of poetry either: I examine the meaning and language of poetry more than I attempt to convey the beauty of its form and expression – whenever possible, I have used available translations.

Linked to the complex relationship between art and reality, Pritchett has further pointed at the issue of sincerity in poetic texts that are constrained by convention: can any 'genuine' emotion be recovered from the Urdu *ġhazal*? Much criticism of the authenticity of feelings in Urdu poetry originated from the strong disapproval of overly romantic and 'unnatural' traditional Urdu poetry by late nineteenth-century poets of the New School of Urdu literature, such as Azad and Hali. They criticised the ornate and metaphorical poetry of their predecessors, claiming that their emotions and subjects were false. In contrast, they proposed new avenues towards simplicity (*sādgī*), truth (*aṣliyat*), and emotion (*josh*). The approach was very much shaped by the Victorian context, and influenced by literary criticism from the British poets Milton and Coleridge.[68]

In his *Muqaddamah-e shiʿr-o shāʿirī* (1890), Hali clearly asserted the highly emotional nature that was to be desired in poetic expression: first, he explained that the inspiration of the poet is *josh* (emotion) that 'springs from the true feelings of the poet'.[69] It is the quality of the poet to feel everything and to express it:

> It is the god-gifted skill of poets to be affected by everything, to partake to everyone's happiness or grief, and to be intoxicated by everyone's feelings (*jazbāt*). He can express in language the state of things that cannot speak in a manner so that even if the things did have a tongue, they would not be able to express their own state any better.[70]

[66] L. Steele, 'Hali and His *Muqaddama*', p. 20.
[67] F. W. Pritchett, 'On Ralph Russell's Reading of the Classical Ghazal', p. 199.
[68] L. Steele, 'Hali and His *Muqaddama*', p. 19; S. R. Faruqi, '*Sādgī, aṣliyat aur josh*'.
[69] Ibid. p. 35; Hali, *Muqaddamah-e shiʿr-o shāʿirī*, p. 112.
[70] Ibid, p. 32; Hali, *Muqaddamah-e shiʿr-o shāʿirī*, p. 65.

It was not enough for Hali that poetry stem from the poet's true feelings. While he argued that 'poetry is dependent (*tābeʿ*) on society',[71] poetry also has the power of *affecting* society, and it is in this respect that poetry could be useful. Through emotions, poetry could mobilise for action, as Arab poets motivated armies before war:

It is not only intended that the poet recite poetry in a state of fervour (*josh*) or that fervour be displayed by the statement of the poem (*shiʿr ke bayān se*), but it is also necessary, in addition to that, that fervour grow in the hearts of the addressees (*mukẖāṯab*).[72]

[...] People listening to poetry are certainly affected by it. Sometimes, through listening to poetry, feelings of enthusiasm and pleasure are elicited, and other times grief and sadness are created. When poetry is effective, it can be very useful.[73]

In fact, if anything, what Hali testified to is the sincerity of the emotion of 'New' Urdu literature. That he claimed his predecessors were not genuine only served to prove that *he* was. His is actually a statement of the sincerity of poetic emotions.

Historians have remarked that unless the sources themselves worry about their own sincerity, we need not worry.[74] Given the intertwined processes of felt and expressed emotions, historians usually agree that historical sources remain 'representations [...] about how some people think that they feel'.[75] What would their 'real' emotion be other than what they express it to be? Is it at all relevant to wonder if Iqbal was sad when he wrote his nostalgic *Ṣiqliyah* ('Sicily')? While we can argue that the very practice of the genre would have elicited *ġham* in him at least temporarily, as a historian, I am more preoccupied with documenting emotional expression and its transformation through time than with recovering whether individuals 'really' felt what they expressed. Throughout the book, I nonetheless indicate as much as possible how texts were said to be delivered (e.g. the 'tone' of poetic recitation) and how the audience was reported to have reacted (e.g. the shedding of tears).

71 Hali, *Muqaddamah-e shiʿr-o shāʿirī*, p. 17.

72 S. R. Faruqi, '*Sādgī, aṣliyat aur josh*', p. 198, quotes Hali, *Muqaddamah-e shiʿr-o shāʿirī* (ed?), p. 68.

73 L. Steele, 'Hali and his *Muqaddamah*', p. 24; Hali, *Muqaddamah-e shiʿr-o shāʿirī*, p. 3.

74 B. Rosenwein, 'Problems and Methods', p. 21. See also J. Plamper, 'The History of Emotions: An Interview', p. 258.

75 Ibid.

The issue of sincerity in fact arises in another way in the corpus: not because actors question their own emotions – that would be an interesting problem – but because the lampooning or challenging of rival communities' emotions occasionally occurred. Those attacks on emotional authenticity would always emanate from adversaries who aimed to discredit the other group, like Hali did when he blamed traditional poets of fraud. This points instead to the delineation of clashing emotional styles and communities and to the marking of distinctions. This is particularly evident in the Aligarh–Congress controversy (Chapter 2), when pro-Congress *Awadh Punch* contributors mocked the grief of Aligarh partisans. It is also conspicuous when the colonial state refused to yield to the claims of 'Young Party' leaders by disbelieving the sincerity of their feelings in 1913, prompting the latter to express them further (Chapter 3).

3 Translating *ġham*

When writing about sadness in Urdu, particularly in relation to the past, scholars have generally used the English 'nostalgia', which is often defined as a melancholic evocation of the past. Nostalgia has indeed received a great deal of scientific attention since the late seventeenth century. The term originally appeared in the work of Johannes Hofer, a doctor from Basel in Switzerland, who was the first to characterise what was then conceived as a serious pathology. Observed among Swiss soldiers abroad, the nostalgic condition (from the Greek *nostos* 'return' and *algia* 'pain') included symptoms such as fever, anxiety, and palpitations.[76] Most patients suffered from hallucinations and 'erroneous representations' that caused them 'to lose touch with the present'.[77] Although death sometimes seemed imminent despite treatments such as 'hypnotic emulsions' or opium, a return home guaranteed prompt and total recovery. Nostalgia as a disease continued to interest physicians throughout the eighteenth and nineteenth centuries: fears of an epidemic scared American doctors in the post–Civil War period, while Scot soldiers were forbidden to play bagpipes and sing native tunes suspected to cause nostalgia.[78] Nostalgia was

[76] G. Rosen, 'Nostalgia: A "Forgotten" Psychological Disorder', p. 342.
[77] S. Boym, *The Future of Nostalgia*, p. 3. [78] Ibid., pp. 4 and 6.

not only perceived to be an individual condition but could become a serious public threat.[79]

Although nostalgia was initially understood as a longing for home – a sort of homesickness – it is now usually thought of in temporal terms.[80] Svetlana Boym argued that 'changing conceptions of time' (modernity, revolutions, the fall of empires) generated nostalgia.[81] She distinguished two main types: one restorative and the other reflective. For Boym, restorative nostalgia focuses on the *nostos* and the restoration of the past, while reflective nostalgia emphasises the *algia* in a more contemplative attitude.[82] Vernacular nostalgia has also been associated in colonial worlds with 'an early stage' of resistance,[83] and with subaltern forms of protest and dissent.[84] As scholars have unanimously remarked, one of the essential elements of nostalgia is idealisation: the past (even if never lived)[85] is always imbued with positive qualities.

Like nostalgia, melancholy historically evokes mental illness and physical disorders, both in the West and in Islamic societies: humoural medicine considered that the accumulation of 'black bile' (melancholy) in the body resulted in different types of mania and depression, depending on the affected body part.[86] The illness also usually included sleeplessness, phobias, and distorted perceptions. On one occasion, Ibn Sina described one of his patients who suffered from melancholy and was convinced they were a cow.[87] In 1918, in his important *Mourning and Melancholia*, Freud contrasted melancholy with the normal work of mourning: he explained that whereas a normal subject grieves an identified loss, a melancholic subject unconsciously reports the loss of the loved object into a loss of ego, which makes the process of mourning impossible. Melancholy was pathological, unresolvable grieving.[88] Melancholy has equivalents in Urdu (*mālīk͟hūliyah*, and *saudā* linking

[79] Ibid., p. 6. [80] A. Santesso, *A Careful Longing*, p. 15.
[81] S. Boym, *The Future of Nostalgia*, p. 7.
[82] Ibid., p. 16. [83] A. Bonnett, *Left in the Past*, p. 91.
[84] P. Ricoeur, *La mémoire, l'histoire, l'oubli*, p. 583.
[85] A. Appadurai calls it 'armchair nostalgia'; see A. Appadurai, *Modernity at Large*, p. 78.
[86] G. Blamberger and V. Nutton, 'Melancholy', online (last accessed 28 March 2022).
[87] I. Abdel-Sattar, 'Saudi Arabia', in *The Oxford Handbook of the History of Psychology*, p. 444.
[88] S. Freud, 'Mourning and Melancholia'.

blackness, madness, and depression),[89] but the concept of nostalgia does not translate easily and straightforwardly: the Qur'anic *ḥuzn* more generically alludes to sorrow,[90] *ḥasrat* evokes regret, *udāsī* solitude, and *yād* ('memory') does not necessarily encapsulate the idea of longing.

Instead, the term that appeared most often in my sources was *ġham*. *Ġham* is an inclusive and generic word for grief in Urdu.[91] It stems from the Arabic root *ġh-m-m*, 'to cover' 'because it veils, or precludes, happiness'.[92] In Arabic, it is associated with darkness, like clouds, and with a veil, like grief. In this book, I generally translate *ġham* into English as grief – although I occasionally use synonyms to vary my prose or to better reflect the contextual usage. Of course, translation is bound to be treason, and it is especially hard to translate accurately, if this is even possible at all, a polysemic umbrella term like *ġham*. While nostalgia and melancholy could occasionally match the emotion expressed in some sources, I have preferred to refrain from uniformly using such semantically loaded terms in order to avoid imposing too tight a framework on the material. Of course, I could, and did sometimes, translate *ġham* as nostalgia, but I usually favoured grief for its etymological connection in English with 'grievance', which the Urdu also sometimes conveyed, but most importantly for its stronger associations with the experience of loss.[93] In traditional ethical treatises (*akh̲lāq*), since al-Kindi (801–873) at least, sadness was closely tied to 'the loss of an object of love or the missing of things desired'[94] – also intrinsically implying some kind of memory or expectation.

That said, *ġham* often did not appear in isolation in the sources but in relation to many terms. It was at the core of rich semantic nods which linked physical suffering and mourning (*dard*, *mātam*) to amorous longing and separation (*armān*, *dāġh*); sad loneliness (*udāsī*) to sympathy (*hamdardī*); hopeless depression (*māyūsī*, *afsurdagī*) to fuming lament (*shikāyat*, *āzurdagī*); anxiety (*fikr*) to regret (*ḥasrat*).

[89] Sayyid Ahmad Dehlawi, *Farhang-e āsafiyah*, vol. 3 (1898).
[90] On *hüzn*, see, for instance, O. Pamuk, *Istanbul: Memories and the City*. *Ḥuzn* is also used to describe the way Muslims must recite the Qur'an, with a certain 'sadness'; see G. S. Gregg, *The Middle East: A Cultural Psychology*, pp. 117–8.
[91] 'Gham', in J. T. Platts, *A Dictionary of Urdu*, p. 173.
[92] E. W. Lane, 'gham', in *Arabic-English Lexicon*, p. 2290.
[93] G. A. Bonanno, L. Goorin, and K. C. Coifman, 'Sadness and Grief', p. 798.
[94] Gh. Jayyusi-Lehn, 'The Epistle of Ya'kub ibn Ishaq al-Kindi', p. 122.

I have remained attentive to the different semantic webs created around *ġham*. In each chapter, I have emphasised how different actors played with different connotations of *ġham* and how this impacted collective activity. At times, *ġham* was described as physical pain, at others as a sign of hopefulness. As psychologists have highlighted, grief is far from a one-dimensional emotional phenomenon, and sometimes rather counter-intuitively involves positive effects – especially perhaps in Islam, where suffering is often valued.[95] Despite the fact that scholars have shown that emotions are often gendered – and *ġham* particularly[96] – I only very briefly allude to gender in Chapter 4.

4 Outline of the Book

This book explores how memory and grief are invoked and interpreted in different ways by different actors, and how this impacted the history of colonial north India. It documents different 'shades' of grief, emphasising a multiplicity of voices, the evolving codes of *shahr āshob*, and the sometimes-debated nature of emotional expression in Urdu, from 1857 to the late 1930s. I start by grounding the study of *ġham* in Chapter 1 by analysing the emotional language deployed by poets after 1857, and by re-tracing the genealogy of the *shahr āshob* genre and post-1857 innovations. I highlight how the aftermath of 1857 was described as traumatic through the adoption of the elegiac (*marṡiyah*) style, the association of *ġham* with *dard* (pain, suffering) and the resort to a graphic vocabulary of physical agony. The contrast between pre-1857 paradise and post-1857 Doomsday materialised in the image of the garden, which was deployed to describe the city as symbol of Mughal political order.

In Chapter 2, I examine the development of the genre in the late 1870s and its contrasts with the post-1857 period. The context of the Russo-Turkish war prompted the circulation of *shahr āshobs* in the periodical press, which expanded to mourn worldwide ruin (*dunyā āshob*; *dahr āshob*). Two distinct practices developed

95 Among others, D. E. Gill, *Melancholic Modalities*, p. 11; S. Mahmood, *Politics of Piety*; B. Grima, *The Performance of Emotion among Paxtun Women*; M. J. Delvecchio Good and B. J. Good, 'Ritual, the State, and the Transformation of Emotional Discourse'; M. Bagheri, 'Conceptualizations of Sadness in Persian'.

96 M. Bagheri, 'Conceptualizations of Sadness in Persian', p. 137; B. Grima, *The Performance of Emotion among Paxtun Women*.

simultaneously: while the *Awadh Punch* built on the inherent plaintive (*shikwah*) dimension of *ġham* to denounce oppression from the colonial state, Aligarh writers linked *ġham* to regret (*afsos*) to call their co-religionists to self-reformation. The emotional style of Altaf Husain Hali's *Musaddas* (1879) and *Shikwah-e Hind* (1888), which I relate to medieval Arabic elegies, was widely popular, and the Aligarh movement of Syed Ahmed Khan used it extensively to bolster (*ashrāf*) community cohesion. It was most noticeable in the anti-Congress campaign of 1888 when Aligarh and Congress partisans clashed in the *Awadh Punch*. Aligarh was then mocked for its manipulative recourse to emotion. The chapter ends by highlighting how Hali's poems were criticised in light of early twentieth-century communal politics.

Chapter 3 comes back to Delhi's urban pasts by examining the emotional registers of Mohamed Ali Jauhar's periodicals *The Comrade* (f. 1911) and *Hamdard* (f. 1913) during the first few years of the construction of New Delhi. Both papers reported, and mobilised Delhi's Muslim population, on the issue of urban planning and demolition works. The emotional expression of *ġham* took an increasingly anticolonial turn with the Kanpur mosque incident in 1913, when authorities denied the sincerity of Muslims' feelings. *Ġham* was no longer turned inwards as in previous reformist movements but decried as the result of colonial oppression. Much of the agitation thereafter aimed at displaying grief, as well as at claiming the right to patriotic feelings, cultivating an emotional identification between memorials of Muslim power and a pan-Indian Muslim political identity in the making.

Exploring the development of *shahr āshob* and *marṡiyah* poetry from roughly the same period and during the Khilafat movement (1919–1924), Chapter 4 looks at the way writers built on grief and lament to reclaim power and agency, and adopted a positive Sufi perception of *ġham*. Martyrdom was then hailed as the expression of love *par excellence* as grief was associated with devotion and masculinity. It is in this respect that *ġham* further nourished anti-colonial mobilisations in the 1910s–1920s. Iqbal's poetry was emblematic in proposing a new positive interpretation of grief as he turned ruins into new beginnings.

Chapter 5 follows with an analysis of the nostalgia deployed in memoirs of Mughal Delhi by local *ashrāf* prose writers in the

1910s–1930s. I argue that the idealisation of the pre-colonial local past, in contrast with a *ġham*-full present, enabled authors to face the displacement lived during the construction of the colonial capital and the growing challenges of communal tension in the city. As heterogeneous texts both recording knowledge and inducing multisensory pleasure in the manner of *qiṣṣahs* (tales), city memoirs aimed at moving the Mughal past permanently into collective fantasy and at maintaining collective identity continuity. Examining the elements of nostalgic recollection, I show that those memoirs responded to the urgencies of the present in articulating a critique of British rule and of the growth of communalism, reflecting a local Muslim collective identity that yearned for power.

1 A Garden Lost
Grief and Pain in 1857 shahr āshob *Poetry*

The Uprising of 1857, and its aftermath, is a watershed event in the history of colonial South Asia. Much has been written on its significance, both for the British and Indians, in terms of population and landscape, relationships and imaginaries. Urdu-speaking elites, particularly, saw their world crumble as quickly as the buildings around them. Many were imprisoned or openly, often collectively, executed. Muslims, thought by the British to be more responsible than Hindu subjects, were usually expelled from Delhi, one of the epicentres of the Uprising, forced to leave their belongings and properties behind.[1] In the aftermath, British officers seized a vast quantity of goods, known as the 'Delhi Prize'. When the government finally agreed to restore the confiscated properties, most Muslims, who were forbidden within the city walls until 1862, were unable to claim theirs back.[2] Like many courtiers, Ghalib (1797–1869), who had been appointed poet laureate of the Mughal court of Delhi from 1854 to 1857, lost his primary source of livelihood. He gave heartrending accounts of his degrading situation and of his daily struggle to survive in his diary, *Dastanbū*, as well as in his letters. On 31 December 1859, he wrote to his friend Husain Mirza: 'Say to yourself: We were never nobles; rank and wealth were never ours; we had no property, and never drew a pension'.[3]

1 N. Gupta, *Delhi between Two Empires*, p. 22; according to Gupta, the measure was partly attributed to the British fear of an epidemic.

2 Home Department, Public, 14 May 1858, no. 97, Proceedings of the Committee assembled at Delhi on 22 January 1858, p. 59 (about the auction of the confiscated goods): 'The Committee however do not anticipate many, if any, claims will be made on the property remaining to be disposed of, as the bulk of the prize was taken from the houses of Mussalmans [*sic*], and their owners being excluded from the town as outlaws, have no opportunity of claiming their property'.

3 Mirza Asadullah Khan Ghalib, *Ghalib, 1797–1869, vol. I: Life and Letters*, p. 226. Ghalib, *K͟hut̤ūt̤-e Ġhālib*, vol. 2, p. 608.

The collapse of the fortunes of Urdu-speaking elites was reflected by the devastation of cityscapes. The finest monuments of Lahore, Agra, Lucknow, and Delhi were destroyed or rehabilitated as chapels, hospitals, railway stations, post offices, or military quarters,[4] 'symbolic of the invincibility of British power'.[5] In Lucknow, while Begum's Kothi (Nawab Amjad Ali Shah's first queen's palace) was used as a post office, many of the Nawabs' buildings were simply pulled down and the city's finest gardens destroyed: Charbagh became a railway station and Alambagh developed as a new colony.[6] Lakhnawis lamented that 'Panch Mahala, Sangi Mahal, Hasan Manzil, etc. and other grand buildings which came under 1500 feet radius of the fort have been razed to the ground. Imambara Hasan Raza Khan, Masjids, etc. were bulldozed to the ground level'.[7] The city was unrecognisable.

In Delhi, the transformation was as dramatic: after 1857, most of the crowded areas around the Red Fort were entirely demolished. The palaces of the Nawabs of Jhajjar, Ballabgarh, Bahadurgarh, and Farrucknagar; the haveli of Nawab Wazir; Akbarabadi Masjid; and many madrasahs were destroyed.[8] Explosions were conducted in March 1859 within the fort itself and most of the remaining buildings were requested for military use. Henry Cole, curator of Ancient Monuments, reported in 1882 that 'the great pillared *Diwan-i Am*, with its fine marble mosaic canopy and throne, is used as a canteen, and on the right of the throne is a bar for serving out liquor! To the left of the throne is an enclosure of bamboo screen-work in which Nubbi Bux keeps a soldiers' coffee shop!'[9]

As Anthony King has shown, demolitions after 1857 were often justified by new colonial ideas in urban planning that mainly aimed at maintaining hygiene and control, and at dividing the urban space between public and private spheres, and native and colonial populations. After the Uprising, the colonial state began to remodel the city by introducing Western technology (railways and later electricity),

4 See *First Report of the Curator of Ancient Monuments in India for the Year 1881–82, Simla, 1882*, pp. xxiii and xxiv.

5 *Lahore Chronicle 1858,* 15 May 1858, p. 309 quoted by N. Gupta, *Delhi between Two Empires*, p. 26.

6 K. Hjortshoj, *Urban Structures and Transformations in Lucknow*, pp. 102–103.

7 N. Masood, 'Discovery of Lost Glory', p. 4.

8 K. Hjortshoj, *Urban Structures and Transformations in Lucknow*, p. 27.

9 *First Report of the Curator*, p. xxiv. For more on the British occupation of the Red Fort in the aftermath of 1857, see M. Rajagopalan, *Building Histories*, pp. 25–51.

sanitising the town (through waste disposal or water supply systems), and modifying the structure of the walled city in creating two distinct and separated spaces: 'one colonial, and primarily military and administrative, the second indigenous, and primarily residential, commercial and industrial'.[10] Apart from racial segregation, one of the most important transformations under British rule was a new emphasis on public spaces: narrow alleys gave way to wide streets, and private gardens to public parks, a novelty that, as Jyoti Hosagrahar demonstrated, did not remain devoid of tension and conflict.[11] Ghalib, who had remained in Delhi during the events, described his despair at seeing the urban landscape manifesting concretely the end of an era. In one letter dated 2 December 1859 to his friend the poet Majruh, he wrote: 'If you are coming, come along. Come and see the new road through Nisar Khan's Chatta, and the new road through Khan Chand's Lane. Come and hear how Bulaqi Begum's Lane is to be demolished and an open expanse cleared to a radius of 70 yards from the Jama Masjid. Come and see Ghalib in all his despondency (*afsurdah dil*). And then go back'.[12]

In this chapter, I investigate how the events were remembered in the decade immediately following 1857 by looking at Urdu poems that described and lamented the devastation of Delhi.[13] The poems were mainly gathered in the compilation entitled *The Lament for Delhi* (*Fuġhān-e Dehlī*, 1863), on which my analysis is based – with a couple of additions in the 1931 enlarged collection *Faryād-e Dehlī* (*The Complaint of Delhi*).[14] Although historians have noticed the existence of *shahr āshob* poetry on 1857, it has generally been neglected in comparison to other sources of the period that have been seen as more

[10] A. D. King, *Colonial Urban Development*, p. 209.

[11] J. Hosagrahar, *Indigenous Modernities: Negotiating Architecture and Urbanism*.

[12] Mirza Asadullah Khan Ghalib, *Ghalib. 1797–1869*, p. 224; Ghalib, *Ḵẖuṭūṭ-e Ġhālib*, vol. 1, p. 369.

[13] J. T. P. de Bruijn, T. S. Halman, and M. Rahman, 'Shahrangiz', *The Encyclopaedia of Islam*, p. 212 quoted by S. Siddique, 'Remembering the Revolt', p. 48. It is noted about Persian *shahr āshobs* that they could also be expressed in prose. Sunil Sharma prefers to see *shahr āshob* as a topos, rather than a 'genre' (S. Sharma, 'The City of Beauties in Indo-Persia Poetic Landscape', p. 73). See also F. Lehmann, 'Urdu Literature and Mughal Decline', p. 127.

[14] Badayuni added nine other contemporary poems found scattered in various poets' *diwāns* and *kulliyāts* to Kaukab's material. The anthology strangely omitted two of Aish's poems but added poems by Husami, Hali, Shamshir, Safir, Abbas, Ghalib, Farhat, and Majruh, some of which were composed after Kaukab's edition of 1863. Hali's poem, for instance, was composed and recited in 1874.

factual. It is only in the last decades that Urdu *shahr āshob* poetry has begun to receive more attention.

This chapter re-assesses this body of texts through a careful analysis of their vocabulary, motifs, and imagery, and highlights their originality compared with previous *shahr āshobs*. Although mid-nineteenth-century poets claimed continuity with the Urdu *shahr āshob* tradition and scholars have generally emphasised pre- and post-1857 connections,[15] the poems of *The Lament for Delhi* also introduced new ways of expressing grief. Through a complex emotional vocabulary and the distinct use of elegiac (*marṡiyah*) literary devices, pain and rupture were emphasised in various ways by the poets and were echoed by a strong attachment to the city's ruined materiality. Ultimately, through the image of the garden, it was a tradition, a political culture that was mourned, along with an ideal vision of enlightened Muslim kingship.

1 *The Lament for Delhi*: Compiling *shahr āshob* Poetry after 1857

In 1863 – six years after the Uprising and a year after Muslims were readmitted into Delhi and former king Bahadur Shah Zafar passed away in Rangoon – the poet Tafazzul Husain Kaukab (1833–1873/4)[16] published an anthology of poems on 1857 entitled *Fuġhān-e Dehlī* (*The Lament for Delhi*)[17] by the Akmal ul-Maṯābeʿ publishing house.[18] *The Lament for Delhi* gathers fifty-nine *shahr āshob* poems written in Urdu by thirty-eight poets,[19] all lamenting the devastation

[15] Kaukab clearly traced the genealogy of 1857 *shahr āshobs* back to Muhammad Rafiʿ Sauda's verses, thus overtly claiming continuity with pre-1857 *shahr āshob* poetry.

[16] We do not know much on Kaukab, besides the fact that he was a disciple of Ghalib and an excellent friend of the poet Salik. Kaukab had two sons and two daughters but three of them died in their early years. See M. Ansarullah, *Jāmaʿ-e taẕkirah*, vol. 3, pp. 467–9.

[17] Tafazzul Husain Kaukab, *Fuġhān-e Dehlī*; Nizami Badayuni, *Faryād-e Dehlī*.

[18] The publishing house was managed by Sayyid Fakharuddin and was situated in Hakim Mahmud Khan's haveli in Ballimaran since 1858. It issued an Urdu weekly entitled *Akma ul-Akhbār* from 1869. See N. A. Khan, *Hindustānī Pres (1556 tā 1900)*, p. 176.

[19] All but three poems are in Urdu: two are in Persian and one is bilingual Persian-Urdu. So Yamame counts 63 poems by more than 40 poets but he might have taken into account the poems added by Nizami Badayuni in 1931. S. Yamame, 'Lamentation Dedicated to the Declining Capital', p. 53.

of Delhi (and, to a much lesser extent, of Lucknow) in 1857. The anthology is divided into three 'sparks' (*sharār*): the first contains four pre-1857 poems (the collection opens with one poem by Bahadur Shah Zafar and three by Sauda); the second, fourteen poems on 1857 in the *musaddas* form with one chronogram (*tārīkh*) by Sozan; and the last thirty-eight *ġhazals* and two *qiṯa*'s. In each section, the poems are arranged according to the alphabetical order of their authors – though the most eminent poets are listed first – and every poet is introduced by a couple of lines in Persian indicating his name, and sometimes the names of his father and *ustād* in the manner of *taẕkirahs*.

In the Persian foreword, Kaukab described the compilation as a 'new' (*navā'iṇ*) type of anthology (*guldastah*) that interwove 'the tears (*ashk*), sighs (*āh*) and heart-burnings (*soz-o gudāz*) of the people of Delhi'.[20] As a matter of fact, *The Lament for Delhi* was presented as an attempt to record the collective grief of the post-1857 period by publishing poems that circulated orally and could otherwise have been lost. In the chronograms[21] presented at the end of the book, Kaukab's work was indeed described by Salik as 'the strange (*'ajīb*) book [...] with which both the educated and uneducated will agree'[22] hence stressing that it mirrored the shared feelings of the time. Kamil further described in his chronogram that:

jab yeh kī tālīf Kaukab ne kitāb
jis se ẕāhir hū'e ḥāl-e ahl-e hind
yūṇ kahī tārīkh Kāmil ne bah sa'ī
daftar-e ranj-o malāl-e ahl-e hind (1279 hijrī).

When Kaukab compiled this book,
From which the condition of the people of Hind was revealed,
Kamil thus composed its chronogram as the endeavour
to record the grief and anguish of the people of Hind (1863).[23]

If *The Lament for Delhi* thus seems to constitute a conscious memory work, the exact way in which the poems were collected, however, remains obscure. In his preface to the book, while emphasising the thriving of oral *shahr āshob* poetry after 1857 despite the decline of

20 See the preface of *Fuġhān-e Dehlī* (ed. 2007), p. 1.
21 For more information on chronograms (*tārīkh*), see M. A. Farooqi, 'The Secret of Letters: Chronograms in Urdu Literary Culture'.
22 See Salik's chronogram: *hū'ī tālīf yeh 'ajīb kitāb.*
23 Kamil, *jab yeh kī tālīf Kaukab ne kitāb.*

state patronage,[24] Salik described Kaukab's efforts in the gathering and publishing of these poems:

It is obvious that when poets are in abundance and such a revolt (*inqilāb*) arises, no seal can be put on the mouth that could restrain speech. And there is no force on the heart that could prevent from feeling pain (*dard*), no manifestation of pain (*iẕhār-e dard*) that could not be expressed poetically. [...] In this city, lots of *musaddases* and *ġhazals* have been composed on this topic, but no one had thought about gathering them and about making a substantial anthology for the public out of them. [...] Munshi Muhammad Tafazzul Husain Khan, *taḵẖalluṣ* Kaukab assembled them with extreme effort and, looking from place to place, had them asked for. He organised them in a compendium, gave it to print to the publishing house Akmal ul-Maṯābeʿ and entitled it *The Lament for Delhi*.[25]

While the compiling of anthologies by post was apparently not uncommon after 1857,[26] Pasha Khan has argued that elements from the poems give evidence of the 'existence of a community of poets interacting amongst themselves' rather than 'of a scattered set of materials which Kaukab ha[d] brought together for the first time'.[27] He noted that almost all of the *ġhazals* of the collection were composed in the same *zamīn* (rhyming element) – 'ān-e Dehlī' which conveniently rhymes with the title of *Fuġhān-e Dehlī* – and also detected examples of intertextuality.[28] He thus pointed to the possibility of the poems being the result of a *ṯaraḥī mushāʿirah*, a poetic assembly that is 'patterned', that is when the rhyme is previously set, a common practice at the time.[29]

Other scholars have indeed argued that the content of *The Lament for Delhi* stemmed from an organised context of composition. Malik Ram, for instance, noted about the context of the compilation that 'after the bloody disturbance of 1857, when peace and calm was reestablished in the city the citizens likely (*ġhāliban*) held a *mushāʿirah*

[24] See C. M. Naim, 'Mughal and English Patronage of Urdu Poetry', p. 269.
[25] Kaukab, *Fuġhān-e Dehlī* (ed. 2007), pp. 40–1.
[26] *NNRNWP&O for 1864*, p. 51, for instance, mentions the undertaking of a certain 'Jewalanath' from Delhi who had gathered ninety pages of Persian poetry 'written from various stations and sent by *ḍāk*' in the prospect of publishing an anthology.
[27] P. M. Khan, 'What Is a Shahr-Ashob', p. 1.
[28] Ibid. Ahsan's *maqṯaʿ* directly quotes an extract from Rizwan's *ġhazal*.
[29] Ibid. See also S. Siddique, 'Remembering the Revolt', p. 77. The mention of the patterned nature of Kaukab's poem, for instance, appears in M. Ram, *Talāmiẕah-e Ġhālib*, p. 469.

during which the major master-poets of the time cried over the devastation of the city'.[30] If, as Ram said, the *mushāʿirah* was held when the situation had improved and after Muslims were readmitted into the city, that would probably date the event just after 1862. Poems of the collection, however, have been attributed to different dates of composition by Badayuni. For instance, Raqam's and Afsurdah's poems are said to date from 1858, and Dagh's *musaddas* is supposed to have been composed in 1859–1860.[31]

The attribution of the poems to one poetic event, while plausible, seems restrictive. Signs of intertextuality in poems that are set in different patterns and the internal mention of oral recitation may also point at the continued liveliness of *shahr āshob* performances in the aftermath of 1857.[32] In his commentary on *shahr āshob* poetry, Arifi indeed argued that 'the tradition of *āshobgo'ī* was still present a few years after 1857'.[33] Even as Urdu poets relocated to their hometowns, to smaller towns (*qaṣbahs*) emerging as new urban centres[34] or to regional courts where patronage was still provided, poetic milieus that sustained the composition of *shahr āshob* poetry undoubtedly persisted. Hyderabad, Alwar, Rampur, Jaipur, and Tonk emerged as popular destinations.[35] Until 1874, when Shivdan Singh died, the court of Alwar employed several of the poets whose poems are gathered in the anthology like Majruh, Salik and Zahir.[36] Communities of poets were thus still close-knit and active, and scholars have shown that the period immediately following 1857 was indeed particularly creative from an artistic point of view.[37]

[30] M. Ram, *Talāmiżah-e Ġhālib*, p. 469. The same idea also came up during an informal discussion with Dr. Mohammad Feroz Dehlawi, retired professor of Urdu on 24 November 2013.

[31] N. Badayuni, *Faryād*, p. 6 and p. 28. About Dagh's poem, see S. M. A. Zaidi, *Muṭʿālah-e Dāġh*, p. 247.

[32] For examples of intertextuality, see, for instance, Tajammul, *Phirte chalte jo meṇ ā niklā beshahr-e Dehlī*, verse 20.

[33] A. Arifi, *Shahr Āshob*, p. 10.

[34] M. Ram, *Talāmiżah-e Ġhālib*, p. 239; N. Badayuni, *Faryād*, p. 56; R. Khan, 'The Social Production of Space and Emotion', p. 622; R. Khan, 'Local Pasts: Space, Emotions and Identities', p. 699.

[35] M. Ram, *Talāmiżah-e Ġhālib*, pp. 474–9.

[36] Ibid., p. 240.

[37] I am thankful to Katherine Butler-Schofield for pointing this out to me during the Urban Emotions workshop (St John's College, Oxford, 27 February 2016). See R. D. Williams, 'Hindustani Music between Awadh and Bengal, c. 1758–1905'.

Although the compilation emphasised the unity and similarity of the poems, enhanced through the shared rhyme, and thus a recurring vocabulary, differences in the authors' expressions and sensitivities can be uncovered. The poets of the anthology evolved in the same literary milieu of interaction (and competition),[38] and the majority of them belonged to the Muslim *ashrāf* of Delhi with some being friends or even kin,[39] except for Lala Ram Parshad Zahir being a Hindu Khatri (and Farhat in *Faryād-e Dehlī* a Kayasth) and some originally coming from other cities like Lucknow, Hyderabad, Agra, Benares, Panipat, and Bijnor. Most were amongst the most famous poets of the time (Sheftah, Azurdah, Salik, Aish, Dagh, and Ghalib) but some would have been of humbler or unknown origin (like Sozan, and Husami,[40] said by Badayuni to have earned a living from storytelling without having had a proper education),[41] sometimes making mistakes of grammar and pronunciation.[42] The poets nonetheless belonged to different generations, earned their living in diverse ways and had distinct experiences of the Mughal court and of the city.

For instance, while Hakim Agha Jan Aish, known for his satire of Ghalib, came from a famous family of physicians and was at the service of the king,[43] Mufti Sadr Uddin Khan Azurdah (1789–1868) held important official posts in the British administration. A figure in the Delhi intelligentsia, he was a member of the Delhi College and the principal Chief Justice of Delhi from 1841. In 1857 Bahadur Shah wished to appoint him as city magistrate, a proposition that he refused, considering the Uprising to be 'ill-advised.'[44] His links with the Mughal court and a (forged?) signature on fatwas

[38] See, for instance, the famous argument between Ghalib and Aish. N. Badayuni, *Faryād*, p. 68.

[39] Dagh and Sha'iq are brothers, like Rizwan and Salik, and Saqib and Talib.

[40] The second edition of *Fuġhān-e Dehlī* added Husami's poem to Kaukab's initial material but there is some debate around authorship: while Nizami claims that it was the rare work of an otherwise unknown poet, Naeem Ahmad argued that it was from the pen of Bahadur Shah Zafar (N. Ahmad, *Shahr Āshob*, p. 181). For a detailed comparison and discussion of Zafar's and Husami's versions, see A. Arifi, *Shahr Āshob*, pp. 233–40, who argued against the attribution to Zafar (see Ibid., p. 238).

[41] N. Badayuni, *Faryād*, p. 19. [42] Kaukab, *Fuġhān-e Dehlī* (ed. 1954), p. 8.

[43] See a description in M. H. Azad, *Ab-e Hayat*, trans. and ed. F. W. Pritchett, pp. 378–9; M. H. Azad, *Āb-e Ḥayāt*, p. 463.

[44] S. Liddle, 'Azurdah: Scholar, Poet, and Judge'.

encouraging jihad against the British led colonial officials to suspect him of sympathy with the *mujāhidīn* and put him on trial. He was eventually released, but had lost his job and half of his property in the process.[45] Part of this situation appeared in his *musaddas*, in which he both recalled the sophistication of the court and of the king, as well as attributed the responsibility of the Uprising to the Fort.[46] The very first couplet of his *musaddas* opened with:

āfat is shahr meṇ qileʿh kī badaulat ā'ī
wāṇ ke ʿamāl se dillī kī bhī shāmat ā'ī.

Misfortune befell on the city because of the royal Fort,
As the result of its misdeed, Delhi too was afflicted.[47]

The sympathies unveiled in the poems thus reflect each of the authors' personal situations, loyalties and, probably, hopes for the future. When Saqib (~1840–1869), son of Nawab Ziauddin Ahmad Khan Loharu,[48] appointed honorary magistrate of Delhi by the British, greatly praised British town improvement projects, Ghalib (1797–1869), resentful towards the British with whom he struggled to secure a pension, saw them as guilty of the bloodshed.[49] Contrary to what some scholars have argued, post-1857 *shahr āshobs* did not seem unanimously anti-British although, of course, censorship was most carefully enforced at the time.[50]

2 1857: Transforming the *shahr āshob* Genre

All the poems of the anthology invariably belong to the *shahr āshob* genre. In Urdu, it was essentially characterised by a particular mood, sadness, and especially a particular subject, the city.[51] In the Islamic world that 'had an overwhelmingly urban focus'[52] the city was usually celebrated through

[45] See A. Powell, 'Questionable Loyalties: Muslim Government Servants and Rebellion', p. 93.
[46] R. Jalil, 'Reflections of 1857 in Contemporary Urdu Literature', p. 122.
[47] First verse from Azurdah's *musaddas*, *āfat is shahr meṇ qileʿh kī badaulat ā'ī.*
[48] N. Badayuni, *Faryād*, p. 18.
[49] See Ghalib's *ġhazal*, *baskeh faʿāl māyurīd hai āj*, in Badayuni, *Faryād-e Dehlī*.
[50] S. Siddique, 'Remembering the Revolt', pp. 67–76.
[51] F. Lehmann, 'Urdu Literature', p. 127.
[52] M. Hermansen, 'Imagining Space and Siting Collective Memory in South Asian Muslim Biographical Literature (Tazkirahs)', p. 5.

the vivacity of urban life and its idealised moral order: cities were often described as gardens of paradise on earth and conveyed particular ideas of harmony and virtue. Although *tażkirahs* and travelogues often described urban landscapes, in one way or another, the genre of *shahr āshob* or *shahr angez* in the Turkish and Persian traditions, which was greatly appreciated in the late Timurid and early Safavid periods,[53] consisted in humorously praising a city by describing the positive uproar caused by its many beautiful young citizens (*shahr āshob* literally meaning 'city-disturbers'). The genre portrayed, sometimes satirically, the inhabitants of various professional, ethnic, and religious backgrounds.[54] The representation of the city as a space where moral values and behaviours were epitomised eventually highlighted the morality and righteousness of its ruler. Seventeenth-century Persian *shahr āshobs* composed in India by Kalim Kashani, Munir Lahori, and Fani Kashmiri, for instance, served to exalt the greatness of the Mughal Empire by describing peaceful cities characterised by the diverse composition and impeccable morality of their inhabitants.[55]

From the eighteenth century, the genre was adapted in Urdu.[56] With the decline of Mughal power, poets increasingly resorted to it to portray the social disarray of north Indian cities. Whereas Turkish and Persian *shahr āshobs* were primarily composed in honour of the 'city-disturbers', the function of the city-poem radically changed to describe and lament the 'disturbed city' and the confused state of affairs of different classes of inhabitants. Such poems were written about Delhi, Agra, Hyderabad, Awadh, Bihar, and Rohilkhand,[57] with the first of this kind having probably been composed by Jaʿfar Zatalli (1659–1713), the famous satirist who was sentenced to death for having ridiculed the king Farrukhsiyar in one of his verses.[58] Often preserving a humorous and satirical tone,[59] Urdu *shahr āshobs*

[53] J. T. P. de Bruijn, T. S. Halman, and M. Rahman, 'Shahrangiz', H. A. R. Gibb (ed.), *Encyclopaedia of Islam*, online version.

[54] See the description of Tabriz by Lissani in A. Bricteux, 'Pasquinade sur la ville de Tébriz, par maître Lissani de Chiraz'.

[55] S. Sharma, '"The Errant Eye" and Mughal Pastoral Poetry'.

[56] The first poem in this trend was probably the *Maṣnawī-e āshob-e Hindustān* composed in Persian by Bihishti at the end of the reign of Shah Jahan.

[57] N. Ahmad, *Shahr Āshob*, p. 10.

[58] On Zatalli's 'obscene' and satirical poetry, see S. R. Faruqi, 'Burning Rage, Icy Scorn: the Poetry of Jaʿfar Zatalli'.

[59] I. Hasan, 'Later Mughals as Represented in Urdu Poetry: A Study of Qa'im's Shahr Ashob', p. 132.

described the disorder and chaos of a 'world turned upside down' and the fall of moral values attached to the Indo-Persian culture.[60] Along with satirical critiques of the power in place, which recalled insult poems (*hajw*),[61] realistic depictions of misery, hunger, and exile were intertwined with complaints about the reversal of fortunes, with morally and occupationally inferiors rising in status.[62] This new development, along with the fact that *shahr āshob* writers usually employed plain and simple language, led the Urdu genre to be considered 'democratic' and historical by later scholars,[63] the change in fortunes pointing, for instance, at the growing social tensions between Hindu commercial groups and the Indo-Persian gentry during the eighteenth century.[64]

Arthur Dudney has recently argued that the Urdu genre was in fact a construction of later critics and editors, early Urdu *shahr āshobs* being in fact *hajw* poems.[65] He thus maintained that mid- and late nineteenth-century poetry 'owed more to engaging with colonial literary aesthetics than to a precolonial Urdu and Persian tradition'.[66] While this is maybe a step too far, if one examines Urdu *shahr āshobs* from Zatalli's to *Fuġhān-e Dehlī*'s poems,[67] a progression in the imagery deployed is indeed noticeable. The earliest poems that display some of what would become the classic imagery of 1857 *shahr āshobs* unsurprisingly emanate from poems deploring the sack of north Indian cities by Nadir Shah (1739) and Ahmad Shah Abdali (1756). At the time, the poems focused on the city proper. Urdu poets gradually abandoned their satirical tone and the caricature of all types of citizens to become more emotional and lament the city's devastation.[68] Sauda (d. 1781) and Hasrat (d. 1793) both wrote *shahr āshobs* on Shah Jahanabad,

60 C. M. Naim, 'A Note on Shahr Ashob', p. 42.

61 For more on that, see, for instance, I. Hasan, 'Later Mughals as Represented in Urdu Poetry: A Study in the Light of Shahr Ashobs from Hatim, Sauda and Nazir', pp. 131–53, or the work of Abdullah Chishti at Jamia Millia Islamia.

62 M. Rahman, 'Shahrangiz'.

63 See, for instance, C. R. Petievich, 'Poetry of the Declining Mughals: The Shahr Ashob', p. 105.

64 C. Bayly, 'Delhi and Other Cities of North India during the "Twilight"', p. 132.

65 A. Dudney, 'Literary Decadence and Imagining the Late Mughal City', p. 192.

66 Ibid., p. 188.

67 Naeem Ahmad collected pre- and post-1857 *shahr āshobs*, on which I have based most of my analysis for pre-1857 poems (N. Ahmad, *Shahr āshob*).

68 See Mir Taqi Mir, *Zikr-e Mir. The Autobiography of the Eighteenth Century Mughal Poet.*

which already talked, albeit allusively, about Paradise, Doomsday, and the city of the past, but it is only gradually that those elements became central and typical of the language of later *shahr āshob* poetry. At the beginning of the nineteenth century, Rasikh's *maśnawī* on Patna (d. 1822) contained a typical description of various types of professions (farmers, traders, soldiers, lawyers) intertwined with the nostalgic recollection of the city as a garden.[69] Mushafi (d. 1824) and Nazir (d. 1830) also used natural metaphors to describe Delhi's and Agra's decline, but Rangin (d. 1835/6) still composed his *maśnawī* on the emblematic listing of professions. In 1857, as we shall see, such lists yielded to the powerful evocation of garden landscapes.

The 1857 *shahr āshobs* were in continuity with these developments of the Urdu tradition, but also reached a climax of nostalgia by narrating collective pain and highlighting rupture. The poems expanded on elements that were already in the bud since the mid-eighteenth century, and even more so from the beginning of the nineteenth century, and cultivated them to a new level. It was no longer only a matter of the world being upside-down, or of cobblers undeservingly wearing gold-embroidered shoes:[70] the whole population, civilisation even, had been devastated was and unable to recover. Several elements in the poems conveyed the idea of trauma and definite rupture with the past: the style of the poems themselves, set in the *musaddas* and *ġhazal* verse forms (also used for the performance of collective mourning); the vocabulary (enhancing longing, physical pain, and indelible scarring); and the imagery used (the ruined garden, the apocalypse).

Before analysing them, however, I should note that the Delhi poems gathered in *The Lament for Delhi*, which form a quite homogeneous lot, were not the first poems displaying these new developments: the political turmoil of 1856 and 1857 in northern India seems to have acted as a catalyst. Perusing the *shahr āshobs* assembled in Naim Ahmad's chronological compilation,[71] one poem, and others thereafter, appears strikingly similar to those of Kaukab's anthology: a

69 N. Ahmad, *Shahr Āshob*, p. 150: 'This garden is now full of thorns; Alas, autumn has come to such a spring': *yeh gulzār ab ho gayā k͟hārzār, k͟hizān ho ga'ī hā'e iskī bahār.*

70 To cite a verse from Jur'at, 'In the Presence of the Nightingale', (S. R. Faruqi) p. 3, and N. Ahmad, *Shahr Āshob*, p. 133.

71 N. Ahmad asserted that the poems have been classified according to chronological order, but dating poems is, more often than not, a difficult task.

musaddas on the devastation of Lucknow by Mirza Muhammad Raza Barq. Besides the use of similar imagery and vocabulary, Barq's poem is also the first *shahr āshob* written in the *musaddas* verse form in Ahmad's collection (previous *shahr āshobs* were usually set in *mukẖammas*, *maṡnawī*, *ġhazal*, or *qaṣīdah* form). This does not seem to be a coincidence, and in fact, it is plausible that the style of 1857 *shahr āshob* poetry on Delhi was heavily influenced by literary and political developments that occurred first in Lucknow. Lucknow may have been the branch out of which the Delhi variety of *shahr āshob* poetry bloomed.

Barq was not an ordinary Urdu Lakhnawi poet. Born in Lucknow probably around 1790, he had become *ustād* and companion of the last king of Awadh, Wajid Ali Shah. After Wajid Ali Shah's deposition in February 1856, he followed him to Matiya Burj, and, when fears that rebels might rally around Wajid Ali Shah spread in 1857, Barq was imprisoned with his king at Fort William College. That is where he died on 17 October 1857.[72] His *musaddas*, Ahmad tells us, was composed only a few months before his death. All of the characteristics of 1857 *shahr āshob* poems on Delhi, which I will detail below, were already present in his poem, and in other such compositions by Lakhnawi peers, like Aman Ali Sahr (d. 1857) and Mir Muhammad Jan Shad (d. 1899).[73]

2.1 Shahr āshobs *as Secular* marṡiyahs

One of the innovative ways in which 1857 poems departed from previous *shahr āshob* tradition was the adoption of particular literary devices which participated in representing 1857 as a rupture and in expressing collective pain. *Shahr āshob* writers generally resorted to a language and framework that was particularly efficient in conveying grief and tales of common dispossession: the *marṡiyah*. While the *marṡiyah* – from the Arabic root *r-ṡ-y* (literally, 'oration in mourning'[74]) – is to be found in the secular Arabic lamentations traditionally recited at the time of the funeral for the mourning of the deceased or

[72] Barq, *Intikẖāb-e ġhazaliyāt-e Barq*, pp. 5–8.
[73] See N. Ahmad, *Shahr Āshob*.
[74] M. Trivedi, 'A Genre of Composite Creativity: Marsiya and Its Performance in Awadh', p. 194.

at the loss of cities like Baghdad or Cordoba,[75] the genre in Urdu and Persian was mainly used in a religious context to commemorate the martyrs of Karbala and especially Imam Husain. Only from the later part of the eighteenth century and especially in the mid-nineteenth century were *shahr āshobs* composed 'in a new way, in which the "colour" of *marśiyah* was prominent.'[76]

From 1857, *shahr āshob* writers used the *musaddas* and *ġhazal* verse forms almost exclusively: of the fifty-nine poems of *The Lament for Delhi*, fifty-two (i.e. almost 90 per cent of them) are either *musaddases*[77] or *ġhazals*. Salik's description in the preface supports the idea that the poets' use of the *musaddas* and *ġhazal* was consciously made, as both verse forms accentuated the feelings of loss and despair, and linked the memory of the Uprising with practices of mourning:

> If you look carefully, every *musaddas* is an elegy (*marśiyah*), and every *ġhazal* is a requiem (*nauḥah*). Who has the power, listening to them, not to cry? Whose heart is not brimming with blood because of this pain (*dard se k̲h̲ūn*)? When one listens to someone's verses on that matter, his ears go dumb (*kān gung ho jāte haiṇ*), he has knots in his stomach (*kalejah munh ko ātā hai*), he remembers his own hardships and that crossing of the desert comes in sight again.[78]

The *ġhazal* originated in Arabic poetry from the panegyric (*qaṣīdah*). The poets of the Hejaz traditionally used it to describe the deserted encampment and to express sorrow at separation.[79] As amorous poetry, it also reflected on the transience of love and on the pain of loss. It was one of the most fashionable styles of poetry at the time and was used for a variety of purposes, including for *nauḥahs* (requiems) as Salik emphasised in the preface. The resort to the *ġhazal* enabled nineteenth-century *shahr āshob* writers to emphasise human finitude. They described the destruction of Delhi allegorised in the figure of the lost lover or of the deceased in a more abstract and condensed tone by elaborately using classical images of loss like autumnal gardens and extinguished candles.

[75] Ch. Pellat, 'Marthiya' in *Encyclopaedia of Islam*.
[76] 'Shahr Āshob', in *Urdū Dā'irah-e Ma'ārīf-e islāmiyah*, p. 820.
[77] The *musaddas* is a six-stanza metre on the model 'aaaabb ccccdd'; see G. Schoeler and M. Rahman, 'Musammat', in H. A. R. Gibb, *Encyclopaedia of Islam*, online version. The adoption of this meter for *shahr āshobs* was an innovation of the time; 'Shahr Āshob', in *Urdū Dā'irah-e Ma'ārīf-e islāmiyah*, p. 825.
[78] Kaukab, *Fuġhān-e Dehlī* (2007), pp. 40–1.
[79] R. Blachère and A. Bausani, 'Ghazal', in *Encyclopaedia of Islam*.

The adoption of the *musaddas* form was even more explicit for the expression of collective suffering. The *musaddas* was originally developed in the Shia kingdom of Awadh for the elegies devoted to Imam Husain and his relatives martyred at Karbala, which were especially recited during the month of Muharram. In nineteenth-century Lucknow, the *marśiyah* was indeed 'invariably' in the *musaddas* form.[80] The *musaddas* under Mir Anis (1803–1874) and Mirza Dabir (1803–1875) was increasingly considered 'the most suitable form for a marsiyah'[81] and had become the fundamental characteristic of nineteenth-century Shia elegies. As C. M. Naim argued, the change was most probably linked to the fact that 'the marsiyah moved indoors' and poets abandoned singing for declaiming (*taḥt ul-lafẕ*).[82] The genre usually consisted in the commemoration of the hardships suffered by the martyrs of Karbala, with detail and realism. In general, the *musaddas* was used in *The Lament for Delhi* to describe the devastation of Delhi in more detail, sometimes even describing the hardship endured by different categories of people, in a classical *shahr āshob* stance.

Azurdah, for instance, gave one detailed account of the fortunes of the nobility in his *musaddas*. First recalling the delicateness of the Mughal court, he lamented its ruin, and finally ended with the memory of two of his friends, the poets Sahba'i and Sheftah, who had been killed and sent to jail by the British, respectively[83]:

zewar almās kā sab jin se nah pahnā jātā
bhārī jhūmar bhī kabhī sar peh nah rakhā jātā
gāch kā jin se dūpaṭṭah nah saṇbhālā jātā
lākh ḥikmat se uṛhāte to nah oṛhā jātā
sar peh woh bojh lī'e chār t̲araf phirte haiṇ
do qadam chalte haiṇ mushkil se to phir girte haiṇ.

Those who could not endure the weight of diamond jewellery
And found the *jhūmars* on their foreheads heavy
They could not even manage the embroidered scarf

[80] Ch. Pellat et al., 'Marthiya', in *Encyclopaedia of Islam*.
[81] C. M. Naim, 'The Art of the Urdu Marsiya', p. 102. [82] Ibid.
[83] Sheftah's property was confiscated, and he was sentenced to a seven-year imprisonment by the lower court, which, however, was eventually dismissed (K. C. Kanda, *Masterpieces of Patriotic Urdu Poetry*, p. 6).

They tried but failed after a thousand attempts,
Now they go everywhere carrying burdens
When they walk a few steps with difficulty they then fall.[84]

roz waḥshat mujhe ṣaḥrā kī t̤araf lātī hai
sar hai aur josh-e junūṇ sang hai aur chhātī hai
ṭukṛe hotā hai jigar jī hī peh ban jātī hai
Muṣt̤afā K͟hān [Sheftah] *kī mulāqāt jo yād ātī hai*
Kyuṇkeh Āzurdah nikal jā'e nah saudā'ī ho
qatl is t̤araḥ se bejurm jo Ṣahbā'ī ho.

Every day, sadness leads me to the barren desert
to beat my heart with great insanity.
My wounded heart and soul are shattered,
When I remember encounters with Mustafa Khan [Sheftah].
How wouldn't I become insane, Azurdah,
When the innocent Sahba'i has been murdered this way.[85]

The use of the *ġhazal* as *nauḥah* and of the *musaddas* as *marṡiyah* for *shahr āshob* poetry was a deliberate choice made by 1857 poets to emphasise suffering. Along with the adoption of the forms usually used for Shia elegies, *shahr āshob* writers adopted the elegists' tasks of weeping and making others weep (*ronā aur rulānā*). With heartrending descriptions of massacre and misery declaimed in a particular way and tone, the Shia *marṡiyah* aimed at generating a particular collective mental and emotional state of mourning, considered religiously rewarding. The main quality of *marṡiyahs* is indeed that of evoking emotions (*haijān k͟hez*) in an audience.[86] With this collective emotional 'contagion' (or 'collective effervescence'), it aimed at reinforcing sentiments of group belonging and solidarity.[87]

Post-1857 *shahr āshob* poetry assuredly shared these characteristics. The poems of *The Lament for Delhi* and *The Complaint of Delhi* swarmed with comparisons between *shahr āshob* poets and elegists (*marṡiyahk͟hwāns*) and pointed to a similar context of recitation during which both the poet and the audience would burst into tears.

[84] Azurdah, *āfat is shahr meṇ qile'h kī badaulat ā'ī*, verse 3. [85] Ibid., verse 11.
[86] M. Trivedi, 'A Genre of Composite Creativity', p. 198; A. Bard, '"No Power of Speech Remains": Tears and Transformation in South Asian Majlis Poetry', p. 156.
[87] C. von Scheve, 'Collective Emotions in Rituals.'

Hali, for instance, indicated a clear equivalence between *shahr āshob* and Shia performances (thus hinting both at the intensity of *shahr āshob* poetry and at the inappropriateness of the situation):

bazm-e mātam to nahīṇ, bazm-e sukhan hai Ḥālī
yāṇ munāsib nahīṇ ro ro ke rulānā har giz.

It is not a mourning assembly, but a poetic symposium, Hali,
It is not appropriate to grieve others with your tears.[88]

With the typical use of interjections of sorrow (*wā'e, hā'e, ḥaif*, etc.), *shahr āshob* writers could transmit deep emotions to the audience and induce collective expressions of mourning but applied to a different, non-religious, context.

The reference to the effect of verses on the audience is an enduring theme in the poems. At least one verse of every poem was dedicated to the description of its capacity to make listeners cry, as Salik had anticipated in the preface. In these two examples from Aish's *musaddas* and the *maqta*ʿ (the final verse) of one of Salik's *ġhazals*, the poets evoked the pain of listening to narratives of 1857:

nahīṇ aisā ko'ī dil jo nahīṇ is ġham se do chār
kis ke dil meṇ nahīṇ is ġham kā yeh batlā'o to khār
sun ke is ḥāl ko sīnah nahīṇ hai kis kā figār
kaun aisā hai jo is ġham se nahīṇ zār-o nizār
kaunsā dil hai jo is ġham meṇ giriftār nahīṇ
kaunsī āṇkh hai is ġham se jo khūṇ bār nahīṇ?

There is not one single heart not traumatised by this sorrow,
Tell me, in whose heart there is no distress,
In listening to this condition, whose heart is not breaking
Who is not agonising because of this sorrow
Which heart is not struck by this grief
Which eyes do not shed tears of blood because of this woe?[89]

sun ke har shiʿr peh kyuṇkar nah hoṇ āṇkheṇ namnāk
sālik-e ġhamzadah hai marṡiyahkhwān-e Dehlī.

In listening to every verse, how can eyes not fill with tears?
Salik, afflicted, becomes the *marṡiyakhwān* of Delhi![90]

88 Hali, *jīte jī maut ke tum muṇh meṇ nah jānā hargiz*, verse 30 (*Faryād-e Dehlī*).
89 Aish, *kyā kahūṇ is falak-e shoʿbdagār ke nairang*, verse 2.
90 Salik, *rū-e jannat meṇ bhī ham kar ke bayān-e Dehlī*, verse 14.

By interweaving emotions and memory in such a powerful way, and by making conspicuous links with Shia rituals, *shahr āshob* poems probably generated similar responses from their audience. The composition and recitation of *shahr āshob* poems in the aftermath of the Uprising may have released some of the tension generated by the trauma in inscribing the experience into collective memory, thus 'allowing the pent-up emotions of loss and mourning to be expressed' through collective acts of commemoration.[91] The fact that *shahr āshob* poems, like Shia elegies, could have been recited or chanted in a way supposed to arouse and heighten emotions could also have resulted in the trope of the 'weeping Hindustani' lamenting the end of the Mughal world, notably developed in early twentieth-century Bengali literature.[92]

2.2 *The Language of Grief*

The emotional vocabulary deployed in 1857 poetry contains an array of emotions like dishonour (*ābrū, ruswā'ī*), bewilderment (*ḥairānī*), fear (*ḍar, k͟hauf*), restlessness (*andeshah, bechainī, beqarārī, taṛap*), helplessness (*bebasī*), and patriotism (*ḥubb-e waṯan*). Compared to previous *shahr āshobs*, the mention of helplessness and surprise seems to be a new addition. One emotion, however, conspicuously dominates: grief. As Sylwia Surdykowska noted in her study of sadness in Iranian culture, its significance is reflected by the richness of its vocabulary in Persian.[93] The same is true in Urdu. Many words convey sadness in the poems, creating a complex and broad semantic and affective web of sorrow. Among the most frequent words are *ġham*, *andoh* (grief), *māyūsī*, *muẓṯar* (despair), *alam*, *ranj*, *dard* (pain), *afsos*, *ḥasrat* (regret), *malāl*, *fasurdagī/afsurdagī* (depression), *saudā* (melancholy), *pareshānī*, *tang* (distress), and *shikastagī* (with the idea of brokenness). Cognates of some of those words also add to the terminology of sadness, such as *dardangez*, *dardmand*, *ġhamgīn*, *ġhamnāk*, *ġhamzadah*, *ġhamzadagān*, and *ġhamkadah*. The variety of words used for sorrow is remarkably broader in 1857 *shahr āshobs*

[91] J. C. Alexander, *Cultural Trauma*, p. 5.
[92] For instance, the figure of Murad Khan in Dilipkumar Mukhopadhyay, *Bhārater Saṅgīta Guṇī*, Part II, pp. 15–27, quoted in R. Williams, 'Hindustani Music between Awadh and Bengal, c. 1758–1905', p. 248.
[93] S. Surdykowska, 'The Idea of Sadness', p. 69.

than previously. Among those, the one that appears repetitively, and through derivatives, is the Arabic word *ġham*, an inclusive and generic term for grief in Urdu.[94]

To understand its meaning in the poems, it is useful to explore the terms and expressions that are used alongside it. In the collections, *ġham* is intimately linked to the physical experience of pain and implies different body reactions: tears (*ashk* 'tear', *ronā* 'cry', *rulānā* 'make others cry', *dil-e giryāṉ* 'weeping heart', *dil rotā hai* 'the heart cries', *baḥr-e ġham* 'ocean of grief', etc.), sometimes made of blood (*chashm se k̲h̲ūn* 'blood from the eye', *k̲h̲ūn ke daryā* 'rivers of blood', etc.)[95]; one's liver being cut to pieces (*jigar kaṭ kaṭ ke girtā hai, tukṛe jigar*); being sick (*munh ko kalejah ātā hai, kalejah munh ko ublā ātā hai*); eating or drinking one's heart and blood (*k̲h̲ūn-e jigar pīnā*); tearing one's collar to pieces (*girebān chāk*); or being pale and emaciated (*ġham se safed honā, ġham se zār-o nizār honā*). Grief is also said to generate two paradoxical responses: both the irrepressible need to lament (*fuġhān*; *faryād*; *josh-e shikāyat, nālah, shikwah*, etc.) and the impossibility of speaking at all (*ġham se sākit honā*; *k̲h̲āmosh*; *munh se kuchh bāt nah nikālnā*). The vocabulary of blood and tears, and of vitals being broken, cut to pieces (*dil/jigar-figār*, *k̲h̲astah dil*), twisted, burned (*sozāṉ*, *sok̲h̲tgān*), or eaten is graphic. Hearts transform into kebabs (*dil-kabāb*). The image is not new, but in this context *ġham* is nothing like 'sweet sorrow' (*ġham-e shīrīn*),[96] nor it is an exclusively mental state of depression, but an emotion linked with acute physical pain.

Some of the expressions quoted above apply to both grief and love. The burning sensation illustrates emotional intensity, and love and sadness thus share a common vocabulary of flame and smoke. Amorous sadness is indeed a prevailing theme in classical Urdu poetry, which most beautifully unfolds in *ġhazals* through a whole system of conventions. As Frances Pritchett notes, 'the garden's death in autumn, the bird's nest struck by lightning, the candle burnt out overnight, and the withering of the rose are images of ultimate separation and loss'.[97] A poetic allegory epitomises this: *dāġh*, the burn mark, the scar, which

[94] 'Gham', in J. T. Platts, *A Dictionary of Urdu*, p. 173.

[95] The image of crying tears of blood is already a topos of Arabic poetry lamenting the loss or ruin of cities. M. Hassen, 'Recherches sur les poèmes inspirés par la perte', p. 44.

[96] S. Surdykowska, 'The Idea of Sadness', p. 73.

[97] F. W. Pritchett, 'Convention in the Classical Urdu Ghazal', pp. 67–8.

is left imprinted on the heart (*dil*, *jigar*, *sīnah*). The literal meanings of *dāġh* in Urdu are a (dis)coloured mark (a bleach mark, a stain), or a scar from a wound or burn. In a more figurative sense, *dāġh* also means sadness, shock, and grief at the loss of a loved one.[98] It is the painful remnant of passionate love when it has vanished. The image of the scar blends the memory of the beloved with grief, and interiorises both pain and a yearning for reunion.

In the last couplets of his *ġhazal*, Ghalib uses an allegory suggesting a collective of mourners who meet and share the same grief. Doing so, he alternates fire and water, between the internal burning in the first couplet quoted (*jal kar*; *sozish-e dāġh*) and the collective tear-shedding in the second (*ro kar*; *giryāṇ*), to end, in the *maqtaʿ*, with the idea that trauma is indelible:

gāh jal kar kyā kī'e shikwah
sozish-e dāġh hā'e pinhāṇ kā
gāh ro kar kahā kī'e bāham
mājrā dīdah hā'e giryāṇ kā
is ṯaraḥ ke wiṣāl se yā rab
kyā miṭe dil se dāġh hijrāṇ kā?

Often we complain in pain about
The agony of hidden scars,
Often together we shed tears and tell
The tale of wailing and lamentation,
With this kind of union, O Lord,
How is erased the scar of separation?[99]

One traditional metaphor for the scar of separation in Turkish, Persian, and Urdu literature is that of the poppy (*lālah*). Also translated as tulip with a similar cup shape, Mélikoff has shown that *lālah* rather evoked the wild red anemone or the poppy.[100] Wild flower *par excellence*, the poppy is the opposite of the *gul* (the rose), the cultivated flower and the flower of Prophet Muhammad. Yet, because of its spelling – which is an anagram of 'Allah' – the *lālah* has also enjoyed a particular status in art history, often decorating mosques and mausoleums.[101] But usually the *lālah* is a metaphor for the suffering heart, its redness evoking

[98] 'Dāġh', in *Urdū Luġhat Tārīḵẖī Uṣūl par*, vol. 8, pp. 946–7.
[99] Ghalib, *baskeh faʿāl māyurīd hai āj*, last three couplets (*Faryād-e Dehlī*).
[100] I. Mélikoff, 'La fleur de la souffrance', pp. 341–60. [101] Ibid., p. 348.

blood and its black centre a burn. According to popular Iranian traditions, Mélikoff tells us, Adam's tears made *lālahs* bloom after his fall from Paradise, symbolising his suffering of being separated from God, just like the tears of blood of Majnun were compared to poppies.[102] The *lālah*, as a symbol of *dāġh*, represents the pain of love, and the common poppy is indeed also sometimes called *lālah-e dāġhdār* (the *lālah* that bears a scar).[103] In his poem collected in Nizami's *Complaint of Delhi*, Safir Dehlawi evokes the image of the scarred poppy and other flowers of the garden, each of which interiorises and characterises *ġham* in its own way:

hai yāsmīṇ hī ġham se nah kuchh zard aur zabūṇ
sosan bhī pīṭ pīṭ ke hotī hai nīlgūṇ
lālah ke dil peh dāġh hai pītā hai apnā k͟hūṇ
aur gul kā jaib chāk to ġhunchah hai sarnigūṇ
nargis ko is ke sog meṇ yarqān ho gayā.

From grief, the jasmine is pale and weak
The iris has become black and blue from beating
In great agony, the poppy drinks its own blood,
And the rose's petals are ripped, the rose bud overturned.
In mourning, the narcissus is jaundiced.[104]

The garden, with its shade trees and fragrant flowers, the place where a poet meets his lover, became incredibly central to the expression of grief in the poems. Love and the garden had traditionally been linked in Persian and Urdu poetry, with nature often mirroring the emotions of the poet, as in Safir's couplets above. Ali Akbar Husain noted that Deccani garden descriptions, like Nusrati's *Garden of Love* (*Gulshan-e ʿishq*), usually 'serve to record and mirror the moments of joy and despair, of spiritual awakening, or the kindling of love'.[105] William Hanaway also highlighted the harmony between the poet's emotions and garden landscape, trees and flowers expressing, and mimicking, human emotions in Persian poetry.[106] As a place of love

[102] Ibid., p. 349. [103] M. Aghamohammadi, 'An Apology for Flowers', p. 34.
[104] Safir, *kyā āsmān āj bad-uʿnwān ho gayā*, verse 4, in *Faryād-e Dehlī* (2007), p. 51.
[105] A. A. Husain, *Scent in the Islamic Garden*, p. 165.
[106] W. Hanaway, 'Paradise on Earth: The Terrestial Garden in Persian Literature', p. 56. See also J. S. Meisami, 'Poetic Microcosms: The Persian Qasida to the End of the Twelfth Century', p. 146.

(and sometimes despair), the garden soon became by extension a metaphor for the beloved, with its roses recalling the beloved's cheeks, narcissis her/his eyes, hyacinths beautiful dark curls, and the cypress her/his slender silhouette.[107] *Shahr āshob* writers clearly identified their lost beloved as the Delhi of the past, and thus naturally resorted to garden imagery, as we shall see in the next section. Aish, in the following *ġhazal*, described how garden flowers reminded the poet of the beloved in very typical garden imagery.

pahnī sosan ne hai nīlī poshāk
khā ke ġham-e mātamiyān-e Dehlī
pech khātī hai yeh sumbul kar yād
zulf-e purpech-e butān-e Dehlī
lālah ho dāġh bah dil kartā hai
yād-e khāl-e pariyān-e Dehlī
yād kar kar ke hai nargis hairāṇ
nighah-e khūsh nigahān-e Dehlī.

The iris is wearing blue (mourning) garments
Sharing the grief of the mourners of Delhi
The hyacinth is coiled by recalling
The entangled curls of the beloved of Delhi
The poppy changes its mark in memory
of the beauty spot of the fairies of Delhi
The narcissus is astonished, remembering
The barren gaze of the beautiful-eyed of Delhi.[108]

In 1857 *shahr āshobs*, Urdu poets thus used a specific vocabulary of sorrow and classical poetic images of afflicted love to narrate a tale of collective grief. *Ġham* was expressed through a complex set of images and contrasts, which accentuated physical pain and projected idealised sensations of blissfulness into the past. Doing so, they created rupture.[109] One of the most interesting and notable innovations of post-1857 *shahr āshob* poetry was its focus on the city *of the past* as much as, if not more than, the city of the present, unlike traditional

[107] M. Subtelny, *Le monde est un jardin*, p. 127.
[108] Aish, *mil ga'ī khāk meṇ shān-e Dehlī*, verses 16 to 19.
[109] Rupture, and its related feelings of loss, is often linked to the arrival of modernity or to the aftermath of revolutions and of the fall of empires and is what characterises nostalgia for most scholars; see S. Boym, *The Future of Nostalgia*, p. 7 and D. Walder, *Postcolonial Nostalgias*, p. 10.

Urdu *shahr āshobs*. The use of the past tense was generalised as poets lingered on descriptions of paradise lost. The juxtaposition of images of glorified past and of dreadful present influenced the representation of 1857 into the early twentieth century. Khwajah Hasan Nizami, for instance, interspersed his *Ġhadar-e Dehlī ke afsāne* ('Stories of the Rebellion of Delhi', from 1914)[110] with 'then and now' drawings similar to those depicted in *shahr āshob* poems, hinting at the intermediality of these motifs.[111]

3 The Garden That Was Delhi: Eulogising Mughal Political Culture

Cultural rupture was emphasised in various ways, but one of the most significant images was the ruined garden. If the metaphor of the garden was already used in pre-1857 *shahr āshobs*, 1857 poetry extended it remarkably. In fact, allegorising the city as a garden became the core of most poems, which focused on beautiful waterways and fragrant flowers soon wasted by autumnal winds and dust. This is of course apparent from the poems' vocabulary. Besides the use of terms evoking garden landscape (*bāġh*, *gulshan*, *lālahzār*, *chaman*, *gulistān*, *chamanistān*, *bistar-e gul*, *farsh-e gul*, etc.), an elaborate lexicon detailing various types of flowers, trees, fruit, birds, sounds, and scents is employed and opposed to a vocabulary of wilderness (*wīrān*, *waḥshat*, *jangal*, *dasht*, *bayābān*), autumn (*k͟hizān* or *zāġh* and *zuḥal*, crows and the planet Saturn, both announcing the change of season) and dust (*miṭṭī*, *k͟hāk*, *ġhubār*). Through its landscape and seasonality, the garden symbolised both the place and temporality of nostalgic longing. As D. Fairchild Ruggles indeed noted, in Islamic traditions, the ruined garden is 'one of the most powerful, romantic metaphors for the passage of time'.[112] Through the growth cycle of trees and plants, and through the daily cycle of sunlight,[113] with the alternate blooming of day and night flowers, the garden enables one to grasp the experience of time and change in a most sensorial way.

However, I argue that the use of garden imagery also more importantly suggested the perfection of Mughal sovereignty. The city

110 For a study of the work, see M. Schleyer, 'Ghadr-e Dehli ke Afsane'.
111 Khwajah Hasan Nizami, *Ġhadar-e Dehlī ke afsāne. Ḥiṣṣah Awwal*, pp. 42, 50, and 98.
112 D. Fairchild-Ruggles, *Islamic Gardens and Landscapes.* 113 Ibid., p. 6.

described in the poems was made of the urban landscape, but also of its inhabitants and especially of the court. The court-city was allegorised in the image of the garden, which was also a traditional symbol of secular power. Describing cities through garden imagery was not uncommon in Islamic literary cultures, as nature invariably evoked the perfection of paradise.[114] Paradise became the archetype for earthly gardens, which were conceived as its rival. One of the most famous examples is the legend of Iram, or the city of the Pillars (mentioned in Surah 89), which 'captured the imagination of poets throughout the Islamic world'.[115] In a bid to surpass the beauty of paradise, the South Arabian king Shaddad created the garden of Iram. God warned the king against challenging Him and eventually destroyed the garden.[116]

Comparing Delhi, or any Muslim city, to paradise was not only a literary trope but also a tool to legitimise and praise its rulers.[117] Julie Meisami indeed argued that it was a standard part of Persian panegyrics to depict garden scenes, to the extent that they were sometimes labelled 'garden *qaṣīdahs*'.[118] Building on pre-Islamic Iranian

[114] As Hämeen-Anttila argued, nature in the Qur'an was also usually mentioned in relation to paradise (J. Hämeen-Anttila, 'Paradise and Nature in the Quran and Pre-Islamic Poetry', p. 136). Lange shows that paradise was also often described in worldly terms (C. Lange, *Paradise and Hell in Islamic Traditions*, p. 3). See also A. Al-Azmeh, 'Rhetoric of the Senses: A Consideration of Muslim Paradise Narratives', p. 223 and A. Schimmel, 'The Celestial Garden in Islam', p. 18.

[115] D. Hanaway, 'Paradise on Earth', p. 46.

[116] Earthly gardens caught the imagination of many, and different interpretations also emerged as to where Adam and Eve's primordial garden was located. Since the garden of Eden refers to both the primordial garden and to the eschatological one promised to believers in the Qur'an, some have argued that it was located in heaven – Adam and Eve are ordered by God to 'descend from paradise' (e.g. Surah 20, 123) – while others have situated it on a mountain top. Because of the mention of peacocks and snakes in paradise, which are indigenous Indian species, South Asia emerged as a likely location (A. Schimmel, 'The Celestial Garden', p. 20). Adam's Peak in Sri Lanka was said to bear the footprints of the first man.

[117] Inheriting these traditions of describing imperial cities as gardens, Indian Muslim authors had described Delhi as the Garden of Eden since Amir Khusrau (1253–1325) at least. See *Qiran al-Saʿdayn*, pp. 22–3, quoted in M. K. Hermansen and B. B. Lawrence, 'Indo-Persian Tazkiras', p. 167, and C. Ernst, 'India as a Sacred Islamic Land', p. 556.

[118] Already in Arabic panegyrics, the enclosed garden symbolised the world and the court, but even more so in Persian. In the eleventh century, Nasir Khusrau, for instance, described the Fatimid court in Cairo in typical garden imagery that was also later used by Urdu *shahr āshob* poets. See J. S. Meisami, 'Poetic Microcosms', p. 166.

beliefs but also on Quranic traditions, the Islamic garden symbolised the king's (or the patron's) fitness, generosity, and justice. The beauty of the garden, its abundance of fruit and flowers, its sophisticated flowing canals and waterfalls, all extolled the king's ability to control nature, to reproduce paradise on earth, and to link 'heaven and earth, divinely ordered cosmos with justly governed world'.[119] The garden was an ultimate symbol of kingly power,[120] and it was not uncommon for medieval Muslim kings to commission miniature representations of themselves sitting in gardens[121] – Mughal miniature painting also contributed to the tradition.

In agricultural societies with arid or semi-arid climates, the ability to create gardens and thus to master irrigation denoted remarkable skill but also a complex system of central administration.[122] The garden represented the quintessence of irrigated culture. It was not used only as an aesthetic landscape but as a space for food production and botanical experiments.[123] With society and the army depending mostly on agricultural revenues, agriculture and irrigation were considered essential elements of royal ideology in ancient Iranian culture. As Maria Subtelny showed, the concept of the 'good king' was intrinsically linked to the good state of the land, and the king was often described as a 'good gardener'.[124] *Pairidaēza* in Avestan or *bāġh* in Persian, the enclosed garden was since Antiquity, as Stronach argued, a 'political statement' and a 'potent vehicle for royal propaganda'.[125]

In Mughal culture too, gardens were essential elements and symbols of courtly life. As Farahani, Motamed and Jamei argued, as a nomadic and nature-loving people, 'the Mughals used their charbaghs as no other great dynasty has used gardens. Neither decorative adjuncts to a palace nor intended simply for visual enjoyment, gardens were used in place of buildings'.[126] Since Babur's arrival in South Asia, gardens had acquired an important status. Riding from garden to garden in

[119] Ibid., p. 145.
[120] J. S. Meisami, 'Ghaznavid Panegyrics: Some Political Implications', p. 34; J. S. Meisami, *Medieval Persian Court Poetry*, p. 292.
[121] M. Subtelny, *Le monde est un jardin*, p. 104. [122] Ibid., pp. 29–52.
[123] Ibid., p. 101 and A. A. Husain, *Scent in the Islamic Garden*.
[124] M. Subtelny, *Le monde est un jardin*, p. 69.
[125] D. Stronach, 'The Garden as a Political Statement', p. 171.
[126] L. M. Farahani, B. Motamed, and E. Jamei, 'Persian Gardens: Meanings, Symbolism, and Design', p. 3.

Central Asia, Babur's discovery of India's lack of running water was a shock, which he strove to overcome. Under his rule, as he illustrated in his memoirs, 'in disorderly Hindustan, plots of garden were seen laid out with order and symmetry, with suitable borders and parterres in every corner, and in every border rose and narcissus in perfect arrangement'.[127] Walled gardens were conceived as delightful open-air palaces,[128] whose architecture and orderly planning reflected and legitimised the new order of Mughal rule in India.[129] As in Persia, but to an even greater extent, gardens were instruments for the legitimacy of power and were also the place where court rituals were celebrated.[130] Gardens were commonly used for public audiences, wine parties and entertainment, political talks, horticultural experiments, and religious rites.[131]

Despite their role in urbanisation and their construction of fine capital cities, the Mughals like the Timurids and Safavids (under whose rule *shahr āshob* literature thrived) were incredibly mobile and retained a nomadic way of ruling.[132] In his *Travels in the Mogul Empire, A.D. 1656–1668*, the French traveller Bernier observed that 'the whole population of Delhi is in fact collected in the camp, [...] it has no alternative but to follow [the court and army] in their march or perish from want during their absence'.[133] Until 1739, Mughal emperors spent around 40 per cent of their time in tours of one year or more.[134] When emperors left with their camp, the city was emptied of its population and dramatically declined, since the entire court (including women, cooks, water-carriers, craftsmen, etc.) followed the emperor. Abul Fazl described in his *A'īn-e Akbarī* the size of each encampment, which required for its carriage '100 elephants, 500

127 Babur, *Babur Nama: Journal of Emperor Babur*, p. 278.
128 E. B. Moynihan, *Paradise as a Garden in Persia and Mughal India*, p. 97.
129 E. Koch, 'My Garden Is Hindustan: The Mughal Padshah's Realization of a Political Metaphor', p. 160.
130 M. Alemi, 'Princely Safavid Gardens: Stage for Rituals of Imperial Display', p. 125.
131 E. B. Moynihan, *Paradise as a Garden*, p. 97. See also A. A. Husain, *Scent in the Islamic Garden* and C. B. Asher, 'Babur and the Timurid Char Bagh: Use and Meaning'.
132 A. Schimmel, *The Empire of the Great Mughals*, p. 77.
133 Bernier, *Travels in the Mogul Empire, A.D. 1656–1668*, pp. 280–1, quoted by S. P. Blake, *Shahjahanabad*, p. 68.
134 S. P. Blake, *Shahjahanabad*, p. 97.

camels, 400 carts, and 100 bearers'.[135] Massive tents were erected as the entire court moved from one place to another, forming a veritable 'tent city' with palaces, streets, and bazaars.[136] As Stronach and Subtelny noted for ancient Persia, one may argue that in Mughal India too 'it was the architecture of the garden that incorporated the palace and not the contrary'.[137] In 1648, the imperial camp/garden as symbol and assertion of Mughal power was so essential that it served as archetype for the construction of the Red Fort of Delhi.[138] As a matter of fact, the palace buildings often reproduced a natural environment, incorporating botanical elements in their architecture with tree-like columns or colourful ever-blooming pietra dura (*parchīn kārī*) flowers.[139] Even in the capital city, tents were still erected in and around buildings, and awnings and canopies were rigged to the palaces until 1857.[140]

In 1857 *shahr āshobs* the descriptions of Delhi as a heavenly garden strongly built on this traditional imagery. They often evoked celestial bodies, fountains, trees, legends like the garden of Iram, and other symbols of eternity (Jamshed's cup, the Water of Life, the elixir of immortality). Although only a couple of passages in pre-1857 *shahr āshob* poetry evoked paradise, from Barq's *musaddas* (1857?) onwards, virtually every 1857 poem mentioned one or several paradisiacal elements. The vocabulary for (earthly and heavenly) paradise was rich: *k͟huld, gulshan-e k͟huld, chaman-e k͟huld, k͟huld-e barīn, firdaus, janān, jannat, bihisht, gulshan-e Riẓwān, roẓah-e Riẓwān, ḥūristān, haft āsmān, maqām-e aman, k͟hudā kī panāh*, and so on but also *Iram-e k͟huld, parīstān*. Adam and Eve were sometimes mentioned, along with houris, fairies (*parī*), angels (*farishtah, malā'ik*), male servants (*ġhilmān*), the gatekeeper Rizwan, the heavenly fountain Tasnīm, the spring of Haiwān, the T̠ūbā tree, and so on.

[135] Abul Fazl, *The Ain-i Akbari*, trans. H. Blochmann, p. 47.
[136] A. Schimmel, *The Empire of the Great Mughals*, p. 80. See also F. Robinson, *The Mughal Emperors*, p. 129.
[137] M. Subtelny, *Le monde est un jardin*, p. 104.
[138] See P. A. Andrews, *Felt Tents and Pavilions*, p. 903 and E. Koch, 'My Garden Is Hindustan', p. 161.
[139] For instance, D. Fairchild-Ruggles, *Islamic Gardens and Landscapes*, p. 84. See also E. Koch, 'Flowers in Mughal Architecture'.
[140] P. A. Andrews, 'The Generous Heart or the Mass of Clouds', p. 151. The continuance of the use of tents under Shah Alam II and Bahadur Shah Zafar is, for instance, attested in Munshi Faizuddin, *Bazm-e āk͟hir*.

Pre-1857 Delhi was idealised as an earthly paradise, sometimes as the centre of Creation and as a most sacred place that rivalled the Islamic city of Mecca. Opening his *musaddas*, Safir, for instance, compared the Delhi of the past to Mecca and to Heaven, asserting its past exalted status:

Yeh shahr ba'd Makkah ke sharaf ul-bilād thā
yeh shahr jumlah shahroṇ meṇ mīnū sawād thā
sākin har ek is kā bihishtī nazhād thā
har ko'ī waṣl-e yār kī mānind shād thā
thā bāġh ab ujaṛ ke bayābān ho gayā.

This city was the noble city after Mecca,
This city was more heavenly than all other cities combined,
Its every inhabitant was of heavenly origin,
Everyone met like cheerful friends,
Now this garden has been ruined and became a desert.[141]

In her investigation of Indian *taẕkirahs*, Marcia Hermansen noted that the sacralisation of cities was a way of memorialising Islam in the urban space and affirming Muslim identity through the configuration of new centres and circuits of pilgrimage.[142] Indo-Persian elites had in fact compared Delhi to a little Mecca (*k͟hurd-e Makkah*) since the beginning of the Muslim rule. In *shahr āshob* poems, however, the sacralisation of the pre-1857 landscape seems to do more than define space as a memorial of religious piety. The objective was to show that Delhi once surpassed the garden of Iram and rivalled Paradise – it was the envy (*rashk*, *ġhairat*) of Iram, or of Heaven, as many poets illustrated. They did not try to exalt places of pilgrimage and worship as in *taẕkirahs*, but to show that the entire Mughal city was the place of God's manifestation. Urdu, the language of Delhi, was compared to Arabic, the language of God spoken in Heaven:

hu'ā iskā jo faṣiḥān-e jahāṇ se nah jawāb
goyā Qurāṇ kī zubāṇ hai yeh zubān-e Dehlī.

In the world there was no rival to its eloquent people,
As if it were the language of the Qur'ān, the language of Delhi.[143]

141 Safir, *kyā āsmān āj bad-u'nwān ho gayā*, verse 2.
142 See M. Hermansen, 'Imagining Space and Siting Collective Memory'.
143 Sipihr, *miṭ gayā safḥah-e 'ālam se nishān-e Dehlī*, verse 10.

In Kamil's *musaddas*, typical of many 1857 poems, the whole of Delhi was described as God's world of pleasure and (the Red Fort especially, with its glowing red sandstone) as Mount Sinai, one of the places of God's appearance on earth.[144]

tamām gulshan-e ʿaish-o surūr thī Dehlī
tamām ʿishrat-o farḥat ẕahūr thī Dehlī
tamām maṯlaʿ-e k͟hūrshīd-e nūr thī Dehlī
tamām ġhairat-e ṣad koh-e ṯūr thī Dehlī
har ek kūchah yahāṇ kā thā ik makān-e ʿaish
yeh shahr thā keh ilāhī ko'ī jahān-e ʿaish.

All of Delhi was a garden of luxury and pleasure,
All of Delhi was a manifestation of gaiety and joy,
All of Delhi was like the glittering sunrise,
All of Delhi was the envy of a hundred Mount Sinai.
Here's every street was an abode of luxury,
This city was one of God's worlds of pleasure.[145]

As this passage illustrates, pre-1857 Delhi was often described with a vocabulary of joy and radiance, with every day resembling the day of Eid and every night Shab-e Barat. It was a world of luxury (*ʿaish-o ʿishrat*), splendour (*shān-o shaukat*), pleasure (*mazā*, *musarrat*, *luṯf*), and happiness (*nishāṯ*, *ṯarab*). Delhi's inhabitants were described as perfect (*kāmil*, *ahl-e kamāl*). It is notable that the world of Delhi was also described in terms of material wealth, recalling the wealth promised in paradise, with much insistence on jewellery (e.g. *jauhar*, *gauhar*, *zewar*, *motī*), embroidered clothes, perfume, and adornments (*ʿiṯr*, sandalwood, *mehndī*, *singhār*). In another example from one of Salik's *musaddases*, different elements of Delhi were gauged in relation to paradise, only to stress that the Mughal city surpassed it.

zamīn-e past yahāṇ kī thī āsmāṇ manẕar
har ek żarrah yahāṇ kā thā mehr kā hamsar
yahāṇ kī k͟hāk thī aksīr se bhī kuchh bahtar
yahāṇ kī āb meṇ āb-e ḥayāt kā thā aṡar
nasīm-e k͟huld se bahtar simūm thī yāṇ kī
yeh woh chaman hai keh dunyā meṇ dhūm thī yāṇ kī.

[144] The Fort, like the Sinai, is red in colour: when God appeared to Moses on Mount Sinai, he appeared surrounded by red light.
[145] Kamil, *tamām gulshan-e ʿaish-o surūr thī Dehlī*, verse 1.

Here low earth was equal to the Heavens,
Here every particle was like a shining sun,
Here dust was even better than elixir,
In here water had the power of the Water of life,
Here Simoom [a dust-laden wind] was better than the paradise's
breeze,
This is the garden whose fame was known to the world.[146]

The comparison of the Red Fort to Mount Sinai, of Delhi to God's paradise, served to praise Mughal rule metaphorically yet purposefully. The emperor's gardens were a matter of political legitimacy and, as the sovereign was able to create and maintain landscapes that matched the heavenly paradise, his title as God's shadow (*z̤ill-e ilāhī*) on earth was confirmed. The ordered setting of the garden acted as a microcosm centred on the figure of the emperor. The garden-court incorporated traditional theories of Islamic architecture, in which the emperor was conceived as the *axis mundi*, the imperial fort acting as a 'symbolic centre of a nested hierarchy: city, empire and universe'.[147] This, of course, was extended to the urban landscape too, since it was initially conceived on the camp's model. Perceived as both the macrocosm of man and the microcosm of the empire, the city was likened to human anatomy (perhaps thereby alluding to the body of the emperor) – with the main market acting as its backbone, the palace as its head, the great mosque as its heart, smaller streets and buildings as ribs and organs, and walls defining the body.[148] Such theories are reproduced in *The Lament for Delhi*, in one of Ahsan's *ġhazals*:

chāndnī chauk ko sīnah kaheṇ aur qileʿh ko sar
masjid-e jāmaʿ ko t̲hahrā'eṇ miyān-e Dehlī.

Let's call Chandni Chowk the breast, and say the Fort's the head,
And let's imagine Jama Masjid is the waist of Delhi.[149]

146 Salik, *jahāṇ meṇ shahr haiṇ jitne jahāṇ jahāṇābād*, verse 3.
147 S. P. Blake, *Shahjahanabad*, p. xiv.
148 N. Ardalan and L. Bakhtiar, *The Sense of Unity: The Sufi Tradition in Persian Architecture*, p. 93 quoted by S. P. Blake, *Shahjahanabad*, p. 35.
149 Ahsan, *hā'e woh log jo the rūh-o rawān-e Dehlī*, verse 3, trans. Pasha Khan, columbia.edu/itc/mealac/pritchett/00urduhindilinks/workshop2009/txt_pasha_fughan.pdf, p. 4.

As Soofia Siddique has shown, the metaphor of the body was an important image in Mughal ideology. Political authority was asserted through the 'ritual and relational hierarchy of the different parts of the body' that materialised in the ceremonious giving of the *k̲h̲ilaʿt* (honorific robe), which incorporated subjects in the body politics.[150] Rosalind O'Hanlon argued that the just emperor and his norms and values were seen as agents of cohesion in the articulation of the different bodies composing the empire and regulating the different spheres of the kingdom, household, and individual.[151] The Mughal emperor was the symbolic centre of the garden city and of the empire as the 'divinely ordained focus [...] of society',[152] and the poems largely perpetuated this vision.

4 Doomsday in Paradise: Loss of Sovereignty

The destruction of the orderly paradise of Mughal Delhi was commonly compared to autumn, to death, and to the apocalypse in the poems. As Annemarie Schimmel noted, the identification between the beloved and paradise 'was all the more appropriate as the poets liked to compare the day of separation to the day of resurrection which extends over centuries, and in which the greatest tumult takes place',[153] Here, of course, 1857 *shahr āshobs* again built on traditional poetic expressions of loss, but, once more, extended them powerfully by resorting to rich apocalyptic symbolism. Besides describing the events of 1857 as a catastrophe, oppression, and injustice, with terms like *āfat*, *hangāmah*, *fitnah*, *inqilāb*, *balā*, *mājrā*, *shāmat*, *jafā*, *barbādī*, *sitam*, *muṣībat*, and so on, a more explicit vocabulary referred to the end of times: *nālah-e ṣūr* (the sound of the apocalyptic trumpet), *malak al-maut* (the angel of death), *qayāmat*, *qayāmat-e ṣuġhrā*, *ṣubh-e qayāmat* (doomsday, resurrection), *roz-e jazā* (doomsday), *roz-e mauʿūd* (the promised day), *ajal* (the appointed time), *ḥashr*, *maḥshar*, *maḥshar-e ġhadar*, *ḥashr kā maidān*, *roz-e ḥashr* (the day or place of final judgment), and *nār-e dozak̲h̲* (the fire of hell). In Islamic eschatological

[150] S. Siddique, 'Remembering the Revolt', p. 50 quotes B. Cohn, 'Representing Authority in Victorian India', p. 168. See also B. Cohn, 'Cloths, Clothes, and Colonialism: India in the Nineteenth Century', pp. 114–5.
[151] R. O'Hanlon, 'Kingdom, Household and Body History', p. 889.
[152] F. W. Pritchett, *Nets of Awareness*, p. 29.
[153] A. Schimmel, 'The Celestial Garden', p. 19.

traditions, the apocalypse is usually predicted by the blowing of the trumpet, the apparition of lesser signs or warnings (*ʿibrat*) like natural disasters, the disintegration of morality, and then of greater signs (the arrival of the Antichrist, his fight with the *Mahdī*). Then follows resurrection (*qayāmat*), the gathering for the final judgment (*ḥashr*), and the crossing of the bridge of Sirat to reach either the Garden or the Fire.[154]

The shock of 1857 and of its aftermath was pictured as the end of times that abruptly concluded Islam's sacred history. Besides comparing the events to Karbala, some poets, like Dagh, also inscribed Delhi's experience within Prophetic history to emphasise fracture. In one instance, he referred to the Prophet Ilyas (Elijah) as the only figure who could have escaped from the events, and, indeed, Ilyas is traditionally seen as a non-mortal prophet with an eschatological dimension, since he predicts the arrival of the Messiah.[155] In another example, Dagh illustrates that everyone cries upon the separation with Delhi, even the sky, so much so that even Noah's ark would not have survived the flood of tears:

Zamīṇ ke ḥāl peh ab āsmān rotā hai
har ik firāq-e makīṇ meṇ makān rotā hai
nah t̲ifl-o aurat-o pīr-o jawān rotā hai
ġharẓ yahāṇ ke lī'e ek jahāṇ rotā hai
jo kahī'e joshish-e t̲ūfān nahīṇ kahī jātī
yahāṇ to Nūḥ kī kashtī bhī ḍūb hī jātī.

The sky now cries at the earth's condition,
Every house cries on the separation with its occupants.
Not (only) babies, and women, old and young cry
In short, the whole world cries for Delhi,
They say that the violence of this tempest is unfathomable,
Here even Noah's ark would sink too.[156]

The events of 1857 were interpreted as death, with the corporeality of the city (encapsulated in the city's material landscape) disappearing to leave only its soul (or its recollection): *gumān-e Dehlī* as most poets

[154] For more on Islamic eschatological representations, see J. Smith and Y. Haddad, *Islamic Understanding of Death and Resurrection*; N. and N. Rustomji, *The Garden and the Fire*; S. Günther and T. Lawson (eds), *Roads to Paradise.*

[155] See, for instance, P. Lory, 'Elie', in M. A. Amir-Moezzi (ed.), *Dictionnaire du Coran*, pp. 244–6.

[156] Dagh, *falak zamīn-o malā'ik janāb thī dillī*, verse 11.

told. With cosmic signs of apocalypse occurring in the poems – particularly tempest (*ṯūfān*) and windstorms (*bād-e tund*), earthquakes (*tazalzul*), a rain of fire (*āg kā barsā*), and the split of the earth (*zamīn-shaq*) – Shah Jahanabad fell into nothingness (or *ʿadmābād*).[157] It was the ultimate separation. While the Day of Resurrection would also traditionally imply reunion with God/the beloved, in the poems here analysed, the Delhi of the past was predominantly described as utterly annihilated. As Delhi surpassed paradise, paradise would pale in comparison, so paradise was lost, so much so that even the otherworldly paradise cried over the loss of Delhi.[158] The violence of the rupture only strengthened the yearning for pre-1857 times.

Many poems tried to explain the events of 1857, to understand why 'doomsday had come before doomsday' (*qayāmat ā'ī qayāmat se kis lī'e pahle?*) as Mubin asked in one of his *musaddases*.[159] The question of why misfortune occurred had been raised by *shahr āshob* poetry well before the events of 1857. As Shamsur Rahman Faruqi noted in his commentary on Jurat's (d. 1810) *shahr āshob*, the sky was often pointed out as 'the traditional perpetrator of crimes of injustice in Urdu poetry'.[160] One of the words for the sky, *charḵẖ*, also means a turning wheel and is a metaphor for time. The idea of the wheel of fortunes, or of fate, was occasionally invoked in Nazir's or Jauhri's verses,[161] as in 1857 poems (*gardish-e taqdīr*, *muqaddar*, *qiṣmat*, *naṣīb*). Usually, 1857 *shahr āshobs* built on convention and blamed the cruel old sky for its injustice and malice (*pīr-e falak*, *charḵẖ-e kuhan*, *falak kī barbādī*, *falak kā ẕulm*, *falak-e kīnah*, *charḵẖ-e bad-kesh*, *charḵẖ-e badbīn*, *charḵẖ-e sitamgar*, etc.); others accused the cold, boisterous winds of winter. Of course, the reference to the sky or to the climate alluded to the change in season that brought autumn to the garden.

Some expressions such as *zuḥal kī ānkh* ('the eye of Saturn') or *naẕar-e ḵẖaṣm-e falak* ('the enemy sky's eye'), along with general

157 For instance, in Sabir's *ġhazal baskeh bedād se ṭūṭe haiṉ makān-e Dehlī*, verse 12.
158 Lange explains in his studies of Islamic eschatological traditions that paradise 'remains accessible, even during one's life on earth', with prophets and mystics sometimes flying to the heavens. Generally speaking, he argues, the Quranic paradise 'co-exists with this world'. C. Lange, 'The Discovery of Paradise in Islam', p. 7.
159 Mubin, *pasand-e ḵẖāṯir har ḵẖāṣ-o ʿām thī Dehlī*, verse 18.
160 Jur'at, 'Jurat's Shahr-ashob' (S. R. Faruqi) p. 13.
161 F. Lehmann, 'Urdu Literature and Mughal Decline', p. 130.

mentions of the evil eye (*naẕar, chashm-e badbīn*), also introduced the idea of jealousy and alien malevolence as the cause of ruin. This resonates particularly with the metaphor of the garden, since gardens are traditionally enclosed in Islamic traditions, and protected from the outside world.[162] As Farahani, Motamed and Jamei argued, this introversion is also incorporated into architecture, so that the eyes of strangers cannot peek easily into Persian gardens.[163] An unauthorised glance into the garden's cherished and well-guarded wealth was thus a powerful symbol. Soofia Siddique has argued that the sky in fact symbolised British oppressors for *shahr āshob* poets, who were particularly wary of colonial censure and retaliation. Given the historical context and the literary conventions too, despite the compelling idea of the external gaze, it is difficult to assess how much of this hypothesis is true. In some of the poems, the Rebels – called *Tilange, kāle* (black), or *bedīn bāġhī* (faithless rebels) in the poems – were condemned.[164]

When explaining decline with the conventional image of the cruel sky, the latter's anger was often emphasised. Other poets attributed the anger to God (*k͟hudā kā qahr, qahr-o ġhaẓab, ġhuṣṣah*) and explained that Delhi's devastation was God's command (*fa'āl-e māyurīd* 'The Accomplisher of what He intends', *Allāh kā hukm*). The anger at Delhi could be read as a second example of God's wrath at human attempts to rival paradise on earth, as in the case of the garden of Iram. But divine or heavenly anger was also attributed by some poets to human wrongdoing and sin, and to the absence of fear of God or lack of faith. In one of his *musaddases*, and the only poem with a chorus, Mubin insisted on the fact that the people of Delhi brought the misfortunes upon themselves by their own attitude, interestingly exonerating both the British (white) and the rebels (black):

Ẕulm goroṇ ne kiyā aur nah sitam kāloṇ ne
ham ko barbād kiyā apne hī ā'māloṇ ne.

The white have not afflicted us, nor the black,
We have ruined ourselves by our own deeds.[165]

[162] J. S. Meisami, 'Allegorical Gardens in the Persian Poetic Tradition', p. 231, or A. Schimmel, 'The Celestial Garden', p. 16.
[163] L. M. Farahani, B. Motamed, and E. Jamei, 'Persian Gardens', p. 8.
[164] On the question of guilt and responsibility for 1857, see also R. Jalil, 'Reflections of 1857 in Contemporary Urdu Literature', pp. 121–4.
[165] Mubin, *dil ġhanī rakkhā sak͟hāwat peh nah zar wāloṇ ne*, chorus.

In any way, 1857 *shahr āshob* writers seem to have articulated a discourse on the loss of power that was symbolised by the apocalypse or the autumn that had devastated a perfectly ordered garden. The garden was the city of Delhi but, more profoundly, the city of Mughal power. In his long *musaddas*, Zahir Dehlawi indeed stated that apocalypse had come on the 'House of Timur' (*k̲h̲āndān-e Tīmūr par qayāmat ā'ī*).[166] A couple of verses before, he qualified Mughal rule, which he calls 'Caliphate', as a ruined garden:

nihāl-e gulshan-e iqbāl pā'emāl hū'e
gul-e riyāẓ-e k̲h̲ilāfat lahū meṇ lāl hū'e.

The trees of this prosperous garden have been trampled
The flowers of Caliphate's garden have been reddened with
blood.[167]

Delhi poets who represented the pre-1857 city as an earthly paradise undoubtedly lamented the loss of the Mughal court, without being overtly sympathetic to the Delhi king. As a matter of fact, the figure of Bahadur Shah Zafar did not appear often in the poems. One notable exception was Zahir Dehlawi's *musaddas*, which directly referred to the king in rather laudatory terms, despite the latter's trial for treason in 1858.

kahāṇ woh k̲h̲usraw-e ʿālī naẕar bahādur shāh
kahāṇ woh sarwar-e neko-siyar bahādur shāh
kahāṇ woh bādshāh-e dādgar bahādur shāh
kahāṇ woh dāwar-e wālā gauhar bahādur shāh
kahāṇ se bāġhī-e bedīn ā ga'e hā'e hā'e
keh nām us kā jahāṇ se miṭā ga'e hā'e hā'e.

Where is the regal benevolent Bahadur Shah?
Where is the courteous monarch Bahadur Shah?
Where is the king of justice Bahadur Shah?
Where is this eminent just sovereign Bahadur Shah?
Alas, wherefrom did these unfaithful rebels come,
Alas, who have erased his name from the world?[168]

[166] Zahir, *farishtah maskan-o jannat nishān thī Dehlī*, verse 30. Divine light was supposed to have descended from Timur to his Mughal descendants. See, for instance, F. Robinson, *The Mughal Emperors*, p. 7.

[167] Zahir, *farishtah maskan-o jannat nishān thī Dehlī*, verse 23.

[168] Ibid., end of verse 24.

The garden, just like imperial monuments, represented the power of Mughal rule and its ability to order the world, an order that was shattered in apocalyptic cataclysm. Despite resorting heavily to metaphors of the city as a garden, 1857 *shahr āshobs* also provide evidence for the increasing significance of the built landscape, as I have shown elsewhere.[169] While ruins were already used as a motif to enhance despair in Mir's and Sauda's verses, they usually remained metaphorical, abstract, and anonymous.[170] Writers of 1857 *shahr āshob* extended the description of the ruins of nameless houses and buildings to the mention of specific monuments by name, sometimes with a description.[171] While Western influence may have accentuated the change in conceptions of the urban, the growth of a sense of place and the emotional investment in the architectural environment were most probably inspired by both the changing nature of Mughal political power from the eighteenth century onwards and the collective expression of grief.[172] As Margrit Pernau argued, such descriptions, like Syed Ahmed Khan's description of the garden of Hayat Bakhsh in the Fort, starting with a comparison to paradise and ending with a depiction of its pitiful present state, allowed 'for the transfer of emotions from the rich archive of poetry onto the experience of a concrete space'.[173]

The theme of the ruins reminding people of the ephemeral nature of human existence was not new and had already given birth to the ancient Persian literary theme of the 'warning' (*'ibrat*), which also appeared in *shahr āshobs*. Ebba Koch showed how popular the theme was in Akbar's epigraphy, as the emperor inscribed the sites of the conquered territories of the Faruqi kings or of the sultans of Mawa. One such epigraphical poem composed by Nami at Mandu illustrated: 'At Dawn I saw an owl sitting on the pinnacle of Shirwan Shah's tomb. Plaintively it uttered the warning: 'Where is all that glory and where

169 E. Tignol, 'Nostalgia and the City'.

170 See, for instance, Sauda, *Mukhammas-e shahr āshob*, verse 28.

171 The poet Shamshir mentioned the Khas market, and Mirza Aziz evoked the Lal Diggi, also known as the Ellenborough tank (1846) in their *ġhazals* (Shamshir, *kaise kaise hū'e barbād makān-e Dehlī*, verses 7 and 8, and Mirza Aziz, *jannatī dekh ke kahte haiṇ khizān-e Dehlī*, verse 13).

172 See E. Tignol, 'Nostalgia and the City', pp. 568–72. About Western and indigenous pictorial representations of the urban landscape, see S. Waraich, 'A City Besieged and a Love Lamented', pp. 153–4.

173 M. Pernau, 'Fluid Temporalities: Saiyid Ahmad Khan and the Concept of modernity', p. 110.

all that splendour?"[174] This type of inscription, she emphasised, was 'employed in a dialectic way to commemorate as well as to symbolise conquest and appropriation of land'.[175] In 1857, the reflective theme of the warning hints at the fact that poets commemorated the change in political power too.

5 Conclusion

The poems on 1857 all developed a language of collective grief through different literary devices: the poetic meters of the *ġhazal* (as *nauḥah*) and *musaddas* (as *marṡiyah*), the deployment of a rich vocabulary of suffering, and the resort to the image of the garden with its inherent representations (paradise, separation from the beloved, apocalyptic chaos).

By adopting the style of the *marṡiyah* and conventions usually associated with mourning and Shia rituals in a non-religious, secular context, 1857 was collectively represented as a historical and cultural rupture that obliterated Mughal identity – the abundance of verbs like *miṭnā* 'to be erased' or *miṭānā* 'to erase' is remarkable. The constant references to orality and to the impact of *shahr āshob* verses on the audience hinted at the fact that *shahr āshob* poets cultivated a culture of '*āshobgo'ī*' which implied collective commemoration and communal weeping. These elements were not entirely new to Urdu poetry, but their full development and combined use became typical of later *shahr āshob* poetry.

In the poems, the expression of *ġham* built on a rich poetic vocabulary of pain and love. But poets did not use a vague depressive mood; rather, they expressed acute physical pain in its most corporal manifestations. The language was graphic: it was all blood, burn, and decomposition. Some poets went so far as to identify the victims of 1857 as a 'people of suffering' (*ahl-e dard*).[176] Loss was apprehended through the poetic pain of amorous separation, where Delhi acted as the beloved, which only left a burning scar (*dāġh*) on the lover's heart. With the grief of loss also came an idealisation of the Delhi of the past.

The garden, a conventional and natural setting for the expression of romantic suffering, was also deployed as an undeniable symbol of

174 J. Horovitz, 'Inscriptions of Dhar and Mandu', pp. 26–7, quoted by E. Koch, 'Shah Jahan's Visit to Delhi prior to 1648', p. 29.
175 Ibid.
176 See, for instance, Zahir, *farishtah maskan-o jannat nishān thī Dehlī*, verse 27.

kingly power in the poems. Resembling the garden descriptions of many medieval Arabic and Persian *qaṣīdahs*, 1857 *shahr āshobs* most certainly articulated a discourse on power. After all, Kaukab's *Lament of Delhi* opened with a poem by the former Delhi king Bahadur Shah Zafar. Similar poetry by Lakhnawi poets, like Barq and others during the same time frame (1856–1857), is perhaps more obviously conceived as straightforward praise to Wajid Ali Shah, but Zahir Dehlawi, who was closely associated with the Mughal court and later wrote a prose account of the events of 1857,[177] nonetheless clearly described the beloved garden in terms of Mughal sovereignty.

As scholars like Daniela Bredi have noted, the choice to remember pre-1857 Delhi as a Mughal city was, however, not entirely accurate.[178] Although the Mughal king still reigned over the Red Fort, his influence had become mostly symbolic and his resources were limited. After Shah Alam II's difficult return to Delhi in 1774 and the British occupation of Delhi from 1803, the proverb used to mock the Mughal 'empire' as stretching only from Delhi to Palam.[179] Delhi from 1803 to 1857 was very much governed by the British, who controlled what happened in the city and fort. Arsh Taimuri remembered in his *Qilaʿh-e muʿallah kī jhalkiyāṇ* (1937, see Chapter 5) that the Mughal court had to obtain permission from the British resident every time the king planned to leave Delhi, even to spend a few days in his hunting lodges on the outskirts of the city.[180] Since their annexation of Delhi in 1803, the British had pacified the territory and made it thrive again.[181] They had adopted the Mughal way of life and manners; founded the Delhi College; and stimulated and commissioned artists, poets and scholars while managing the city. The city bloomed again in what Andrews called the 'Delhi Renaissance'.[182]

In an article arguing against the idea of Muslim estrangement from the British and hostility towards Western knowledge before 1857,

[177] Zahir Dehlawi, *Dastān-e ġhadar, yaʿnī hangāmah-e 1857 ke chashamdīd ḥālāt;* Zahir Dehlavi, *Dastan-e ghadar: the tale of the mutiny*, trans. R. Safvi.

[178] D. Bredi, 'Nostalgia in the Re-construction of Muslim Identity'.

[179] As the Persian saying goes, 'Ṣulṯanat-i Shāh ʿĀlam, az Dehlī tā Palam.' Palam is now a southwest suburb of New Delhi.

[180] Arsh Taimuri, *Qilaʿh-e muʿallah kī jhalkiyāṇ*, p. 48.

[181] *Fraser Papers*, vol. 33, AF to his mother, p. 338, 6 December 1811, on the Ganges quoted by W. Dalrymple, *The Last Mughal: The Fall of a Dynasty*, p. 74.

[182] N. Gupta, *Delhi between Two Empires*, p. 6.

Mushirul Hasan emphasised the fact that during the Delhi Renaissance, Muslim elites had in fact begun to adapt to Western ideas and power, and had little interest in the Mughal king and his fort. He further argued that 'not many shed tears over the collapse of the Mughal Empire or the defeat of Bahadur Shah, a decrepit old man who took refuge in Urdu lyrical poetry'.[183] Further, as Syed Ahmed Khan's *Āṡār uṣ-Ṣanādīd* illustrated, Shahjahanabad's built heritage was already in a state of disrepair before the Uprising.[184]

Shahr āshob poems in the aftermath of 1857, however, wailed over the end of the Mughal world. As Daniela Bredi put it, the Delhi Renaissance period was indeed usually read by Indo-Muslim elites as 'an imagined place embodying the final splendour of the Mughal age'.[185] Recently, Nishtha Singh has shown that the sedentarisation of the Mughal court in Delhi enabled the development of a 'city-centered patriotism' (Dehlviyat),[186] in which the role of the emperor was revived so as to become a 'Dehlvi institution', precisely at the time when 'he was most powerless in administrative terms'.[187] As Ghalib indeed lamented in a letter when remembering the world before 1857, 'all these things lasted only so long as the king reigned'.[188] Poets of 1857 *shahr āshob* usually did not shed tears over Bahadur Shah specifically, but over the Mughal court/garden of which he was a symbol. The profound longing for the pre-1857 period as a time of Mughal splendour certainly did not wait until the 1930s to develop.[189]

Shahr āshob poets also expressed the shock of 1857 with a greater emphasis on the city's built landscape, which concretely gave evidence for the extent of the devastation. The Mughal city was always described as a sacred space of order and pleasure that had been trampled upon. Ruined buildings were used to cleverly echo collective grief when human life had been lost. The poems' new emphasis on buildings and urban planning projects reflects the growing preoccupation with

[183] M. Hasan, 'The Legacies of 1857 among the Muslim Intelligentsia of North India', p. 111.

[184] See M. Rajagopalan, 'Loss and Longing at the Qila Mu'alla', pp. 233–54.

[185] D. Bredi, 'Nostalgia in the Re-construction', p. 145.

[186] N. G. Singh, 'Dehliviyat: The Making and Un-making of Delhi's Indo-Muslim Urban Culture', p. 5.

[187] Ibid., p. 11.

[188] R. Russell and K. Islam, Ghalib, p. 291, quoted by F. W. Pritchett, *Nets of Awareness*, p. 21.

[189] D. Bredi, 'Nostalgia', p. 146.

the protection of heritage sites and town improvement measures in the aftermath of the Uprising. If some poems appraised positive urban changes under British rule, the large majority lingered on lamentations over urban destruction. Other sources, such as Ghalib's letters and the *Native Newspapers Reports*, well highlight the fact that after 1857, issues around urban development were often raised by Urdu litterateurs and editors who frequently lamented and opposed the destruction of some garden, mosque, or ancient gate. Although Chapter 3 will explore the early twentieth-century political implications of urban planning by the British government, Delhi's monuments had already acquired much importance as reminders of Mughal power.

2 *Useful Grief*
The Aligarh Movement

In the decades that followed 1857, the distinctive elite 'family life, language, ideology, and religion all came into question'.[1] As scholars of the period have highlighted, a split between the dwindling Indo-Persian elite and the burgeoning Hindu merchant culture marked the post-1857 era,[2] which was further widened by new government measures in education and government jobs. Competitive recruitment, new mandatory qualifications, quotas, and the gradual establishment of elective government – first through local committees – opened public offices to new English-proficient graduates who directly competed with the Urdu-speaking elite.[3] New examinations to enter public offices directly threatened the maintenance of the *kachahrī* milieu – the complex of court and administrative offices – which relied on kin-like alliances and preserved *ashrāf* privileges and heritage.[4]

From the late 1860s, the Hindi–Urdu language controversy also strained the Urdu-speaking elite. The clash of interests took an increasingly communal form in the late nineteenth century and beyond, despite the fact that Urdu remained the language of administration.[5] The anxiety of seeing other social groups accessing public service increased the Urdu-speaking elite's sense of urgency and fear of lagging behind those who had been prompter to adapt to the new policies. These sentiments were reinforced in the early 1870s by the widespread

[1] D. Lelyveld, *Aligarh's First Generation*, p. 68. See also F. Robinson, *Separatism*, p. 84.

[2] C. R. King, *One Language, Two Scripts*, p. 182.

[3] See F. Robinson, *Separatism*, pp. 36–50.

[4] D. Lelyveld, *Aligarh's First Generation*, p. 68.

[5] See C. R. King, *One Language, Two Scripts*, p. 186. Many petitions in the late 1860s and early 1870s asked for a change of policy regarding the use of the Persian alphabet in courts (V. Dalmia, *The Nationalisation of Hindu Traditions*, p. 181). Much of the controversy revolved around script rather than language; see C. R. King, 'Forging a New Linguistic Identity: The Hindi Movement in Banaras', p. 188.

colonial image of the 'backward Muslim'[6] incapable of adapting to the modern world that was later backed by colonial statistics and reports from the Hunter Commission.[7] While historians of British India have argued that this perception was largely a 'myth', with many upper-class Muslims in fact gaining much from British rule,[8] the new pressures were increasingly addressed by a number of associations of the Urdu-speaking elite.[9] Of these organisations, the modernist and loyalist Muhammadan Anglo-Oriental College founded in 1875 by Syed Ahmed Khan had the most enduring impact on Urdu-speaking groups and especially on the Muslim *ashrāf*.[10]

This chapter focuses on the development of *shahr āshob* poetry into *āshob* poetry, particularly by the Aligarh movement. In the late 1870s, in the middle of the Russo-Turkish war, *shahr āshob* poetry gave way to *dahr/dunyā āshob* poetry, which encouraged visions of a global Muslim community unified in grief. Aligarh poets, such as Altaf Husain Hali (1837–1914), partook in this narration of worldwide Muslim decline and re-engaged with Arab heritage as an impulse for Muslim cultural regeneration. While the adaptation of Arabic classics was part of the articulation of new 'strategies of authority', *ġham* and the remembrance of the origins of Islam were instrumental in creating community and encouraging reform. In contrast with 1857 poetry that emphasised physical pain and burning hearts, the grief of Aligarh writers activated different semantic nets that correlated regret, longing, and repentance. Grief and (imaginary) memory were closely linked to reform.

6 See W. Hunter, *Indian Musalmans*, 1876 (3rd ed.), London. The book focused on Bengali Muslims.

7 S. Seth, 'Constituting the "Backward but Proud Muslim"', p. 129. Statistics putting all Muslims – nobles or poor – in a same religious category highlighted the disinterest of Muslims in the government-sponsored school system.

8 See Ibid. and P. Hardy, *The Muslims of British India*.

9 K. Pant, *The Kashmiri Pandit*, p. 143.

10 By the 1870s, the number of such organisations in the UP numbered more than twenty (F. Robinson, *Separatism*, p. 85). Societies such as the *Benares Institute* (1861), the *Jalsah-e Tahżīb* (1868), and the *Anjuman-e Hind* (1868) were not communal in nature and did not aim for 'sanskritisation' but rather for Westernisation through modernist reform. See K. Pant, *The Kashmiri Pandit*, p. 160; L. C. Stout, 'The Hindustani Kayasthas', p. 78; L. Carroll, 'Origins of the Kayastha Temperance Movement', p. 432. Muslim government servants and landlords supported the Kayastha conference just as Kayasths participated in Muslim institutions and constituted a fair portion of Aligarh graduates. See L. Stout, 'The Hindustani Kayasthas', p. 173; D. Lelyveld, *Aligarh's First Generation*, p. 171; and F. Robinson, *Separatism*, p. 85.

As Aligarh's poetic expression and amplification of Muslim collective grief attained popular success in the late 1880s and beyond, its potential for the creation of emotional communities appeared more clearly. In 1888, Hali's *Complaint to India* (*Shikwah-e Hind*) and the resort to *āshob* poetry in the satirical magazine *Awadh Punch* for anti- and pro-Congress propaganda showed that the elicitation of *ġham* by Aligarh writers not only served the project of reform but also promoted the cohesion of an aristocratic community – a 'strategy' which was highly criticised by the cosmopolitan milieu of *Awadh Punch* contributors who mocked Aligarh's opportunistic recourse to feeling.

The chapter ends by showing that Aligarh's grief and articulation of a nostalgic-reformist discourse in which India appeared as the place of Muslim downfall was gradually read outside of its immediate reformist and polemical context of composition. In the early twentieth century, *Awadh Punch* contributors criticised Hali's *Musaddas* and *Shikwah-e Hind* for their lack of patriotic dedication and their misrepresentation of Indo-Muslim history. At the beginning of the twentieth century, such works resonated as instances of 'emotional dissociation' from the Indian motherland. Despite aiming at creating community, *ġham* and imaginings of a glorious Islamic past also created estrangement.

1 From *shahr āshob* to *āshob* Poetry in the 1870s

When war was declared between the Russian and Ottoman empires in 1877, the Urdu press bloomed. News from the world and especially from Turkey inundated the Indian public sphere and left Urdu-speaking elites aghast, especially Muslim *ashrāf* who saw in the Ottoman Empire the last 'spark' of Islamic glory. In the *Urdū Ak͟hbār*, a year before the war, the fate of Indian Muslims was already described as intertwined with that of the Ottoman empire: 'if that Empire ceased to exist, the Muhammadans will at once fall into insignificance and be utterly neglected.'[11] Newspapers played a tremendous role in mobilising Indian Muslims. While pro-Turkish feelings had appeared in the Delhi press since the 1840s,[12] this time, news about Turkey

[11] Urdu Akhbar, 17 August 1876, L/R/5/53, *IOR* quoted by A. Özcan, *Indian Muslims, the Ottomans and Britain (1877–1924)*, p. 65.
[12] N. Qureshi, *Pan-Islam in British Indian Politics*, p. 30.

overflowed the expanding Urdu press to the extent that many papers started devoting special space to cover the events and to appeal to the compassion and generosity of fellow countrymen.[13] As Qureshi notes, journals such as *Shams ul-Akhbār* and the *Awadh Punch* (Lucknow), *Aḥsan ul-Akhbār* (Allahabad), and newspapers published by Hindus like *Awadh Akhbār* (Lucknow) and *Akhbār-e ʿām* (Lahore) overtly expressed their support for Turkey.[14] Local newspapers issued daily editions to broadcast the latest developments in the war, meetings were organised all over India to raise money for the Turkey Relief Fund (more than 10 lakhs of rupees were collected),[15] and Indian volunteers joined the Turkish army.[16] However, in December 1877, after months of siege and enthusiasm for Gazi Osman Pasha's heroic resistance, the fall of the city of Plevna shattered the hopes of many.

Shahr āshob poems that had until then mourned the devastation of Mughal cities started lamenting the condition of the whole world. Urdu poets extended the genre to what was now called *āshob* (on disturbance), *dunyā āshob* (on the disturbance of the world), and *dahr* or *zamānah āshob* (on the disturbance of the age). Although *āshob*s were still written on local issues and class problems, more and more poems alluded to global developments. Almost since the beginning of its creation, the newly founded satirical magazine *Awadh Punch* – published from Lucknow by Munshi Sajjad Husain, Rais of Kakori (1856–1915) – started publishing *āshob* poems alongside news of the Russo-Turkish war and of the southern India famine (1876–1878).[17]

On 18 December 1877 (one week after the fall of Plevna), the *Awadh Punch* published a *ġhazal* entitled *dunyā āshob* (Figure 2.1). In the introduction to the poem, the poet Khushgap[18] explained that 'until now poets of the whole world have recited *shahr āshob*s, now

[13] A. Özcan, *Indian Muslims*, p. 64. [14] N. Qureshi, *Pan-Islam*, p. 30.

[15] A. Özcan, *Indian Muslims*, p. 69.

[16] Even Syed Ahmed Khan, despite disagreeing with the widespread view of the Ottoman emperor as caliph, organised a meeting at his house to collect funds. See G. Minault, *The Khilafat Movement*, pp. 5–7.

[17] The *Awadh Punch* was published from 16 January 1877 to 1936. See M. Hasan, *Wit and Humour in Colonial North India*, p. 11 and *A Selection from the Illustrations Which Have Appeared in the* Oudh Punch *from 1877 to 1881*.

[18] The full name of the poet Khushgap is Rashak Khaqani Fakhar Salman. He was probably a regular contributor or worked as assistant manager for the magazine, as his name is followed by the epithet *munshī-e Awadh Punch*.

Figure 2.1 Decorated title for Khushgap's *dunyā āshob*, *Awadh Punch*, 18 December 1877

your devoted servant will put together and recite a *dunyā āshob*'.[19] Similarly, in an explanation to one *dahr āshob* written in 1928, Safi Lakhnawi explained that 'while others used to write *shahr āshobs*, I am writing *dahr āshobs*'.[20] Urdu poets saw *āshob* poetry as an evolution of the *shahr āshob* genre: they did not claim to create something new but placed themselves in an already recognised tradition, the exact formal literary modes of which were yet fluctuating. As such, in addition to borrowing *shahr āshob* metres and motifs, poets also tended to identify their verses nominally as pertaining to that tradition by titling or introducing their works as *dunyā* or *dahr āshob* poems.

The development of *shahr āshob* into *āshob* poetry in the late 1870s illustrated what Francis Robinson highlighted as a 'symbiotic relationship between the growth of pan-Islamic consciousness and of the press'.[21] Khushgap's *dunyā āshob* of 1877, for instance, strengthened feelings of belonging to a pan-Indian community and to a wider world that shared the same grief and was linked via the print media. Such poems not only put Indian news and more general world affairs on the same level but also sometimes mentioned the role of the press (here the *Deccan Punch*) in the spreading of feelings of worldwide despair.

[19] Khushgap, '*Dunyā āshob*', *Awadh Punch*, 18 December 1877, p. 313.
[20] A. Arifi, *Shahr āshob: Ek tajziyah*, p. 259.
[21] F. Robinson, 'Islam and the Impact of Print', p. 79.

Turk tū zor āzmānā chhoṛ de
Rūs-e nāzuk ko satānā chhoṛ de
[...] hai siyāhī se hameṇ żillat khudā
rang tū kālā banānā chhoṛ de
[...] yunhī nā sarkār ham se māng le
fīs-o ṭeks kā bahānā chhoṛ de
[...] likh chukā bas ahliyān nauḥah ko
Ay Dakkan Punch, ab rūlānā chhoṛ de

Turks, stop giving a trial of strength,
Stop tormenting the delicate Russia!
[...] From our blackness comes our disgrace, O God,
Stop blackening everything!
[...] May the government stop demanding from us without reason,
Stop making pleas about fees and taxes!
[...] People have written enough elegies,
O Deccan Punch, now stop making us cry![22]

The juxtaposition of the Great Famine of 1876–1878 with the imposition of relief measures[23] and the Russo-Turkish war in the poem mirrored the very format of newspapers, which united various snippets of world news on a same page, helping the Indian Muslims identify with their Turkish coreligionists. Already a few months earlier, in the 4 September 1877 issue, a poem simply entitled *Nauḥah* (Lamentation) and signed 'F.' typically lamented the Russo-Turkish war while apposing it to the contemporary Indian famine. The lack of food that spread both in Turkish trenches and in north India tied Muslims in the same hardships, with a similar aesthetic of apocalyptic chaos:

ġhallah kī girānī hai qayāmat kī nishānī
paṛtā nahīn pānī
sarkār ne aur ūspeh hai yeh ṭaks jamāyā

[22] Khushgap, '*Dunyā āshob*', p. 313.
[23] About the Great Indian Famine of 1876–1878 see *Imperial Gazetteer of India, vol. 3: Economic*, Oxford, 1908, p. 488. The famine first broke out in the south, affecting Madras, Hyderabad, Mysore, and Bombay, and spread to the north in the Central and United Provinces and in the Punjab from 1877 to winter 1878, affecting a population of 58.5 million overall. The government imposed new taxes to address the situation, which eventually led large numbers of Bombay relief workers to strike. For a discussion on the representation of Indian famines in the *Awadh Punch*, see M. Hasan, *Wit and Humour*, pp. 53–57.

faryād khudāyā
wahān Rūm meṇ Awadh meṇ laṛne kī ṭhanī hai
jānoṇ peh banī hai
yān qahṯ ne hai morchah ab apnā jamāyā
faryād khudāyā
[...] khāne kī tawaqqoʿ hai nah hai pānī kī ummīd
Ay ḥasrat-e jāwed
is sāl meṇ māh-e Ramẓān kisī'e āyā?

This scarcity of grain is a sign of Doomsday,
  Rain too doesn't fall
And the government has imposed taxes again,
  Help us God!
There in Rum [Turkey], in Awadh, a war is going on,
  Lives are in danger
Here famine entrenches in every direction,
  Help us God!
[...] There is no expectation for food, no hope for water,
  O, eternal regret!
Why, has the month of Ramzan come this year?[24]

As Jennifer Dubrow also remarked in a *zamānah āshob* published on 23 April 1878 (still during the Indian famine) by Shauq Qidwai (1852–1925), the magazine 'reframed [the genre] [...] to conjure up a shared landscape of suffering'.[25]

Global news and the newspaper press undoubtedly played a role in the development of *dahr āshob* poetry as in the Urdu poets' growing awareness of pan-Indian and world politics. From the adoption of print in the early nineteenth century and with the introduction of new techniques and the diminution of production costs in the 1840s,[26] printed material became mass produced in India. Locally produced periodicals quickly started stirring enthusiasm among Urdu-speaking elites, so much so that 'in the last thirty years of the [nineteenth] century, over seven hundred newspapers and magazines in Urdu were started'.[27] As scholars have shown, the press opened spaces of circulation and exchange – although it also built on and reinforced

[24] F., '*Nauḥah*', *Awadh Punch*, 4 September 1877, p. 211.
[25] J. Dubrow, *Cosmopolitan Dreams*, p. 77.
[26] See U. Stark, *An Empire of Books*, p. 3.
[27] F. Robinson, 'Islam and the Impact of Print', p. 67.

pre-colonial forms and contents of communication and information of the 'Indian ecumene'.[28] Periodicals quickly became one of the 'main forums for public debate'[29] and 'fostered cosmopolitan debate, reform and social mobilisation that triggered new kinds of associational life', as Vivek Bhandari highlighted.[30] From the second half of the nineteenth century, periodicals increasingly played a role in the formation of class and community consciousness and were conceived as 'a particularly appropriate medium in the creation of a public sphere' thanks to their interactive and adaptable nature, as Samarpita Mitra noted in the case of Bengal.[31]

Yet, contrary to Jürgen Habermas' characterisation of seventeenth- and eighteenth-century Western public spheres as initially apolitical,[32] the Indian vernacular periodical press had been political in nature since its very beginnings. As Christopher Bayly remarked, a number of newspapers (e.g. *T̤ilism* of Farangi Mahall in Lucknow and the *Dehlī Urdū Ak͟hbār* in Delhi) were already critical of the British well before 1857.[33] As networks of interactions linked newspapers (e.g. Khushgap's mention of the *Deccan Punch* above, a confluence which was common to *Punch* magazines),[34] Muslim political opinion started forming too, and that was increasingly out of the government's control.

In the 1870s, the *Awadh Punch* still took part in what Jennifer Dubrow has called the 'Urdu cosmopolis', a community of interaction based on language but not on religion.[35] A product of the sons of former elites now engaged in educational or legal professions,[36] the *Awadh Punch* was part of a transcultural Asian phenomenon of

[28] See C. Bayly, *Empire and Information*. On pre-colonial forms of information, see also M. Pernau and Y. Jaffery, *Information and the Public Sphere*. For a recent study of the periodical press and the formation of an Urdu public, see M. Robb, *Print and the Urdu Public*.
[29] R. Perkins, 'From the Mehfil to the Printed Word', pp. 47–76.
[30] V. Bhandari, 'Print and the Emergence of Multiple Publics in Nineteenth-Century Punjab', p. 276.
[31] S. Mitra, *Periodicals, Readers and the Making of Modern Literary Culture*, p. 5.
[32] J. Habermas, *The Structural Transformation of the Public Sphere*.
[33] See, for instance, C. Bayly, *Empire and Information*, pp. 240 and 322–3.
[34] S. Mitra, *Periodicals, Readers and the Making of Modern Literary Culture*, p. 15. About the confluence of *Punch* papers, see H. Harder and B. Mittler, *Asian Punches*, pp. 441–3.
[35] J. Dubrow, *Cosmopolitan Dreams*, p. 19, referring to S. S. Rizvī, *Awadh Punch aur Punch Nigār*, Karachi, 1995, pp. 10–11.
[36] J. Dubrow, *Cosmopolitan Dreams*, p. 17.

satirical journalism inspired by the British *Punch*, and it lasted from the 1860s and 1870s to the beginning of World War II. From its first years of publication, *Awadh Punch* was one of the most popular *Punches* – probably also thanks to its sophisticated illustrations.[37] From issuing 230 copies it quickly reached 400, although, as Ritu Khanduri noted, 'the subscription and circulation of these newspapers was unstable'.[38] Its format enabled the reader to engage with the effects of colonialism while circumventing censorship.[39] As such, as Barbara Mittler concluded, the Asian *Punches* indeed tended 'to be much more radically political' than their British model.[40]

The appearance and type of *āshob* poems in the *Awadh Punch* well reflected the political predilection of *Punch* magazines. Instead of focusing on the romantic and idealising elements inherent in post-1857 *shahr āshob* poetry, *Awadh Punch* poems cultivated the potentiality of the secular *marṡiyah* to lament and complaint. They accentuated the semantic links between grief and grievances. The focus on worldwide oppression was used to voice dissatisfaction with God and the vicissitudes of time, but it actually denounced government policies and the colonial state, more or less obliquely. In 1878, the government did in fact ask for a list of *Awadh Punch* subscribers, 'raising fears in certain circles of a government backlash' but, in the end, no measure was taken.[41] On 12 March 1878, a *ġhazal* entitled 'Lament on the taxes' (*Tax par hā'e hā'e*) by a correspondent in Peshawar, Kh. B. Farogh, was published. The poem complained about the *chaukīdārī* (watchmen) tax in Kakori in the typical language of the *marṡiyah* in order to voice criticism towards government measures. It was reprinted in the *Akhbār-e ʿālam* of Meerut and was also noticed as worthy of attention by the colonial authorities under the new Vernacular Press Act.[42]

[37] *A Selection from the Illustrations Which Have Appeared in the* Oudh Punch *from 1877 to 1881*; R. G. Khanduri, *Caricaturing Culture in India.*

[38] R. G. Khanduri, '*Punch* in India', in H. Harder and B. Mittler, *Asian Punches*, p. 180; see also R. G. Khanduri, *Caricaturing Culture in India.*

[39] See H. Harder and B. Mittler, *Asian Punches*, pp. 2 and 6.

[40] B. Mittler, 'Epilogue' in H. Harder and B. Mittler, *Asian Punches*, p. 440.

[41] M. Hasan, *Wit and Humour*, p. 82.

[42] Ibid., p. 61. See *NNR for the Punjab, North-West Provinces, Oudh, Central Provinces, Central India and Rajputana* for 12 March 1878, p. 204, quoted in Ibid., footnote 109.

dārogīr-o hasht masht-o jor-o ẕulm-e lāta'd[ād]
ho nahīṉ saktī bayān tafṣīl-e k͟hwārī hā'e hā'e
hāth k͟hālī kīsah [=kāsah] k͟hālī fāqahkash zār-o nizār
ṭaks ke qābil thī yeh hālat hamārī hā'e hā'e
[...] marte marte thī ummīd-e dastagīrī hamko āh
mil ga'ī miṭṭī meṉ sab ummīdwārī hā'e hā'e
kyā ġhaẓab suntā nahīṉ faryād ko'ī ṭaks kī
be asar kyūṉ ho ga'ī is ratbah zārī hā'e hā'e

Tumult, and strife, tyranny and countless oppression
Cannot describe in full our misery, alas!
Our hands are empty, our begging bowl empty, starved and weak!
Did it deserve taxes, this condition of ours? Alas!
[...] Alas! At the very time of our death we cry for help,
But all hope has been ruined, alas!
How irritating, no one listens to the complaint of the taxes!
Why is this lamentation useless? Alas![43]

In the late 1870s, *shahr āshob* poetry had given way to an elegiac genre on the condition of India and of the whole world. This development was very symptomatic of the new awareness of belonging to a wider world that was now accessible through daily news. The nostalgic, retrospective dimension of post-1857 *shahr āshob* poetry was usually absent from the *āshob* poems published in the *Awadh Punch*, which adopted the devices of the secular *marsiyah* to voice discontent. At the very same time, the Aligarh movement was to develop the genre in another perspective and to a new level. Again, the periodical press played a tremendous role in those new trends and styles.

2 *Āshob* Poetry and the Aligarh Movement

In 1878, a few weeks after the fall of Plevna that had prompted the composition of Khushgap's *dunyā āshob* in the *Awadh Punch*, Syed Ahmed Khan commissioned Altaf Husain Hali (1837–1914)[44] to write the *Musaddas on the Ebb and Flow of Islam* (*Musaddas-e Madd-o Jazr-e Islām*), which was to become the most famous poem

[43] B. Kh. B. Farogh, '*Tax par hā'e hā'e*', *Awadh Punch*, 12 March 1878, p. 2.

[44] C. Shackle and J. Majeed, *Hali's Musaddas*, p. 2. For an excellent and detailed biography of Altaf Husain Hali Panipati, see S. Anjum, *Monogrāf K͟hwājah Alt̲āf Ḥusain Ḥālī*.

of the Aligarh movement. The poem met such popularity that soon 'it became the recognised function of Hali to write and often recite poems dwelling on the glorious past of Islam'.[45] While nostalgia might seem paradoxical with Syed Ahmed Khan's forward-looking and modernist project, the Aligarh movement became famous for its poetic grieving of the past. Besides Aligarh's renowned scholarly interest in history and archaeology,[46] almost every project undertaken by Syed Ahmed Khan was accompanied by the recitation of sorrowful verses: the memory of glorious forebears whose educational qualities and modern outlook were emphasised and the description of present-day decline aimed at encouraging Urdu-speaking elites to take lessons from the past and join the Muhammadan Anglo-Oriental College at Aligarh, bolstering Muslim *ashrāf*'s claims and interests, and, more pragmatically, attracting funds.

Syed Ahmed Khan frequently used the melancholic rhetoric of decline in a variety of ways to promote and fund his projects. In *Ḥayāt-e Jāwed*, Hali explained how the latter proceeded to convince Nawab Mukhtar ul-Mulk Turab Ali Khan (Salar Jang I, 1829–1883) to support the Muhammadan Anglo-Oriental College. A picture was painted of Sir Syed standing near a tree on the seashore, worried. In the ocean, a ship (the Muslim community) was sinking, with some of the men already drowning. Fortunately, a boat (the MAO College) was coming to save the shipwrecked from the storm. Words in English were written on the flag of the rescue boat: 'One lakh rupees', to which Syed Ahmad replied, 'Not Sufficient'. An angel was drawn in the sky, holding his hand, pointing to Mukhtar ul-Mulk, and saying, 'Look at this noble man' – still in English. The whole scene was supposedly inspired by an Urdu couplet: 'Succour gives a glimpse from afar, a boat approaches to save the sinking fleet!' (*dūr se ummīd ne jhalkī sī ik dikhlā'ī hai, ek kashtī ḍūbte beṛe ko lene ā'ī hai*).[47] The painting was sent to Nawab Mukhtar ul-Mulk and persuaded him to contribute to the extent that a part of his private estate (*k̲h̲āṣ jāgīr*) was allocated to funding the College.[48]

45 A. Qadir, *Famous Urdu Poets and Writers*, p. 138.

46 See, for example, I. H. Siddiqui, 'Sir Syed Ahmad Khan's Approach to History and History Writing'; A. Ahmad, *Islamic Modernism in India and Pakistan*, p. 40.

47 Hali, *Ḥayāt-e Jāwed*, part I, pp. 182–3 and part II, p. 416 translated into English: Hali, *Hayat-i Jawed*, pp. 119 and 484–5.

48 Hali, *Ḥayāt-e Jāwed*, part I, pp. 182–3.

Such discourse, especially through poetry, promptly entered political meetings and assemblies, particularly community gatherings such as the Muhammadan Educational Conference, which was established by Syed Ahmed Khan in 1886. As Francis Robinson has shown, the emphasis on past glory and present ruin continued to resonate throughout the late nineteenth and early twentieth centuries, as Aligarh leaders strove to gain advantages from colonial authorities according to their so-called political importance – particularly between 1900 and 1909.[49] It became a feature of the organisation of Muslim political associations, such as the Muslim League in 1906. While the resort to *āshob* poetry and the invocation of collective sadness served many purposes for Aligarh partisans, it also more essentially helped create a political community of feeling, through a utilitarian and reformist interpretation of *ġham*.

2.1 *Hali's* Musaddas *and Andalusian Elegies*

On 10 June 1879, after having received a first copy of the *Musaddas*, Syed Ahmed Khan explained that one could not read the book without 'getting one's eyes filled with tears (*be-chashm-e nam paṛhe nahīṇ jā sakte*)' and that, coming from the heart, it truly 'touched the heart'.[50] Syed Ahmed Khan was the mastermind behind this reformist work of art. As I have shown, it was he who emphatically requested Hali to write a *marṡiyah* on his community, similar to the thirteenth-century Arabic *Lament for the Fall of Seville* in January 1878.[51] In his preface to the work, Hali also alluded to how Syed Ahmed Khan had convinced him to write the poem and spoke of the long process of writing that had been interrupted by illness – more than a year had passed between the publication of the first dozen lines in the *Aligarh Institute Gazette* in early 1878 and the full poem in *Tahż̤īb ul-Ak̲h̲lāq* in 1879.[52]

[49] See F. Robinson, 'The Memory of Power'.

[50] Letter from Syed Ahmed Khan to Hali, Shimla, Park Hotel, 10 June 1879, 10 edited by M. A. Mannan (ed.), *Selected Letters*, 11 and *K̲h̲uṭūṭ-e Sir Sayyid*, p. 166.

[51] E. Tignol, 'A Note on the Origins of Hali's *Musaddas*'. S. S. Hameed also mentioned the fact that the *Musaddas* was inspired by Andalusi elegies without identifying the source: '"Write something like *Marsiya-e Andalus* (dirge for Spain)," Sir Saiyad is reported to have said'. S. S. Hameed, *Hali's Musaddas*, p. 30

[52] Hali, 'First Preface'; see C. Shackle and J. Majeed, *Hali's Musaddas*, p. 93.

The description of the inception of Hali's *Musaddas* in the *Aligarh Institute Gazette* came out in the middle of the Russo-Turkish war, after weeks of lengthy reports on the situation in Plevna from December 1877. In its seventy-eighth issue, the *Gazette* announced that the city had eventually fallen to the Russian forces on 11 December.[53] In the next couple of weeks, descriptions of Gazi Osman's bravery – of the garrison's heroic struggle and sacrifice – were accompanied by accounts of the slaughter carried out by the Russian army, of its cowardice, of the horror of mass graves where the living had also been tossed indiscriminately, and of the establishment of various relief funds for the sick and wounded Turkish soldiers. Finally, on 26 January 1878, it published the thirteenth-century Arabic elegy, its Urdu translation, and a couple of lines from an early version of Hali's *Musaddas*, a rare instance of poetic presence in the *College Gazette*.

The extraordinary appearance of a medieval Arabic *marśiyah* when relating the contemporary events taking place in the Ottoman Empire was probably not a mere accident. The text in Syed Ahmed Khan's possession likely circulated in Arabic milieus at that time. The attribution of the *marśiyah* – also known as *Rithā' al-Andalus* of al-Rundi (1204–1285)[54] – to Sayyid Yahya Qurtubi Andalusi was widespread among Arabic scholars,[55] but not in the West: the poem had been translated into French and German in 1828 and 1865 and was attributed to al-Rundi instead.[56] Interestingly, Sharif al-Din al-Khafaji's 1856 anthology of Arabic poetry *Rayḥānat al-alibbā fī zahrat al-ḥayāt al-dunyā*, which comprised the *Lament* with al-Qurtubi's attribution,

53 *Aligarh Institute Gazette*, vol. XII, 78, 15 December 1877, p. 1.

54 Some scholars date the composition from 1248 while others date it from 1267. See J. El Gharbi, « Thrène de Séville », pp. 26–30. Not much is known about al-Rundi's life: he probably lived in Granada, is thought to have been a judge and would have composed a number of treatises on poetics, metrics and law, see J. S. Meisami and P. Starkey, *Encyclopedia of Arabic Literature*, p. 372.

55 Both Sharif al-Din Mahmud al-Khafaji (d. 1657) and the *Fihrist al-makhṭūṭāṭ* of the *Dār al-Kutub* in Cairo had ascribed the text to al-Qurtubi. See R. Y. Ebied and M. J. L. Young, 'Abū'l-Baqā' al-Rundi and his elegy on Muslim Spain', pp. 30–31; E. Tignol, 'A Note on the Origins of Hali's *Musaddas*'; S. Meisami and P. Starkey (eds.), *Encyclopedia of Arabic Literature*, p. 194.

56 R. Y. Ebied and M. J. L. Young, 'Abū'l-Baqā' al-Rundi', p. 30: the text and its French translation first appeared in Lagrange's *Anthologie Arabe*, dedicated to the famous French Orientalist scholar Silvestre de Sacy in 1828, pp. 141–148.

was reprinted by the Būlāq Press in Cairo in 1877 precisely.[57] While the date of the reprint is a striking concurrence, the only available copy of the anthology at Maulana Azad Library in Aligarh today is a later reprint from Egypt dated 1306 Hijri (1888). Minor variations between the 1878 *Aligarh Institute Gazette* version and the 1888 reprint make it a less likely source, although it may still be a second-hand source.[58]

Another more plausible avenue is that the poem was reproduced in a contemporary foreign newspaper. An examination of the newspapers mentioned in the *Aligarh Institute Gazette* around that time (December 1877–January 1878) shows that the journal relied on a network of Western and Indian newspapers. Turkish papers were rarely mentioned, although we know that at that particular time foreign newspapers and especially those from Turkey were eagerly read in India. Syed Ameer Ali (1849–1928), for instance, remembered that he excitedly read the Arabic paper *Dār ul-K̲h̲ilāfat*, which was published from Constantinople.[59] As Naeem Qureshi remarked, in the late 1870s and 1880s, 'Indian journals had been regularly publishing material culled and translated from several Turkish and Arabic newspapers, such as *al-Jawaib*, the *Tercuman-i Rum*, the *Akhbar Dar al-Khilafat* and the *Tercuman-i Mashriq*'.[60]

In an article of the *Aligarh Institute Gazette* dated a week earlier on 19 January 1878, the anonymous author (Syed Ahmed Khan?) explained that the catastrophe (*āfat*) in Plevna might develop into some unforeseen benefit (*fāʿedah*). He went on to say that it might hide divine plans for the betterment of Muslim communities and compared the situation with that of the Muslims in India and of the subsequent beneficial foundation of the Muhammadan Anglo-Oriental College in Aligarh.[61] In the article, one contemporary Turkish newspaper was specifically named and described as the 'special journal of Constantinople': *Al-Jawā'ib*.

This Arabic language newspaper published in Constantinople by Ahmad Faris al-Shidyaq from 1860 was indeed popular. Sponsored

[57] I am grateful to Simon Leese for pointing this out to me.

[58] al-Khafaji, *Rayḥānat al-alibbā fī zahrat al-ḥayāt al-dunyā*, reprint Misr, 1888, pp. 178–181.

[59] G. Minault, *The Khilafat Movement*, pp. 6–7 quoting Ali, *Memoirs and Other Writings of Syed Ameer Ali* (Wasti, S. R., ed.), p. 107.

[60] N. Qureshi, *Pan-Islam in British Indian Politics*, p. 42.

[61] *Aligarh Institute Gazette*, vol. XIII, 6, 19 January 1878, pp. 78–9.

by the Ottoman government and subsidised by the British government too from 1877,[62] *Al-Jawā'ib* press had ambitions to be the major distributor of Islamic books in Turkey, and its books and newspaper were widely read across the Middle East and India.[63] Its editor, Faris al-Shidyaq, a pioneer of the movement of the Arab Renaissance (*al-Naḥdah*),[64] was particularly interested in publishing classical Arabic works and books on Arabic language and literature and, as Mohammed Alwan noted, *Al-Jawā'ib* quickly became instrumental in the growth of Arabic studies.[65] Although Syed Ahmed Khan did not mention his source, the Arabic elegy is certainly the kind of material that could appear in *Al-Jawā'ib*.[66]

Regardless of the way the *Lament for the Fall of Seville* reached Syed Ahmed Khan, it is likely that the discovery of the Arabic poem and the idea of the *Musaddas* were connected to the cultural renaissance occurring in Egypt and Ottoman-ruled territories. The importance of contacts with other Muslim countries was amplifying for Indian Muslims, as was the drive of Aligarh scholars to connect with the Arabic tradition and the intellectual awakening of the *Naḥdah*. As Francis Robinson argued, the 'embracing of Arab models' was not only a means through which Islamic modernism could be achieved but also part of broader 'strategies of authority' that were developed by leaders like Syed Ahmed Khan.[67] These new strategies emphasised Arabic authoritative texts like the Qur'an and the Hadiths as well as the figure of the Prophet – and the *Musaddas* was a perfect example. Although not discarding Persian heritage,[68] the poem concretely embodied the fact that Arabic literary traditions were increasingly compelling for Indian Muslim elites who were looking

[62] On the relation between *Al-Jawa'ib* and the British government, see C. Uçan, 'Breaking the News: A Case Study', p. 2.

[63] Mohammed B. Alwan, 'The History and Publications of al-Jawā'ib Press', pp. 4–7 and N. Vanelli, 'Al-Jawaib: Exploring an Arabic Newspaper'.

[64] G. Roper, 'Aḥmad Fāris al-Shidyāq and the Libraries of Europe', pp. 233–48.

[65] M. Alwan, 'The History and Publications of al-Jawā'ib Press', p. 6.

[66] Further work is needed to confirm whether the Andalusian elegy was indeed reproduced in *Al-Jawā'ib*, or any other Turkish paper, around that time.

[67] F. Robinson, 'Strategies of Authority', p. 193.

[68] About the rejection of the Persian literary heritage see Ibid. Interestingly, Hali did not choose to use the same metre used by al-Rundi (the *basiṭ* metre) but instead used the *mutaqārib* metre; see C. Shackle and J. Majeed, *Hali's Musaddas*, pp. 28–9.

for a new impulse. It exemplified the rich literary influences and transfers between Arabic and Urdu, and the complex processes of literary creation and cultural renaissance in the late nineteenth-century Middle East and north India. The simple and effective language of the *Musaddas*, which excited many writers of the New School, was inspired not by English models but by Arabic ones.

The publication of Arabic verses with their juxtaposed translation into Urdu was extremely rare in the *Aligarh Institute Gazette*, and the fact that the poem occupied several pages shows how much the Andalusian elegy had inspired Sir Syed. The instruction for the *Musaddas* to follow the model of an Arabic elegy explains that Hali's poem was imbued with a rare Arabic flavour.[69] Through the imitation of the Andalusian elegy, Syed Ahmed Khan's hope was that Hali's 'tears will fall into the heart of mankind (*tumhārā ānsū insān ke dil meṇ jāwegā*)' and that 'after [describing the community's] flow and progress (*numū aur taraqqī*), its decline (*tanazzul*) would have much impact on the heart and our sleepy community would wake up and worry about their own offspring's welfare, progress and education'.[70] The *Musaddas* was imagined as a powerful tool to awaken the community through heartfelt emotion and tears.

The Arabic Andalusi genre of *rithā' al-mudun* (city elegy),[71] and *The Lament for the Fall of Seville* in particular, contained specificities which were particularly interesting for a modernist leader trying to popularise his message: the evocation of exotic and once-glorious Islamic places, the warning of the sleeper who needs to wake up, and – especially – the call for jihad. One of the first aspects of the Arabic *rithā' al-mudun* that irrevocably marked the reformist poem was the idea of the ebb and flow of Islam, which directly influenced the title of Hali's *Musaddas*. *The Lament for the Fall of Seville* lamented the fall of Andalusian cities by intimately linking them with other once-glorious Muslim kingdoms in a broader historical narrative of Islamic accomplishment and decline.

As Alexander Elinson noted in his study of elegies on Al-Andalus, 'the *rithā' al-mudun* for a particular location is literally built on the ruins of other historical losses that locate it within a larger context of

[69] C. Shackle and J. Majeed, *Hali's Musaddas*, pp. 29–32.
[70] Ibid. [71] See A. E. Elinson, *Looking Back at al-Andalus*.

the genre, resulting in a complex and richly textured effect.'[72] Through this 'layering and recalling of past elegies'[73] Andalusian poets interwove their immediate local circumstances with a greater and more distant Arab past. They typically invoked the legendary landscapes of the Najd plateau; the Nile; Mecca; and Damascus, 'the mere mention of [which] conjures up a host of images and emotional responses that carry the audience far beyond the boundaries of the actual words'.[74] Via a vocabulary emphasising wealth and power, the Andalusian *Lament* published in the *Aligarh Institute Gazette* did not solely lament the devastation of a particular city or dynasty but remembered and grieved Muslim supremacy worldwide.[75]

In the *Musaddas*, as in the Arabic elegy, Hali relocated the history of the rise and fall of Indian Islam within the long history of Muslim sovereignty, thus uniting all Islamic civilisations – which further echoed contemporary awareness of being part of an increasingly global world and the burgeoning ideology of pan-Islamism. This was quite new, since Urdu *shahr āshobs* on Delhi or Lucknow did not usually compare Indian cities with other Muslim ones (with the exception of Mecca), or the Mughal Empire with other famous dynasties in or outside India. The *Musaddas* thus adopted the Arabic literary device 'of establishing a framework for nostalgia through the citation of exotic proper names' and linked the fate of Muslim India with other historical instances of cultural loss.[76] India was included as one of the great historical places of Muslim sovereignty. Nostalgia thus not only flowed from a romanticised vision of the Indian Muslim past but also from the suggestive description of global Muslim power:

nahīṇ is ṯabaq par ko'ī barr-e ʿaẕam
na hoṇ jis meṇ un kī ʿimārāt-e mohkam
ʿarab, hind, miṣr, andalus, shām, dailam
binā'oṇ se haiṇ un kī maʿmūr ʿālam
sar koh-e Ādam se tā koh-e baiẓā
jahāṇ jā'oge khoj pā'oge un kā
[...] huwaidā hai ġharnāṯah se shaukat un kī
ʿiyāṇ hai balansiyah se qudrat un kī

[72] Ibid., p. 61. [73] Ibid. [74] Ibid., p. 30.
[75] Abu al-Baqa al-Rundi, 'Lament for the Fall of Seville', pp. 220–1.
[76] C. Shackle and J. Majeed, *Hali's Musaddas*, p. 31.

baṯaliyūs ko yād hai ʿaẕmat un kī
paṭaktī hai qādis meṇ sar ḥasrat un kī
naṣīb un kā ishbīliyyah meṇ hai sotā
shab-o roz hai qurṯubah un ko rotā

There is no continent upon this globe
In which their buildings do not stand firm.
Arabia, India, Egypt, Spain, Syria, and Dailam,
The whole world is filled with their foundations.
From the summit of Adam's Peak to the Sierra Nevada,
You will find their traces wherever you go.
[...] Their majesty is manifest from Granada,
Their greatness is made apparent by Valencia,
Their glory is recalled by Badajoz,
Cadiz throbs with longing for them.
Their fortune sleeps in Seville,
And Cordoba weeps for them night and day.[77]

By relating the history of Muslim India to that of other Islamic lands, the *Musaddas* represented Muslim *ashrāf*'s past, present, and future as not only Indian but global and Islamic. While *ashrāf* had always emphasised their extra-Indian origins through elaborate pedigrees and *shajrah*s,[78] genealogies and pre-modern histories rather tended to highlight family and small group inheritance. As Faisal Devji noted, the past in Hali's verses was, on the contrary, not 'filiative' but still 'conceived of temporal succession and historical transmission in genealogical terms'.[79] The poem offered a grand meta-narrative of the Muslim history of power and relocated the sense of cultural dispossession in a broader tale of Islamic ebb and flow which encouraged the shaping of a unified, pan-Indian Muslim elite identity beyond sub-groups – such as Sayyids, Shaikhs, or Pathans – or family/*birādarī* membership.[80]

Yet, the most interesting aspect of al-Rundi's elegy for nineteenth-century Indian reformers was that the trope of the ebb and flow not only participated in creating a particular aesthetic, but also served a

[77] Hali, *Musaddas*, verses 80 and 83, trans. C. Shackle and J. Majeed, *Hali's Musaddas*, pp. 131 and 133.
[78] P. Hardy, 'Modern Muslim Historical Writing on Medieval Muslim India', p. 295.
[79] F. Devji, 'Muslim Nationalism: Founding Identity in Colonial India', p. 157.
[80] See, for instance, A. F. Buehler, 'Trends of ashrāfization in India'; T. Wright, 'The Changing Role of the sādāt in India and Pakistan'; J. Levesque and L. Gautier, *Historicizing Sayyid-ness.*

very practical purpose: a call for jihad. Muslim fellows were questioned for their lack of faith, bravery, and care. The sleeper was prompted to wake up: the process could be reversed. By enhancing emotions of grief and shame, Andalusian elegies, such as the one composed by Ibn Sahl al-Ishbili in 1242 to request Muslim support at Seville, called for action since 'through action, tears can be turned into freshwater, and death into life'.[81]

The *Musaddas* built on the same interpretation. In his first introduction to the *Musaddas*, Hali explained that Arabic elegies were particularly useful to raise fervour (*josh*), regretting that until now 'no one has yet written poetry [in Urdu], which makes a natural appeal to all, and has been bequeathed to the Muslims as a legacy from the Arabs, for the purpose of awakening the community'.[82] As Hali also noted in his *Muqaddamah-e shi'r-o shā'irī*, 'in Arabia, [...] poets would recite their verses, setting hearts on fire, and the tribesmen would be ready to sacrifice their lives'.[83] The aim of the *Musaddas* was, like *The Lament for the Fall of Seville*, to enhance collective grief for mobilisation and reform.

2.2 Aligarh's Interpretation of Grief

The importance of *ġham* in the *Musaddas*, and in Aligarhian discourse in the following decades, calls for a more detailed understanding of its value and of the semantic webs it activated, which, I argue, were significantly different from those of 1857 *shahr āshob* poetry, or contemporary *āshob* poems of the *Awadh Punch*. Margrit Pernau has demonstrated that late nineteenth-century north Indian *ashrāf* conceptualised emotions through both Islamic ethical (and also medical) and Sufi traditions.[84] However, as Orhan Pamuk noted about Turkish *hüzün* – it is also true for Arabic, Persian and Urdu *ḥuzn* – the two traditions had different perceptions of grief. While in Sufism *ḥuzn* is to be cultivated, it has to be cured in traditional ethical treatises. For Hali, who inherited from both traditions, *ġham* was good as long as it was transformative, but it was to be eventually 'cured' by adapting to the times, as *akhlāq* treatises advised. He offered a sort of synthesis

81 A. E. Elinson, *Looking Back at Al-Andalus*, p. 36.
82 Hali, 'First Preface'; see C. Shackle and J. Majeed, *Hali's Musaddas*, p. 93.
83 L. Steele, 'Hali and His Muqaddamah: The Creation of a Literary Attitude in Nineteenth Century India', p. 24.
84 See M. Pernau, *Emotions and Modernity*, p. 56.

by emphasising the 'useful' dimension of the emotion, which also mirrored the utilitarian thought that infused much of contemporary vernacular literature.[85]

Sadness was closely related to memory in Islam. Many scholars have argued that Islam (like Judaism and Christianity) puts special emphasis on remembering as 'a fundamental religious duty',[86] and 'a primary mode of divine-human interaction'.[87] In the Qur'an, the people of the Book are also called *ahl ul-żikr*, 'the people of remembrance', and a number of Quranic injunctions assert the need for believers to remember God (e.g. Q2, 152; 18, 24; 33, 41). Religious remembrance has been described as the greatest virtue, with the development of the practice of *żikr* (invoking the names of God, or reciting the Qur'an) seen as essential in uniting with God (*ittiṣāl*, *fanā'*).[88] In Sufism, a strong sentiment of longing is associated with the practice and the desire to reach God. This emotion is then considered a positive experience. As the Turkish writer Orhan Pamuk beautifully summarised, 'it is the absence, not the presence, of hüzün that causes distress'.[89] Sylwia Surdykowska remarked that, in Persian cultures, sadness was also generally perceived as a transforming emotion that led to the perfecting of oneself, since 'the experience of pain allows one to see the depth and value of life, to understand what is really important and what is not'.[90] Aligarh reformist contemporaries of Hali shared this conception of grief; Deputy Nazir Ahmad, for instance, underlined the high value of that emotion in his novel *Mirāt ul-ʿurūs* (1869):

> It is in the order of this world that no human being is exempt from sorrow (*ranj se k͟hālī nahīṇ*), and doubtless this has been so ordained by Providence, since if any person were happy in all respect, he would not remember his God even in his moments of leisure, nor think of himself as only God's servant.[91]

Feeling grief was a way to connect with God and to improve oneself.

[85] C. M. Naim, 'Prize-Winning adab'.
[86] Le Goff, *Histoire et Mémoire*, p. 131.
[87] M. A. Sells, 'Memory', in *Encyclopaedia of the Qur'an Online.*
[88] See, for instance, B. M. Ahmad, *Remembrance of Allah. Zikr-i Ilahi*, p. 3 and L. Gardet, 'Dhikr', in *The Encyclopaedia of Islam.*
[89] O. Pamuk, *Istanbul: Memories and the City*, p. 81. About melancholy in Turkish culture and affective practices, especially in classical music, see D. Gill, *Melancholic Modalities.*
[90] S. Surdykowska, 'The Idea of Sadness', p. 74.
[91] N. Ahmad, *The Bride's Mirror*, p. 119; for the Urdu see Nazir Ahmad, *Mirāt ul-ʿurūs*, p. 91.

Looking more closely at the vocabulary and motifs used in the *Musaddas* is revealing. While, as far as I know, Hali did not describe the *Musaddas* as a *shahr āshob*, it displayed similar motifs: the meter of the *musaddas*, the description of past kingship, the satirical depiction of categories of people. One of the high points of the *Musaddas* was the image of the ruined garden,[92] which was typical of nineteenth-century *shahr āshob* poetry. But his way of expressing grief was strikingly different, as it was also different from late 1870s *Awadh Punch āshob* poems that emphasised complaint. For Hali, *ġham* was described less in terms of physical pain or political grievance; rather, it related to repentance.

One can note that along with the usual polysemic term of *ġham* – with derivatives (*ġham-khāne wālā*, *ġhamk̲h̲wār*, *ġhamgīn*, *purġham*) – Hali mostly used *dard*, *māyūs*, *ranj*, *ḥasrat*, *majrūḥ*, and *afsos*. While *māyūs* evoked despair and *dard* pain, *ḥasrat* and *afsos* rather related to regret, and *majrūḥ* to hurt honour. Instead of linking *ġham* to the burning experience of amorous separation or to the assertive denunciation of oppression, Hali operated a shift. He conjured up a different inherent sense of *ġham*: the concept of regret/repentance that naturally shared semantic features with shame – which also repeatedly occur in the poem.

As I have shown elsewhere, *sharm* (one of the words for shame) had a positive dimension in didactic magazines of the early twentieth century. It implied remorse and operated as a powerful incentive for social reparation and self-improvement.[93] Both idiomatically 'black', shame and grief are close.[94] Benedict Grima's study of the performance of *ġham* and its links with the question of collective honour among Pashtuns showed too that, in comparison with women, 'a man's *gham* refers more to his financial and honor-related worries than to his internal state of grief or sorrow'.[95] While of course the situation of the colonial North-Western Provinces was different from that of the modern-day Swat valley, Hali too interwove both emotions. Their combined use further stressed their semantic overlaps.

[92] Hali, *Musaddas*, v. 110–3, trans. C. Shackle and J. Majeed, *Hali's Musaddas*, pp. 143–5.

[93] E. Tignol 'The Language of Shame'.

[94] Ibid., p. 230.

[95] B. Grima, *The Performance of Emotions among Paxtun Women*, p. 36.

In the introduction, Hali explained that he did in fact write the poem 'to make my friends and fellows feel a sense of outrage and shame (*ġhairat aur sharm*)'.[96] Through the idealisation of an Islamic past and the subsequent pathetic descriptions of collective ruin, Indian Muslims were reprimanded for the fall of inherited secular power:

hamārī har ik bāt meṇ siflapan hai
kamīnoṇ se badtar hamārā chalan hai
lagā nām ābā ko ham se gaihan hai
hamārā qadam nang ahl-e waṯan hai
buzurgoṇ kī tauqīr kho'ī hai ham ne
'arab kī sharāfat ḍubo'ī hai ham ne

There is meanness in everything we do
Our ways are worse than those of the most base
Our forefathers' reputation has been eaten away by us
Our step makes our countrymen ashamed
We have thrown away our ancestors' credit
And sunk the nobility of the Arabs.[97]

Regret and shame were meant to lead to individual and collective reform. Of course, the significance of the experience of colonisation should not be downplayed when considering the concept of shame/humiliation in Aligarhian writings.[98] Syed Ahmed Khan was very much impacted by European discourse of progress, morality, and behaviour, sometimes contrasting Western 'civility' with Eastern 'barbarity'. It is noteworthy, as Mana Kia emphasised, that mid-nineteenth-century Iran also linked 'individual moral abasement to the abrogation of political sovereignty'.[99] Likewise, the *Musaddas* related the loss of secular power to the lack of individual morality. It aimed at making everybody accountable by evoking 'a strong sense of personal dishonour and shame for the state of the community'.[100]

The first centuries of Islam, a time of glory and expansion, had always been invested with emotions by Muslims, and not only in South Asia.[101] In Muslim history, the coming of the Prophet was a

[96] Hali, 'First Preface', in C. Shackle and J. Majeed, *Hali's Musaddas*, p. 97.
[97] Hali, *Musaddas*, v. 121, trans. C. Shackle and J. Majeed, *Hali's Musaddas*, p. 147.
[98] See S. A. Zaidi, *Making a Muslim*.
[99] M. Kia 'Moral Refinement and Manhood in Persian', p. 146.
[100] C. Oesterheld, 'Campaigning for a Community', p. 48.
[101] See, most recently, M. Pernau, 'The Time of the Prophet and the Future of the Community'.

unique event in the history of humanity. As 'Seal of the Prophets', He brought the last revelation before the end of times.[102] Despite a few episodes of opposition and martyrdom around the Hegira, Ira Lapidus emphasised that the beginnings of Islam were glorious times of rapid conquest and unification under the leadership of the Prophet and his rightly guided caliphs until the first Islamic civil war (*Fitnah*) of the mid-seventh century.[103] Sacred history thus culminated with the time of the Prophet and his four enlightened successors, and was conceived as 'the history of a constant progress of men towards salvation',[104] the period thereafter often being perceived as a long and gradual decline.

Many modern scholars hence characterised Islam – more than Christianity and Judaism – as a religion of nostalgia and regret.[105] While scholars have since complicated this view, notably by engaging more closely with the concept of temporality in Islam,[106] the age of the Prophet generally remained the 'yardstick by which the Muslims measure their present situation'.[107] The prophetic period constitutes the primary frame for evaluating Islamic practice – although one should not discredit the significance of local Islamic pasts[108] – as the words and deeds of the Prophet continue to be the reference point for contemporary conduct. The second half of the nineteenth century in north India, particularly, saw the blooming of devotional practices and of *sīrat* literature focusing on the figure of the Prophet.[109]

A large portion of the *Musaddas* centred on the original teachings of Islam and on a correlated social critique of contemporary times. The description of the ebb and flow was narrated with a reformist prism: Muslims thrived as long as they followed the Prophet and declined as soon as they strayed from His principles. Indian Muslims were described as forgetful and negligent (*ġhaflat*). To regain past glory, a return to

[102] See, for instance, F. Rosenthal, *A History of Muslim Historiography*, p. 26.
[103] I. M. Lapidus, 'The Golden Age: The Political Concepts of Islam', p. 229.
[104] M. Turki, 'Erinnerung und Identität', p. 60.
[105] See J. Wansbrough, *The Sectarian Milieu*; G. Hendrich, 'Identitätskonstruktion und Geschichtsbilder', p. 236; and M. Turki, 'Erinnerung und Identität'.
[106] See, for instance, Wansbrough's own reserves and Calder's objections in N. Calder, 'History and Nostalgia', p. 250. About concepts of Islamic temporalities, see, for instance, G. Böwering, 'The Concept of Time in Islam'.
[107] A. Schimmel, *And Muhammad Is His Messenger*, p. 221.
[108] See, among others, D. A. Birchok, 'Sojourning on Mecca's Verandah', p. 4.
[109] A. Dey, *The Image of the Prophet in Bengali Muslim Piety*; M. H. Katz, *The Birth of the Prophet Muhammad.*

the roots was justified. Yet, as many have shown, Hali's depiction of the past was invested with a modernist perspective. The moral virtues praised in the contemporary world were projected back into the past. The *Musaddas* focused 'on the social aspects of the Prophet's message'[110] and insisted on the fact that Islamic glory stemmed from the *ummah's* unquenchable quest for knowledge, and that regeneration could only come from the same principle. Muslims were to live with their times.[111]

Hali undoubtedly praised emotions for their ability to transform those who experienced them, and, accordingly, tried to elicit them in his audience. He deplored that his contemporaries did not feel regret (*afsos*).[112] But, at the same time, he criticised depressive lethargy. In his first introduction, he explained that mourning the ruin of the Indian Muslim community was not enough; it needed to be acted upon (*ham ko kuchh karnā chāhīe*).[113] The power, and purpose, of emotion was the 'awakening of the community'.[114] Emotion, for him, was conceived as *josh* ('fervour, emotion, excitement'); it should lead to action, not to despondency. In fact, when he introduced a new edition of the *Musaddas* in 1886, Hali appreciated the emotional impact of the poem (*qaum ke dil meṇ mutāṡir*) but precisely regretted that 'while this manner of expression was calculated to arouse a sense of shame (*ġhairat dilāne wālā thā*), it was equally one to encourage despair (*isī qadar māyūs karne wālā bhī thā*). [...] The poem concluded with verses so gloomy as to terminate all hopes (*tamām ummīdeṇ munqateʿ ho gayīṇ*)'.[115]

Hali valued grief, not despair. The emotion was positive as long as it was transformative and led to self-reformation; otherwise, it was disorder. This reflected classical Islamic knowledge, and the *Musaddas* indeed opened with a medical dialogue with Hippocrates. Islamic treatises, both ethical and medical, like Greek medicine and philosophy, considered sorrow to be a psychical pain. Sometimes distinguishing between 'reactive sorrow' (usually called *ḥuzn*) and

[110] M. A. Raja, *Constructing Pakistan*, p. 61.
[111] Hali, *Musaddas*, v. 139, trans. C. Shackle and J. Majeed, *Hali's Musaddas*, p. 153.
[112] 'They feel not the slightest sorrow at their degradation' (*nah afsos unheṇ apnī żillat peh hai kuchh*) in Hali, *Musaddas*, v. 5, in C. Shackle and J. Majeed, *Hali's Musaddas*, pp. 104–5.
[113] See 'First Introduction', in C. Shackle and J. Majeed, *Hali's Musaddas*, pp. 93–4.
[114] C. Shackle and J. Majeed, *Hali's Musaddas*, p. 93.
[115] 'Second Introduction', in C. Shackle and J. Majeed, *Hali's Musaddas*, p. 100.

true 'physiological disorder' (*mālīkẖūliyā, saudā*),[116] common grief was generally understood in classical Islamic treatises as

a mental suffering produced by losing something desired, or missing something pursued, the cause of it being a greediness of desire after animal gratifications and bodily delights.[117]

Nasirean ethics typically saw *ḥuzn* (sometimes *ḥasrat*, 'regret') as the inability to control one's appetites and to believe in God's plans.[118] Grief was connected with greed. As one Ottoman poem by Mustafa Ali said in the sixteenth century: 'Cupidity is a special, horrid affection; Melancholia is difficult to cure'.[119] In *The Art of Averting Sorrows*, al-Kindi (c. 801–873) had prescribed to cultivate right habits (*tarbiyat*) by accepting things as they are, reducing possessions, and being 'content with every situation'.[120] Nasir al-Din al-Tusi (1201–1274) also concluded that one should be content with what is available and adapt to changing circumstances.[121] Otherwise, one needed to be treated through diet, drugs, cauterization, or even surgery.

The idea that one should put efforts into adapting to the modern world also appeared in an article by Ahsanullah from Allahabad entitled *Ranj-o muṣībat* ('Sorrow and Affliction') published in the *Aligarh Institute Gazette* on 18 October 1879, the year of the publication of Hali's *Musaddas*.[122] The article opened with the question of whether sadness was inborn or learned. Did it come from nature or nurture? Ahsanullah reiterated the idea that it emanated from the lack of engagement with tradition and of love for one's community, and that it came out of an inadequacy with nature and with the times. Grief was branded

---

[116] The distinction was introduced by Ahmed Ibn Sahl al-Balkhi in his *Maṣāliḥ al-abdān wa al-anfus* ('Sustenance for Body and Soul'); see I. Abdel-Sattar, 'Saudi Arabia', p. 447.

[117] Dawani, *Practical Philosophy of the Muhammadan People*, p. 236. On *akẖlāq* treatises, see particularly B. Metcalf, *Moral Conduct and Authority*; A. Powell, 'Old Books in New Bindings'; M. E. Subtelny, 'A Late Medieval Persian *Summa* on Ethics'; M. Pernau, *Emotions and Modernity*, Chapters 2 and 3.

[118] Nasir ad-Din Tusi, *The Nasirean Ethics*, p. 124; for the Urdu, see Nasir ad-Din Tusi, *Akẖlāq-e Nāṣirī*, p. 272.

[119] Mustafa 'Ali, *Kühn ul-Akẖbār* (sixteenth century), trans. in C. Fleischer, 'Royal Authority, Dynastic Cyclism, and Ibn Khaldunism', p. 213. I have not had access to the original.

[120] Gh. Jayyusi-Lehn, 'The Epistle of Yaʿqūb ibn Isḥāq al-Kindī', p. 123.

[121] Tusi, *The Nasirean Ethics*, p. 145.

[122] *Aligarh Institute Gazette*, 18 October 1879, pp. 1163–5.

a 'crime against the law of nature' (*qānūn-e qudrat kī k͟hilāf warzī*), a 'misunderstanding (*ġhalat͟fahmī*) of the law of nature'.[123] Building on Qur'an 35,43 ('You will find no change in the way of Allah'), the author urged his readers to open their eyes and conform to the requirements of the age: 'the walk of time will not change: if you want to prosper, you need to change your own walk yourself' (*zamāne kī chāl nah badlegī, agar tum falāḥ chāhte ho to tum ko k͟hud apnī chāl badalnī chāhī'e*).[124] This, of course, was the message of the *Musaddas* too.

2.3 *Creating Community: The Political Uses of Grief*

The *Musaddas* enchanted Syed Ahmed Khan, so much so that he recommended it to be published and also performed by singing boys *qawwals* and dancing girls (*ranḍiyāṇ*).[125] It rapidly became an integral part of the Urdu-speaking elites' lives[126] – 'no poem', Bailey noted, 'has had so great an effect on the Urdu-speaking world'.[127] In addition to various imitations, a number of translations of the *Musaddas* also appeared in Pashto, Gujarati, and Punjabi.[128] Many authors started to write *Musaddas*-like poems lamenting present backwardness and using the same literary devices that had been developed in Urdu by Hali. The *Musaddas* represented a milestone not only because 'it supplied the new school [of Urdu literature] with a model and directed poetry into a new and fruitful channel'[129] but also because it gave poetry, and emotions, a clear purpose and use.[130]

123 Ibid., p. 1163. 124 Ibid., p. 1165.
125 Letter from Syed Ahmed Khan to Hali, M. A. Mannan (ed.), *Selected Letters*, 11 and *K͟huṭūṭ-e Sir Sayyid*, pp. 166–7.
126 A. Qadir, *The New School of Urdu Literature*, p. 20.
127 T. G. Bailey, *A History of Urdu Literature*, p. 93.
128 C. Shackle and J. Majeed, *Hali's Musaddas*, p. 45.
129 T. G. Bailey, *A History of Urdu Literature*, p. 349. This new style received criticism, for instance, from Chiryakoti, Shibli's mentor, who published an anti-*Musaddas* in 1901 in opposition to Hali's natural style (J. A. Khan, *Muhammad Shibli Nomani*, p. 84).
130 See C. Shackle and J. Majeed, *Hali's Musaddas*, pp. 40, 42. *Musaddases* were also written by Hindus, such as Lala Kidari Lal Nirbhai Ram in his *Musaddas-e Nirbhai Prakāsh*, Pandit Brij Kaifi in his *Musaddas-e Kaifī*, and Munshi Prashad Shafaq in his Arya Samaji poem significantly entitled *Musaddas-e Shafaq, Madd-o Jazr-e Aryā* (Ibid., p. 44). Brij Narain Chakbast (1882–1926) also adapted the *musaddas* to encourage Hindu religious reforms (A. Schimmel, *Classical Urdu Literature*, p. 240).

The political implications of such practice most forcefully materialised starting in 1888 as the Indian National Congress (INC) was preparing its annual session in Allahabad and anti-Congress propaganda intensified in north India. The Indian National Congress, founded in 1885, had until then held its annual sessions in east and south India but in the winter of 1887, it developed new centres in Lucknow and Allahabad, and Madan Mohan Malaviya started to tour in the region to recruit new members.[131] The Indian National Congress, which aimed at representing the interests of all Indian subjects,[132] appealed to more and more Muslim *ashrāf*. The main demands of the INC, however, worked against Aligarh's aim to maintain their political influence in north India.[133] Members of the Aligarh movement felt threatened by demands for elective government and competitive examinations, as well as by the intensification of communal tensions with the Hindi–Urdu language controversy and the increasing convergence of religious–political interests in the Western Doab area.[134] During the Muslim Educational Conference in winter 1887, after a year of fierce campaigning, Syed Ahmed Khan clearly positioned himself against the Congress in his Lucknow speech[135] – despite the fact that the Conference also highlighted a number of disagreements among Urdu-speaking *ashrāf*[136] – notably with Munshi Sajjad Husain, editor of the then ten-year-old *Awadh Punch*.[137]

In 1888, just after the Lucknow speech, Syed Ahmed Khan launched an anti-Congress campaign under the direction of Theodore Beck and founded the United Indian Patriotic Association, with Shiva Prasad and other rajas, which regularly published pamphlets and 'claimed a monopoly on loyalty to British rule and purported to represent the

[131] C. A. Bayly, *The Local Roots of Indian Politics*, p. 139.

[132] The Congress propaganda was often criticised by Muslim opponents as pro-Hindu (C. A. Bayly, *The Local Roots*, pp. 123, 142).

[133] Robinson, *Separatism*, p. 116.

[134] Communal tension had started to agitate the Allahabad municipal board in the 1870s; see F. Robinson, 'Municipal Government and Muslim Separatism', p. 410. See also M. Robb, *Print and the Urdu Public*, p. 3.

[135] Syed Ahmed Khan, *The Present State of Indian Politics*: Speech at Lucknow on 28 December 1887, pp. 10–1.

[136] See M. S. Jain, *The Aligarh Movement*, p. 93 and the *Proceedings of the Muslim Educational Conference*, Aligarh, 1887, Resolution 3, p. 42.

[137] For more about his political stance, see S. K. Das, *History of Indian Literature*, p. 506 and S. Naeem, *Shināsan-e Sir Syed*, vol. 2, pp. 26–27.

politically significant sections of the population'.[138] In March, April, and May 1888, the anti-Congress and Congress campaigns got more intense: while Ajudhia Nath recruited new Congress members among the province's elite, Aligarh partisans persuaded associations of landlords and government servants to make public declarations against the Congress.[139]

The same year, Hali published a poem entitled *Complaint to India* (*Shikwah-e Hind*), which was filled with anguish and bitterness. Thirty-four pages long and written in *tarkīb band*,[140] the *ġhazal* was written on the model of a petition (*shikwah*), a form of Islamic legal address of a petitioner to the ruler to ask for justice that was particularly used during the period of the Delhi Sultanate.[141] The poem displayed the tropes of traditional *ġhazal* poetry, with lovers complaining to their unfaithful beloved.[142] Relating the love story between India and the Muslims since its beginning to its 'end', Hali represented India as an 'overpoweringly, cruelly, even fatally beautiful'[143] beloved for a naïve lover, unprepared though aware of his tragic destiny. Oscillating between recollections of past glory and fears of annihilation, Hali emphasised the need to remember: he mourned the Muslim *ashrāf*'s cultural death in India, accusing the country of their ruin. In *Complaint to India*, this cultural death was also interpreted as resulting from the loss of Muslim cultural specificities:

jab tak, ay Hindūstāṇ, hindī nah kahlāte the ham
kuchh adā'eṇ āp meṇ sab se judā pāte the ham
ḥāl apnā sak͟ht ʿibratnāk tū ne kar diyā
āg the, ay Hind, hamko k͟hāk tū ne kar diyā!

[138] D. Lelyveld, *Aligarh's First Generation*, p. 309.

[139] Robinson, *Separatism*, p. 120. See also *Pamphlets Issued by the United Indian Patriotic Association, n°2: Showing the Seditious Character of the Indian National Congress and the Opinions Held y Eminent Natives of India Who Are OPPOSED to the Movement*, p. 96 and *Civil and Military Gazette* of 19 May 1888 quoted in *Pamphlets Issued by the United Indian Patriotic Association*, appendix, vi.

[140] The *tarkīb band* is a style of *ġhazal* in which every stanza has its own rhyme. It also displays a break in the middle of each couplet in which a common rhyme often appears. See B. D. Metcalf, 'Reflections on Iqbal's Mosque', p. 166.

[141] A. V. Taneja, *Jinnealogy*, pp. 3, 62.

[142] On this and Hali's use of the *Shikwah*, see A. Khan Mahmudabad, *Poetry of Belonging*, pp. 184–5.

[143] F. Pritchett, *Nets of Awareness*, p. 93.

O Hindustan, as long as we were not called Indians,
We had etiquettes that distinguished us from all
You have made of our condition dreadful
We were fire; you made us ashes, O Hind![144]

Nonetheless, Ali Khan Mahmudabad rightly argued, the form of the *shikwah* also revealed a space of intimacy between Muslims and India. The petitioning style of the first half of Hali's poem could well point to the hope that justice would somehow be done and Muslim grievances acknowledged. Contrary to the second edition of the *Musaddas*, which Hali wanted to be more optimistic in 1886, *Shikwah-e Hind* reflected Aligarh's political anxieties around the Congress propaganda. The powerful images of India reducing Muslims to ashes mirrored fears that Muslim political influence would disappear in the shadow of elective government and make the Muslim *ashrāf* a subordinate minority.

Around the middle of the poem, however, the finger started pointing less at India and more at Muslims for their own negligence and, again, need for reform.[145] Hali's *Complaint to India* undoubtedly built on the same literary devices used in the *Musaddas* and was indeed a reformist piece as well.

Bazm ko bar ham hū'e muddat nahīṇ guẓrī bahut
uṭh rahā hai gul se sham'-e bazm ke abtak dhū'āṇ
kah rahe haiṇ naqsh-e pā'e rahravāṇ, ay k̲h̲āk-e Hind
yahāṇ se guẓrā hai abhī ik bātajjamul kārawāṇ
go yaqīṇ hai – raftah raftah yād-e ayyām-e salaf
dil se chhoṛegī miṭā kar gardish-e daur-e zamāṇ
bhūl jā'enge keh the kin ḍālyūṇ ke ham ṡamar
ṭūṭ kar ā'e kahāṇ se aur bike ā kar kahāṇ

Smoke is still rising from the snuffing of the gathering's candle
The traces of the travellers' footprints still reveal, O dust of Hind,
That a magnificent caravan has just passed this way
It is certain that, blurred by the passage of time,
Our ancestors' memory will gradually leave our heart,
We will forget of which branches we were the fruit,
Whence we fell and where we came to be sold.[146]

[144] Hali, *Shikwah-e Hind*, band 7.
[145] A. Khan Mahmudabad, *Poetry of Belonging*, p. 184.
[146] Hali, *Shikwah-e Hind*, band 13.

Against the traumatic narration of Muslim cultural death equated with the loss of power, Hali emphasised glorious origins and genealogical ties with ancestors who belonged to different lands but were united 'all under the banner of Islam'.[147] The lengthy descriptions of the respective qualities of ancestors of various origins, which the Muslim *ashrāf* would have inherited indiscriminately, helped to create a sense of belonging – something that Hali further highlighted by the constant use of the personal pronoun 'we' (*ham*).[148]

The memory of a perfect past and the grief for its loss that Hali erected as shared heritage in *Shikwah-e Hind* called on the Muslim elites' imagination to create a sense of unified community when it was actually fragmented. He summoned a community of imagination, a community of feeling, rather than addressed a community that was already cohesive. This, of course, reflected the immediate context of composition when uniting the *ashrāf* was a priority.

Like the *Musaddas*, *Complaint to India* generated enthusiasm among the Urdu-speaking elite and was copied by poets, who sometimes even borrowed its title.[149] In 1888, *āshob* poems like Hali's *Complaint to India* appeared on the front pages of north Indian newspapers. Through the elicitation of collective grief, memory, and imagination, such discourse strove both to promote social reform and to strengthen social bonds through collective feelings. *Ashrāf* were associated with grief – and grief, with *ashrāf*. In Shauq Qidwai's *Lail-o Nahār* that was recited at the Muhammadan Educational Conference in 1889, this process of emotional/social identification was obvious. Like Hali's poems, it built on evocations of extra-Indian landscapes and the inheritance of 'Muslim' virtues, but also clearly described grief as community practice:

ham haiṇ ġham se tang ham ko ġham se chhuṭkārā nahīṇ
ġham hai ham se tang ġham ko ham se chhuṭkārā nahīṇ

We are sick of grief, grief doesn't let us free
Grief is sick of us, we don't let it free.[150]

147 Hali, *Shikwah-e Hind*, band 10.
148 See, for instance, Hali, *Shikwah-e Hind*, band 3.
149 See, for instance, the *Āgrah Aḵḫbār* of 14 July 1899 that published a *Complaint against India* by one Sayyid Aijaz ud-Din Faiq. *NNRNWP&O*, p. 372.
150 Shauq Qidwai, *Lail-o Nahār*, p. 30.

One year later, Shibli Numani (1857–1914) composed a similar poem entitled *Tamāshā-e ʿibrat yaʿnī Qaumī Musaddas*, which was recited in a very mournful tone (*pur-dard-o pur-soz*) at a public performance in Aligarh.[151] Such poems expressing the grief of the *ashrāf* were often titled *qaumī marṡiyah* or *qaumī musaddas*. Unsurprisingly, these were widely popular amongst the Urdu-speaking elites, and hence also became objects of controversy,[152] especially in the *Awadh Punch*. The main element of mockery was precisely the identification of *ġham* with a specific (elitist) community (*qaum*).

The *Awadh Punch*, like many *Punch* magazines, frequently caricatured Westernised Indians. Considering themselves the safeguards of vernacular culture, they criticised those who imitated Europe and promoted Anglo-Muslim entente.[153] The ambivalent 'not quite/not white'[154] effect was a cause of mockery by traditionalists. As Hali remarked in *Ḥayāt-e Jāwed*,

> The *Punch* newspapers mostly discussed Sir Syed. Their editors and proprietors were usually Muslims, and the sale of those papers depended on the degree to which they disgraced him (*phabtiyāṇ uṛā'eṇ*), how much they presented him in cartoons, how many satirical verses (*hajw ke ashāʿr*) they carried against him, and how they portrayed his merits as demerits. Thus, they exposed not only Sir Syed but the entire community to disgrace and ridicule (*ruswā aur badnām*).[155]

In the 1880s, a great point of contention was politics: the *Awadh Punch* was a pro-Congress magazine, with its editor Sajjad Husain, and many on its team, joining from 1887.[156] It did much to promote the organisation and fight against its opponents. In the late 1880s, the

[151] Shibli Numani, *Kulliyāt-e Shiblī*, p. 39, trans. C. Shackle and J. Majeed, *Hali's Musaddas*, pp. 39–40.

[152] S. F. Ahmad, *Sir Syed Ahmad Khan, Beck and the Indian National Congress*, p. 9. Fatwas denouncing Syed Ahmad Khan's 'heresy' were composed in Mecca. For an excellent description of contemporary Indian critiques, see A. Zaidi, *Making a Muslim*, pp. 106–109.

[153] On the milieu of the *Awadh Punch*, see J. Dubrow, *Cosmopolitan Dreams*.

[154] To borrow the words of H. Bhabha, 'Of Mimicry and Man: The Ambivalence of the Colonial Discourse'.

[155] Hali, *Hayat-e Jawed*, p. 382. For the Urdu: Hali, *Ḥayāt-e Jāwed*, part II, p. 271.

[156] Sarshar attended the Madras session in 1887, and Chakbast agreed with Gopal Krishna Gokhale's nationalist ideology. M. Hasan, *Wit and Humour*, p. 71; M. Islam, 'The Conscious Poet of Nationalism: Chakbast', p. 192.

Awadh Punch hence resisted attempts of Aligarh partisans to create a political community and claim leadership for the north Indian Muslim *ashrāf* through emotional discourse. Part of this process is visible as the *Awadh Punch* engaged in an '*āshob* dispute' in three rounds in 1888.

The dispute in the *Awadh Punch* started with the publication of one *āshob* poem in the Kanpur newspaper *Akẖbār-e ʿAlam-e Ṯaswīr* by an opponent of the Indian National Congress entitled 'Community Warning' (*Qaumī ʿibrat*). The *Awadh Punch* quickly reacted to the poem by publishing another poem, *The Drum of Islam* (*Naqqārah-e Islām*), in the edition of 5 April 1888, written by Munshi Abdul Basir Huzur, a Congress partisan. An anti-Congress reader from Mirzapur then responded with a thirty-seven-verse *musaddas* entitled *The Horn of Israfel* (*Sūr-e Isrāfīl*), which was published on 3 May by Sajjad Husain, claiming to give his reader the chance to 'establish their own opinion',[157] but interspersing the verses with literary and political criticism. Finally, a pro-Congress poem by Mirza Muhammad Murtaza Ashiq, *The Sun of Doomsday* (*Aftāb-e Qayāmat*), concluded the dispute in the magazine on 31 May.[158]

The poems, published over a two-month period, clearly replied to each other in what increasingly became aggressive campaigning. It is noteworthy that all three poems evoked the apocalypse in their titles (drums, the trumpet, and finally the Judgment), and used the same *musaddas* meter. They directly mentioned and responded to the preceding poems and used identical images (sometimes borrowing each other's verses) that were constantly ridiculed, and which certainly found their origin in the *Community Warning* of Kanpur.[159] The last poem mainly resorted to smear tactics to undermine the credibility of the Aligarh anti-Congress campaign rather than engaged with the arguments put forward by previous poets.

In the magazine, *āshob* poetry was clearly branded 'Aligarhian', and Congress partisans did not hesitate to pastiche the language of their opponents to mock them. The expression of grief for propaganda was

[157] Introduction to 'Sūr-e Isrāfīl', *Awadh Punch*, 3 May 1888.

[158] For more about the dispute, see E. Tignol, 'Genealogy, Authority and Political Representation'.

[159] The second poem, *The Horn of Israfel*, mentioned *Qaumī ʿibrat* in its last verse (verse 37), which would have been published by a Muslim and which I have unfortunately been unable to find in the pages of the *Awadh Punch*.

caricatured. Resorting to the same rhymes and metre, the *Drum of Islam* thus lampooned Aligarh partisans as depressed reactionaries:

Yehī ahl-e nechar ko din-rāt hai ġham
ūnheṇ ghere rahtī hai yeh fikr har dam
'banenge ġhulām ahl-e Bangāl ke ham
yeh har ṣūbeh meṇ jā ke honge farāham
zamāne meṇ koī rahegā nah bāqī
yehī honge maikash yehī honge sāqī!'

These people of Nechar are day and night engulfed in sorrow,
They always remain surrounded by this worry
'We'll become the slaves of the Bengalis,
They'll come and spread in every province,
None will remain in this world,
Neither the drunkard, nor the cupbearer!'[160]

In all the poems, Aligarhian *ashrāf* were described as afflicted by loss and worry.[161] Each side argued for different causes of worry. On one hand, Congress poems typically argued that Aligarh was responsible for the loss of faith.[162] On the other hand, Aligarh poems, like *The Horn of Israfel*, accused 'low born' members of the Indian National Congress of wanting to eliminate both Muslim *ashrāf* and Islam:

Bahut sach keh hai kul sharīfoṇ meṇ yeh ġham
ūnheṇ ghere rahtī hai yeh fikr har dam
banenge ġhulām ahl-e Bangāl ke ham
kamīne naẕar āte beshak haiṇ k͟hurram
yehī hogī paidā aṡar Congress kī
k͟hudāwand-e ʿālam woh sāʿat nah lā'e!

It is true that all the nobles bear this grief,
Always they are surrounded by this worry:

160 Huzur, '*Naqqārah-e Islām*', *Awadh Punch*, verse 30.

161 The fourth verse of *The Horn of Israfel* lamented, 'We've been harassed by destruction such that what was ours became the property of others, these thoughts have accumulated in our hearts that we should relieve the ruin of the nation: everyone wants Islam and the name of Muhammad to be erased from this country'.

162 Verse 11, for instance, says, 'Can I summarise who has brought this calamity? Nechar, Nechar, Nechar!'; verse 12: 'Now the Muslims are aware of who are responsible for the spread of this rebellion: those Necharis are in fact the enemies of Islam'; verse 22: 'They have erased the honour of the Shariʿah, they have wiped out Islam's modesty and bashfulness'.

We'll become the slaves of the Bengalis
These low born people are indeed cheerful
This will be the effect of the Congress
May God never bring such a time![163]

In any case, *ġham* was clearly highlighted as an emotion that characterised and performatively created community belonging. The grief of noble men was opposed to the delight (*k͟hurram*) of 'low born' Congress members, implying that being noble was bound to feeling sad. The dispute did not oppose Hindus and Muslims, but 'noble' and 'popular' classes; it was, first and foremost, about class and political leadership.

Writers like Akbar Allahabadi (1846–1921), a regular contributor to the *Awadh Punch* and nonetheless an admirer of Syed Ahmed Khan, were quick to highlight the opportunism of Aligarh leaders who 'manipulated' collective emotions for their own vested interests. In one undated satirical couplet, Allahabadi emphasised the discrepancy between discourse and practice, as Aligarh leaders mourned decline while enjoying success:

qaum ke ġham meṇ ḍinar khāte haiṇ hukkām ke sāth
ranj līḍar ko bahut hai magar ārām ke sāth

Our leaders, in pain for the nation, are guests of the rulers for dinner;
In their suffering situation, it's strange they're not looking thinner.[164]

The question of the authenticity of sentiments is important. At the same time as Aligarh worked at uniting an elite community through shared feelings, it also demarcated community boundaries. Those who did not identify with Aligarhian emotions were excluded. It is thus unsurprising that the question of emotional authenticity should emanate from adversaries who did not share the same valuations of emotions.

The emphasis on collective grief in Aligarh writings certainly contrasted with the fact that educated Aligarh elites usually prospered under colonial rule. Syed Ahmed Khan and Hali often celebrated

163 Anonymous, '*Sūr-e Isrāfīl*', *Awadh Punch*, verse 26.
164 Unfortunately I have not been able to trace the date of composition of the couplet which appears under 'Miscellaneous', number 1349, in *Kulliyāt-e Akbar Allahābādī*, p. 167, trans. M. H. Case, 'The Social and Political Satire of Akbar Allahabadi', p. 18.

colonial rule as a world of new and exciting opportunities, and they certainly benefitted most from it – nothing to be sad about for *Awadh Punch* contributors.[165] However, the *ġham* that Aligarh writers practised was not the despair that was mocked by Allahabadi and *Awadh Punch* poets, and that would manifest itself through lethargy or misery. It was one full of energy and self-rehabilitation. The *āshob* dispute nevertheless illustrated well the growing tensions between Aligarh's and the Congress' attempts at securing leadership, and the existence of conflicting emotional communities.

As reports from *Native Newspapers Reports* demonstrated, the late nineteenth-century press was full of this new type of literature intertwining descriptions of decline and collective grief.[166] Hindus composed similar poems, and the theme of present decline and past glory also developed in Bengal in the second half of the nineteenth century. This rhetoric was extensively used in community organisations such as the Muhammadan Educational Conference from its beginnings in 1886.[167] It became such an important feature of the Aligarh movement that in 1904 – only two years before the creation of the All India Muslim League and the use of the argument of the Muslims' political importance to gain advantages for representation in the colonial government – controversy arose about community *marṡiyahs* and the overpowering role that *āshob* poetry had come to play in community politics.[168]

In one letter to Maulvi Mahbub Alam, editor of the *Paisah Ak̲h̲bār*, Lahore, in 1904, following some controversy around one such *qaumī marṡiyah*,[169] Hali responded to an article published in the 19 April 1904 issue of the paper entitled 'The Excess of Poetry in Community Gatherings'. As M. S. Jain highlighted in his study of the Aligarh movement, the Muslim Educational Conference had been increasingly criticised since the last decade of the nineteenth century for resembling

165 For a summary of Akbar Allahabadi's perception of Aligarh, see S. R. Faruqi, 'The Power Politics of Culture'.

166 See, for instance, *Āgrah Ak̲h̲bār* of 7 December 1895, *NNRNWP&O*, p. 616, or such poems by, for instance, M. A. Tonki, Nazim, *Musaddas-e Nazim*, Lahore, 1900.

167 F. Robinson, 'The Memory of Power'.

168 Letter from Hali to Maulvi Mahbub Alam, editor of the *Paisah Ak̲h̲bār* in Hali, *Makātīb-e Ḥālī*, pp. 49–51.

169 Such controversy seems to have involved a Persian poem from Lucknow. See *Awadh Punch*, 14 June 1904, p. 5.

a *mushāʿirah* to the extent that, in 1899 at Calcutta, the chair refused the recitation of poems.[170] Although Hali agreed with the author that poetry had taken up too much space in those organisations, he traced the beginning of the practice back to Syed Ahmed Khan and justified its use in some instances. Besides postulating that poets saw in community gatherings opportunities to recite poetry after the abolition of traditional platforms (*mushāʿirahs*), he also explained 'it was necessary to provide an atmosphere to these conferences with which Muslims are naturally familiar so that they come to join these meetings with great pleasure and eagerness'.[171] In his biography of Syed Ahmed Khan published a couple of years earlier, Hali had indeed rejoiced in comparing the great flux of people attending the Muhammadan Educational Conference with the crowds at Delhi's festival of the flower-sellers (*phūlwāloṇ kī sair*).[172]

Despite deploring in the letter the fact that poets exclusively composed work on the decline of Islam,[173] Hali argued for the usefulness of *āshob* poetry in some cases; for instance, for the meetings of the *Anjuman-e Himāyat-e Islām* that crucially needed financial support.[174] *Āshob* poetry clearly served to convey a sense of belonging and messages of reform, but also to attract audiences and funds. While the letter was critical of the use of such practices – Hali suggested they be abolished in favour of religious sermons and moral lectures – it attested to their success in the early twentieth century.

Kayasths and Kashmiri Pandits also used *āshob*-type literature for propaganda.[175] The majority of such poems aimed at encouraging Urdu-speaking elites to 'devote themselves heart and soul to the study of modern arts and sciences'.[176] The success of Aligarh's *āshob* poetry

[170] *Report of the Conference for 1899*, p. 93, quoted in M. S. Jain, *The Aligarh Movement*, p. 173.
[171] Letter from Hali to Maulvi Mahbub Alam, p. 51. My emphasis.
[172] Hali, *Ḥayāt-e Jāwed*, p. 107. [173] Hali, *Makātīb-e Ḥālī*, p. 50.
[174] The *Anjuman-e Ḥimayāt-e Islām* (Society for the Support of Islam) was an educational organisation inspired by the Aligarh movement and founded in the Punjab in 1886 in the wake of the Muslim Educational Conferences. For more about the Society, see M. M. Fuchs, 'Islamic Modernism in Colonial Punjab'.
[175] See, for instance, *Rahbar* of 1 May 1900, *NNRNWP&O*, p. 227, or *Kayasth Hitkari* of 8 July 1900, *NNRNWP&O*, p. 364.
[176] See the *Kshatriya Mitra* of 16 February 1910, *NNRNWP&O*, p. 199.

seems to have gradually extended to other groups looking for higher social status in the colonial world.[177] By the end of the nineteenth century and until the middle of the twentieth century, the memory of past glory and the grief at present backwardness reached groups that were not necessarily of noble descent but nonetheless aspired to a good position in British India. They identified with the emotional practices of the elite in attempts at upward social mobility. The *Kshattriya* of 20 May 1918, for instance, noted that 'though the Jat community are in a very depressed condition it is gratifying to note that they still have some of the prototypes of their illustrious forebears. We should therefore bear in mind the following poem [published in the paper] and learn to hope for the educational future of our community'.[178] The *āshob* dispute in the *Awadh Punch* and more generally the expression of *ġham* by Aligarh partisans illustrated the ability of emotions to create and sustain communities, although the demarcation of community boundaries necessarily implied the exclusion of others.[179]

3 India as the Land of Muslim Downfall: Letters from the *Awadh Punch* (1904)

The 1857 *shahr āshob* gradually developed into *dunyā āshob* and eventually into *qaum āshob* poetry in Aligarhian milieus, in which 'a renewed focus [wa]s placed on the religious identity of the community'.[180] The longing for an imaginary extra-Indian Islamic past came at a crucial time when a Muslim political community was being created, with the support of the newspaper press. If Dubrow argues that print was 'an emotional, affective experience' which united an Urdu cosmopolis that 'consciously resisted national borders or religious identities',[181] it was less and less the case at the turn of the twentieth century. While a word like *qaum* (community, nation) had assumed different meanings even in the mouth of Syed Ahmed Khan, scholarship has highlighted that the colonial apparatus of spatial mapping,

[177] S. Anjum, *Monogrāf*, pp. 82–3. [178] *NNRNWP&O* for 1918, p. 407.
[179] About social bonding and dissociation in the aftermath of trauma, see M. T. Fullilove, *Root Shock: How Tearing Up City Neighborhoods Hurts America*, quoted in J. Saul, *Collective Trauma, Collective Healing*, p. 4.
[180] A. Khan Mahmudabad, *Poetry of Belonging*, p. 181.
[181] J. Dubrow, *Cosmopolitan Dreams*, pp. 2 and 7.

census, and print – as well as the emergence of representative politics – increasingly enabled the shaping of 'comprehensive, abstract and agentive' identities, such as the Indian Muslim *qaum*.[182]

Aligarh's poetic works, and Hali's in particular, were increasingly read as 'separatists' in the following decades. Historians have argued that the powerful Muslim 'pull' towards an extra-Indian past that was notably displayed in Hali's *Musaddas* and more radically in his *Complaint to India* translated the *ashrāf's* growing 'reluctance to receive and participate in the cultural experience of India's history'.[183] As we have seen, the particular historical context surrounding these works should not be downplayed, and the emphasis on extra-Indian origins revealed the desire of Aligarh poets to reinforce the status and authority of the Muslim *ashrāf* by insisting on their noble ancestors – genealogies, after all, had always played a prominent part in Indo-Muslim aristocratic culture. *Shikwah-e Hind* also reflected the polemical context of the anti-Congress campaign and was first of all a reformist piece. It was not designed to fuel Hindu–Muslim tension, and as Ali Khan Mahmudabad remarks, it was 'symbolic of closeness rather than estrangement, for real complaint is proof of intimacy rather than separation'.[184]

The representation of India as corrupt, or as the land of Muslim downfall, had been used in Aligarhian discourse as a way to promote a reformist return to the origins of Islam, and was probably also a reaction to the very experience of colonialism. On 22 October 1873, Mohsin ul-Mulk gave a lecture at the Mirzapur Institute, in which he asserted that '[w]hat especially has caused the decline of the unfortunate Indian Muslims has been their adoption of India as a homeland, and their forsaking of their original homes.'[185] Along with the desire to reconnect with the roots of Islam, the humiliation of now belonging to a subjected nation certainly enhanced the aspiration to dissociate oneself from the place of submission. As Faisal Devji argued, the colonial state had forced Indian Muslims to 'abandon the idea of territorial nationality, which defined them as second-class subjects in

182 S. Kaviraj, 'A Strange Love of the Land', p. 7.
183 A. B. M. Habibullah, 'Historical Writing in Urdu: A Survey of Tendencies', p. 485.
184 A. Khan Mahmudabad, *Poetry of Belonging*, p. 184.
185 Mahdi Ali Khan, *Majmu'ah-e Lectures-o Speeches*, p. 33, quoted by F. Devji, 'India in the Muslim Imagination', p. 3.

a state where they were unfree instead of free, a minority instead of a majority'.[186] At the time, emerging as a unified and distinct community was part of an effort to 'overcome the ravages of colonialism'.[187]

Yet, as I argued, Aligarh's *āshob* poetry emphasised *ġham* as repentance to lead to cultural improvement, and to recover part of the honour that was said to have been lost.[188] In Hali's poems, the memory of Arab origins replaced 'the imperfect present with a perfect past'.[189] Instead of directing anger towards the colonial state and risking being labelled as disloyal – something that loyalists like Syed Ahmed Khan tried to avoid at all costs – Hali and others rather blamed themselves (and sometimes India) for the traumatic loss.

Hindu Kayasths actually seem to have responded in a similar manner to the impact of colonisation. They engaged in the same collective reconfiguration process by emotionally recalling their glorious Hindu origins and putting their collective past into writing, giving birth to numerous 'caste histories' in attempts to create community belonging.[190] Kayasth community newspapers regularly announced projects of writing the history of their communities, which usually claimed to be Hindu Kshatriyas.[191] As Sender noted, some Kashmiri Pandits also 'adopted an historical perspective'[192] and, like many Muslim *ashrāf*, tended to express grief and emotional 'dissociation' from Hindustan around the same period. They increasingly longed for a Kashmir homeland that was described as paradise on earth, perhaps in a similar attempt to escape the colonial world and to return to their roots for the construction of a

[186] F. Devji, 'A Shadow Nation', p. 126.

[187] Ibid., p. 131. See also F. Devji, 'India in the Muslim Imagination', p. 3.

[188] This process would also be quite common in reaction to cultural traumas. See, for instance, S. Schneider and H. Weinberg, *The Large Group Re-Visited*; I. Kogan, *The Struggle against Mourning*; V. D. Volkan, 'Not Letting Go'; V. D. Volkan, 'The Next Chapter: Consequences of Societal Trauma'.

[189] J. Damousi, *Living with the Aftermath: Trauma, Nostalgia and Grief*, p. 68, quotes J. Rutherford, *Men's Silences: Predicaments in Masculinity*, p. 127.

[190] On this, see L. C. Stout, *The Hindustani Kayasthas*.

[191] The *Kayastha Samachar*, for instance, advertised at least three such publications over the course of three years (1903–1906): the *Kayastha Sarvasva* (February 1903, vol. VII, 2, p. 199), the *Miftāḥ ul-Makhzan ul-Ansāb* (May–June 1904, vol. IX, 5–6, p. 554), and the work of Pandey Ram Saran Lall of Ghazipur (July 1906, vol. 14, 83, p. 103). Such works were usually written in Urdu. A look at the list of the publications by the Nawal Kishore Press shows the success of such enterprises. See U. Stark, *An Empire of Books*, p. 461 ff.

[192] H. Sender, 'The Kashmiri Brahmins (Pandits) up to 1930', p. 137.

new collective identity. As Brij Mohan Dattatreya Kaifi (1866–1955), for instance, wrote in autumn 1891, 'Leaving Kashmir was like leaving Eden, it was our downfall'.[193]

If the Urdu-speaking elite often expressed such sentiments in the late nineteenth century, they resounded quite differently in the early twentieth century.[194] The 1900s saw the growth of communal tension in north India. Political agitation and consequent colonial concessions to Hindu revivalist claims in the United Provinces led to more assertive demands from Muslim leaders who were anxiously looking at new administrative policies.[195] In 1900, for instance, Sir Anthony MacDonnell, then Lieutenant Governor of the United Provinces, agreed to the use of Devanagari in courts after having received a Hindu deputation, which stirred Muslim agitation in Aligarh and led to the foundation of the Urdu Defence Association by Mohsin ul-Mulk.[196] In the south, communal tension also increased. At the end of the nineteenth century, the nationalist leader Bal Gangadhar Tilak organised an annual national festival in honour of the birth anniversary of the Marathi ruler Shivaji, which eventually (and unintentionally) sparked Muslim indignation.[197] The festival that was intended to 'create national feeling'[198] and was held in different parts of India in fact created a 'history war'.[199] It polarised Hindu and Muslim communities as 'two great monolithic political communities divided by memories of masterhood and subjecthood, and by the pride of the one at the humiliation of the other'.[200] In 1906, Muslim leaders from Aligarh who had just founded the All India Muslim League definitely refused to join in the yearly celebrations, arguing that

[193] *Safar-e Kashmīr*, October–November 1891, quoted in Ibid., p. 137.

[194] Pant has noted that while the north Indian Kashmiri Pandits who had emigrated in the eighteenth and nineteenth centuries continued to adhere to the Indo-Muslim culture and fought for the cause of Urdu in the late nineteenth century, newly immigrated Kashmiri Pandits in the late nineteenth century and early twentieth centuries were more aggressive in their religious assertions: K. Pant, *The Kashmiri Pandit*, pp. 154–6.

[195] F. Robinson, *Separatism*, p. 133.

[196] P. Hardy, *The Muslims of British India*, p. 143.

[197] As Hardy noted, the festival was intentionally conceived as nationalist but was not intended to 'exacerbate Hindu-Muslim relations' (Ibid., p. 142).

[198] The *Hindustani* (Lucknow), 2 July 1901, *NNRNWP&O*, p. 431.

[199] D. Chakrabarty, 'The Public Life of History'.

[200] P. Hardy, *The Muslims of British India*, p. 142.

while every community is free to celebrate its great men, in order to create a national feeling among its members, it has no right to ask men of another community to take part in such celebrations, especially when the hero celebrated happens to be regarded as an enemy by the members of that community.[201]

In retaliation, they proposed celebrating Ahmad Shah Abdali, who had defeated the Mahrattas. Suggestions to commemorate Akbar instead to 'promote a feeling of common fellowship'[202] amongst members of all communities were also put forward, but after the partition of Bengal in 1905, communal tension was already in full swing.

Then Hali's *Musaddas* and *Complaint to India* were read with different lenses: the pull away from India was no longer interpreted only as part of a discourse on community status and reform, but as a vigorous assertion of communal antagonism and as a lack of dedication to India's past and future. Although Ayesha Jalal argued that 'Hali's *Shikwa-e-Hind* did not stir a public controversy over his, or for that matter his community's, putative lack of allegiance to India',[203] in the early twentieth century, strong criticism was voiced. Disapproval would come again from papers like the *Awadh Punch*, whose contributors promoted Hindu–Muslim cooperation. Since 1903, Brij Narain Chakbast (1882–1926), a Kashmiri Brahmin from Faizabad who was traditionally educated in Urdu and Persian, was drawn into the *Awadh Punch* 'anti-Hali campaign', and, despite having been influenced by Hali's works,[204] started routinely ridiculing his style of poetry in the magazine's articles.[205] Chakbast was representative of the *Awadh Punch*'s cosmopolitan team of columnists who were against the representation of Urdu as a Muslim language.[206]

[201] *Aligarh Institute Gazette*, 11 July 1906, *NNRNWP&O*, p. 426.
[202] *Awadh Akhbār*, 10 November 1906, *NNRNWP&O*, p. 788.
[203] A. Jalal, 'Exploding Communalism: The Politics of Muslim Identity in South Asia', tcd.ie/iiis/documents/archive/pdf/communalismayesha.pdf, p. 4.
[204] S. S. Kaif, *Chakbast: Makers of Indian Literature*, p. 14.
[205] Ibid., p. 42. Notably, according to Kaif, in an article on 27 August 1903.
[206] After Chakbast's new edition of *Gulzār-e Nasīm*, a *maśnawī* written by Pandit Daya Shankar Kaul Nasim. A Kashmiri Brahmin Urdu poet, Sharar published a review in which he expressed his doubts about authorship. A dispute followed, highlighting the ongoing process of making Urdu a Muslim language, which divided Urdu-speaking opinion but which Chakbast eventually won. See C. R. Perkins, 'Partitioning History', pp. 209–54. See also the full publication of the dispute: M. M. Shafi Shirazi, *Maʻrakah-e Chakbast-o Sharar*.

In 1904, Hali was awarded the title of *Shams ul-ʿulamā'* by the British government. This official recognition and praise of his literary achievements certainly added further fuel to the fire in the *Awadh Punch*. Articles that year frequently mocked Hali for being *K͟hālī* ('empty', a pun with his pen name *Ḥālī*),[207] for reciting poems using meaningless words (*be-maʿnī lafẕoṇ kā istiʿmāl*) in a sad voice (*dardnāk āwāz meṇ*) at the Educational Conference,[208] or for having 'tarnished Urdu poetry' as went the chorus of an insult poem of 'Mister Careless' (*Mirzā Lā-ubālī*).[209] The two letters that appeared against Hali and Aligarh leaders in July and August 1904 thus emerged in a context in which Hali was already a first-hand target of *Awadh Punch* satirists.[210] The *Awadh Punch* made it clear: Hali was not worthy of public acknowledgment.[211]

The letters – one signed 'Hindustan' (28 July 1904) and the second 'The Islamic faith' (4 August 1904) – particularly targeted the *Musaddas* and *Shikwah-e Hind* and their representation of Indo-Muslim history. The 'letter' format was then in fashion in the next issues too and recalled Sajjad Husain's use of the style to address famous personalities (the Nizam of Hyderabad, Gladstone, Queen Victoria, the Begum of Bhopal, etc.).[212] The letters, however, were anonymous. At the core of their preoccupations were the representation of the Muslims' arrival and 'degeneration' in India and the emotional rejection of India in Hali's poems. The author of Hindustan's letter expressed his discontent with not having spoken earlier and not having directly addressed Syed Ahmed Khan, but the granting of the *Shams ul-ʿulamā'* title rekindled his eagerness to express what seemed to have been a long-standing critique.[213]

207 *Awadh Punch*, 3 March 1904, pp. 1–2; also on 26 May 1904.
208 *Awadh Punch*, 21 April 1904, pp. 1–2.
209 *Awadh Punch*, 16 June 1904, p. 1.
210 The *Awadh Punch*, as Jennifer Dubrow noted, was already specialised as an organ for 'correct and proper language use' (J. Dubrow, *Cosmopolitan Dreams*, p. 104).
211 '*Islām kā k͟hat̤*', *Awadh Punch*, 4 August 1904, p. 7: 'These days, the issue [...] is that you should receive some title from the government for good service to your community. Your service to the community, what is it? Why should you receive this title?'
212 See Awadh Punch, *Intik͟hāb-e Awadh Punch* (R. Kazmi, ed.) on Sajjad Husain, pp. 25–74.
213 'It is sad that Sir Syed has passed away otherwise today I would cling to his clothes and reply to him face to face. But fortunately, you and Mahdi Ali [Mohsin ul Mulk] are alive'. '*Hindustān kā k͟hat̤*', *Awadh Punch*, 28 July 1904, p. 2.

Both letters accused Hali's representations of being offensive and his attitude irreligious; they noted that the Muslims whom Hali mourned in fact still existed and that Muslim virtues and sciences had never disappeared but were being trampled by Aligarh's anxious search.[214] This had been a common critique since the 1880s. In Hindustan's letter, the author beautifully refuted Hali's accusation that India was responsible for Muslim decline by showing that Syed Ahmed Khan's modernist (i.e. 'faithless') ideas were responsible for the Muslims' cultural downfall:

In which ways have I been so perfidious that you wrote that I have taught Muslims selfishness (*k̲h̲udġharẓī*); that I am selfish; that I have ruined Muslims? There still remains today Muslims of the old times and the children who have obtained education from them should not plant new saplings from their own hands that would confront the old branches. Look now, if you have obtained in so doing the qualities that you lament in your *Musaddas* and *Shikwah-e Hind* or not.

In reality, if you look attentively then [you will see that] the hands of your *Pīr Nechar* [Syed Ahmed Khan] were spoiled, and you put the blame on me! Pay attention: these Muslim qualities that you search for in *Shikwah-e Hind*, where are they? Look at the hospitality (*mehmān-nawāzī*), the morality (*ak̲h̲lāq*), and the togetherness. Remember that religion is what removes difficulties in the world. As much someone loves religion and is devoted, as close he will be to God and love His servants. When one is devoted (*pāband*) then he automatically obtains all the best virtues as God's reward.[215]

But besides the usual critique of Aligarh's irreligiousness, Hindustan's letter also more broadly opposed Hali's representation of Muslim interactions with India in both *Shikwah-e Hind* and the *Musaddas*. It criticised the representation of India as being a cruel and plundering lover by emphasising the violence of Islam's arrival in India:

This is pure accusation and a consequence of weak faith to consider me as the resolute maker [i.e. God]. I did not give wealth to your community (*qaum*), nor did I give it sovereignty. Neither houses were given, nor drums nor seals [here, the author refers to one of *Shikwah-e Hind*'s verses]; your community arrived by itself in my abode and entered it by force without asking. It snatched the bread from my children's hands and, trespassing, it

[214] '*Islām kā k̲h̲aṭ*', *Awadh Punch*, 4 August 1904, p. 7.
[215] '*Hindustān kā k̲h̲aṭ*', p. 5.

penetrated [my] houses to such an extent that not even a piece of paper was left that was not taken by force.

The author's response to Hali's poems was far from being less antagonistic than Hali's initial words. Muslims' arrival in India was described as a most violent phenomenon; but the real focus was not so much on the brutality of the event as on the violence of Hali's dissociation from India. While Muslims had been friends with Hindus for centuries to the extent that they were considered equal, Hali was now ungratefully turning against his adopted kin. What the author criticised was not so much Hali's communal representations as the Muslim *ashrāf's* rejection of India and their lack of dedication to what had long become their homeland:

I [India] submitted to the command of the sultanate and I respectfully made room. Because of their [the Muslims'] continued stay, they started revering me like my own sons and became so friendly with my sons that I began to think of them as real brothers. But these friends kept an account of mutually exchanged gifts; in reality, records were kept of what was yours and what was mine. The wealth and goods that were theirs remained theirs. I neither took anything from them, nor did they give me anything.[216]

Emphasising the Muslims' violent separation from India, the letter operated an important shift by representing India as a mother – an image that had become popular in nationalist circles since Bankim Chandra Chattopadhyay's novel *Ānandamaṭh* and its *Vande Mātaram* hymn (1882) at least. Already in the 1870s, the Bengali elite had resorted to the image of the mother for nationalist propaganda, an image that soon circulated in art forms too.[217] As several scholars have shown, in early works such as Kiran Chandra Bandyopadhyay's *Bhārat Melā* (1873) or in one of Chattopadhyay's early piece on *Dasamāhavidyā* published in his journal *Bangadarshan* in 1873, India's contemporary condition was allegorised in the wretched condition of a widow trying to wake her sleeping sons to recover her honour.

Probably inspired by Western anthropomorphic representations of territories, the *Awadh Punch* also regularly pictured India (or other countries and regions) as a female, though not specifically as a mother,

[216] Ibid. [217] See S. Ramaswamy, *The Goddess and the Nation.*

from its creation.[218] In the late 1880s, at the time of the publication of Hali's *Shikwah-e Hind*, India was in fact regularly presented in the *Awadh Punch* as a lady whose love was coveted by others, like the Russian government, for instance.[219] So, while certainly building on the recent fashionable image of the motherland that gained prominence in the United Provinces,[220] the transfer of the representation of India as a lover who deluded a vigorous and proud Muslim male in *Shikwah-e Hind* to one of India as the adoption mother of a selfish Muslim boy in the 1904 *Awadh Punch* was harsh. The *Awadh Punch* accused Hali's works of egotism and ungratefulness towards a mother's loving dedication. The transfer could easily be seen as emasculating and castrative.[221] Of course, almost twenty years had passed between the 1888 poem and the 1904 critique in *Awadh Punch*, and the political context had changed. By transforming what was first described as a deceptive romantic relation into a tragic family discord, the magazine argued for the impossible justification of Muslim separatist claims.

4 Conclusion

The expression of grief underwent a change in north India in the late nineteenth century. The *shahr āshob* genre that until then lamented the destruction of cities developed into *dunyā āshob* and *qaum āshob* poetry in the late 1870s in the print media. In 1877 or 1878, just after the fall of Plevna, *āshob* poetry enabled the expression of discontent in the *Awadh Punch*, and served the purpose of reform at Aligarh.

The 'unearthing' of a thirteenth-century Andalusi poem belonging to the Arabic genre of *rithā' al-mudun* by Syed Ahmed Khan changed the way *ġham* was expressed and used in late nineteenth-century north India. Taking the Andalusian poem as an example, Hali relocated India's Muslim past within a broader narrative of Islamic glory, and

[218] For Hind as a man or an animal, see, for instance, respectively, M. Hasan, *Wit and Humour*, pp. 44 and 98. For India as a woman, see Ibid., p. 38, and *A Selection from the Illustrations Which Have Appeared in the* Oudh Punch *from 1877 to 1881*.

[219] M. Hasan, *Wit and Humour*, p. 75, quotes *Awadh Punch*, 1 September 1887, p. 541.

[220] C. Gupta, 'The Icon of the Mother in Late Colonial India', p. 4298.

[221] Ibid., p. 4293.

built on a different meaning of *ġham*, which semantically linked grief to shame, and repentance. The emotion was to be transformative and to lead to self-reformation. Through the elicitation of *ġham*, interwoven with powerful memory narratives, Aligarh writers worked at both promoting reform and shaping community belonging, especially during the 1888 anti-Congress propaganda.

The propaganda demonstrated that *ġham* was powerful in summoning an emotional community into being: grief and respectability were intertwined. *Awadh Punch* contributors then criticised the resort to emotion as being opportunistic and interest-oriented. Yet, at the end of the nineteenth century, the success of *āshob* poetry increasingly impacted the political sphere, so much so that Hali eventually disapproved of its excessive use in community meetings forty years later. While Aligarh's imagination of the past mainly aimed at strengthening social bonds and promoting cultural regeneration among the Muslim *ashrāf*, it appealed more and more to lower-class groups who strove to secure a good position in the colonial world.

In the early twentieth century, the representation of India as the place of Muslim decline was increasingly read as a lack of allegiance to contemporary politics, a blind loyalty to the colonial state, and a passive rejection of India's composite heritage. Even more so after the foundation of the Muslim League in 1906, many Urdu-speaking elites expressed their disapproval of Muslims' lack of dedication to the Indian nationalist cause, and, for instance, argued in the *Kayastha Samachar* that 'the Indian Mussulman is the product of mixed influences in which the indigenous Hindu element preponderates'.[222] As Shackle has shown, Kaifi copied the *Musaddas* style to encourage modern education while emphasising India's rich heritage against Muslim claims of precedence.[223] The *Kayasth Samachar and Hindustan Review* further lamented in 1902:

> [The Muslims] do not yet believe that India is their home for all ages to come, though they have been living here for nearly nine centuries. [...] Some of them have vague hopes of regaining their lost supremacy—not by physical power, but by some miracle. Others there are who look to Mecca and

222 *The Kayastha Samachar and Hindustan Review*, March 1901, vol. 3, 3, p. 124

223 C. Shackle, 'Brij Mohan Dattatreya "Kaifi" (1866–1955): A Mirror for India', p. 103.

Constantinople and even to Kabul for making their homes. There is yet another section which is haunted by the chimera of Pan-Islamism and is 'hatching vain Empires'. Foolish men and foolish dreams![224]

Of course, Muslims voiced similar critiques. In his biography of Maulvi Muhammad Zakaullah (1832–1911), Charles F. Andrews explained that he 'objected vehemently to Musalmans, whose forefathers had been in India for many generations, regarding themselves as foreigners, or making a line of separation between their own interests, as Musalmans, and the interests of India itself'.[225] In the early 1910s, as we shall see next, some young educated Aligarh Muslim leaders also disapproved of the 'passivity' of the Muslim *ashrāf* whose nostalgic recollections prevented them from engaging with Indian nationalist causes.[226] In fact, the *ġham* of Aligarhian writings was, on the contrary, supposed to be self-transformative, but its reformist stance was certainly less attractive to the next generation of Muslim leaders.

224 *The Kayastha Samachar and Hindustan Review*, November 1902, vol. 6, 5, p. 399.
225 C. F. Andrews, *Zaka Ullah of Delhi*, p. 110.
226 See, for instance, *The Comrade*, 14 January 1911, vol. 1, 1, p. 1.

3 Memorials, Feelings, and Public Recognition, c. 1911–1915

On 12 December 1911, during his lavish Coronation Durbar in Delhi, George V revealed that the capital of the British Raj would soon be transferred from Calcutta to Delhi.[1] With the news still resounding through the stupefied audience, the king-emperor also announced the construction of a new Delhi, meant to 'convey the idea of peaceful domination and dignified rule over the traditions and life of India by the British Raj'[2] of which he laid the foundation stones two days later. This 'royal boon' to the people of India was accompanied by the annulment of the partition of Bengal and the creation of a new governorship for the presidency of Bengal, Orissa, and Assam, which were prompted by a tense political climate and the rise of anti-colonial activism – the Swadeshi movement.[3] Transferring the seat of government offered the opportunity for the new Viceroy Charles Hardinge (1910–1916) to move away from nationalist agitators, as well as to enhance and stabilise colonial authority.[4] Not everyone received the news with enthusiasm; several British residents and government officers, among them Lord Curzon (1899–1905) – who had presided over the partition of Bengal in 1905 – strongly criticised the state's decision.[5] He and others did not agree with the expenditure that the construction of the new city would imply, especially a city that was full of ruins and tombs and was dubbed by pro-Calcutta partisans 'the grave of empires'.[6] 'The activities of a modern State would be

[1] *Parliamentary Papers*, 'Announcement by and on Behalf of His Majesty the King-Emperor', 3, p. 6, quoted in R. G. Irving, *Indian Summer*, p. 11.

[2] *Parliamentary Papers*, 'Second Report of the Delhi Town Planning Committee', Cd. 6888, p. 5, and *Parliamentary Papers*, 'Final Report of the Delhi Town Planning Committee', Cd. 6889, p. 2, quoted by R. G. Irving, *Indian Summer*, p. 52.

[3] S. Chattopadhyay, 'Cities of Power and Protest', p. 41.

[4] E. A. Christensen, 'Government Architecture and British Imperialism', pp. 67–8.

[5] R. G. Irving, *Indian Summer*, p. 32.

[6] S. Chattophadyay, 'Cities of Power and Protest', p. 42; *The Comrade*, 28 March 1914, vol. 7, 13, p. 253.

unconsciously affected in the atmosphere of a vast, silent graveyard, with its haunting memories', they argued.[7]

While late nineteenth-century nostalgic writings turned towards an extra-Indian heritage for cultural regeneration, after the transfer of the capital of the British Raj from Calcutta to Delhi, fantasies of a glorious past reinvigorated the Indian soil. The peculiar climate of the 1910s and the construction of New Delhi awakened a growing urge among young Indian Muslim elites to preserve the past and its local manifestations in the urban landscape. They called for proper public memorialisation – a process through which buildings were turned into political and emotional objects of memory. As scholarship has emphasised, during the construction of New Delhi, 'Young Party'[8] Muslims exploited Mughal landscapes as pan-Indian Muslim sites of paramount importance. They broke off with the loyal stance of Aligarh's first generation and increasingly mobilised around anti-colonial nationalist issues, thus gaining broader popular support. Through an analysis of articles published in Mohamed Ali Jauhar's twin papers *The Comrade* and *Hamdard* ('Comrade, Sympathiser') from 1911 to 1915, this chapter shows that from its foundation, *The Comrade* frequently stated a willingness to participate in the reconfiguration of the city landscape, notably by founding Ghalib's Grave Fund from Calcutta and by advising the destruction of Delhi's Kashmiri Gate. Mohamed Ali's papers strove to rehabilitate an Indian memory of the Uprising by durably commemorating it in the cityscape – even before proper construction work began. Local and private sites, however, soon became spaces of public debate and bargaining chips that could mobilise a pan-Indian Muslim political community in the making and force the government to recognise its importance publicly.

Besides underlining 'how the Mughal mosques of Delhi became critical spaces to resist British power',[9] this chapter highlights the way Mohamed Ali's papers successfully resorted to emotional and memory practices. The grief (*ġham*) that infringements on Muslim religious

[7] 'Vested Interests and New Delhi', *The Comrade*, 28 March 1914, vol. 7, 13, p. 253.

[8] Francis Robinson has noted that the 'Young Party' group was not a party in a narrow sense, since it had no formal organisation and also displayed differences, but the term was often used at the time to represent one major interest group of north Indian Muslims. F. Robinson, *Separatism*, p. 6.

[9] S. Kavuri-Bauer, *Monumental Matters*, p. 15. Emphasis mine.

sites elicited was not guiltily turned towards Muslims themselves as in late nineteenth-century reformist discourse, but voiced as proof of oppression, with the theme of Karbala and martyrdom emerging at centre stage. The representation of Indian Muslims as a poor and oppressed community departed from previous reformist works, and enabled them, as Sandria Freitag and others have shown, 'to successfully bridge the gap, at least temporarily, between *sharif* Indo-Persian culture and the combative sense of community felt by lower-class Muslims'.[10] Collective *ġham* and patriotic sentiments allowed Indian Muslims to mobilise and to bargain with the colonial state by playing with the legal recognition of feelings. First negotiating, then opposing or subverting British practices, Mohamed Ali's press constantly engaged with monuments as emotional symbols that were to be indelible, and acknowledged.

1 *The Comrade* and the Early Coverage of the Construction of New Delhi

With the construction of colonial Delhi, criticism of British town planning projects became strong, especially in the English weekly and Urdu daily newspapers *The Comrade* and *Hamdard*, both published by Mohamed Ali's press. Mohamed Ali Jauhar (1878–1931)[11] was an Urdu poet and journalist who studied English at Bareilly and then at Aligarh, where he developed 'communal consciousness [which] was far more secular than religious'.[12] In 1898, he received a government scholarship to read an Honours Degree in Modern History at Oxford, but he failed to enter the Indian Civil Service, the Allahabad Bar examination, or the faculty at Aligarh, and turned instead to a career in the Native States civil service. He nonetheless continued to be absorbed in Aligarh affairs,[13] notably supporting (and maybe initiating) a student strike in 1907 against the college's British professors.[14] After some time in the education department in Rampur, he entered the service of

[10] S. Freitag, 'The Roots of Muslim Separatism in South Asia', p. 121.
[11] M. Ali, *My Life a Fragment*, introduction by Mushirul Hasan, p. 15. His grandfather, Sheikh Ali Baksh, served as an official in the court of Nawab Muhammad Yusuf Khan until his death in 1867.
[12] M. R. Rahman, 'We Can Leave Neither', p. 257.
[13] F. Robinson, *Separatism*, p. 180; D. Lelyveld, *Aligarh's First Generation*, p. 331.
[14] D. Lelyveld, *Aligarh's First Generation*, p. 331.

the Gaekwar of Baroda, a job that he found unrewarding and that he eventually left in 1911 to devote his efforts and passion to journalism.

Aided financially by Ali Imam and the Aga Khan, *The Comrade* was launched in Calcutta on 14 January 1911. Mohamed Ali later explained in his autobiography that he took up journalism to 'assist [his] community in taking its proper share in the political life of the country'[15] two years after Indian Muslims had gained special political representation as a distinct community via the Morley–Minto reforms. Mohamed Ali was actively involved in the Muslim League and eagerly participated in the Muslim Educational Conference, two activities that his papers frequently documented. *The Comrade* responded to the call of the Muslim League for a strong 'Muslim press', especially in English, by which the Aga Khan believed 'national regeneration' could be achieved.[16] Mohamed Ali was also a fervent defender of Hindu–Muslim cooperation: *The Comrade* was a secular, nationalist periodical.[17]

From its beginnings, the journal was a huge success. It was unmatched in its polemical tone and its wide initial circulation of 1,200, which easily doubled by May 1912.[18] In May 1911, the *Kayastha Samachar* appraised *The Comrade* as 'one of the best-written weeklies in the country',[19] but it also described it as an organ of the Muslim League and not as the 'bit of neutral ground where war shall cease and passions shall subside and whereon the belligerents shall meet together'[20] that it had promised in its first issue.[21] What was announced as intending to be a 'comrade of all and partisan of none' quickly started to prepare Indian Muslim elites 'to make their proper contribution to territorial patriotism.'[22] As Francis Robinson highlighted, *The Comrade* provided a platform for the educated Muslim middle classes, and

[15] M. Ali, *My Life a Fragment*, p. 74.
[16] The Third Session of the All-India Muslim League held at Delhi, 29–30 January 1910, inaugural address by His Highness the Aga Khan in M. Shan, *The Indian Muslims: A Documentary Record*, vol. 2, p. 242.
[17] M. R. Rahman, 'We Can Leave Neither', p. 258.
[18] D. Ferrell, 'Delhi, 1911–1922', pp. 215 and 224.
[19] 'The English Press in India in 1910–1911: I', *Kayastha Samachar*, May 1911, vol. 23, 141, p. 399.
[20] Ibid., p. 400.
[21] 'We Are Partisans of None, Comrades of All', *The Comrade*, vol. 1, 1, 14 January 1911, p. 1.
[22] M. Ali, *My Life a Fragment*, p. 75.

Mohamed Ali was emblematic of the 'Young Party' Muslims dissatisfied by the politics of 'Old Party' Muslims who depended on government favour.[23] Faridah Zaman highlighted that, in November 1911,[24] Mohamed Ali contrasted his forward-looking vision with previous reformist projects:

> India wants not 're-formers' but revolutionaries who would release the heart and mind of the people from the thraldom of a dead past and turn them confidently ahead. The nature of the appeal has got to be completely changed. They should be roused to activity, not for the sake of what they were but what they can be.[25]

A week after the Durbar and the annulment of the partition of Bengal, Nawab Waqar ul-Mulk had indeed stated that

> It is now manifest like the midday sun, that after seeing what has happened lately, it is futile to ask the Muslims to place their reliance on Government. [...] What we should rely on, after the grace of God, is the strength of our right arm.[26]

In February 1912, *The Comrade* further described agitation amongst Bengali Muslims as 'the only effective method for converting [the Government]'.[27]

From the middle of 1912 Mohamed Ali was increasingly described by the authorities as 'utterly unscrupulous',[28] 'a quite typical specimen, full of incurable vanity',[29] leaving trouble wherever he went. From 1912, Abdul Bari of Farangi Mahall in Lucknow became his *pīr*, and Mohamed Ali started considering the ulama as potential political allies.[30] In the following years, growing as a 'professional politician',[31] he increasingly resorted to Islamic

[23] F. Robinson, *Separatism*, p. 176.
[24] F. Zaman, 'Beyond Nostalgia', p. 646.
[25] 'Illusions', *The Comrade*, 25 November 1911, p. 453.
[26] Waqar ul-Mulk, 'The Fate of Muslims in India' published in the *Aligarh Institute Gazette* of 20 December 1911, quoted in F. Robinson, *Separatism*, p. 203.
[27] 'The Viceroy at Dacca', *The Comrade*, 3 February 1912, p. 105.
[28] Letter from Butler to Hardinge, 3 November 1912 (Hardinge Papers, 1912), quoted by M. Shan, *The Indian Muslims: A Documentary Record*, vol. 2, p. 132.
[29] Edwin Montagu to Chelmsford, 23 June 1920, file 6, Chelmsford Papers, quoted in M. Hasan's introduction of M. Ali, *My Life a Fragment*, p. 43.
[30] D. Lelyveld, *Aligarh's First Generation*, p. 340.
[31] G. Minault, *The Khilafat Movement*, p. 189.

symbols to mobilise and he developed, with his brother Shaukat Ali, a 'blend of religion and politics, not always subtle', which 'was to become their specialty'.[32]

From the launch of *The Comrade* in 1911, the attention of readers (and of the authorities) was frequently directed towards the question of the preservation of Indian heritage, and especially the restoration of the tombs of great men. What preoccupied *The Comrade*, even before the announcement of the transfer of capital, was a still unresolved and disputed past: that of the Uprising. In March 1911, an article published under the title 'The Care of Tombs' lauded the fact that the mausoleums of Nur Jahan and Shivaji were receiving 'due attention' and praised Lord Curzon for his 'great service to the country in the preservation of ancient monuments'.[33] But the article also raised the burning question of the last Mughal's grave in Rangoon.[34] *The Comrade*, in fact, conjured up a demand that had regularly appeared in Indian newspapers since the beginning of the twentieth century and that was linked to the state's treatment of 1857-related issues. In late 1903 and early 1904, several newspapers from the North-Western Provinces and UP published a letter by Maulvi Abdus Salam of the *Anjuman-e Islām* of Lahore to Lord Curzon complaining about the condition of Bahadur Shah's tomb. A correspondent reported that the grave consisted in a 'mud' mound located in a ruined garden, with grass growing over it.[35] Despite the fact that the Lieutenant Governor of Burma had expressed his willingness to let the king's offspring repair the tomb, their indigence did not enable them to do so. The *Ṣaḥīfah* of Bijnor protested that 'it is a pity that while Government itself undertakes to keep the ancient royal buildings in repair, it should relegate the duty of repairing the tomb of Bahadur Shah to his penniless descendants'.[36]

The controversy around the king's tomb, which seemed to affect colonial opinion too,[37] in fact more broadly questioned the latter's role (and that of the Mughal nobility) in the Uprising, and demonstrated

[32] Ibid., p. 202.
[33] 'The Care of Tombs', *The Comrade*, 11 March 1911, vol. 1, 9, p. 165.
[34] Ibid.
[35] The *Naiyar-i Azam* (Moradabad) of 26 November 1903; see *NNRNWP&O*, p. 469.
[36] The *Sahifa* (Bijnor) of 26 January 1904, in *NNRNWP&O*, p. 34.
[37] The *Oudh Akhbar* of 10 November, for instance, refers to a debate between Mr. Hyndman and Mac-Minn about the matter; see *NNRNWP&O* for 1903, p. 774.

the desire of north Indian editors to rehabilitate his memory around the time of the Uprising's fifty-year anniversary. Although the government seems to have permitted the Muslim community to erect a memorial on the spot in 1907,[38] the *Urdū-e Muʿallah* (Aligarh) brought up the issue again in January 1910.[39] *The Comrade* article in March 1911 thus resumed a recurring discussion in Indian newspapers. Demands for a tomb befitting the king also highlighted the need to come to terms with 1857. The article indeed asked, '[H]ave we not left those terrible times far behind, and need they interfere with the rights of the dead and the duties of the living?'[40] The paper demonstrated a willingness to bury the painful past in order to move forward.

Not long after this first piece, a series of articles appeared on a weekly basis about the preservation and repair of Ghalib's tomb that was located close to Nizamuddin Auliya's *dargāh*. The first article was published in June 1911 under the title 'Ghalib's Grave' and mentioned Dr Morton's suggestion to erect a suitable monument over the grave of the famous nineteenth-century poet.[41] *The Comrade* was quick to react to the suggestion. From the office in Calcutta, it asked its readers to visit the tomb in Delhi, report on its state, and put forward an estimate of the cost of urgent repairs to be carried out before the construction of an adequate memorial. Two weeks later, *The Comrade* reported again on the matter. One reader, perhaps Tasadduq Husain,[42] had gone to the tomb and suggested an estimate for the repairs 'on a very modest scale', although *The Comrade* proposed instead the construction of stone fencing and the hiring of a gardener 'to plant a small flower-garden and tend the grave'.[43]

The article announced the launch of a 'Ghalib's Grave Fund' to raise 'a worthy monument over the last remains of Mirza Naushah'.[44] With the first sums coming from the staff and amounting at Rs. 50, *The Comrade* also declared that Altaf Husain Hali would be asked 'to

38 The *Advocate* (Lucknow) of 29 August 1907, in *NNRNWP&O*, p. 1042.
39 *Urdu-i Mualla* (Aligarh), January 1910, in *NNRNWP&O*, p. 162.
40 'The Care of Tombs', *The Comrade*, 11 March 1911, p. 165.
41 'Ghalib's Grave', *The Comrade*, 17 June 1911, vol. 1, 23, p. 444.
42 A letter from Tasadduq Husain mentions his going to the grave and making an estimate. It also mentions Hali for the fundraising campaign (see Maulana Mohamed Ali Papers, JMI, 464–5). The letter, however, is dated 25 July 1911, i.e. two weeks after the publication of the article.
43 'Ghalib's Grave', *The Comrade*, 8 July 1911, vol. 2, 2, p. 27.
44 Ibid.

nominate a small committee representing every province of India' to collect local subscriptions.[45] A week later, however, the paper complained about the lack of response to its appeal. The fund was now only Rs. 30 richer.[46] The next appeal hoped to raise local subscriptions,[47] but the next after that lamented again that the response was so feeble.[48] In the middle of August, the fund was starting to receive some attention, notably thanks to the generous contributions of Tej Bahadur Sapru, the Old Boys and Bombay Barrister M. K. Azad, and Newab Gholam Ahmad Khan of Madras.[49] The sums received continued to increase over the following weeks to reach Rs. 677 in December 1911.[50] The matter, however, ended abruptly: while acknowledging the (relative) success of *The Comrade*'s fundraising campaign, the last article on Ghalib's Grave Fund mentioned that some of Ghalib's relatives had decided to repair the tomb at their own expense and that they 'would not like the idea of their great ancestor's grave being repaired by public subscription'.[51] It is difficult to know what happened with the money raised. In any case, Ghalib's Grave Fund demonstrated that *The Comrade* had support from English-educated middle-classes from all over India (contributions came from Bengal, UP, Punjab, Madras, Bombay, etc.).

After the Coronation Durbar of 1911, Mohamed Ali decided to leave Calcutta for Delhi, and in October 1912 he settled in Kucha Chelan, a famous neighbourhood of Shahjahanabad. Just before the move, one of his friends, writing under the pen name Birbal, warned him of the danger of Delhi's atmosphere for his future growth:

> There is such a thing as a spirit of the ruins, which peacefully reigns over fallen greatness, and if disturbed, takes its revenge on meddlesome humanity by possessing their souls. [...] I only hope that you will be able to resist the subtle and all-pervading charm of the dead and buried past, and preserve your impishness in the midst of the Tombs of Delhi.[52]

[45] Ibid. [46] 'Ghalib's Grave', *The Comrade*, 15 July 1911, vol. 2, 3, p. 46.
[47] 'Ghalib's Grave', *The Comrade*, 22 July 1911, vol. 2, 4, p. 67.
[48] 'Ghalib's Grave', *The Comrade*, 29 July 1911, vol. 2, 5, p. 88.
[49] I am using here the names as transliterated in *The Comrade*, 12 August 1911, vol. 2, 7, p. 126.
[50] 'Ghalib's Grave', *The Comrade*, 2 December 1911, vol. 2, 23, p. 474.
[51] Ibid.
[52] '*The Comrade*: A Review' by Birbal, Calcutta, 17 September 1912, *The Comrade*, 19 October 1912, vol. 4, 13, p. 301.

Delhi was often described as 'really one vast graveyard',[53] an argument that would still resonate in post-independence India, as Anand Taneja showed.[54] This was the case especially after May 1912, when it was decided that the imperial capital would be constructed at the south of Shahjahanabad where the remains of previous cities could be found.[55] While British architect Edwin Lutyens found major monuments of the ancient capitals useful when drawing the layout of the city,[56] the newly acquired lands had the great disadvantage of being honeycombed with mosques, temples, and tombs.

Santhi Kavuri-Bauer rightly argued that restoration projects alienated Indians from their own cultural heritage by disrupting traditional activities taking place in and around monuments, distributing repair funds arbitrarily, establishing opposing categories such as 'functional' versus 'non-functional' buildings, and yielding Indian aesthetics to Victorian tastes.[57] Yet, the major issues for Urdu-speaking elites were not only the colonial reconfiguration of monuments but their very preservation.[58] Minor monuments which did not fit into Lutyens' hexagonal plan were said to be 'awkwardly situated',[59] and were only dubbed

[53] Demi-official letter from Major H. C. Beadon to the Hon'ble Mr. H. Wheeler, Delhi, 31 August 1912, in Home, Delhi, September 1912, Deposit 9: 'Question of the Treatment of Mosques, Temples and Tombs in Connection with Land Acquisition Proceedings at Delhi', p. 1.

[54] A. V. Taneja, *Jinnealogy*, p. 35, referring to discussions between Prime Minister Nehru and Abul Kalam Azad about construction work in Delhi.

[55] The place was judged to be better than the northern site (where the foundation stones had been laid) in all respects, and it had 'views across old Delhi to that wilderness of ruined tombs that form the remains of the 7 older Delhis.' R. G. Irving, *Indian Summer*, p. 46.

[56] R. G. Irving, *Indian Summer*, p. 80. The restoration of historic sites was central to their incorporation into the design of the city, which, after all, was conceived to absorb and safeguard India's cultural heritage (letter from L. Dane, 18 January 1912, Home, Delhi, A Proceedings, April 1912, p. 43).

[57] See S. Kavuri-Bauer, *Monumental Matters*.

[58] Demolition works had been eagerly followed – even anticipated – since 1858, and rumours around the destruction of the Khooni Darwaza in Delhi appeared in 1865. Urdu editors regularly denounced disrespect towards tombs, improper uses of mosques, and negligence towards gardens and mausoleums. The *NNRNWP&O* show examples of opposition to the dilapidated state of *nuzul* gardens in Lucknow (3 November 1868, p. 428); to the disrespect for tombs in Lucknow (25 November 1872, p. 76); to the improper use of mosques in Lucknow (28 September 1872, p. 619); etc.

[59] Letter from L. Dane, 18 January 1912, Home, Delhi, A Proceedings, April 1912, p. 43.

a nuisance, 'nameless uncared-for erections' which 'interfere everywhere', spoiling Lutyens' designs.[60] It soon appeared that building the new colonial city would naturally entail choices as to what would be preserved (and more problematically what would *not*) of Delhi's edifices.[61] In August 1912, Major Beadon, Deputy Commissioner of Delhi, tried to tackle the problem by composing three lists of the buildings that were located within the building area, specifying what should be done with them. List Z included the buildings and tombs that did not need to be preserved; list Y contained those which did not need to be destroyed forthwith; and, finally, list X contained those which ought to be preserved – all the structures that were not listed 'would fall naturally into list Z'.[62] The document revealed that, for British officers, the deportation of local populations and the gradual discontinuance of local practices were seen as participating in the process through which land and buildings could be acquired and eventually destroyed.[63]

One of the first articles published from Delhi precisely demonstrated Mohamed Ali's willingness to participate in the careful selection process of what was to be remembered of Delhi's past.[64] As in its previous articles on Bahadur Shah's and Ghalib's tombs, the past that *The Comrade* considered was that of the Uprising. Coming to Delhi certainly brought back painful memories of the history of 1857 that had been dominated by British officers and historians. In the decades after the Uprising, besides the erection of memorials and commemorative plaques for British civilians and soldiers,[65] 'Mutiny tours' guided foreign tourists through Delhi, Lucknow, and Kanpur thanks to travelogues and history books that narrated gruesome massacres.[66] There was no place for Indian narratives of the events.

[60] Ibid. Lutyens apparently mentioned the matter to his wife Emily in late 1913. See E. A. Christensen, 'Government Architecture', p. 211.

[61] Home, Public, B, December 1913, 170: 'Questions and Answers in the Imperial Legislative Council Regarding the Acquisition of Muslim Mosques etc. and Regarding the Preservation of Religious Edifices', p. 2.

[62] Ibid.

[63] Demi-official letter from Major H. C. Beadon, Home, Delhi, September 1912, Deposit 9, p. 1.

[64] 'Bury the Past', *The Comrade*, 19 October 1912, vol. 4, 13, pp. 295–6.

[65] See R. Nanda and N. Gupta, *Delhi: The Built Heritage*, pp. 5, 37, 54, 78; *First Report of the Curator of Ancient Monuments in India for the year 1881–82, Simla, 1882*, pp. cix–cx; A. D. King, *Colonial Urban Development*, p. 215.

[66] See S. Kavuri-Bauer, *Monumental Matters*; M. Goswami, '"Englishness" on the Imperial Circuit', pp. 54–84.

The Comrade's first suggestion for New Delhi town planners was to rehabilitate the honour and presence of Indian subjects in the urbanscape: 'while the English have a distinguished roll of heroes who owe their fame to the courage displayed during the Mutiny, the names of their Indian comrades are forgotten'.[67] With the necessity of commemorating Indian bravery also came the desire to erase memorials of Indian disloyalty, and especially the Kashmiri Gate:

> If an officer of Government residing in the temporary quarters now being erected in the Civil Lines approaches the town where the Indian population resides, the first sight that greets him is the shot-riddled Kashmir Gate, which brings back memories that should fade and disappear rather than be revived. [...] The first official act that [His Excellency the Viceroy] should perform after taking over the charge of India's historic Capital should be the demolition of the Kashmir Gate and its reconstruction as monument of the desire of Great Britain to bury the carrion of the dead and dread past and of the resolve of the Government to trust that it may itself be trusted.[68]

2 'City of Tombs': Mobilisations in *The Comrade* and *Hamdard*

With the move to Delhi, Mohamed Ali planned to launch *The Comrade*'s sister paper in Urdu, *Hamdard*, which he had announced on 27 April 1912. If *The Comrade* was conceived as 'the medium between [the people] and their rulers', *Hamdard* was seen as a means 'to educate the people'.[69] Thanks to encouragement from Nawab Waqar ul-Mulk (1841–1917), *Hamdard*'s debut was much anticipated, but technical problems soon arose.[70] Daily issues started 23 February 1913, but the official (and second) launch took place only on 1 June 1913. Despite Mohamed Ali's discontent with the unusual and expensive *naskh* Beirut typeset, which got damaged in just one year of use and was eventually replaced by lithography,[71] advertisements in

[67] 'Bury the Past', *The Comrade*, 19 October 1912, vol. 4, 13, p. 295.
[68] Ibid.
[69] M. Ali, *My Life a Fragment*, p. 97.
[70] 'Bismillah', *Hamdard*, 1 June 1913, reproduced in S. Umar, *Intik͟h͟āb-e Hamdard*, Lucknow, 1988, p. 23.
[71] On the typeface used by *Hamdard*, see M. Ali, *My Life a Fragment*, pp. 94–6 and also S. Ahmad, *Urdū Ṣaḥāfat aur Taḥrīk-e Āzādī*, p. 110.

Abul Kalam Azad's *Al-Hilāl* praised the success of the paper amongst the public who read it 'with interest (*shauq*) and pleasure (*żauq*)'.[72] By 1914, *Hamdard* had gotten so popular that its circulation was four to five times that of its vernacular rivals.[73]

The Balkan wars (October 1912–August 1913) provided the backdrop for the launch of *Hamdard* and for the impressive increase in the circulation of *The Comrade* (from 2,500 in May 1912 to 8,500 in 1913).[74] As Francis Robinson argued, it was the Balkan wars that 'saved the *Comrade* from liquidation and Mohamed Ali from ignominious return to the obscurity of Baroda.'[75] The office of *The Comrade* press in Old Delhi soon 'became a political salon'.[76] Of course, the newspapers were not the only means used to rally public opinion and unite the various sections of the Muslim public. From 1912, Mohamed Ali particularly valued the importance of public displays and societies that were promoted in the papers, illustrating the close relationship between print and new forms of associational activity.[77] Mohamed Ali's press eagerly followed the fundraising campaign for the Turkish Relief Fund, and launched both the Red Crescent Medical Mission with Dr Ansari in 1912 and the *Anjuman-e Khuddām-e Kaʿbah* with Maulana Abdul Bari in 1913. While Mohamed Ali could count on the support of 'Young Party' Muslims starting in 1911, via these new activities he also rallied around him established leaders of Delhi; teachers and students of various Delhi madrasahs; as well as (Punjabi) hide and shoe merchants, butchers and artisans.[78]

From spring 1913, construction work was followed by *The Comrade* and *Hamdard*, which strongly condemned the legal processes used by the state to acquire land in Delhi. As soon as the New Delhi Scheme was announced, the Punjab government had decided to buy 'with the least possible delay all land and houses [...] as far

[72] '*Hamdard-Dehlī*', *Al-Hilāl*, 16 July 1913.
[73] R. Rahman, *Mohamed Ali: A Sketch of His Life, His Writings and Speeches*, p. 4, quoted in R. Rahman, 'We Can Leave Neither', p. 259.
[74] M. Ali, *My Life a Fragment*, p. 18.
[75] F. Robinson, *Separatism*, p. 186. [76] M. Ali, *My Life a Fragment*, p. 18.
[77] V. Horne, 'The Politicisation of Muslim Delhi in the 1910s', p. 238.
[78] See A. Basu, 'Mohamed Ali in Delhi: The Comrade Phase'; D. Ferrell, 'Delhi, 1911–1922', pp. 183–235 and 246–75.

as the Kutub Minar and Tughlukabad',[79] a process that resulted in a dramatic decrease in the area's property values.[80] Although the government already owned 31,381 acres of land – mostly the result of confiscations after the Uprising – by the end of the Coronation Durbar, 113,821 acres had been notified for acquisition under the Land Acquisition Act.[81] Entire families were expelled from their properties while immigrants, particularly from the Punjab, settled in the city.

The first article on the topic, which appeared on 24 May 1913, noted the great agitation that the New Delhi project had created in the local population because of the 'remarkable diminution of the value of house property' and 'the fear that their houses would be acquired without adequate compensation for the improvement of the town'.[82] *The Comrade* further suggested it should act as representative in the Municipal Corporation meetings regarding urban planning.[83] The article ended by lamenting 'It is not only the houses of the living that are in danger, but also the resting places of the dead', accusing the Government of 'destroying every trace' of Delhi's past.[84]

It was followed up a month later in *The Comrade* and *Hamdard* by what became a series of feature articles entitled 'City of Tombs' and 'Delhi's Ancient Graves and Mosques'.[85] *Hamdard* began by introducing Delhi as a crucial location of Muslim rule, alluding to the various dynasties and destructions that the city had witnessed, and to the 'rivers of Muslim blood' that had flowed on several occasions. The most recent Delhi was of course Shahjahanabad 'on the places where dust used to whirl started blooming fields of greenery and flowers'.[86] The article then focused on a memorandum by Major Beadon to rearrange Delhi's Muslim burial grounds, which had been reproduced three days earlier by

[79] Home, Delhi, A Proceedings, April 1912, 103–39: 'Acquisition of Land at Delhi and the Planning and Building of the New City of Delhi', pp. 1 and 12.
[80] 'The City of Tombs', *The Comrade,* 24 May 1913, vol. 5, 20, p. 418.
[81] A. Earle 15-1-12, quoting Letter 253-c, 16 December 1911, in Home, Delhi, A Proceedings, April 1912, 103–39, p. 12.
[82] 'The City of Tombs', *The Comrade,* 24 May 1913, vol. 5, 20, p. 418.
[83] Ibid. [84] Ibid.
[85] 'Ancient Tombs and Mosques' (*Qadīmī maqābir-o masājid*), *Hamdard*, 29 June 1913, pp. 2–3.
[86] Ibid., p. 2

the secretary of the *Anjuman-e Mu'ayid ul-Islām*.[87] Behind the necessity to 'respect the dead', sanitation and health issues, as well as future city improvement measures, the main stake was of course the acquisition of land. Major Beadon proposed reorganising the Muslims' 'unmethodical'[88] burial practices by simply discontinuing the use of burial grounds in areas within the New Delhi area (such as Qadim Sharif in Paharganj, an area mainly populated by indigent Muslim labourers) and to provide three big enclosed cemeteries to be used by the whole city's Muslim population on the outskirts of the town instead.[89] The cost of the adjustments, which was estimated at around Rs. 20,000, was to be raised by the Muslims themselves, a task that Beadon expected to be easy.[90]

The Comrade called the question of Muslims raising money for their own graveyards unheard-of and sordid, and despised the 'considerable ignorance of Moslem views about burial grounds and graves and Moslem funeral arrangements' that the memorandum displayed.[91] Tombs and mosques were particularly at the forefront, since infringements on their structures were seen as infringements on the most basic respect. *Hamdard* and *The Comrade* did not oppose the construction of New Delhi, but only asked that 'those who sleep should not be awaken[ed]' in the process.[92] The article in *Hamdard* further invoked the 'deep relevance' of tombs and mosques 'for the history of Muslims'

[87] This was probably Abdul Ahad, then Municipal Commissioner of Delhi (1912–1915) and honorary secretary of the Anjuman that had been founded in 1888 by Hakim Ajmal Khan and Sayyid Ahmad, Imam of the Jama Masjid to support poor children, preserve old mosques, and bury isolated citizens. See D. Ferrell, 'Delhi, 1911–1922', pp. 130 and 147.

[88] Beadon noted that 'the bodies are buried in no methodical order' and 'in any scrap of waste land which happens to be near a mosque, without any regard to order or anything else' (File 77/1915 B, Education, CC: *Mohammadan Graveyards in Delhi*, pp. 1–2).

[89] One cemetery of thirty acres was situated near Nizamuddin, for the population of Paharganj and old Delhi; another cemetery of the same amount of land was near Dhoralia Nullah, for the people of Sadar Bazar and the new city; finally, the third cemetery of twenty acres was planned near the Azam road and the Najafgarh Branch canal for the people of Sabzimandi and the Civil Lines. See File 77/1915 B, Education, CC and 'The City of Tombs', *The Comrade*, 24 May 1913, vol. 5, 20, p. 419.

[90] Ibid.

[91] Ibid. *The Comrade* explains that the need for Muslims to be able to bury their dead day or night, without transporting the corpses by carts or horses. Those practices thus necessitated relative proximity between Muslim dwellings and burial grounds.

[92] '*Qadīmī maqābir-o masājid*', *Hamdard*, 29 June 1913, p. 3.

as well as their significance 'in the Muslim religious mind'.[93] As Nile Green and others have indeed emphasised, Sufi shrines and sacred topography served to 'maintain an Islamic and Islamicate sense of history and identity', interweaving past and present, and royal and saintly pasts of 'Muslim grandeur and self-rule'.[94] Anand Vivek Taneja also argued in his study of Delhi's Firoz Shah Kotla that graves were paramount places of Muslim presence where communities were shaped and genealogies passed on.[95] Transformations of the city's landscape had profound repercussions on religious landscapes of memory.

Serious discussions with Mr. Hailey, Chief Commissioner of Delhi, about the selection of the buildings and tombs to be demolished were initiated and the latter consequently aimed at clarifying the process of land acquisition. He brought to the readers' attention that the committee would respect 'all religious buildings to which importance attaches' and that 'where the sites of religious buildings and graveyards have been acquired it must not be understood that they have necessarily been acquired for demolition'.[96] He further announced that officers had been appointed to look into the matter and that any person interested in the fate of any building should directly address the Deputy Commissioner.[97] As Hailey later wrote, he had been forced to take these further measures:

> Since April last [1913] interested persons have continued to throw a fierce light of publicity on any demolition proceedings connected with the new sites. Remains are being invested with a sometimes real and sometimes spurious association of religion or importance which their owners did not put forward a few months ago.[98]

The local anti-demolition resistance that *The Comrade* and *Hamdard* supported was finally being taken into account. But although both

93 Ibid., p. 2. 94 N. Green, *Making Space: Sufis and Settlers*, pp. 265–6.
95 A. V. Taneja, *Jinnealogy*, p. 26.
96 'The City of Tombs', *The Comrade*, 21 June 1913, vol. 5, 24, pp. 494–5.
97 'The City of Tombs', *The Comrade*, 21 June 1913, p. 495.
98 Home, Public, Deposit 36, August 1913: letter from Hailey to Wheeler, 12 August 1913, p. 2. Hailey explained that Beadon's list was being examined cautiously and that the engineering staff had been ordered to obtain a written authorisation before demolishing any religious or historic monument. The land acquisition officer was also requested to make a list of all such buildings and enquire as to their history and the reverence in which they were held. After the lists were composed, Mr Hailey would himself check personally with the local notables and a surveyor about which buildings would be preserved.

newspapers quickly pointed at the ambiguous terms 'importance' and 'necessity' used in Hailey's note,[99] they more generally argued that

> It is impossible to draw any distinction between religious buildings. An old neglected mosque, whose walls have fallen and whose history we do not know is, according to our religious conceptions, equal to Delhi's grand Jama Masjid. [...] Each and every particle which has been consecrated *waqf* in the name of God, whether prayer is thereon read or whether ablutions are performed, is worth of reverence.'[100]

On 21 June 1913, as the whole conversation on graveyards unfolded, *The Comrade* and *Hamdard* reported a 'distressing sacrilege':[101] the demolition of a historic mosque near Kokī Bridge, where the famous Maulana Shah Abdul Haq Muhaddis (1551–1642) taught for fifty years in the time of Akbar, Jahangir, and Shah Jahan. The newspapers lamented that the descendants of the saint had been in government service for decades and kept the mosque and its adjoining cemetery in good repair. The mosque, which was situated near the canal from Delhi to Okhla and was still used for prayers by passers-by, was demolished by the Imperial Public Works Department while demarcating road boundaries.[102] Villagers had removed the stones so quickly that local people had to 'assist [the Chief Commissioner] in locating the spot where the famous mosque had stood for centuries amidst the ruins of earlier Delhi'.[103] Although the remains of the famous Shaikh had long been transferred to Hauz Shamsi, the place was still said to retain an aura of sacredness.[104] On 24 June, Mubin ul-Haq, a descendant of Abdul Haq Muhaddis, having been alerted by the press, wrote to the Chief Commissioner to enquire about the rumours that had reached him in Shimla about the destruction of his ancestor's mosque:

99 '*Qadīmī maqābir-o masājid – ḥissah dawam*', *Hamdard*, 1 July 1913, p. 3.
100 Ibid. See also 'More Apprehension', *The Comrade*, 21 June 1913, vol. 5, 24, p. 495; '*Qadīmī maqābir-o masājid – ḥissah dawam*', *Hamdard*, 1 July 1913, p. 3.
101 'Distressing Sacrilege', *The Comrade*, 21 June 1913, vol. 5, 24, p. 495; see also '*Qadīmī maqābir-o masājid*', *Hamdard*, 29 June 1913, p. 2.
102 See CC, Revenue and Agriculture, 39/1915 B: 'Demolition and Restoration of Maulana Abdul Haq's Mosque near Okhla', p. 3.
103 'Distressing Sacrilege', *The Comrade*, 21 June 1913, vol. 5, 24, p. 495.
104 CC, Revenue and Agriculture, 39/1915 B, p. 11, extract from p. 99 of 'Miratul Haqayaq', printed at Rampur State in 1902.

I heard that our ancestral mosque had actually been pulled down. My enquiries seem to establish the correctness of the news, and it has pained me to hear of the fate of the place. [...] We have always held the place in reverence owing to the family associations and to the fact that our ancestor, whose name is known and respected throughout India, lived, studied and worked there, and it is there that my grandfather and other relations and my own child lie buried.[105]

Mr. Hailey enquired about the reasons behind the demolition of the mosque, which had occurred against the normal procedure and without the necessary written permission that such an operation now required.[106] The demolition was a sorry mistake: the mosque was listed 'Y' ('structures not to be demolished forthwith'). Mr. W. R. Robson, in charge of the works, explained to the executive engineer, 4th Division that, in order 'to clear all roads and to dismantle all buildings that came in the way',[107] he gave the order on 4 June to demolish the compound wall of the mosque, but certainly not the mosque itself.

The authorities decided to sweep the matter under the rug. As *The Comrade* gladly reported, Mr. Hailey 'expressed every readiness to make full amends for the sacrilege which, we need hardly say, was in no way authorised by him'.[108] He also promised to punish the people guilty of the mistake and to treat the new building as an 'Ancient Monument'.[109] Abdul Haq Muhaddis' descendants were offered the rebuilding of the mosque (the cost was estimated at Rs. 800–1,000) and the fencing of the graveyard.[110] On 14 July, the family of the saint wrote a letter of gratitude to the government, announcing their readiness to cooperate with the Public Works Department staff to supervise the rebuilding and asking for permission to erect a tablet in the mosque acknowledging the government's kindness.[111] Mohamed Ali's papers approved: the *waqf* was left intact and the mosque would now

105 CC, Revenue and Agriculture, 39/1915 B, pp. 27–9: 24/06/1913: to CC from Simla descendant of Abdul Haq (Mubin ul-Haq)

106 CC, Revenue and Agriculture, 39/1915 B, p. 25: letter of CC to chief engineer, 21 June 1913.

107 CC, Revenue and Agriculture, 39/1915 B, p. 42: from W. R. Robson to the executive engineer, 4th Division.

108 'Distressing Sacrilege', *The Comrade*, 21 June 1913, vol. 5, 24, p. 495

109 According to 'Distressing Sacrilege', *The Comrade*, 21 June 1913, vol. 5, 24, p. 495. I have not been able to corroborate the information with colonial records.

110 CC, Revenue and Agriculture, 39/1915 B, p. 42: letter from G. F. Demontmorency to M. I. Hak, 2 July 1913.

111 CC, Revenue and Agriculture, 39/1915 B, p. 47.

be new. But Mohamed Ali's report ended with the sad news of yet another sacrilege in Delhi.[112]

The emphasis in *The Comrade* and *Hamdard* on the Kokī Bridge mosque being listed as an 'Ancient Monument' reveals one of the motives of the operation. The importance was not so much on the archaeological preservation of what was a historic mosque as on the recognition by the government of the importance of preserving Muslim presence in the city landscape. While the coverage of the case enabled Mohamed Ali to gain popular support, especially among the *ashrāf*,[113] it is noteworthy that, in other cases, local populations and elites did not always agree to the addition of Muslim monuments to the list of 'Protected' monuments.[114] In June 1918, for instance, the granting of the 'Ancient Monument' category to the tomb of Bahlol Lodhi implied the evacuation of the place and was sternly objected to by the locals, who denied that the property was the tomb of the dynasty founder; they complained that the identification provided by Syed Ahmed Khan's *Āṡār uṣ-Ṣanādīd* was not reliable.[115] In 1929, a certain Mohammad Abdul Ghafar also wrote a petition to the Chief Commissioner of Delhi to ask permission to lay out afresh the Shalamar Garden, which had been his ancestor's property, and bring it to its original condition by repairing the tomb that was situated within, thus asking the Archaeological Department to remove a board that had been fixed upon the tomb's dome. The authorities replied that the tomb had been declared a Protected Monument since 1914 and hence could not be renovated by the petitioner.[116] As Hilal Ahmed pointed out, the categorisation of Ancient and Protected Monuments prevented the owners from enjoying their rights fully, and, notably, from altering their properties.[117]

[112] 'Distressing Sacrilege', *The Comrade*, 21 June 1913, vol. 5, 24, p. 495 and 'Ancient Tombs and Mosques' (*Qadīmī maqābir-o masājid*), *Hamdard*, 29 June 1913, p. 2 mention the demolition of another stone mosque in the area of Paharganj.

[113] D. Ferrell, 'Delhi, 1911–1922', p. 235.

[114] *The Comrade* and *Hamdard* always cheered when a monument made it onto the list of Ancient or Protected Monuments and supported government scientific research on the Muslim monuments of Delhi. See notably *Hamdard*, 5 July 1913, p. 5.

[115] CC, Education, 24/1918 B 'Protection of Monuments in Delhi Province', pp. 53–4, objecting to notification 4414 dated 24 June 1918.

[116] See CC/Education, 1(6)/1930 (B): petition from Muhammad Abdul Ghafar regarding exemption of his property at Qutab from the Ancient Monuments Act of 1904.

[117] H. Ahmed, *Muslim Political Discourse*, p. 84.

Beyond the problem of the preservation of built structures, one of the important stakes for Mohamed Ali's press in the 1910s was space. Since the Land Acquisition Act of 1894, the government had been able to acquire any land (including places of worship) in the name of public good and decide which ancient monuments deserved to be protected.[118] As Hilal Ahmed and Santhi Kavuri-Bauer have shown, the state's distinction between functional and non-functional (described as dead, 'without owner') monuments further enabled the government to overlook their complex religious status.[119] For Muslims, however, a space that had been consecrated as *waqf* – functional or not – was unalterable; it could neither be sold nor acquired.[120] In any case, a *waqf* endowed for the construction of a mosque could not be revoked, since the land was God's.

1913 was a particularly sensitive time, and both *The Comrade* and *Hamdard* showed anxiety for the respect of 'God's Acre'.[121] On 7 March 1913, the Mussalman Wakf Validating Act elaborated by Mohammad Ali Jinnah was passed. The act rallied the opinion of Muslims and of the ulamas of the three great theological schools for the restoration of the institution of private endowments.[122] In 1879, disputes over Muslim endowments led the government to distinguish between endowments that were 'religious' and 'charitable' and those which served the interests of particular families.[123] In Allahabad in the years 1907–1912, Karamat Husain was critical of family endowments

[118] See Ibid. [119] Ibid., p. 83.

[120] Z. Abbasi, 'The Classical Islamic Law of Waqf', p. 124. Hanbali Muslims allow the sale of a *waqf* property that is either damaged or destroyed, but most South Asian Muslims belong to the Hanafi school, which does not permit such actions.

[121] To quote the expression used in 'More Apprehension', *The Comrade*, 21 June 1913, p. 495.

[122] G. C. Kozlowski, *Muslim Endowments and Society in British India*, p. 181; L. Carroll, 'Life Interests and Inter-generational Transfer of Property', p. 263.

[123] D. S. Power, 'Orientalism, Colonialism and Legal History', p. 557; G. C. Kozlowski, *Muslim Endowments*, pp. 95 and 142. As scholarship has shown, the adoption of a rigid and 'orthodox' view of Islamic law by Anglo-Indian courts in fact encouraged Muslim elites to create *awqāf*. In an 1877 article in *Tahẕīb ul-Akẖlāq* entitled 'A Plan for Saving Muslim Families from Destruction and Extinction', Syed Ahmed Khan viewed the institution of family *waqf* as a way to preserve landed estates in British India. See G. C. Kozlowski, *Muslim Endowments*, p. 40 and L. Carroll, 'Life Interests and Inter-generational Transfer of Property', p. 257.

as attempts to preserve family wealth, to the extent that his British colleagues sometimes overturned his decisions, judging them too radical.[124] From 1908, on the impulse of Shibli Numani,[125] however, reflections on the institution were organised at the Nadwatul Ulama, which already 'showed how easily the traditional methods used by religious scholars mingled with the political protocol of the period.'[126] With the Act of 1913, the institution of family endowments was restored, although land reforms, taxation, and limitations in the legislation limited its appeal.[127] While after the Indian Councils Act of 1909 various reforms generated the need for concerted Muslim opinion, the newly acquired agency of local governments also needed to be tested.[128]

3 The Kanpur Mosque and the Political Manifestation of Muslim Grief

At the same time as *The Comrade* and *Hamdard* reported on the desecration of mosques across British India,[129] the situation in Kanpur started getting the full attention of Mohamed Ali's press over the course of July 1913. The press coverage of the 'Cawnpore Sacrilege' on 5 July coincided with the return of Dr Ansari's Medical mission the day before in Bombay. The lesson of the Medical Mission that 'the sharing of the common sorrow and the sense of the common task will prove, in the fulness [sic] of time, assets of vital importance to the future of Islam' compensated for the 'deep sense of pain'[130] triggered by the demolition.[131] As Faridah Zaman noted, the description of Dr Ansari's welcome at the station and procession to the Jama Masjid and then to the Fatehpuri mosque emphasised the massive participation of all of Delhi's Muslims.[132] 'The enthusiasm of the immense crowds' was 'indescribable';[133] the timing was ideal.

124 G. C. Kozlowski, *Muslim Endowments*, p. 144.
125 Shibli Numani, '*Waqf-e Aulād*', in *Maqālāt-e Shiblī*, vol. 1, pp. 81–102.
126 G. C. Kozlowski, *Muslim Endowments*, p. 170.
127 L. Carroll, 'Life Interests and Inter-generational Transfer of Property', p. 264.
128 M. Pernau, *Emotions and Modernity*, 224.
129 See, for instance, '*Āgrah meṇ inhidām-e masjid*', *Hamdard,* 22 July 1913, p. 5.
130 'The Cawnpore Sacrilege', *The Comrade*, 5 July 1913, vol. 6, 1, p. 6.
131 'The Return of the Mission', *The Comrade*, 5 July 1913, vol. 6, 1, p. 8.
132 F. Zaman, 'Beyond Nostalgia', p. 637; 'Delhi's Welcome', *Comrade*, 12 July 1913, vol. 6, 2, p. 27.
133 'Delhi's Welcome', *Comrade*, 12 July 1913, vol. 6, 2, p. 27.

shows the temple and Mosque at close quarters. The small
demolished portion of the mosque is plainly visible in the
right hand corner of the photo.

Figure 3.1 The Teli temple and the Macchli Bazar mosque, IOR/L/PJ/6/1256, File 2826, photograph 2, © The British Library Board

The Kanpur case started in 1909 with notification that land would be acquired to build a new road between Mouleganj and the Dufferin Hospital, in the congested area of Macchli Bazar.[134] Land plans were inspected and implied the destruction of the Teli temple, a 'handsome' Hindu structure. Opposition was voiced and, in November 1912, the authorities decided that the new road would be splayed, and the temple fenced and 'left as an island in the middle of the roadway'.[135] This rearrangement implied the removal of a part of the outer eastern courtyard of the Macchli Bazar mosque (Figure 3.1). As government records note, some Muslim gentlemen started asking whether

[134] Home, Political, A, October 1913, Proceedings 100–18: 'Riot at Cawnpore in Connection with the Demolition of a Mosque in Machli Bazar: State of Muhammadan Feeling in India', Appendix A, press communiqué by R. Burn, 25 July 1913, p. 57.
[135] Ibid.

the mosque would be affected and were assured that the only portion of the mosque that would be removed was the vestibule (*dālān*). In February 1913, the Improvement Trust Committee decided to compensate the demolition by giving a plot for the construction of a new washing place along the northern wall of the building.[136] Towards the end of March 1913, articles began to appear in Mohamed Ali's papers protesting against any interference with the mosque's structure, but the authorities claimed that the destruction of the *dālān* had been approved by the mosque's *mutawallīs* (administrators) since 1911.[137]

The Comrade and *Hamdard*, as well as other Urdu newspapers such as Abul Kalam Azad's *Al-Hilāl*, eagerly followed local news and the process of negotiation that took place between the government and a coalition of ulama, zamindars, and Muslim Leaguers who mobilised against the destruction of the *dālān*. *The Comrade* argued that the acquisition procedure was vague and that the members of the board, 'not conversant with English',[138] had been unable to study the map properly. In April 1913, a petition was sent to the UP government, containing fatwas from local ulamas against the alienation of any part of the mosque and asking that the proceedings be stopped. Although the Raja of Mahmudabad and Mohamed Ali both entered in correspondence with Sir James Meston, Lieutenant Governor of the UP, to persuade him to consult with the ulamas, he remained unyielding. He maintained that the washing place was not sacred, since when the chairman of the Municipal Committee visited the place a few months earlier 'the Muhammadans who were with him wore boots inside'.[139] At the end of June, the Raja of Mahmudabad wrote again that he was sending a memorial from the Muslims of Kanpur suggesting the appointment of an investigative committee to look into the matter.[140] The letter was slow to reach Shimla and on the morning of 1 July, the *dālān* was demolished.[141]

[136] Ibid.

[137] Home, Political, A, October 1913, Proceedings 105, p. 65: telegram dated 7 August 1913 from the Chief Secretary to the government of the UP to the Secretary to the government of India, Home Department.

[138] Ibid.

[139] Home, Political, A, October 1913, Proceedings 100–18: telegram from Lieutenant Governor of the UP to Viceroy, Naini Tal, 24 July 1913, p. 1.

[140] Home, Political, A, October 1913, Proceedings 100–18, p. 82.

[141] Ibid. The letter was sent on the 21 June and reached Meston on 28 June, but the demolition of the washing place had already been ordered for 1 July and the reply could not be sent in time.

The demolition created commotion among the local Muslim population, but official reports asserted that no action would be taken and a telegram asking for permission to rebuild the vestibule was sent to the Viceroy.[142] On 5 July, *The Comrade* nonetheless wrote:

> A great blow has been dealt to their religious feelings, but they [Kanpur Muslims] are expected to bear themselves manfully. Let them prove for once that they can act with courage, determination, sustained energy in time of need. [...] What counsel we can give now to Cawnpore Moslems except that they should trust their God alone and act with vigour.[143]

That same issue, Mohamed Ali reproduced his correspondence with Sir James Meston. In it, Meston described the agitation as 'an afterthought suggested by the concession to the Hindus and by the desire to secure some corresponding privilege by the Muhammadan community',[144] an idea that Mohamed Ali strongly opposed, underlining Hindu–Muslim support in the matter and dubbing the insinuation 'as mischievous as it is false'.[145]

More importantly, Meston's letters revealed that while Hindu feelings regarding the temple were judged genuine, the Lieutenant Governor believed Muslim 'grievance to be largely imaginary',[146] as well as 'exaggerated and not wholly sincere'.[147] Should there have been any doubt about its seriousness, Meston would have been 'most scrupulous to avoid anything which would wound genuine susceptibilities'.[148] In a letter dated 2 July 1913 – the day after the demolition – the Lieutenant Governor further concluded that a deflection of the road to spare the mosque would have been a 'small matter' but that minor sacrifices needed to be made for public good.[149] Once the agitation was over, an enquiry would be conducted to settle for the future 'what are the sacred limits of a mosque generally and what is the religious law about

[142] Home, Political, A, October 1913, Proceedings 100–18, p. 92.
[143] 'The Cawnpore Sacrilege', *The Comrade*, 5 July 1913, vol. 6, 1, p. 8.
[144] Letter by J. B. Meston, Naini Tal, 2 July 1913 published in 'The Cawnpore Sacrilege', *The Comrade*, 5 July 1913, vol. 6, 1, p. 10.
[145] 'The Cawnpore Sacrilege', *The Comrade*, 5 July 1913, vol. 6, 1, p. 6.
[146] Letter by J. B. Meston, Naini Tal, 23 May 1913, in 'The Cawnpore Sacrilege', *The Comrade*, 5 July 1913, vol. 6, 1, p. 10.
[147] Ibid., p. 11.
[148] Letter by J. B. Meston, Naini Tal, 23 May 1913, Ibid., p. 10.
[149] Letter by J. B. Meston, Naini Tal, 2 July 1913, Ibid., p. 10.

compensation'.[150] The protest against the demolition of the *dālān* indeed revealed that Muslim opinion was divided on the question.[151]

Religious feelings and their alleged sincerity became a point of contention but also a bargaining chip. The press indeed cultivated 'emotional registers'.[152] Since the very end of June 1913, *Hamdard* regularly emphasised the despair that town-planning projects kindled among Muslims and insisted on the need for them 'to express the[ir] true feelings (*aṣlī jażbāt*)' to the authorities.[153] On 1 July, alluding to the Macchli Bazar mosque of Kanpur, *Hamdard* warned, in emotional terms: 'we hope that, for the beauty of streets, breaking the hearts of Muslims (*musalmānoṇ kī dilshikanī*) will not be permitted'.[154] While some could read this emotionality as sensationalism, Margrit Pernau has observed that feelings could well be 'strategically evoked and deeply felt at the same time'.[155] The correspondence underscored that if religious feelings were displayed enough to be considered sincere, colonial authorities could bow, as in the case of the Teli temple. It then appeared crucial to make grief public in order to be acknowledged.

Although the Land Acquisition Act of 1894 allowed for the destruction of religious sites, Chapter XV of the Indian Penal Code (1860) considered hurting 'religious feelings' a serious offence.[156] Lord Macaulay, who drafted the Code, took feelings into account, since they were deemed likely to cause riots and unrest.[157] As Ahmed

150 Ibid.
151 While some ulama considered the whole structure of a mosque unalterable, others agreed to the conversion of parts of a mosque into a road if for the public good. See, for instance, Confidential Records, Home, 1914, B, 8: pamphlet entitled *Ahkam ul-Masjid Regarding the Demolition of Mosques* (by Janab Abu Al-Makarram Muhammad Rifaʿat Ali Khan of Shahjahanpur). See Home, Political, A, October 1913, Proceedings 100–18, statement by Mr. Sanderson, superintendent of Muhammadan Monuments in the Northern Circle, p. 89.
152 F. Zaman, 'Beyond Nostalgia', p. 640.
153 '*Qadīmī maqābir-o masājid*', *Hamdard*, 29 June 1913, p. 3
154 '*Qadīmī maqābir-o masājid – ḥissah dawam*', *Hamdard*, 1 July 1913, p. 4.
155 M. Pernau, 'Nostalgia: Tears of Blood', p. 97, quoted by F. Zaman, 'Beyond Nostalgia', p. 639.
156 Chapter XV 'Offences Relating to Religion', *Indian Penal Code (Act XLV of 1860): With Notes*, ed. W. Morgan and A. G. Macpherson, Calcutta, 1863, pp. 217–21.
157 On this, see, for instance, A. A. Ahmed, 'Specters of Macaulay: Blasphemy, the Indian Penal Code, and Pakistan's Postcolonial Predicament', pp. 177–82.

and Stephens noted, laws on religious sentiments very much shaped and constituted them.[158] Mohamed Ali's political mobilisation around Muslim grief certainly fed on the state's legal recognition of sentiments. But for it to work, as James Meston highlighted, feelings had to be made visible and unquestionable. Pernau has demonstrated that much of the agitation thereafter aimed at displaying and exacerbating the *josh* (fervour) of the Muslim community for Islamic places of worship.[159]

A look at contemporary newspapers, like *Al-Hilāl*, shows that after the demolition of the *dālān*, much emphasis was put on the fact that Kanpur Muslims had been wrongly prevented from demonstrating grief, pointing, for instance, at the responsibility of the *mutawallī* for having inhibited Kanpur Muslims' heartfelt feelings (*dilī jażbāt kā iẓhār karnā*) to the government when crowds gathered at his door agitating against the demolition, and for having persuaded shopkeepers to reopen the businesses they had closed as a sign of grief (*ranj-o alam meṇ*).[160] The emotion emphasised in Urdu was invariably grief. In *Kānpūr kī k͟hūnī dāstān* ('The bloody tale of Kanpur'), which was largely circulated and soon prohibited under the Indian Press Act, Khwajah Hasan Nizami explained how Meston's letters stating the lack of interest (*josh*) of Kanpur Muslims had created such '*ġham-o alam*' (grief) that they wished to display their fervour (*josh numā'īsh*).[161] At the same time, mass meetings started to spring up in mid-July, notably in Madras, against the desecration of mosques in Kanpur and Delhi, as the agitation went well beyond the realm of local governments.[162] Manifesting feelings became a political act: through grief, justice could be achieved.

The papers continued to negotiate with the authorities when, on the morning of 3 August, the infamous incident occurred. The issue of *The Comrade* that week was unusually delayed in order to cover the

158 Ibid., p. 177 and J. Stephens, 'The Politics of Muslim Rage: Secular Law and Religious Sentiment in Late Colonial India', p. 47. See also M. Pernau, 'Riots, Masculinity, and the Desire for Passions', pp. 253–4.
159 M. Pernau, *Emotions and Modernity*, p. 226.
160 '*Ḥādṡa-e masjid-e Kānpūr kī masūliyah*' by Janab Mahmud Ahmad (Alig.), *Al Hilāl*, 23 July 1913, p. 79.
161 Khwajah Hasan Nizami, *Kānpūr kī k͟hūnī dāstān*, pp. 1–2.
162 From Madras to CC Delhi 17 July 1913 in CC, Revenue and Agriculture, 39/1915 B, p. 66.

news: after a mass meeting (of around 10,000–15,000 people)[163] at the '*Idgāh* of Kanpur, a group of Muslims, filled with anguish at the sight of the desecrated portion of the mosque,[164] or excited by the recitation of pathetic verses,[165] began to pile up the bricks of the demolished wall that were still lying there. The police were called and blank cartridges were fired to spread the crowd, but stones were thrown in retaliation. At half past ten, Mr. Tyler, district magistrate and superintendent of police, ordered the police to fire. The operation, which lasted ten minutes, ended with seventeen men killed, thirty-three injured, and many more arrested.[166] The fact that an official deputation was supposed to meet local Muslim representatives on 9 August seemed to support the idea that the riot had been provoked by malevolent people – the Delhi press according to Meston,[167] the police according to *The Comrade*:

> The Cawnpore Mussalmans were, as a matter of fact, being continuously urged by *responsible 'outside' Moslems* to take no action till the result of the deputation, which was to wait on Sir James Meston, had been made known. They had accepted the advice, and the local leaders appeared calm and cool and were waiting the forthcoming interview with His Honour the Lieutenant-Governor in a spirit of hopefulness. It is difficult, in view of all this, to believe that the Cawnpore Moslems would have broken the peace *without grave police provocation*.[168]

As Mohamed Ali insisted, it was not the religious fervour of Muslims – which the press could hardly deny to have sustained[169] – that had led to the riot but the involvement of adverserial troublemakers that had nothing to do with local Muslims. A week later, *The Comrade*

163 See J. S. Meston, *Minute by the Lieutenant Governor on the Cawnpore Mosque and Riot*, 21 August 1913, pp. 74–112 in Home, Political, A, October 1913, Proceedings 100–18, p. 95.

164 'The Cawnpore Tragedy', *The Comrade*, 2 August 1913, vol. 6, 4, p. 73.

165 See *Minute by the Lieutenant Governor*, Home, Political, A, October 1913, Proceedings 100–18, pp. 96–7.

166 Home, Political, A, October 1913, Proceedings 100–18, p. 2: telegram from the Lieutenant Governor of the UP to the Private Secretary to Viceroy, Bareilly, 3 August 1913. According to government records, 118 rioters were trialled in connection with the Kanpur mosque incident; see Home, Political, A, October 1913, Proceedings 100–18, p. 71.

167 Ibid.

168 'The Cawnpore Tragedy', *The Comrade*, 2 August 1913, p. 73. My emphasis.

169 As Margrit Pernau highlighted, it is not clear how much the press initiated the agitation or conceded to the insistence of the reading public. M. Pernau, *Emotions and Modernity*, p. 225.

Figure 3.2 The Macchli Bazar mosque with the demolished wall, IOR/L/PJ/6/1256, File 2826, photograph 4, © The British Library Board

further supported the idea, put forward by one Kanpur correspondent, that 'the riot was carefully engineered by the police themselves and the "Kabulia" [who had started the riot] were the police hire links'.[170] The article infuriated the authorities and a demand of security (amounting at Rs. 2,000, the maximum permissible) under section 3 of the Indian Press Act (1910) was immediately requested from Mohamed Ali.[171]

The Macchli Bazar mosque became a test case for the local government as much as for Mohamed Ali's press (Figure 3.2). For the colonial

[170] 'The Cawnpore Tragedy', *The Comrade*, 9 August 1913, vol. 6, 5, p. 93. The suggestion also appeared in *Tauḥīd*. See Home, Political A, October 1913, Proceedings 142–9, p. 2.

[171] Home, Political A, October 1913, Proceedings 142–9, pp. 1 and 8. The security was paid on 11 August. On 8 August, Mr. H. Wheeler advised Mr. W. M. Hailey to bring to his notice any infringement on the provisions of the Press Act by either *The Comrade* or *Hamdard*. See demi-official letter from Mr. H. Wheeler to Mr. W. M. Hailey, Simla, 8 August 1913, in Home, Political, A, October 1913, Proceedings 100–18, p. 4.

officers in charge, the agitation in Kanpur was clearly 'fomented from outside and from Delhi in particular',[172] 'in order to embarrass us with contemplated Delhi improvement'.[173] As Meston confessed, the fact that he believed the agitation had roots in Delhi 'where so much work of the highest importance is now being undertaken' made him 'particularly unwilling to make any concession'.[174] By Delhi, the authorities truly meant 'Young Party' Muslims.[175] For Mohamed Ali, on the other hand, 'the Cawnpore mosque furnishe[d] a test case through which the principle of freedom of Muslim places of worship from outrage and desecration has to be vindicated once for all'.[176] With the indignation that *The Comrade* notably spread (among many other Indian newspapers like *Zamīndār*, *Al-Hilāl*, *Tauḥīd*, and *Madīnah*)[177] across all sections of Muslims, the case rapidly emerged as an example of what could be achieved politically through the expression of Muslims' collective grief.[178]

Quickly after the incident, *The Comrade* and *Hamdard* started a 'Cawnpore Moslem Relief Fund'; reported on Dr Ansari and Shaukat Ali's visits to the wounded and prisoners; and described the site where the tragedy had taken place, with portrayals of bloodstains and bullet impacts on the walls of the martyred mosque.[179] Poems lamenting the martyrdom of men and buildings were published and recited at meetings devoted to the collection of funds all over British India.[180] Black banners were waved by groups of protesters; mosques threatened to close in religious strikes.[181] Photographs were taken, bought,

[172] Home, Political, A, October 1913, Proceedings 100–18: telegram from Lieutenant Governor of the UP to Viceroy, Naini Tal, 24 July 1913.
[173] Ibid., R. H. C (Raddock), 7-9-13, p. 11.
[174] Ibid., telegram from Lieutenant Governor of the UP to Viceroy, Naini Tal, 24 July 1913, p. 90.
[175] See Ibid., p. 20: extract from a fortnightly demi-official letter, 3 September 1913, from the Commissioner, Rohilkhand division, p. 21.
[176] 'The Cawnpore Tragedy', *The Comrade*, 9 August 1913, vol. 6, 5, p. 8.
[177] For an excellent study of the covering of the Kanpur incident by *Madīnah* see S. Kavuri-Bauer, *Monumental Matters*, pp. 113–5.
[178] G. Minault, *The Khilafat Movement*, pp. 46–7.
[179] 'The Cawnpore Tragedy', *The Comrade*, 9 August 1913, vol. 6, 5, p. 96.
[180] See, for instance, Home, Political A, October 1913, p. 54.
[181] See Mohamed Ali Papers, JMI, 1007–1008, 15 July 1913, from Shah Baz Khan Meerut Cantonment. The latter solicited Mohamed Ali's views on the possibility of leading religious strikes.

and held up in assemblies to raise financial support for the victims.[182] Sets of photographs taken by Mazurul Haque of Mittra and Sous Photographers were advertised.[183] Mosques were turned into political platforms,[184] and fiery speeches and pamphlets prompted Muslims to wake up and protect religious sites.[185] Cases of desecration of mosques and graveyards in Delhi resurfaced and stirred public opinion.[186]

In the mobilisation against the demolition of the *dālān*, the themes of Karbala and of martyrdom were extensively referred to so as to nourish a strong anti-British agitation. Soon after the bloody event, *Al-Hilāl* indeed described 'the morning of 3 August to be the 10th of Muharram' and 'the date of the revolution (*inqilāb*) of the British Government'.[187] As in the 1870s, the fate of the Muslims of Kanpur was linked to the fate of Muslims around the world, and the incident at Kanpur was reframed as 'not just the incident of Kanpur, but the incident of the world of Islam'.[188]

> The earth is thirsty, it needs blood, but whose? The Muslims'. Whose blood waters the earth of Tripoli? The Muslims'. Whose blood dyes Morocco? The Muslims'. Whose corpses writhe on the soil of Iran? The Muslims'. Whose blood flows on the land of the Balkans? The Muslims'. The earth of Hindustan too is thirsty for blood, whose? The Muslims'. Eventually, blood inundated Kanpur, and watered the soil of Hindustan.[189]

182 Home, Political A, October 1913, Proceedings 100–18, p. 41: demi-official letter from the Hon'ble Mr. H. Le Mesurier CSI CIE, to the Hon'ble Mr. H. Wheeler CIE, 82-c, Ranchi, 27 Sept. 1913: '[about a meeting at Bankipore on the 31 July] Mr Mazhar ul Haq was said to have stimulated excitement by showing photographs of the demolished portion of the mosque and by spreading statements regarding the conduct of the Cawnpore officials'.

183 Mohamed Ali Papers, NMML Reel 2, from Mittra and Sous Photographers to Mohamed Ali, Cawnpore, 23 September 1913 in response to letter 11619, dated 22 September. The company proposed two different sets, one of seventeen photographs at Rs. 15, and one of nineteen photographs at Rs. 18.

184 Home, Political A, October 1913: demi-official letter from the Hon'ble Mr. C. A. Barron CIE to the Hon'ble Mr. H. Wheeler CIE 1660-S.B. Simla, 11 October 1913, p. 44.

185 Home, Political A, October 1913: weekly report of the Director of Criminal Intelligence, Simla, 2 September 1913, pp. 3–4.

186 Home, Political A, October 1913: demi-official letter from Mr C. Q. Barron: 'the old charges against the Delhi authorities of demolishing graveyards and other sacred enclosures were revived'.

187 '*3 August kī ṣūbah*', *Al Hilāl*, 13 August 1913, p. 117.

188 Ibid., p. 122. See also M. Pernau, *Emotions and Modernity*, p. 239.

189 '*E'ānat-e Maẕlūmān-e Kānpūr*', *Al-Hilāl*, 13 August 1913, p. 120.

Newspapers and pamphlets clearly participated in the identification of Indian Muslims (and Muslims in general) as a poor and oppressed community that needed protection. Nizami's popular *Kānpūr kī k̲h̲ūnī dāstān* reproduced speeches, articles, and poetry on Kanpur that heavily built on a symbolism of innocence, martyrdom, blood, and poverty – but also hope and solidarity, as will be emphasised further in the next chapter. Descriptions full of pathos of the dead and wounded were interspersed with reflections on poor and famished orphans, and on the blood-stained robes of elders,[190] almost giving the impression that the crowd at Kanpur was primarily composed of innocent children and frail patriarchs. The speech of Maulana Azad Subhani, a local Arabic teacher who was being tried in Kanpur, also recalled to the audience the tough childhood of Prophet Muhammad, 'also reared up in the arms of a poor mother, but [whose] voice [...] shook the pinnacles of the Emperor's palace'.[191]

This discourse quickly gained popular support, and, as Nandini Gooptu showed, coincided with feelings that had begun to spread among the Muslim urban poor whose economic and social situation had worsened since the beginning of the twentieth century with the rise of competitive Hindu commercial classes who 'were also aggressive in their religious and cultural expression'.[192] The Muslim poor, Gooptu argued, started to 'ma[k]e sense of their plight in dialogue with a projected history of decline of the Indian Muslims and of Islam worldwide'[193] that gave a new centrality to religion as a way to articulate political action and construct identity. At the time, as Ferrell showed, Mohamed Ali's support extended from traditionalist Muslim middle classes to wealthy Punjabi merchants as well as to Delhi's butchers and leatherworkers.[194]

190 See Nizami, *Kānpūr kī k̲h̲ūnī dāstān*, for instance, pp. 1, 10, and the speech by Nizami on 8 August at Meerut, p. 21.

191 Ibid., p. 28, trans. Home, Political A, October 1913, p. 49: proscription under the Indian Press Act (I of 1910) of the pamphlet entitled *Cawnpur ki khuni dastan* (*The Bloody Massacre of Cawnpore*) – demi-official letter from Mr W.H. Hailey to Mr H. Wheeler, 7104 Home, 17 September 1913. As Max Stille has shown, similar imagery of the Prophet as an orphan is used in present-day Bengali sermons to elicit compassion from the audience; see M. Stille, 'Between the Numinous and the Melodramatic'.

192 N. Gooptu, *The Politics of the Urban Poor*, p. 261.

193 Ibid., p. 268.

194 D. Ferrell, 'Delhi 1911–1922', p. 247.

The popularity of the mobilisation can be measured by the amount of funds raised (around Rs. 80,000, of which Rs. 12,000 came directly from Mohamed Ali's press)[195] and by the growing anxiety of colonial officers. In September 1913, the government noted:

> This unfortunate case has greater potentiality for trouble than any since 1857. It is uniting all sections of the Muhammadan community of India into a common belief that their 'deen' is in danger. [...] An appreciable loss of life, including the old, the young and the child, has stirred Muhammadan sentiment to its deepest depths. The literate and illiterate, the orthodox and the heterodox, the men of the new school and those of the old – have been equally affected. My latest information is that the idea of 'the sacrilege' and 'the martyrdom' has entered into the zenanas, and the influence of the women is on the side of the ill-considered but popular grievance.[196]

The Comrade and other north Indian newspapers had not only succeeded to rally and unify Muslim opinion and feelings but had also proven their power to the colonial state. Finally, in October 1913, Lord Hardinge decided to put an end to it all. Charges against the rioters were dropped, the *dālān* was reconstructed, and the government reassured its subjects and hoped that the incident would be soon forgotten.[197] Muslim feelings were acknowledged.

4 Emotions and Memorials

Beyond the success of the mobilisation, the Kanpur mosque case also crystallised new conceptions of memorials as emotional and political objects. At the end of July 1913, as the Kokī Bridge and Kanpur mosques cases unfolded, an unsigned article in *Hamdard* entitled 'Qaumī Yādgāreṇ' (Community Memorials) precisely addressed the significance of historic buildings for collective memory, feelings,

[195] Home, Political, A Proceedings 100–18, October 1913: weekly report of 23 September, p. 1. As Robinson noted, however, the Rs. 80,000 of the fund stayed in the keeping of lawyer-politician Mazhar ul Haq and 'never reached the mosque' (Robinson, *Separatism*, p. 187).

[196] Home, Political, A, October 1913, Proceedings 113: letter to the India Office, 14 (Police), 4 September 1913, p. 11.

[197] Home, Political, A Proceedings 100–18, October 1913: Appendix D: extract from the *Statesman*, Calcutta, 16 October, the viceroy at Cawnpore: Moslem Deputation and Lord Hardinge's reply, p. 61.

and identity.[198] The article reported on the erection of a new British memorial in Selkirk (Scotland) to commemorate the 400-year anniversary of the battle of Flodden Field, which opposed Scottish and English armies. It described the unveiling of the two memorial statues by Lord Rosebery, and displayed particular sympathy for the Scots. The author argued that even though the monument memorialised a defeat, it nonetheless acknowledged the bravery of the Scottish mind, and warned Englishmen of the danger of confronting them. The situation was cunningly paralleled with the situation in India, suggesting that memorials for 'defeated' populations were essential for community identity.

The anniversary of the battle came at a crucial moment. In May 1913, the House of Commons had finally passed the second reading of the Government of Scotland Bill (or Scottish Home Rule Bill) by 204 votes to 159. It was the result of years of political campaigning: in 1894 a resolution had been proposed by Sir H. Dalziel to give the legislatures of Ireland, Scotland, Wales, and England control over and management of their own affairs, and the beginning of the twentieth century was further marked by the appearance of the 'Young Scots', an offshoot of the Liberal party which had as its main objective Scottish Home Rule.[199] In 1912, the Irish Home Rule Bill was passed, and Scottish Home Rule was agreed upon too. It was a great achievement for Scotland and an inspiration for India. After all, the 'Young Party' aspired to the same thing that Scotland had just obtained.

Built memorials not only commemorated the past but also had patriotic values and embodied the state's recognition of the communities for which they stood. As already mentioned, memorials – particularly of 1857 – had been a frequent matter of concern in northern India. In May 1876, for instance, an incident at Shahjahanpur in the North-Western Provinces revealed the uneasiness with which British memorials were often viewed: during a parade, a soldier of the 22nd regiment at Shahjahanpur had suddenly left the ranks, opened fire, and killed three Indians. After his arrest, when he was asked the reasons behind his act, he replied that since he had seen the Kanpur

198 '*Qaumī Yādgāreṇ*', *Hamdard*, 29 July 1913, p. 4.

199 Hansard (1803–2005) online, Commons Sitting, Orders of the Day, 'Government of Scotland Bill', House of Commons, 30 May 1913, vol. 53, pp. 471–551.

Memorial Well (in memory of British civilians killed in 1857), a great enmity towards Indians had been aroused in him.[200] The incident triggered a discussion on the significance of these memorials and on their emotional impact. As the *Punjābī Akhbār* noted, 'Hindustanis imbibe extreme fear from them [memorials], and tremble in the same degree as the European savage raves and fumes at [the] sight of them'.[201] The *Aligarh Institute Gazette* also argued:

> Such memorials (*yādgāreṇ*) will always rekindle rancour (*kīnah*) and create trouble; we now put forward the idea that it is necessary for our Government that, for the maintenance of peace and order, all such memorials be destroyed (*nīst-o nābūd kar de*), and if it is necessary to keep such memorials for the reason that they recall historical events, then we think that it would be necessary to complete thoroughly the written history of 1857.[202]

In 1911, *The Comrade* had also demanded the destruction of the Kashmiri Gate for the same reasons, but now *Hamdard* enhanced the positive emotional (and political) impact of public memorialisation. Monuments were described not only as reminders of collective history but also as 'the best established means for the community's wakefulness (*qaumī bedārī kā bahtarīn żarī'ah s̱ābit*)'. They acted as 'as a warning whip and a spur of pride (*tāzyānah-e 'ibrat aur mahmez-e ġhairat*)'.[203] Monuments were not 'dead' structures but active sites where the past was enacted and made present for future generations.

As scholars have argued, the spirit of forebears is considered to continue living in historical sites, and they can enter in contact with the living, a phenomenon to which many traditional practices attest.[204] Those sites are not considered mere mementos but places where memory is performed. Apart from describing the beauty of dilapidated graves, the author referred to recitations of the *fātihah* at the mausoleums of Data Ganj Bakhsh Hujwiri in Lahore; of Khwajah Moinuddin Chishti in Ajmer; and of Khwajah Baqibillah, Sultan Nizamuddin, or Khwajah Qutubuddin in Delhi as moments that stir collective emotions and memories most powerfully. The author of 'Qaumī Yādgāreṇ' explained:

200 '*Shāhjahānpūr kā wāqi'ah*', *Aligarh Institute Gazette*, 12 May 1876, p. 285.
201 Ibid., pp. 285–86. 202 Ibid., p. 286.
203 '*Qaumī Yādgāreṇ*', *Hamdard*, 29 July 1913, p. 4.
204 R. Kurin, 'Morality, Personhood, and the Exemplary Life', p. 202. See also A. V. Taneja, *Jinnealogy*.

In Delhi, the Red Fort, the Jama Masjid, Nizamuddin's *dargāh*, Qutubuddin's *rozah*, Baqibillah's grave, Humayun's tomb, etc., are, with hundreds such similar monuments, edifices from which men instantly learn the lesson of the impermanence of their existence and refresh their faith (*imān ko tāzah kar detī haiṇ*). Go to Old Delhi, and see how many tombs and how many religious edifices there are, some in good repairs, some broken and dilapidated, and from a silent voice what a lesson of warning (*ʿibrat kī sabaq*) they teach! Look at the height of the Qutub Minar, look at the forlorn beauty and terrible grandeur of the mosque Quwwat-ul Islam! If we don't weep tears of blood, then we are accountable (*żimmedār*). These are the tombs and religious edifices whose every particle should be the collyrium on the eye of the mystic, which wake up men from their negligent slumber (*k͟hwāb-e ġhaflat*); they teach wisdom and increase piety.[205]

The article emphasised both the power that those sites still retained and the complex networks they maintained with holy places throughout the Islamic world.[206] As in Hali's *Musaddas*, Delhi was put in relationship with Karbala, Meshhed, Baghdad, Constantinople, Cordoba, Bukhara, Ajmer, Sirhind, and Lahore, and the Haramain Sharifain which, of course, were 'the best memorials, which can make the blood boil, heat the bodies (*jism ko garmā*) and render the souls restless (*rūḥ ko taṛpā sakte haiṇ*)'.[207] Religious and secular buildings were said to inspire great pride among the population and to act as 'an incitement and a means of progress for the nations to come'.[208]

The emotional importance given to architecture (perhaps inspired by English thinkers)[209] was increasingly popular in north Indian newspapers and magazines. In one article entitled 'Upper Indian Architecture' published in *Kayastha Samachar* by Mr. Niaz Mohammad, reader at the Oriental College of Lahore,[210] in 1906, architecture was said to teach 'noble thoughts' and to 'perforce remind man of the immensity of the Creator of the Universe and incline his heart to humility'.[211] The sentimental and patriotic value of architecture justified the need to

[205] 'Community Memorials' (*Qaumī Yādgāreṇ*), *Hamdard*, 29 July 1913, p. 4.
[206] Home, Political, A Proceedings 100–18, October 1913: weekly report, 16 September, Peshawar, p. 3.
[207] 'Community Memorials' (*Qaumī Yādgāreṇ*), *Hamdard*, 29 July 1913, p. 4.
[208] Ibid. [209] For instance, Ruskin's *Seven Lamps of Architecture* (1849).
[210] 'Upper Indian Architecture', *Kayastha Samachar*, July 1906, vol. 14, 83, pp. 37–48.
[211] Ibid., p. 38.

preserve patrimony at a time that was characterised by intense modernisation, which echoed similar developments in Victorian Britain. Yet, as Mrinalini Rajagopalan explained, British attitude to memorials and monuments was very different in Britain and in India. When Britain enhanced the patriotic value of memorials, or of ruins, in the metropolis, it strove instead to strip Indian monuments of the same emotions that could jeopardise colonial rule.[212] Colonial heritage management consequently worked at preserving monuments as inanimate objects of a disconnected past. Mohamed Ali's press, in contrast, reclaimed the agency and the emotional value of memorials by demanding the right to maintain or to erect them for the sake of collective identity.

Early twentieth-century poems from an Urdu literary magazine such as *Zamānah* show that Hindu and Muslim Urdu poets alike increasingly associated monuments with strong patriotic feelings. Poems entitled 'Community Building' (*Qaumī ʿimarat*, 1908), 'The Mausoleum of Nur Jahan' (*Nūr Jahāṇ kā mazār*, 1909), and 'The Tombstone' (*sang-e mazār*, 1910), respectively composed by Kaifi, Sayyid Mahmud Faruq, and Ram Parshad, romantically depicted monuments as the resilient reminders of past power.[213] In 1910 too, Muhammad Iqbal composed his beautiful poem *Goristān-e Shāhī* ('The Royal Cemetery'), probably after his visit to Hyderabad, in which he romantically reflected on time, longing, and ruins, operating a link between royal monuments and Muslim collective feelings: the 'grief of the *Millat* is always fresh' (*ġham-e millat hameshah tāzah hai*), 'this *Ummah* cannot erase its kings' memories' (*apne shāhoṇ ko yeh ʿummat bhūlnewālī nahīṇ*).[214]

It is noteworthy that buildings such as the Red Fort, Jama Masjid, and Nizamuddin's shrine were not called 'monuments' (*āṡār*)[215] but 'memorials' (*yādgār*) in the article, perhaps in an attempt to restore their agency.[216] Monuments were conceived as 'relics', in Annabel

212 M. Rajagopalan, *Building Histories*, 16.

213 See, respectively, *Zamānah*, May 1908, pp. 347–50; *Zamānah*, July 1909, pp. 49–50; and *Zamānah*, July 1910, p. 72.

214 Iqbal, '*Goristān-e Shāhī*', in *Bang-e Darā*, p. 387, translation in *Call of the Marching Bell*, p. 176.

215 The word *āṡār* was, for instance, used to translate into Urdu the colonial categories of 'Ancient Monuments' or 'Protected Monuments'.

216 The word *yādgār* can be used for monuments but its primary meaning is 'conveyer of memory'. It can also refer to anthologies, memoirs, or keepsakes which act as reminders.

Jane Wharton's understanding, as signs of a previous power that can be revived.[217] It was precisely the present emotional relevance of ancient buildings that was highlighted in *Hamdard* as the primary reason they needed to be preserved and protected by the state – not because of their archaeological value, although that could be an argument too. Kavuri-Bauer noted that mosques (and more generally anything that was considered *waqf*) were increasingly seen as 'symbolic spaces of Muslim social identity' in the Muslim press.[218] While this was certainly the case, for the author of 'Qaumī Yādgāreṇ', religious and royal monuments were equally considered to elicit community belonging through emotions and memory.

Having underlined the value of community memorials, the author pursued that they should be granted the same protection that newly constructed British memorials enjoyed:

> For Muslims, as for poor communities (*qaum*), it is useless to hope to build new memorials for their ancestors like the other religions, civilisations and wealthy nations of the world; but there is no doubt that the protection of our ancestors' memorials, which our ancestors and their successors have built, must be arranged.[219]

As Indian subjects were to respect British memorials,[220] 'Qaumī Yādgāreṇ' demanded that the opposite be enforced as well: if the defacement of a memorial for King Edward was translated by colonial authorities as an attack on British rule, how could destroying a Muslim monument not be interpreted as an attack on the Muslim community? The article finished on a heated note:

> This [the destruction of Muslim monuments] will make us weep, yes! We will cry tears of blood (*k͟hūn ke ānsū*), but they will not be useless: they will water the field of patriotism (*millat parastī*) and will make the flowerbeds of fraternity bloom! Although whole neighbourhoods are being demolished, there are still thousands of reminders of the grandeur of the community

[217] Quoted in M. Rajagopalan, *Building Histories*, p. 54.
[218] S. Kavuri-Bauer, *Monumental matters*, p. 117.
[219] '*Qaumī Yādgāreṇ*', *Hamdard*, 29 July 1913, p. 4.
[220] The state was particularly anxious about defacement, particularly of 1857 memorials and during the construction of New Delhi. See, for instance, Commissioner Office, 68/1894: Defacement of Tombs of British Officers on the Ridge and Confidential/Home/25/1921 (B): Safeguarding of Monuments and Statues from Defacement.

(*millat*); some are manifest in some ruined monuments and some are visible in some fallen wall or in the silence of some dilapidated cemetery embracing the grandeur of former [generations].[221]

The respect due to memorials could indeed become another strategy to resist colonial presence in Delhi. That same month, July 1913, an article by an anonymous 'Ex-Citizen' in *The Comrade* precisely opened an opportunity for further resistance.[222] Arguing that British public opinion was generally hostile to the construction of the new imperial capital on the bones of the dead, and highlighting that further demolition would necessarily take place,[223] the author suggested fixing memorial plaques to preserve the memory of important men. The 'Ex-Citizen' insisted that it was the responsibility of the people to ensure that their heritage be preserved.[224] At Rs. 15 per marble tablet, the suggested scheme was not thought too expensive and the author assumed that the population would be able to participate without the need to inform the government or town planning engineers. It was quite an odd suggestion and somewhat different from the usual polemical tone of *The Comrade*: the author did not openly criticise the government for the destruction of buildings but rather directly called on the population for support.

The proposal was not commented upon in the next issues of the paper. Then on 14 February 1914 two connected articles appeared in *The Comrade*: one by the same 'Ex-Citizen' entitled 'The New Capital' and the second by J. Ramsay MacDonald, future British prime minister, entitled 'City of Ruins and Tombs', which was reproduced from the *Daily Citizen*. MacDonald's article on Delhi complained of the recent practice among Delhi's population of fixing memorial tablets that was said to delay the work of city town planners significantly:

[221] '*Qaumī Yādgāreṇ*', *Hamdard*, 29 July 1913, pp. 4–5.
[222] 'Old Delhi – A Memorial Tablet Scheme' by Ex-Citizen, *The Comrade*, 5 July 1913, vol. 6, 1, p. 13.
[223] Ibid.
[224] Idem: 'Does it not, in the circumstances, behove us all, Hindus and Moslems and others, to make one supreme effort to preserve some marks showing the spot where so many great men of India had lived, whom Delhi had produced or otherwise attracted to its courts and concerns throughout its centuries of chequered career. [...] With a view to preserving the memory of these great men and of their homes and habitations, I suggest that we should institute a scheme of memorial tablets – bearing names and dates. These marble tablets may be fixed up in the walls, or when homes have or will disappear, on stone posts on a side of the road nearest to the actual post.'

Every step the builders take has to be considered lest their foot falls upon a tomb. A platform under a tree shade becomes sacred in these days when holy places have to be purchased so that roads may be made and foundations dug; a new industry has sprung up in the *bazar* for the making of tablets informing the surveyors that this and that that is the resting place of this Khan and that Shah. Nobody but a skilful and patient diplomatist could have emerged from the maze of holiness, false and real, which lay on the ground.[225]

The new 'industry' mentioned in MacDonald's article reminded the Ex-Citizen's suggestion in *The Comrade* six months earlier. It led the latter to justify himself in the same issue of the paper. The Ex-Citizen denied that 'a sudden and desperate movement for a wholesale and indiscriminate bestowal of sanctity to the many thousands of crumbling and decaying tombs' had 'sprung up', arguing that it only consisted of a modest action by a small local organisation led by a certain Shah Abdus Samad Sahib who 'has at some few places supplied tablets and carried out repairs, but that is nothing very unusual for him to do'.[226] He also denied Ramsay MacDonald's insinuation that the process had been undertaken with the intention of disturbing the progress of the town planning projects, but justified it thusly:

All that has happened is that the wild and unauthorised rumours of the last year relating to the scheme for the making of the new town alarmed the people and caused uneasiness as to the fate of public burial places, shrines and important tombs. A mosque had already been demolished and there were persistent rumours that other *khanqas* and shrines were similarly threatened, and naturally there was much anxiety prevailing at the time. Out of this, a society was then formed for taking steps for the preservation of important shrines and tombs, but it has not been able to do any substantial work so far. [...] In the circumstances and in view of the impending complete transformation of the place [i.e. Delhi], it seems quite possible that an effort will be made to secure important places and tombs, such as can be located, from disappearing altogether.[227]

The article further argued that the 'Indian mind' had now awakened to the history of Delhi and had developed a sense of collective duty

225 Mr R. MacDonald, 'City of Ruins and Tombs', *The Comrade*, 14 February 1914, vol. 7, 7, p. 141.
226 Ex-Citizen, 'The New Capital' *The Comrade*, 14 February 1914, vol. 7, 7, p. 133.
227 Ibid.

for its preservation. It would thus be unfair for the British government, which put so much emphasis on the protection of its own glorious past, to deny a similar feeling and desire among Indian people.[228] The article emphasised that memory had become an important stake among the local Muslim population. This time, the article received a response from *The Comrade* that praised the Ex-Citizen and emphatically dubbed him 'one of the most intelligent and patriotic citizens of Delhi'.[229] An 'innocent' practice had eventually turned into an act of local contestation. Marking the Muslim presence permanently in the urbanscape was possible, even when buildings had already been taken down.

By then, *The Comrade* and *Hamdard* had gained wide public support in Delhi and astounding confidence. On 7 May 1914, *Hamdard* published an article on the Akbarabadi mosque in Delhi that was built by Akbari Begum (one of Shah Jahan's wives) and destroyed by the British during the Uprising.[230] Although the exact situation of the centuries-old mosque was unknown,[231] *Hamdard* suggested that it was most probably beneath the Edward Memorial Park during whose construction 'the foundations of the mosque had emerged'.[232] *Hamdard* called on the government to turn its attention to the matter. A petition was sent to the Chief Commissioner to add the mosque to the list of Protected Monuments and excavate the park, signalling that the *waqf* ground should 'not be used in an inappropriate way'.[233] The suggestion to excavate a British memorial park to unearth a supposed Mughal mosque was a bold move. It showed well how far Mohamed Ali was prepared to go in his show of strength to defend the Muslim royal past against the British, and to assert the Muslim presence in the new colonial capital.[234]

228 Ibid. 229 Ibid.

230 '*Masjid-e Akbarābādī – Dehlī*', *Hamdard*, 7 May 1914, p. 4.

231 2012 excavations for the Subhash Park Metro Station in Delhi, which may have unearthed the remains of the famous mosque, sparked a dispute between the Archaeological Survey of India and the North Delhi Municipal Corporation, pushing for demolition over summer 2012. See M. Rajagopalan, *Building Histories*, p. 1.

232 '*Masjid-e Akbarābādī – Dehlī*', *Hamdard*, 7 May 1914, p. 4.

233 See *Hamdard*, 21 May 1914, p. 6.

234 I have not yet been able to trace the outcome of this case in either *Hamdard* or in government records.

5 Conclusion

Muslims were not the only ones to oppose the destruction of religious buildings during the construction of the new imperial capital,[235] yet they became the most vocal, certainly due to the city's long history of Muslim rule and the increasing need for pan-Indian Muslim political representation and unity. From 1911 to 1915, the attitude of *The Comrade* and *Hamdard* towards monuments evolved from one of dialogue and cooperation with the colonial state to one of opposition and subversion. The papers not only highlighted and successfully politicised the feelings that emerged in relation to the built landscape, but they also used them to pressure the state by resorting to, and sometimes subverting, its own arguments. As Santhi Kavuri-Bauer argued in the Kanpur mosque case, but it is also true for Delhi mosques and tombs, Islamic sites 'had become a pivot on which the power relations of Muslims and their government now turned': from local sites, they had become 'a national space for the formation of a Muslim community'.[236]

Mohamed Ali's press highlighted 'the agency of non-human actors'[237] and reclaimed their dynamic status as guardians of a collective (and pan-Indian) Muslim identity against colonial readings of Muslim monuments as 'dead' artefacts. Feelings, and especially the grief that demolition works inflicted on an Indian Muslim *qaum* in the making, were paramount to that process of claiming rights in the colonial world. Grief, and especially its public manifestations, became political. In one poem that appeared in the *Ukẖuwwat* of Lucknow in April 1919, a certain 'Mahwi' complained that sadness had become threatening for the authorities: 'The expression of grief is forbidden in this regime; we are suspected, our grief is suspected'.[238]

Agitations around religious buildings such as the Kanpur mosque brought 'Young Party' Muslims and their association with ulamas to

[235] See, for instance, the question of the demolition of a wall of the Gurdwara Rakib Ganj in 1920. Fortnightly Report, Delhi: 2nd Fortnight September 1920: CDD Annual Home File 3 for 1920, quoted by S. Singh, *Freedom Movement in Delhi (1859–1919)*, pp. 201–15. See M. Rajagopalan, *Building Histories*, p. 68, for an explanation of the incident: it is that particular protest that seems to have prompted the Archaeological Survey of India to compile a list of the ancient monuments of Delhi by Zafar Hasan.

[236] S. Kavuri-Bauer, *Monumental Matters*, p. 115.

[237] M. Rajagopalan, *Building Histories*, p. 100.

[238] *Ukhuwat*, Lucknow, 26 April 1919, in *NNRNWP&O* for 1919, p. 158.

the forefront of Muslim politics and inaugurated the political participation of non-elite populations. They confirmed Mohamed Ali's power in efficiently compelling the authorities to accept political claims and remained, even after the Viceroy settled the question, a way to pressure the government and threaten New Delhi city planners. As Edwin Lutyens related to his wife in late 1913, whilst Keeling, the city engineer, was standing talking near a building 'an Indian man appeared over a wall and cautioned him to "Remember Cawnpore" [thereby perhaps alluding both to 1857 and to the mosque incident]'.[239] Emotions and memory had truly become powerful instruments.

[239] E. A. Christensen, *Government Architecture*, p. 211, quoting a letter to Emily, November and December 1913.

4 *Empowering Grief*
Poetry and Anti-colonial Sentiments in the Early Twentieth Century

The continuation of Urdu *āshob* poetry into the twentieth century and beyond is a phenomenon that has received little attention in Western scholarship and only marginally in Urdu. Yet, with the outbreak of the Balkan and First World Wars in the 1910s and the subsequent defeat and dismantlement of the Ottoman Empire, the aesthetics of *āshob* poetry and of the *qaumī marṡiyah* – both being closely intertwined – continued to be popular. This chapter examines a set of texts by Hindu and Muslim Urdu poets to document the evolution of the way grief was expressed in the early twentieth century. The poetic expression of *ġham* continued to develop as a powerful discourse of anti-colonial mass mobilisation used in pan-Islamic fundraising campaigns, but an important change was perceptible: the emphasis on martyrdom and on complaint in *āshob* poetry opened up a window for empowerment, solidarity, and resistance. Increasingly, Urdu writers expressed the desire to reclaim agency. Looking at the changing role of *āshob*/secular *marṡiyah* poetry in the emergence of a political poetry of optimism from the 1910s, I show how poets built on lament to address power.

Increasingly in the 1920s Islam was felt to be able to rise from its ashes: cries of 'Islam in danger' were accompanied by supportive yells for its irrepressible force against Western onslaught. The symbol of Karbala, in particular, was no longer seen as a historical example of oppression but as a model of love, dedication, hope, and political self-sacrifice; it built not on Shia interpretations of martyrdom but on Sufi understandings. Grief could be transcended. Through a selection of poetic works by Shibli Numani, Mohamed Ali Jauhar, Muhammad Iqbal, and their contemporaries, I discuss how Islam was emphasised as a force for action and social cohesion at a time when an Indian Muslim political community was still being shaped.

From the mid-1910s, Iqbal particularly grappled with providing a new vision of Islam and of time, God, and the Self. He traced a way to immortality through self-assertion. Doing so, he strikingly erected ruins as examples of collective resilience, a process that culminated in his famous *Masjid-e Qurṯubah* (1932) after the failure of the Khilafat movement and the collapse of pan-Islamic dreams.

1 Grief and Grievances in the Early Twentieth Century

In the early hours of 28 September 1908, after days of unusual monsoon rainfall and storms, the saturated upstream water tanks of the Musi river collapsed one after the other, and the powerful rush of water submerged the old city of Hyderabad. The unstoppable torrent destroyed everything in its path, washed away entire portions of the city walls, and claimed the lives of 10,000 to 15,000 people.[1] The water subsided around midday, but the city lay in ruins. Nizam Mahbub Ali Pasha quickly implemented relief measures and rehabilitation works, but the flood permanently transformed Hyderabad and fundamentally changed the city's socio-economic landscape as the nobility relocated to the safer left bank.[2] As Harriet Lynton and Mohini Rajan recounted, 'for many months after the flood, wandering minstrels roamed the city with their stringed instruments, collecting alms by singing stories of the tragedy'.[3]

Urdu poets composed *shahr āshob* poems, in particular those who came from or had lived for some time in the city, such as Amjad Hyderabadi (1878–1961), Zafar Ali Khan (1873–1956), and Ali Hyder Tabatabai (1854–1933).[4] In his *musaddas* entitled *Qayāmat-e ṣuġhrā* ('Lesser Doomsday'), Amjad Hyderabadi poignantly mourned the loss of his home and of his mother, wife, and daughter, as he miraculously survived by holding onto a centuries-old tamarind tree.[5] Designated as a *shahr āshob*, Amjad's *musaddas* was descriptive and

[1] See H. R. Lynton and M. Rajan, *Days of the Beloved*, p. 18.

[2] B. Cohen, 'Modernising the Urban Environment: The Musi River Flood', p. 411.

[3] H. R. Lynton and M. Rajan, *Days of the Beloved*, p. 20. H. R. Lynton and M. Rajan indicate that a full special *Ṯūfān numbar* of *Adīb* (Hyderabad) in 1908 was devoted to testimonies of the Musi flood along with poems, but I could not access that issue of the magazine. H. R. Lynton and M. Rajan, *Days of the Beloved*, p. 14.

[4] I am grateful to Prof. Ashraf Rafi for discussing Hyderabad's Urdu poetry with me and sharing one of her articles that was published on the topic in a local Urdu paper.

[5] Amjad Hyderabadi, *Qayāmat-e ṣuġhrā* in M. A. Siddiqui, *Yādgār-e Amjad*, pp. 83–4.

emphasised grief with references to mourning and Doomsday but did not typically resort to the image of the garden as Tabatabai's *Shahr āshob Marg-e Anboh* (a *nazm*) did, narrating how 'dust whirls where there used to be gardens' (*kẖāk urṭī hai wahāṇ jahāṇ the gulzār*).[6] Several poems on the destruction of Hyderabad (*Haidarābād kī tabāhī*) also appeared in north Indian literary magazines such as Daya Narain Nigam's *Zamānah* in December 1908.

The poems on Hyderabad, a princely state under British indirect rule, continued the tradition of *shahr āshob* poetry in the wake of natural disaster, but *āshob* poetry in British India, in contrast, increasingly expressed political views and nationalist feelings at the 'decline' of India under colonial rule. At the turn of the century, poems entitled *shahr*, *ʿālam*, *jahāṇ*, *dahr*, or *Islām āshob*s appeared regularly in the press, usually with a strong dimension of complaint. In 1907, for instance, *Zamānah* published a *musaddas* entitled *Shahr āshob* by Surur Jahanabadi.[7] The poem reflected the strong political unrest around the Punjab Land Alienation Act (1900) and the Colonisation Bill (1906) that spread in the region. Following the introduction of the new agrarian reforms in the canal colonies,[8] the *Anjuman-e Muḥibbān-e Waṯan* ('The Society of the Lovers of the Motherland') was created in 1906 by Ajit Singh and others who, with Lala Lajpat Rai, toured the region to protest and unite the population against British oppression (*ẕūlm*).[9] The mobilisation was not communal in nature and rallied with Swadeshi claims of the newly partitioned Bengal, taking an anti-British stance and penetrating the army too. In May 1907, Lala Lajpat Rai, along with Ajit Singh, was accused of fuelling agitation in Rawalpindi and was deported to Burma.[10] While evoking autumnal gardens in the typical 1857 fashion, the *shahr āshob* published in December 1907 complained about the arrests of Lajpat Rai and of the editors of the

6 Tabatabai, *Naẕm-e Ṯabaṯabāʾī*, p. 135.
7 Surur Jahanabadi, '*Shahr āshob*', *Zamānah*, December 1907, pp. 383–90.
8 About the reform and the subsequent unrest, see particularly S. S. Sohal, 'Patterns of Political Mobilization in the Colonial Punjab'; N. G. Barrier, 'Punjab Disturbances of 1907'.
9 N. G. Barrier, 'Punjab Disturbances of 1907', p. 365; S. S. Sohal, 'Patterns of Political Mobilization in the Colonial Punjab', p. 467. See also G. Singh, *Deportation of Lala Lajpat Rai and Sardar Ajit Singh*.
10 Lala Lajpat Rai (LLR) was released in November 1907, a month before the publication of the poem in *Zamānah*. On the deportation of LLR, an American missionary reported 'disaffection between Delhi and Rawalpindi among the

Punjabi paper *Hindustān* and the Bengali *Yugāntar*, mentioned the mobilisation in partitioned Bengal, and criticised the police and Lord Morley for 'Punjab's grief': it was a political poem.

Woh lālahzār, woh phūloṇ kī anjuman hī kahāṇ?
woh k͟hush sunbul-o rehān, woh yāsman hī kahāṇ?
nokīlī kalyoṇ meṇ woh dilrubā phaban hī kahāṇ?
woh kamsinī kī ādā'eṇ, woh bāṇkpan hī kahāṇ?
woh rang-rūp 'urūs-e bahār kā nah rahā
shabāb ḍhal gayā, 'ālam ubhār kā nah rahā
[...] Pūlis kī āh! yeh k͟hufiyah haiṇ sāzisheṇ kaisī
yeh Morley kī haiṇ ham par nawāzisheṇ kaisī!
[...] chaman meṇ gīt inheṇ āzādiyoṇ ke gāne de
waṯan ke phūloṇ peh ṣayyād! chahchahāne de
falak ko in peh nah barq-e sitam girāne de
keh un kī kisht-e tamannā ko lahlahāne de
asīr-e dām-e muḥabbat yeh murġh haiṇ ṣayyād
karam! keh dar k͟hūr-e shafqat yeh murġh haiṇ ṣayyād!

Where is that bed of tulips, that assembly of flowers?
Where are those beautiful hyacinths and sweet basil, where the jasmine?
Where is the ravishing grace in the sharpened buds?
Where are the charms of the tender age, where the elegance?
The complexion of the nuptial spring did not remain
Youth withered, the glory of the world did not last.
[...] Alas, what kind of sentences from the Police!
What good favours for us from Morley!
[...] Let them free to sing songs in the garden!
Let them warble on the flowers of the motherland, Hunter!
Don't let the lightning bolt of oppression fall upon them!
So let their fields of desire bloom!
These birds are prisoners in the snare of love, Hunter,
Be gracious: these birds are suited for love, Hunter!

In 1908, a poem published in the *Sunder Shringar* by Radha Krishna Bhargava also lamented India's ruin that was attributed to their fellow countrymen's 'love for foreign-made articles'.[11] In 1907 and 1909, the *Native Newspapers Reports* show that the genre was also used

educated classes' (Home Political B/N0, 39–117, July 1907, p. 118 in S. S. Sohal, 'Patterns of Political Mobilization in the Colonial Punjab', p. 468.)

[11] *NNRNWP&O* for 1908, p. 258.

to condemn the attitude of the Nawab of Dacca and to criticise the Reform Scheme regarding separate electorates for Muslims.[12] Like those issued in the *Awadh Punch* in the late 1870s to express discontent at government measures, those poems continued to assimilate to secular elegies, so the boundaries between a *shahr āshob* and a *qaumī marṡiyah* are difficult to draw.

The political dimension of secular elegiac poetry was undeniable, especially since grief and grievance went hand in hand. This was of course already implicit in late nineteenth-century poetry, but the connection between grief and lament was emphasised further. Although grief had also been associated with silence in 1857, writers now recommended that the emotion be expressed and grievances voiced. Already before leaving for Europe in 1905, Iqbal beautifully described pain as something that could be luminous, when transformed through complaint, in his *Taṣwīr-e Dard* ('Picture of Sorrow'):

żarā dekh is ko kuchh ho rahā hai honewālā hai
dharā kyā hai bhalā ʿahd-e kuhan kī dāstānoṇ meṇ?
yeh k͟hāmoshī kahāṇ tak? lażżat-e faryād paidā kar
zamīn par tū ho aur terī ṣadā ho āsmānoṇ meṇ.
[...] jalānā dil kā hai goyā sarāpā nūr ho jānā
yeh parwānah jo sozāṇ ho to shamʿ-e anjuman bhī hai.

Pay attention to what is happening and what is going to happen
What good there is in repeating the tales of the old glories?
How long will you remain silent? Create a taste for complaint!
You should be on earth, so your cries be in the heavens![13]
[...] The heart's pathos in a way is to become embodiment of Light
If this moth burns it is also the assembly's candle.[14]

In his *Shikwah* too, recited in 1909 at the *Anjuman-e Ḥimayāt-e Islām*, he opened the poem with the reflection that grief should not be silenced but channelled into lament ('*hamnawā! maiṇ bhī ko'ī gul hūṇ keh k͟hāmosh rahūṇ?*' 'Friend, am I a flower that I must remain silent?'),[15] with the rest of the poem consisting in a complaint to God for his

[12] The *Hind* for 4 April 1907, *NNRNWP&O*, p. 485; the *Hindi Pradip* for December 1909, *NNRNWP&O*, p. 82.
[13] '*Taṣwīr-e Dard*', *The Call of the Marching Bell*, p. 146.
[14] Ibid., p. 148. [15] Iqbal, *Shikwah*, 1st verse.

injustice and 'unfaithfulness' to the Muslim community.[16] In 1913, Iqbal provided God's harsh response to the complaint of 1909 (*Jawāb-e Shikwah*, 'Answer to the Complaint').[17] Although Iqbal emphasised the responsibility of Muslims in their ordeal in a reformist fashion and aimed at turning nostalgia into religious fervour by encouraging Muslims to renew their faith and fight for Islamic unity,[18] most of the popular *āshob/marṡiyah* poetry that accompanied the news of the Italo-Turkish and Balkan wars in the 1912–13 and of the Kanpur mosque incident in summer 1913 was more directly anti-British. Muslims were less frequently described as the idle and negligent actors of their own ruin than as the oppressed martyrs of Western imperialism.

Since the Russo-Turkish war of 1877–1879 pan-Islamic feelings in India had intensified. When news of the victory of Turkey over Greece reached India after the Greco-Turkish war of 1897, for instance, Muslim mosques had been illuminated in celebration and the Turkish fez had become popular. As Nanda indeed noted, 'at the turn of the century, Turkey had come to occupy a place in the minds and hearts of large sections of the Muslim community'.[19] Despite Hali's letter to the editor of the *Paisah Akhbār*, who complained about the excess of poetry in community gatherings in 1904,[20] elegies continued to be a popular way to attract people and funds. Poets supplied community platforms with heartrending verses that galvanised the audience and helped raise funds for Turkish and Indian Muslims.

Among others, Muhammad Iqbal regularly took part in community gatherings and emphasised worldwide Muslim grandeur and decline in the fashion typically developed by Hali, especially after his return from Europe in 1908.[21] Usually, the garden that was mourned

16 Khushwant Singh notes that the use of the term 'unfaithful' for God by Iqbal was vehemently criticised in orthodox milieus. See M. Iqbal, *Shikwa and Jawab-i Shikwa*, p. 25.
17 The poem is said to have sold thousands of copies and the money sent to Constantinople. See Ibid., p. 59.
18 *Jawāb-e Shikwah*, verse 11, trans. M. Iqbal, *Shikwa and Jawab-i Shikwa*, trans. K. Singh, p. 71.
19 B. R. Nanda, *Gandhi: pan-Islamism, Imperialism and Nationalism in India*, p. 107.
20 Letter from Hali to Maulvi Mahbub Alam, editor of the *Paisah Akhbār* in *Makātīb-e Ḥālī*, pp. 49–51; see Chapter 2.
21 His poem *Sicily* ('*Ṣiqliyah*' in *Call of the Marching Bell*, pp. 212–3) was particularly emblematic as he placed himself in the tradition of Muslim city elegies like Sa'di for Baghdad, Dagh Dehlawi (his *ustād*) for Delhi, and Ibn Badrun for Granada. As Mustansir noted, Ibn Badrun was not actually the

was that of Islam. In 1912, Shibli Numani composed a poem entitled *Shahr āshob-e Islām*,[22] which again tied the fall of the Ottoman Empire to the fall of the Muslim community (*millat*) worldwide, while denouncing Western powers as the oppressors. It was recited at the Jama Masjid by Mohamed Ali in July 1913 when Dr Ansari and the Red Crescent Medical Mission returned to Delhi. The *shahr āshob* not only mourned decline but pointed accusingly to the aggressor (*tum*), opposing Indian grief to the state's contentment.

yeh mānā qiṣṣah-e ġham se tumhārā jī bahaltā hai
sunā'eṇ tum ko apne dard-e dil kī dāstāṇ kab tak?
yeh mānā tum ko shikwah hai falak se k͟hushk sālī kā
ham apne k͟hūn se sīncheṇ tumhārī khetiyāṇ kab tak?
[...] samajh kar yeh keh dhundle se nishān-e raftagāṇ haiṇ ham
miṭā'oge hamārā is ṯarah nām-o nishāṇ kab tak?
zawāl-e daulat-e ʿuṡmān zawāl-e sharaʿ-o millat hai
ʿazīzo! fikr-e farzand-o ʿiyāl-o k͟hān-o mān kab tak?

Yes, you are pleased with the tale of woe and sorrow
We should tell you the tale of our sad heart how long?
Yes, your fields are dry and parched as there is no rain
But we should water your fields with our blood how long?
[...] Thinking we are the shadow of our past glory
You will go on erasing our traces how long?
The fall of Ottomans is the fall of Islam
Our concern for kith and kin, hearth and home how long?[23]

The manifestation of grief was accompanied by feelings of sympathy that were uniting the Muslim world as well as recriminations against injustice. In one *musaddas* published in *Al-Hilāl* on 22 January 1913, under the title *Qaṯrāt-e ashk yā shahr āshob-e islām* ('Teardrops, or shahr āshob of Islam'), Niaz Fatehpuri (1884–1966) related the disaster in the Balkans and the impact its description had on Muslims. The poem talked of corpses and bloodied robes, and of how it all only

writer of the lament on Granada (rather, it was composed by Ibn Abdun), but his commentator. See M. Mustansir, *Tulip in the Desert*, p. 141. See also Ch. Pellat, 'Marthiya' p. 606.

22 On Shibli Numani, see J. A. Khan, *Muhammad Shibli Nomani* and M. A. Murad, *Intellectual Modernism of Shibli Nuʿmani.*

23 Shibli Numani, *Kulliyāt-e Shiblī*, p. 65, trans. Khan, *Muhammad Shibli Nomani*, pp. 54–5.

made faith grow firmer in the hearts of believers. The narration of ruin and massacre was preceded by an exhortation to speak up and to find in grief the impulse to rise:

ay merī nuṯq-e zubān! nālah-o afġhāṇ ho jā!
ay merī nok-e qalam! hamsar-e pekāṇ ho jā!
ay merī āh! nikal dil se pareshāṇ ho jā!
quwwat-e ẕabṯ-e fuġhāṇ! jā, kahīṇ pinhāṇ ho jā!
rang-e k̲h̲ūṇ ānkh se ṭapke żarā gahrā ho kar
ashk-e dāman meṇ jo ā'e, to kalejā ho kar.
[...] ay musalmān! hameṇ tujh se hazāroṇ haiṇ gile
sun le 'mumkin hai keh phir ham ko mile yā nah mile'
chaman-e dahr meṇ ġhunche tere naġhmoṇ se khile
tere nāloṇ se jabal kyā falak-o ʿarsh hile
āj hangāmah-e hastī terā k̲h̲āmosh hai kyūṇ?
naġhmah-e ṣuḥbat-e doshīnah farāmosh hai kyūṇ?

O my speech-empowered tongue, lament and bewail!
O tip of my pen, become like an arrowhead
O my sighs, leave the heart and become restless
And power-constraining laments, hide yourselves!
Let the colour of blood that trickles from my eyes deepen,
Let my heart come out on my robe of tears.
[...] O Muslims, I complained to you a hundred times,
Listen, it's possible that we won't remain.
In the garden of the world buds open by your melodies
May you rise to the heavens with your lamentations
Today why do you stay silent in the world's tumult?
Why have you forgotten the melody of last night's assembly?[24]

By constructing a discourse on loss and ruins, and by identifying the colonial state as the agent of devastation, *āshob* poetry became a discourse of anti-colonial mobilisation. As Nandini Gooptu argued, the political poetry of the early twentieth century 'was reminiscent of and resonated with the matam (mourning) and marsiyah (a lament) traditions of Islamic verse, and related to the elegiac hymn and ritual mourning of Mohurram'.[25] It deployed a narrative of loss and religion that sometimes synergised with the daily experiences of the urban poor.[26] Contrary to what Gooptu suggested, however, the development of the political

[24] *Al-Hilāl*, 22 January 1913, pp. 74–5.
[25] N. Gooptu, *The Politics of the Urban Poor*, p. 270. [26] Ibid., p. 271.

marśiyah did not directly build on the Shia elegiac genre but emerged in conjunction with the *shahr āshob* genre that indeed owed much to Shia *marśiyah*s since 1857. That the poems above were branded *shahr āshobs* is telling: poets built on the aesthetics of the *marśiyah* and put special emphasis on Islam, but the association with *āshob* particularly highlights the fact that the denunciation of oppression came together with the experience of loss of power in the colonial world, and the desire to reclaim it. Islam was not exalted as a religious or spiritual category, but as a political one. Although the link with the city, which constituted one of the characteristics of early Urdu *shahr āshob* poetry and still occasionally appeared in the title of the poems, was becoming more tenuous, the genre was still about power (or powerlessness) and grief.

2 Muslim Martyrs: New Karbalas

As we have seen in Chapter 3, historians of the events surrounding the Kanpur mosque incident in summer 1913 have noted contemporary journalists and writers resorting to Karbala imagery. The *Native Newspapers Reports* listed many poems written on the occasion, especially in September 1913, almost everywhere in the North-Western Provinces and Oudh.[27] Numerous pamphlets were published from Lahore to Benares, notably S. Aminuddin's *Barq-e Islām*, Shaikh Rahmatullah's *Thunderbolt of Islam* (Benares, 1913), and Shaikh Mahmud Ali's *Muraqqaʿ-e Ṯarābulus* (Lucknow, 1914).[28] Papers like *Al-Hilāl* frequently described the Kanpur massacre as a great place of martyrdom of buildings and men,[29] whose 'pure souls' had reached 'the presence of God'.[30] Kanpur was a new Karbala, 3 August a new Ashura.[31] Official reports noted the way mournful verses were read during assemblies as a 'strategy' to collect a heap of 'money, turbans, and superfluous articles of clothing'[32]

27 *NNRNWP&O* for 1913, p. 1016.
28 Z. Umer, 'Maulana Shibli Numani', p. 343.
29 '*Mashhad-e Akbar*', *Al-Hilāl*, 6 August 1913, p. 98.
30 '*Eʿānat-e Maẕlūmān-e Kānpūr*', *Al-Hilāl*, 13 August 1913, p. 117.
31 The article, entitled 'Mashhad-e Akbar and the Pitiful Sight of Aderna (Tripoli)', was reproduced in the *Union Gazette* of 21 and 22 August 1913. See *NNRNWP&O* for 1913, p. 896.
32 Home, Political B, November 1912, Proceedings 82–6: weekly reports of the Director of Criminal Intelligence on the political situation for the month of October 1912, report for 30 October.

from the enthusiastic public. Sayyid Raza Ali, for instance, was said to use always the same *modus operandi*:

He prefaced his remarks in each instance by shedding tears, and then burst into lamentations, upon the innocent men slaughtered at Cawnpore for the sake of their religion, but then declared that 'no they are not dead, but they live as martyrs, as example to all others.' [...] The conclusion was an appeal for funds.[33]

An analysis of the popular and soon censured booklet published by Khwajah Hasan Nizami in 1913 – *Kānpūr kī k̲h̲ūnī dāstān* – shows well the insistence on Muslim martyrdom (although Hindus were also amongst the wounded) at the hands of the government of Kanpur.[34] Of course, the description of the dead and injured was full of pathos, with graphic portrayals of violence. However, the blood of martyrs was also described as rejuvenating. As the dead entered the paradise of martyrs, so the bloodshed contained a glimpse of immortality. One poem in Nizami's booklet exemplified the process through which martyrdom was disconnected from grief and magnified. As other poems of the collection illustrated, sacrifice would be remembered and suffering would not be 'unsuccessful' (*nah nāmurād raheṇ*).[35] In *K̲h̲ūn-e Shahīdāṇ* ('The Blood of Martyrs') by an 'English-educated Muslim', martyrdom first brought distress as blood drops turned into a sea and indelibly tinted the sky. Yet, blood soon turned into wine in the cups of poppies, and eventually beautified and nourished the world:

nahīṇ miṭṭā nishān-e k̲h̲ūṇ kabhī dāmān-e qātil se
likhī jātī hai ik taḥrīr-e k̲h̲ūnīṇ k̲h̲ūṇ-e bismil se
usī kā ek qaṯrah bahr ko k̲h̲ūnāb kartā hai
yehī gardish meṇ ākar qalb ko betāb kartā hai
shafaq ban kar falak par roz-o shab maujūd rahtā hai
usī se dāman-e chark̲h̲-e kuhan ālūd rahtā hai
yehī mai ban ke rahtā hai sadā lāle ke pyāle meṇ
usī kā nūr roshan hai andhere meṇ ujāle meṇ
yehī rang-e ḥinā ban kar kisī dast-e sitam meṇ hai

[33] Home, Political, A, October 1913, Proceedings 100–18: extract from a fortnightly demi-official letter, dated 19 Aug 1913, from the Commissioner, Allahabad division, p. 20

[34] Khwajah Hasan Nizami, *Kānpūr kī k̲h̲ūnī dāstān*, p. 1. See also the poems and others reproduced in R. Kumar Parti, *Āshob*.

[35] "*ishq-e bāzoṇ kī sarfaroshī*', in Ibid., p. 3.

yehī gulgonah ban kar rang-e ruk̲h̲sār-e ṣanam meṇ hai
dahān-e zak̲h̲m se bah kar kuchh aisā rang lātā hai
keh sairābī se us kī bāġh-e 'ālam lahlahātā hai
yehī k̲h̲ūṇ sīnchtā hai nak̲h̲l-e barbād-e tamannā ko
usī se zindagī miltī hai qalb-e hā'ī be jāṇ ko
[...] ġhiżā pā kar isī se kisht-e qaumī phūl lātī hai
yehī woh maut hai jis se yeh dunyā jān pātī hai.

Bloodstains cannot be erased off from the murderer's dress
One bloody tale is written with the victims' blood
With one drop, the ocean turns into a sea of blood
In such circumstances, the heart becomes restless
Day and night, twilight colours the firmament
Thus the robe of the old sky is stained
It has become wine in the cups of poppies[36]
Its light remains in the dark and in the day
It has become the colour of henna on the hand of injustice
It has become blush on the cheeks of the beloved
From the wound's opening, it brings such colour
That irrigates and makes the garden of the world bloom
This blood waters the tree of ravaged desire
From it, the dead heart finds life again
[...] Nourishing, it brings flowers to the community field
It is the death from which the world is made alive.[37]

Blood and tears – metaphorically transposed to garden imagery with its powerful evocations of paradise, prosperity, desire and eternity – were exalted as fruitful and triumphal. The turning point of the poem, the transformation of blood into wine in the cups of poppies, symbols of martyrdom by excellence, clearly drew on Sufi symbolism.

Scholars of martyrology like David Cook have emphasised that while martyrdom usually arouses grief in a Shia context, the attitude is different in Sunni and in Sufi traditions, where martyrs are, respectively, exalted as victorious and as the true divine lovers as death concretises their union with God.[38] Martyrdom is the ultimate assertion, the epitome of faith. With the model of the Sufi love martyr al-Hallaj

[36] I translate *lālah* as poppy to emphasise the symbolism of martyrdom that it conveys, notably by its red colour. For a reflection on what *lālah* represents in Indo-Persian culture, see Chapter 1 and I. Mélikoff, 'La fleur de la souffrance'.
[37] '*K̲h̲ūn-e Shahīdāṇ*', in Khwajah Hasan Nizami, *Kānpūr kī k̲h̲ūnī dāstān*, p. 26.
[38] D. Cook, *Martyrdom in Islam*, p. 58.

(858–922), grief and pain have been considered essential elements of divine love in Sufism. Annemarie Schimmel summarised that the longing for death among mystics 'is combined with longing for pain, for the pain of love is in itself the greatest happiness'.[39] Longing and suffering were usually seen through gendered lenses as true masculinity supposedly allowed one to overcome the mystical experience of suffering. This was particularly emphasised by the linguistic association between *mard* 'man' and *dard* 'pain'.[40]

The mystical interpretation of grief as an intrinsically positive amorous longing for perfection, union, and immortality that we have already considered in the Chapter 2 was beautifully exposed in Iqbal's post-1908 poem *Falsafah-e ġham* ('Philosophy of Grief') addressed to his Lahore friend Mian Fazl-i Husain:

ḥādis̤āt-e ġham se hai insān kī fiṯrat ko kamāl
ġhāzah hai ā'īnah-e dil ke lī'e gard-e malāl
ġham jawānī ko jagā detā hai luṯf-e k͟hwāb se
sāz yeh bedār hotā hai isī miẓrāb se
[...] ʿishq kuchh maḥbūb ke marne se mar jātā nahīṇ
rūḥ meṇ ġham ban ke rahtā hai magar jātā nahīṇ
hai baqā-e ʿishq se paidā baqā maḥbūb kī
zindagānī hai ʿadm nā āshnā maḥbūb kī

Incidents of grief give perfection to human nature
The dust of anguish is rouge for the heart's mirror
Youth is awakened from sleep's pleasure by grief
This orchestra wakes up with this plectrum alone.
[...] Love does not die by the beloved's death
It stays in the soul as grief but does not die
Lover's immortality is the beloved's immortality
The beloved's life is unacquainted with mortality.[41]

With death and grief being considered in a Sufi light, so was martyrdom. As Syed Akbar Hyder demonstrated in his excellent study of early twentieth-century Sunni reformist poets, the symbol of Karbala was dislodged from a Shia ritualistic perspective in favour of a transsectarian, ecumenical Sufi reading of Imam Husain's struggle as a sacrifice against oppression and falsehood during the Indian nationalist

[39] A. Schimmel, *As Through a Veil*, p. 70. [40] Ibid., p. 73.
[41] '*Falsafah-e ġham*', *The Call of the Marching Bell*, p. 117.

movement.[42] Karbala was read as a jihad for truth and justice, which resonated particularly strongly from the 1910s.[43] Iqbal also erected Imam Husain as the paradigm of the true believer who emerges from and is entranced in love, thus 'building upon the Sufi hermeneutics of Karbala',[44] an aspect that had already been developed by Rumi, for instance.[45] For Iqbal, Husain's struggle at Karbala encapsulated the action of love *par excellence* within his concepts of *khudī* and communal ego, and constituted a model for contemporary Muslims.[46]

Already in 1913, the Urdu political *marṡiyah* became an important means of communication and mobilisation.[47] It used the language of martyrdom and the assertion of faith as a core element of anti-colonial politics and as a way to transform grief into positive action. The message of Karbala as an example of righteous struggle against injustice went well beyond an exclusive Muslim vision of contemporary events to become a universal symbol of anti-colonial contest, as Syed Akbar Hyder showed. Even Hindu Urdu writers, such as Munshi Premchand, exploited the theme to encourage Hindu–Muslim cooperation.[48] In his 1924 drama, Premchand narrated that a Hindu caravan was passing near Karbala: 'when they learnt that Imam Husain's party was fighting for truth and justice against an oppressive army, they decided to help Imam Husain's side.'[49] Martyrdom continued to be, in the verses of political poets, an instrument of hope and love and Karbala reinterpreted as the paradigm of resilience in adversity, as 'a medium of hope and strength',[50] as a positive symbol of collective self-reassertion.[51]

Justin Jones also showed in his study of *Shahīd-e Insāniyat* ('The Martyr of Humanity', 1942) that Sayyid Ali Naqi Naqvi (1905–1988) sought to emphasise the contemporary relevance of Imam Husain as 'the model of the perfected human Self'.[52] Although Naqvi was apolitical,

[42] S. A. Hyder, *Reliving Karbala*, p. 149.
[43] See also M. Pernau, *Emotions and Modernity*, p. 230.
[44] S. A. Hyder, *Reliving Karbala*, p. 141. [45] Ibid., p. 143.
[46] See, for instance, M. Iqbal, *The Mysteries of Selflessness*, p. 28.
[47] G. Minault, 'Urdu Political Poetry', p. 461.
[48] S. A. Hyder, *Reliving Karbala*, p. 171 ff. See for instance the Hindi and Urdu drama by Munshi Premchand, *Karbalā*, Delhi, 1974 [1924].
[49] Q. Ra'is, *Premchand*, p. 30.
[50] M. Umar, *National Movement in India. The role of Hasrat Mohani*, p. 63.
[51] Quoted by Syed Akbar Hyder, 'Recasting Karbala in the Genre of Urdu Marsiya', p. 149.
[52] J. Jones, 'Shi'ism, Humanity and Revolution in Twentieth-Century India', p. 420.

his work resonated in the context of the Quit India Movement of the 1940s, notably with the founding of the Husain Day Committee which promoted the commemoration of Imam Husain among all creeds. At the time, Husain and Karbala had become inspirational symbols of self-sacrifice for political protest and satyagraha: as Jones and Hyder have remarked, it participated in the defiant effort 'for the replacement of the regime of "Yazidiyat" with that of "Husainiyat", [and] carried an obvious contemporary message that nevertheless remained uncensored by government restrictions'.[53] During the freedom struggle, non-Muslim Congress leaders like Jawaharlal Nehru celebrated the figure of Imam Husain and hoped that Karbala would 'become not a memory of great sorrow but rather a great triumph, the triumph of the human spirit against overwhelming odds'.[54] Grief was turned into triumph. More often than before, convinced sounds of 'our glory can never be erased' resonated in Urdu.[55] If this discourse developed against the colonial state, it also sustained Muslim solidarity starting in the 1910s.

3 Faith and Solidarity: Political Poetry and the Khilafat Movement

While Indian subjects remained on the whole loyal to the British crown during World War I,[56] the defeat of Turkey and the subsequent dismantling of the Ottoman Empire brought distress to Indian Muslims. With the Armistice of Mudros on 30 October 1918, all Ottoman territory passed to Western occupation.[57] Even after the war and the release of the pro-Turkish 'Young Party' Muslim leaders from prison, the political climate remained tense in British India: in February 1919, the Rowlatt committee proposed extending the emergency measures of the Defence of India Act of 1915 that enabled the authorities to

[53] Ibid., p. 428.
[54] Jawaharlal Nehru Papers (NMML), Messages, 9 March 1942, S. 144 (Allahabad).
[55] Poem by Ahmad (Aligarh) n.d., in R. Kumar Parti, *Āshob*, p. 163.
[56] Even leaders like Mohamed Ali and Dr Ansari advocated loyalty for a time, and the Muslim League cancelled its annual session to avoid bringing trouble to the government. See F. Robinson, *Separatism*, p. 239.
[57] See, for instance, P. Helmreich, *From Paris to Sèvres: The Partition of the Ottoman Empire at the Peace Conference*; D. Fromkin, *A Peace to End all Peace: The Fall of the Ottoman Empire.*

arrest and detain individuals suspected of conspiracy without trial during World War I. The Anarchical and Revolutionary Crimes Act – commonly known as the Rowlatt Act from the name of the judge who supervised the advisory committee – roused widespread indignation.

Discontent grew against the British government, and Gandhi, with leaders such as Mohamed Ali, decided to organise mass satyagraha protests (*hartāl*) against the bill that was passed by the Imperial Legislative Council in Delhi on 18 March 1919. Although the strike was planned for 6 April, the success of the propaganda in Delhi was such that it started on 30 March – and ended on 18 April. Hindu merchants, also displeased with taxation reforms, mostly led the *hartāl*, which Ferrell argued was rather characterised by its 'lack of organised activity'.[58] The old city was empty and still; shops were closed. Police were deployed everywhere from the Jama Masjid to Lal Kuan Bazar and from Ajmeri Gate to Sadar Bazar.[59] Soon, however, news that food could still be purchased in the Old Delhi railway station reached the city and people marched towards it to close the stalls. An altercation between satyagrahis and the British stationmaster ensued. The police were called and shots fired. Panic and tension spread to Chandni Chowk, where police opened fire too. All in all, fourteen people were killed.[60]

The satyagraha protest of 1919 in Delhi inspired Mohamed Ali Jauhar to write an *āshob* poem that he provocatively entitled *Fuġhān-e Dehlī* ('The Lament for Delhi'), a title that conjured the memory of Kaukab's famous anthology of 1857 *shahr āshob* poems that I have analysed in Chapter 1. Jauhar's *ġhazal* used precisely the same language and form as most of the *ġhazal*s of the 1863 collection, thus clearly placing itself in the continuity of that tradition: it used the same *zamīn* – 'ān-e Dehlī' to match the title. The message of the six-couplet poem, however, reflected changes in the way *āshob* poetry was used during the non-cooperation and Khilafat movements, which Mohamed Ali, his brother Shaukat, and their *pīr* Maulana Abdul Bari with his Farangi Mahal clique, as well as Abul Kalam Azad and Mahmud ul-Hasan Deobandi, founded a couple of months later in September 1919.[61] While the poem denounced oppression, it

[58] D. Ferrell, 'Delhi 1911–1922', p. 379.
[59] D. Nath, *Dehlī aur Āzādī*, p. 107. [60] Ibid., p. 110.
[61] See G. Minault, *The Khilafat Movement*; G. Minault, 'Khilafat Movement'.

also – more importantly – displayed determination. Mohamed Ali confidently stated after the incident of the 30 March strike:

Kalimah-e ḥaq hai agar wird-e zubān-e Dehlī
miṭ sakegā nah kabhī nām-o nishān-e Dehlī
lab peh ā'e nah kabhī shikwah-e jor-e aġhyār
ho zamāne se alag ṯarz fuġhān-e Dehlī
Allah ul-ḥamd kushādah hai rah-e ṣabr-o ṣalāt
ho ke be-k͟hauf baṛheṇ rāh-e rawān-e Dehlī
sarfaroshī ke lī'e pīr-o jawān haiṇ tayyār
āj raunaq peh hai kis darjah dukān-e Dehlī
sangrezoṇ se zyādah nahīṇ golī chharre
yūṇ rukegā nah kabhī sail-e rawān-e Dehlī
ḥaq ke āte hī hū'ā ka'bah se bāṯil ruk͟hṣat
chand din aur haiṇ Dehlī meṇ butān-e Dehlī

If the declaration of faith is chanted by Delhi
Never can be erased the name and trace of Delhi
Don't let the complaint of the tyranny of strangers reach our lips
Let it be unique the style of the lament of Delhi
Praises to God for great patience and compassion
Fearless they grow the people of Delhi
Young and old are ready for rebellion
Today there are in such commotion the shops of Delhi
Bullets are not more than pebbles
They will never dam the gushing flow of Delhi
As soon as Truth arrived, falsehood departed the Ka'bah
For a few more days in Delhi, there are idols of Delhi.[62]

The emphasis on faith as the resisting force and the conviction that erasure was impossible were fundamentally different from the tone of 1857 *shahr āshobs*. This not only transpired in the *ġhazal* by references to the *kalimah* and prayers, but also in the quotation from Surah al-Isrā' on the departure of falsehood from the Ka'bah (Q17:81) and the comparison with the British as the idols of Delhi. Mohamed Ali's poem displayed the confidence that what does not kill makes stronger: ruin was impossible with the strength of faith.

With the rise of the Khilafat and nationalist movements, Urdu poets continued to build on the collective emotion of grief to express confidence in Islam's cultural force, a rebellious force that gave meaning

[62] Mohamed Ali Jauhar, *Kalām-e Jauhar*, p. 42.

and social cohesion. Although *āshob* poems continued to bemoan worldwide ruin,[63] the solidarity of Indian Muslims at the beginning of the Khilafat movement and since the Kanpur mosque incident in 1913 undoubtedly intensified the feeling that Muslim India was powerful. The foundation of the Khilafat movement not long after the Rowlatt Act agitation, which benefitted from Hindu–Muslim cooperation, aimed at pressing the government and influencing the treaty-making process against the dismembering of the Ottoman Empire, and at demanding the restoration of the ante-bellum status quo, the preservation of the Islamic caliphate, and the protection of the holy places of Islam.[64] One of the main objectives of the Khilafat movement from 1919 to 1924 was to secure a safe haven for Islam and to protect religious sites that were now in the hands of Western powers.

Khilafat leaders stressed the impossibility of distinguishing between temporal and spiritual leadership in Islam.[65] This discourse concurred with the entrance of the ulama in politics, who 'could transcend many of the divisions of Islamic society',[66] and saw an opportunity to present themselves as authorities and representatives of Indian Muslims.[67] Already in the 1910s, several pan-Islamic organisations had been founded in collaboration with the ulama such as the *Anjuman-e Khuddām-e Ka'bah* for the defence of Islamic Holy sites,[68] but the latter really became a 'driving force' after the World War I, as part of the new political style of the non-cooperation movement of the early 1920s.[69] That period (1919–1923) saw what Francis Robinson called the 'marvellous growth of Muslim influence in Indian politics'.[70] Although the

[63] See, for instance, '*Jahāṇ āshob*', *Zamīndār* (Lahore), 17 July 1920.

[64] Speech by Mohamed Ali in *Report of an Interview with the Right Honourable H. A. L. Fisher, on Behalf of the Right Honourable Edwin S. Montagu, Secretary of State for India, at the Board of Education on March 2nd 1920*, p. 17.

[65] Letter from M. Ali to the Viceroy, Chhindwara (CP), 24 April 1919, in Home Department, July 1919, in M. Shan (ed.), *Unpublished Letters of the Ali Brothers*, pp. 156–7. As scholars have shown, not all 'Young Party' Muslims agreed that the caliphate was a primary religious duty, and the main stake of Khilafatist leaders was their own position in India rather than the situation in Turkey. (See, for instance, G. Minault, *The Khilafat Movement*; F. Robinson, *Separatism*, p. 291 ff.)

[66] F. Robinson, *Separatism*, p. 272.

[67] F. Shaikh, *Community and Consensus*, p. 175.

[68] As F. Robinson noted, other organisations, such as the Indo-Ottoman Colonisation Society (1914), also emerged. See F. Robinson, 'The British Empire and Muslim Identity in South Asia', p. 282.

[69] F. Robinson, *Separatism*, p. 342. [70] Ibid.

Khilafat delegation returned to India unsuccessful in 1920, describing Muslims as victims of the 'insatiable ambitions of unscrupulous politicians, ever greedy for an extension of their empires',[71] it came back more passionate than ever. Political *marṡiyahs* continued to depict oppression as leaders toured north India holding multiple local conferences and raising funds,[72] but the optimism that the sacrifice would not be in vain invariably percolated through.

The political and cultural climate of the early 1920s provided a unique occasion for bonding around religion and emphasising collective inner strength and optimism among Urdu-speaking intellectuals and political leaders. Public health and anthropology scholars have often emphasised the role of religion as a 'key driver' for providing community cohesion and for sustaining collective resilience,[73] that is, the ability to adapt and to 'rebound'.[74] The success and popularity of the Kanpur mosque mobilisation and later of the Khilafat movement in unifying Muslim opinion opened new perspectives for the construction of a collective political identity through a renewed emphasis on religion. Political poetry emphasised pan-Islamic sympathy (*hamdardī*): grief was not to be felt alone but shared. It was a basis for community and solidarity. This discourse that fed political activism during the Khilafat movement strove to articulate alternative perspectives to bolster individual and collective selves by turning the grim context of early twentieth-century colonial north India into an empowering environment.

In *Kh̲iẓr-e Rāh*, a poem that was recited at a session of the *Anjuman-e Ḥimayāt-e Islām* in 1921,[75] Iqbal addressed collective grief by

[71] Speech by Maulana Syed Sulaiman Nadvi in *Justice for Islam and Turkey: Speeches*, p. 23.

[72] The government grew wary of those 'nationalist' poems, which they sometimes penalised as seditious under the Press Act. See *NNRNWP&O* for 1918, p. 710 and for 1919, p. 167 ff.

[73] C. G. Burton, 'A Validation of Metrics', pp. 79–81.

[74] See, for instance, G. A. Wilson, 'Community Resilience and Social Memory', p. 227; C. G. Burton, 'A Validation of Metrics for Community Resilience', p. 69; A. Chandra, *Building Community Resilience to Disasters*; B. Dugassa, 'Colonial Trauma, Community Resiliency and Community Health Development'.

[75] A. Hashmi, 'Three Poems of Iqbal: A Psychological Interpretation', p. 113. Iqbal started to actively participate in politics only in 1923 (R. Wasti, 'Dr Muhammad Iqbal from Nationalism to Universalism', p. 40), and, as F. Shaikh remarked, he was more concerned with the power of the Khilafat issue to produce Muslim solidarity than with its preservation as an institution (F. Shaikh, *Community and Consensus*, p. 180).

highlighting the possibility of regeneration.[76] He argued for the pan-organisation of the 'Muslim nations' as a way forward, and sought to mobilise and energise Muslims. In *Ṯulūʿ-e Islām*, recited a year later – probably after Mustafa Kamal Atatürk's victory over Greek armies – Iqbal again turned melancholy into hope by showing that adversity only made Muslims more precious. Decline was turned into an advantage, a challenge through which a new sense of self-awareness could emerge, a trial of life that highlighted the things that truly mattered. The Islamic faith was clearly identified as the way to counter the forces of history.

Musalmān ko musalmān kar diyā ṯūfān-e maġhrib ne
talāṯum hā'e daryā hī se hai gauhar kī sairābī
[...] agar ʿuṡmānyoṇ par koh-e ġham ṭūṭā to kyā ġham hai
keh kḫūn-e ṣad hazār anjum se hotī hai saḥar paidā
[...] ṡabāt-e zindagī īmān-e moḥkam se hai dunyā meṇ
keh almānī se bhī pā'indatar niklā hai tūrānī.

The storm of the West has made the Muslim into a real Muslim
Only the upheavals of the sea bring the pearl's beauty to its perfection
[...] The avalanche of calamity over Uthmanis is not to be bereaved
As the dawn is produced after destruction of myriads of stars!
[...] Stability of life in this world is bestowed by firm faith
The Turanian has proved even longer lasting than the German![77]

Iqbal's poetry addressed the 'Islam in danger' rhetoric by perceiving the Muslim community as 'a stable point' in the flow of history.[78]

As Muhammad Sadiq observed, Iqbal emphasised 'man's unbounded capacity for self-improvement and power',[79] while still holding onto tradition and old values. Like many of the Khilafatist poets, he looked onto the past when envisioning the future. Daniela Bredi has viewed this attitude (especially in *Sicily* and *The Mosque of Cordoba*) as an example of 'restorative nostalgia',[80] a strategy 'in which the resort

76 '*Kḫiẓr-e Rāh*', *The Call of the Marching Bell*, p. 353.
77 '*Ṯulūʿ-e Islām*', *The Call of the Marching Bell*, pp. 360–1.
78 A. Bausani, 'The Concept of Time in the Religious Philosophy of Muhammad Iqbal', p. 167.
79 M. Sadiq, *History of Urdu Literature*, p. 362.
80 D. Bredi, 'Nostalgia 'restauratrice' all'opera: 'Sicilia' e 'La Moschea di Cordova' di Muhammad Iqbal'.

to the past is a means to carve out a space of legitimacy for oneself in the present'.[81] As Svetlana Boym theorised, restorative nostalgia is focused on the *nostos* (literally, 'return'), its prime interest being the restoration of this idealised past (often in opposition to other competing groups).[82] In the case of Iqbal and of Khilafatist poets such as Mohamed Ali Jauhar, it was not only the past and its 'reconstruction' that provided the opportunity for transformation but the emotion itself. As Javed Majeed observed in the case of Iqbal, 'the rehearsal of grief at decline is tied to the creation of future possibilities'.[83] The language of grief and suffering that was popular was used to pass on a different message, a message of hope that promoted a positive vision of Islam, and stressed Muslim solidarity and action, especially because grief was intrinsically linked to love again.

4 Pain, Love, and Immortal Ruins in Iqbal

Iqbal was certainly the Urdu author who most admirably promoted community resilience through the bolstering of collective and individual selves. More than any other writer of the time, he strove to provide new visions of Islam and to counter pessimism by constructing a Muslim collective identity through a re-interpretation of Islamic history and ethics – especially after his return from England, whose 'climate made [him] a Muslim'.[84] Already in 1915, he articulated his new vision in Persian in his *Asrār-e K̲h̲udī* ('Secrets of the Self'), in which he developed a philosophical reinterpretation of Islam in light of his discoveries of Western philosophy and particularly of Bergson's theory of time and duration. Three years later, he complemented his first volume with another philosophical poem in Persian, *Rumūz-e Bek̲h̲udī* ('Mysteries of Selflessness', 1918). While the former defended a theory of the self, the latter focused on the individual in relation to society, exploring the concept of the ideal community and Islamic ethics. Despite the three-year gap, the poems were closely intertwined so that they have sometimes been published as one volume under the title *Asrār-o Rumūz* ('Secrets and Mysteries').[85] In the first part of *Asrār*,

[81] Ibid., p. 320. [82] S. Boym, *The Future of Nostalgia*.
[83] J. Majeed, *Muhammad Iqbal: Islam, Aesthetics and Postcolonialism*, p. 10.
[84] Letter to Wahid Ahmad 'Naqib', quoted in G. H. Zulfiqar, *Iqbāl*, p. 67.
[85] See M. Iqbal, *Maṣnawī-e Asrār-o Rumūz*.

Iqbal paid homage to Rumi as the one who prompted him to write the two books, guiding him out of his fruitless despondency. In the first verses, Iqbal described the apparition that came to him in a dream – a common *topos* in Sufi traditions – thus inscribing his philosophical project in line with Rumi's mystical works and explaining his own intellectual and poetic project as one that would transform and 'put aside the passionate melancholy of old'.[86]

One of the aspects that influenced Iqbal in his articulation of a new Islamic philosophy was his encounter with Henri Bergson, first with his eager reading of Bergson's masterpiece *L'évolution créatrice* (1907) and, later, with their meeting in 1931. Bergson's theory of duration and creative evolution that supported a philosophy of life and movement in contrast with a contemplative philosophy inherited from the Greek tradition deeply impressed the young Iqbal as well as generations of Western scholars.[87] The years following the publication of *L'évolution créatrice* saw the emergence of a 'Bergsonian cult' in Europe, and Bergson's lectures at the Collège de France 'were filled to capacity'.[88] Bergson's vitalism developed against the theory of spatialised time to contest the ascendancy of nature and science on the living that was largely adopted by physics, biology, and the social sciences. He distinguished pure 'duration' from spatialised (or serial) time, not as a succession of independent moments but as a heterogeneous and interpenetrative qualitative multiplicity that forms the very texture of life.[89] This particular essence of life makes it capable of perpetual creation and led Bergson to develop his theory of the *élan vital* as life constantly fighting fixation by evolving in irreducibly new, creative, and unexpected ways.[90]

Iqbal developed his reconstruction of Islamic philosophy by reinterpreting Bergson's theories of time in light of the Qur'an and other European and Islamic thinkers and by articulating them as a theology. In *Asrār* and *Rumūz*, Iqbal both aimed at reconciling Western science and philosophy with the Qur'an – thus conforming to Syed Ahmed Khan's previous endeavours – and sought to counter contemporary

[86] M. Iqbal, *The Secrets of the Self: Asrar-i Khudi*, trans. R. A. Nicholson, p. 10.
[87] N. Hautemanière, 'Mohamed Iqbal, penseur d'un autre Islam'.
[88] L. Lawlor and V. Moulard Leonard, 'Henri Bergson'. [89] See Ibid.
[90] I am particularly grateful to Céline Tignol for explaining and discussing the topic by sharing her research on Bergson with me.

interpretations of Muslim decline by offering a new Islamic praxis. Against fears of seeing the Muslim community disappear in the modern world, Iqbal proposed a reassessment of the significance of time and of the 'forces of history',[91] on the basis of Bergson's fundamental theory of duration and *élan vital*.[92] Like Bergson, Iqbal argued that the serial time of natural sciences is 'utterly inadequate to explain the innermost experiences of our consciousness'[93] and that it is, instead, twofold: one is the (false) time of the material world (what Bergson described as 'spatialised time') and the other, the time of God (Bergson's 'duration'), infinite and ever growing.[94] For Iqbal, man (or rather, what Iqbal calls *k̲h̲udī*, the 'ego', the innermost being)[95] is called upon to participate in this movement of endless creation, because it is, in fact, his true essence. To discover his true personal Self, man thus needs to 'tear his girdle'[96] and realise that he is in fact imprisoned in serial time.[97]

For Iqbal, *k̲h̲udī* is timeless and is urged to take part, with God, in the movement of life; it is, as Souleymane Bachir Diagne framed it, a 'co-worker' of God.[98] But, while writing in a mystical way and interpreting Bergson's theories in a religious manner – for Iqbal, for instance, creative evolution necessarily takes place in God; otherwise, it would end in pure chaos[99] – Iqbal argued against the Sufi concept of *fanā'* (annihilation of the Self in God).[100] On the contrary, Iqbal saw the ideal of *k̲h̲udī* not in self-negation, but in self-affirmation. It is through becoming more and more individual that *k̲h̲udī* fortifies itself and takes part in the forward assimilative movement (*'ishq*) that is life.[101] According to Iqbal, in participating in God's evolving creation, man becomes Perfect (*mard-e momin*, *mard-e k̲h̲udā* 'Man of God'). He evolves in divine presence and transcends serial time: he overcomes

91 J. Majeed, *Muhammad Iqbal: Islam, Aesthetics and Postcolonialism*, p. 35.
92 For more on the use of Bergson by Iqbal see, for instance, D. Howard, *Being Human in Islam*.
93 A. Bausani, 'The Concept of Time', p. 160.
94 See A. Schimmel, *The Secrets of Creative Love*, p. 30.
95 Rumi also used the term in the same way; see M. Iqbal, *The Reconstruction*, p. 15; A. Schimmel, *The Secrets of Creative Love*, p. 23.
96 Ibid., p. 31. 97 M. Iqbal, *The Secrets of the Self*, pp.137–8.
98 See S. B. Diagne, 'Bergson in the Colony', pp. 125–45.
99 A. Bausani, 'The Concept of Time' p. 161.
100 See, for instance, J. Majeed, *Muhammad Iqbal*, p. 20.
101 See, for instance, M. Iqbal, *The Secrets of the Self*, p. 23.

death and becomes immortal.[102] For such a man, death is not an end but a new beginning, a new life.[103]

Iqbal thus offered a creative solution to the problem of death: it can be overcome, as immortality can be achieved within the self. By re-interpreting Islamic philosophy with Western metaphysics and the Qur'an, Iqbal opposed the Western view of Islam as 'a fatalistic doctrine of predestination'[104] and interpreted time as a '*genuinely creative* movement and *not* a movement whose path is already determined'.[105] As Iqbal argued in *Asrār*, the key for attaining the status of Perfect Man and for reaching immortality was to fortify the *k͟hudī* through assimilative love (i.e. action) and adherence to the concept of the unity of God (*tauḥīd*). He strongly criticised 'pessimistic mysticism'[106] and inaction that would weaken the self.[107]

Three years later, in *Rumūz-i Bek͟hudī*, Iqbal focused on the relationship between individuals and the Muslim community. He argued that while the self is individual by nature, 'only in society he finds security and preservation', as individuals are linked to each other 'like jewels threaded on a single cord'.[108] Contrary to his previous focus on the individual self, in *Rumūz*, Iqbal advocated that individuals could strengthen themselves only by creating an ideal community,

[102] For more on Iqbal's theories on immortality, see M. Iqbal, 'The Human Ego: His Freedom and Immortality' in *The Reconstruction of Religious Thought in Islam*, pp. 90–117.

[103] '*Jāwednāmah*', quoted by A. Bausani, 'The Concept of Time', p. 176.

[104] S. B. Diagne, 'Bergson in the Colony', p. 141.

[105] M. Iqbal, *Lectures*, p. 196, quoted by A. Bausani, 'The Concept of Time', p. 165.

[106] Quoted by A. Schimmel, *The Secrets of Creative Love*, p. 16.

[107] M. Iqbal, *The Secrets of the Self*, p. 39. Most of the criticism of Iqbal's thought came from Sufis. Writers like Khwajah Hasan Nizami, Pirzadah Muzaffar Ahmad (who wrote *Rāz-e Bek͟hudī* in 1918), and Maulvi Hakim Fizaruddin Tughrai (who wrote *Lisān ul-ġhaib*) strongly reacted to Iqbal's *Asrār*, sometimes representing Iqbal as an enemy of Islam (A. Schimmel, *Gabriel's Wing*, p. 389; Vahid, 'Iqbal and His Critics', p. 8). Iqbal argued that he was not opposed to Sufism in general but to the decadence of mystic leaders who supported ascetic inaction. In a letter to Hafiz Muhammad Islam Jairajpuri, he said that Pirzada Muzaffar Ahmad 'did not understand my real intent at all. If *taṣawwuf* means sincerity of action (and this is what it meant in the earlier centuries of Islam), then no Muslim should object to it' (*Iqbālnāmah*, vol. 1, Shaikh Ataullah, pp. 53–4, quoted by A. Ali Engineer, 'A Critical Appraisal of Iqbal's Reconstruction of Religious Thought in Islam"', pp. 122–3).

[108] M. Iqbal, *The Mysteries of Selflessness*, p. 8.

thereby learning the true meaning of love, within a communal tradition. Only in this context could the Muslim 'develop and hone his or her selfhood'.[109] Iqbal reasserted the importance of following and preserving tradition and Islamic values as a way to bolster community resilience. He called on his co-religionists to 'fix in firm bond today with yesterday' and tomorrow, life being 'a wave of consciousness of continuity'.[110] The values and ideals that Iqbal advocated in *Rumūz* crystallised in well-defined institutions: the *sharīʿah*, Mecca as the centre of the Muslim community, the five ritual prayers, and so on – in other words, historical, concrete, and fixed institutions. For Alessandro Bausani, this was 'a central contradiction in Iqbal's thought.'[111] In fact, if the emphasis on the community's religious history and traditions may have represented a pitfall of Iqbal's philosophico-religious system, it was not in contradiction with his project of self-reconstruction. Underlining the unity, continuity, and community of Islamic practices helped rebound the community around religion. As Reynold Nicholson said in the preface to his English translation of *Asrār-e K̲h̲udī* in 1920, Iqbal's work indeed immediately caught the attention of young Muslims, and many saw him as 'a Messiah [who] stirred the dead with life'.[112]

The ideas developed in Persian in *Asrār-o Rumūz* were later expressed in Urdu poetry in Iqbal's famous *Mosque of Cordoba*, written after his return from Europe, a decade after the failure of the Khilafat movement.[113] On 3 March 1924, the institution of the Khilafat was definitely abolished by Turkey's Grand National Assembly. The news was received in the Muslim world and particularly in India, where the mobilisation had been considerable, with shock and disappointment. In a speech at Aligarh on 8 March 1924, Mohamed Ali condemned the action of the Turks who had acted 'irreligiously' and alluded to a

[109] J. Majeed, 'Muhammad Iqbal: Rumuz-e Bekhudi', litencyc.com/php/sworks.php?rec=true&UID=30671 (accessed 11 May 2021). See also J. Majeed, 'Muhammad Iqbal: Islam, Aesthetics and Postcolonialism', pp. 35–47.

[110] M. Iqbal, *The Mysteries*, p. 62.

[111] A. Bausani, 'The Concept of Time', p. 168. On the question of *ijtihād*, see also A. and A. Abdul Rahim, 'A Study on Muhammad Iqbal's Framework of *Ijtihad*', pp. 5–13.

[112] See Iqbal, *The Secrets of the Self*, introduction by R. A. Nicholson, p. xxx and xxxi.

[113] He also explained his theories in the *Six Lectures on the Reconstruction of Religious Thought in Islam*, published in Lahore in 1930.

proposition from Hindu friends to provide an asylum for the Khilafat in India.[114] The post-Khilafat period indeed showed frail attempts to restore the caliphate, but all proved unsuccessful.[115] Despite the failure of the Khilafat movement and financial difficulties, the Khilafat Committee was still holding conferences as late as 1928. With the collapse of the movement, Hindu–Muslim cooperation also fell apart, especially in the Punjab, where 'the Arya Samaj activists and their Muslim counterparts who had orchestrated the *khilafat* and non-cooperation agitation [...] had by 1923 turned to *shuddhi-sangathan* and *tabligh-tanzim* respectively'.[116] Muhammad Iqbal, who entered the Punjab Legislative Council in November 1926 and grasped the deadlock of communal harmony, argued that the caliphate did not need to be embodied in one person only but that 'according to the spirit of Islam the caliphate or imamate can be vested in a body of persons, or an elected assembly'.[117] The abolition of the Khilafat undoubtedly put the future of Muslims into question, an issue that Iqbal increasingly addressed in the 1930s: since the consolidation of Muslim Selves relied on the free exercise of their faith, a safe haven for Islam had to be found, in or outside India.[118]

On his way back from the Round Table Conferences in London, Iqbal stopped in Madrid, where he had been invited by the orientalist Miguel Palacios.[119] He took the opportunity to visit the mosque of Cordoba and was even exceptionally permitted to give *namāz*, a unique moment that was captured on camera.[120] Out of this experience, Iqbal

[114] Quoted in *Civil and Military Gazette*, Lahore, 11 March 1924, in K. K. Aziz (ed.), *The Indian Khilafat Movement*, p. 289.

[115] A. Schimmel, *Gabriel's Wing*, p. 240.

[116] A. Jalal, *Self and Sovereignty*, p. 257. Jalal noted that the Hindu–Muslim entente had always been more difficult in the Punjab due to the 'hopelessly narrow-minded' leaders in Lahore. See A. Jalal, *Self and Sovereignty*, p. 254 ff.

[117] M. Iqbal, *Six Lectures*, ed. 1958, p. 157 quoted in A. Schimmel, *Gabriel's Wing*, p. 240.

[118] For more on the Pakistan movement, see, for instance, F. Shaikh, *Making Sense of Pakistan*; A. Jalal, *Self and Sovereignty*; Iqbal, *Presidential Address by Dr. Sir Muhammad Iqbal, Barrister-at-Law, Lahore*, All India Muslim League, Allahabad Session, December 1930.

[119] R. Latif, 'Divergent Trajectories of "Masjid-e Qurtuba"', p. 124.

[120] To this day, Spanish Muslims continue to lobby the Roman Catholic Church to allow them to pray inside the building, a request that has always been refused. See, for instance, theguardian.com/world/2004/apr/19/spain (accessed 18 May 2016).

composed one of his most famous poems in Urdu – *Masjid-e Qurṯubah* ('The Mosque of Cordoba', 1933) – which was published two years later in the collection *Bāl-e Jabrīl* ('Gabriel's Wing'). The poem, which described the mosque of Cordoba as the finest embodiment of love, encapsulated both his philosophy and his vision of Muslim cultural renaissance.[121] The mosque personified Iqbal's concept of the *mard-e k͟hudā*, who transformed death into immortality. Since the mosque was turned into a church after the Reconquista, the building also concretely embodied the permanence and timelessness of the Muslim spirit that stands against the assaults of Western colonialism, a particularly strong image in the aftermath of the Khilafat failure.

The poem first opened with a reflection on the impermanence of time and the certainty of death. This recalled Hali's *Musaddas* that began with a similar observation. In the first part of the poem, Iqbal thus positioned himself within a tradition of mourning that he then broke with the description of his concept of love, which holds, indelible and eternal, outside of history. It is from this timeless love that the mosque of Cordoba emerges:

Tund-o subuk sair hai garcheh zamāne kī rau
ʿishq k͟hud ik sail hai sail ko letā hai thām
ʿishq kī taqwīm meṇ ʿaṣr-e rawāṇ ke siwā
aur zamāne bhī haiṇ jin kā nahīṇ koʾī nām
[...] ay ḥaram-e Qurṯubah! ʿishq se terā wajūd
ʿishq sarāpā dawām, jis meṇ nahīṇ raft-o būd

Fast and free flows the tide of time,
But Love itself is a tide that stems all tides.
In the chronicle of Love there are times other than the past, the present and the future;
Times for which no names have yet been coined.
[...] To Love, you owe your being, O, Holy Place of Cordoba,
To Love, that is eternal; Never waning, never fading.[122]

The poem exalts the monument in the manner of a *qaṣīdah* and belongs, according to Yaseen Noorani, to the poetic genre of *waṣf* (descriptive verse).[123] The mosque is indeed at the centre of the poem,

[121] See B. D. Metcalf, 'Reflections on Iqbal's Mosque', pp. 165–70.
[122] '*Masjid-e Qurṯubah*', in M. Iqbal, *Gabriel's Wing*, pp. 277–8. I substituted 'Harem' for 'Holy Place' in the translation.
[123] See Y. Noorani, 'The Lost Garden of Al-Andalus', pp. 237–54.

but is only incidentally described. References to the edifice, its columns and foundations, only act as the 'material conduit for avowing the creative surge of the generic figure of Iqbal's masculine *mard-e k͟hudā*, the exemplary Man of God whose dynamic love, drawn from the kernel of majestic Islamic conduct, has made this expression possible'.[124]

> *tujh se hu'ā āshkār bandah-e momin kā rāz*
> *us ke dinoṇ kī tapish, us kī shaboṇ kā gudāz*
> *[...] hāth hai Allah kā bandah-e momin kā hāth*
> *ġhālib-o kār-āfrīṇ, kār-kushā, kārsāz*
>
> Your edifice unravels the mystery of the faithful;
> The fire of his fervent days, the bliss of his tender nights.
> [...] The might of the man of faith is the might of the Almighty:
> Dominant, creative, resourceful, consummate.[125]

This gendered reading was inherited both from Nietzsche's concept of the *Übermensch* (Super-Man) reinterpreted in a religious light,[126] and from Sufi traditions, which emphasised that only strong men were able to cope with the suffering of divine love.[127] As Markus Daechsel emphasised, the popularisation of this concept fed the ideologies of 'hyper-masculine activism' of political self-expression like the Khaksar movement led by Allama Mashriqi in the 1930s, although it deviated from Iqbal's vision and intention.[128] In *The Mosque of Cordoba*, Iqbal showed that the true Muslim (virtually any man) – terrestrial with a celestial aspect – can reach immortality through faith; that he 'is destined to last as his *azan* holds the key to the mysteries of the perennial message of Abraham and Moses'.[129]

Although Noorani argued that the emphasis on the individual self in the poem aimed at envisioning 'a utopian political order',[130] it undoubtedly also reflected the growing contemporary emphasis on self-realisation. Javed Majeed, for instance, highlighted the importance that the concept of self assumed in the first half of the twentieth

[124] R. Latif, 'Divergent Trajectories of 'Masjid-e Qurtuba', pp. 124–5.
[125] M. Iqbal, '*Masjid-e Qurṯubah*', in *Gabriel's Wing*, p. 278.
[126] See A. Schimmel, *The Secrets of Creative Love*, p. 26. There were influences from Nietzsche even in Bergson.
[127] A. Schimmel, *Through the Veil*, p. 73.
[128] M. Daechsel, *The Politics of Self-expression*, pp. 116–7.
[129] Ibid. [130] Y. Noorani, 'The Lost Garden of Al-Andalus', p. 238.

century in the work of Gandhi, Jawaharlal Nehru, and Iqbal as a way to articulate alternative visions of the nation and resist the objectifying colonial gaze.[131] Francis Robinson has, on the other hand, suggested that this development likely stemmed from the major shift from 'other-worldly' to 'this-worldly' Islam from the nineteenth century, which encouraged Muslims to 'take action for Islam on earth' and 'set in motion processes that might underpin the development of more individualistic Muslim self'.[132] The insistence on self-assertion certainly also reflected transformations taking place in the political sphere when a new sense of confidence grew among Indian political leaders after the end of the war as they sought further devolution of power and, increasingly, self-government.[133]

As we have seen in Chapter 3, *The Comrade* had already expressed doubts in 1911 about the idea of representing Muslims vis-à-vis their so-called political importance and rather displayed the desire for self-fulfilment. Discouraging a sole reliance on the achievements of their ancestors, a rhetoric that had been extensively used by 'Old Party' leaders,[134] the paper instead extolled attitudes of self-help.[135] In 1919, after the defeat of Turkey and during the satyagraha agitation, Sahibzadah Abdul Wahid Khan expressed the same idea:

> Believe me, the time has come when the deeds of our fathers and forefathers have lost their value. Now the only question is—what qualifications do *you* possess? Yesterday we could very well say 'oh! we are nothing but look at the great Muhammadan Empire in Asia!!!' That is nothing but vanity, and in my humble opinion that idea worked mischief more than good, for until a man relies upon the strength of his own shoulder-blade he cannot acquire experience of any value, nor can he attain much success.[136]

[131] J. Majeed, *Autobiography, Travel and Postnational Identity*.
[132] F. Robinson, 'The British Empire and Muslim Identity', p. 287.
[133] During the war, UP 'Young Party' leaders of the Muslim League worked together with the Congress to reach agreements in the hope of progressive self-rule and negotiated the Nehru Pact in 1916, conceding separate representation. F. Robinson, *Separatism*, p. 250 ff. The Pact nonetheless attracted local opposition.
[134] See F. Robinson, 'Memory of Power'.
[135] *The Comrade*, 18 February 1911, vol. 1, 6, p. 103.
[136] Home, Political A, June 1919, Proceedings 362–76: 'Question of the Effect upon Muhammadan Opinion in This Country of the Forthcoming Announcement of the Terms of Peace in Relation to Turkey'; speech of Sahibzada Abdul Wahid Khan, p. 17.

As Margrit Pernau argued, what she calls 'a perception of temporalities' impacted political mobilisation in the first half of the twentieth century, when the future was indeed seen as something that people could shape with their own hands.[137] *The Mosque of Cordoba* was emblematic not only because it expressed Iqbal's thought comprehensively but also because it exemplified the attempt to re-write the poetry of ruins in Urdu. In his verses, the defeated monument, Cordoba's church-converted mosque, was no longer a warning sign (*ʿibrat*) of God's (or of Time's) egotistic whims but an enduring symbol of God's love on earth. Time was no longer unbeatable, Islam no longer in danger of annihilation.

5 Conclusion

Iqbal, and Khilafatist poets, sought to provide Muslims with a positive vision of Islam and of its future, in a context that was otherwise characterised by struggle. Doing so, they transformed the poetry of lament into a revolutionary poetry of resilience. Grief was to be shared and to provide a basis for collective action, a power against the state and for the cohesion of an Indian Muslim community.

Of course, not everyone welcomed Iqbal's message nor interpreted it in the same ways. Many of his contemporaries and successors understood his thoughts in diametrically opposite directions,[138] partly because he sometimes contradicted himself, partly because he did not always clearly articulate his thoughts. As Wilfred Cantwell Smith also illustrated, maybe Iqbal 'was less devoted to enunciating what one ought to do, than to lashing one into doing it with all one's might'.[139] What Iqbal envisioned was Muslim regeneration through faith, action, and love, in which community bonds would naturally act as a cure. He did not establish rules of behaviour through which one could concretely become the Perfect Man that he dreamt of. This was all left to interpretation (*ijtihād*). Yet, Iqbal's positive poetry influenced many of his contemporaries. In 1911, when Mohamed Ali Jauhar published an appraisal of Iqbal's poetry, and especially of his *Tarānah-e Millī*, which was applauded in many Muslim circles, he said that as Hali had

[137] M. Pernau 'Riots, Masculinities, and the Desire for Passion', p. 251.
[138] A. Schimmel, *Gabriel's Wing*, p. 378.
[139] W. C. Smith, *Islam in Modern History*, p. 122.

been acclaimed as 'the poet of our *mazi* [past]', Iqbal had become 'the singer of our *Istiqbal* [future]':[140] 'the poet has felt the pathos of the fallen race', he continued, 'but his message, how joyous, how full of faith and celestial fire!'[141]

Iqbal's poetry resonated deeply in the political climate of early twentieth-century British India. While *āshob* poetry continued to be written on local or global developments, with deep political implications thanks to its dimension of complaint, from the Kanpur mosque incident, Sufi interpretations of sadness and martyrdom turned Karbala into a triumphal symbol of collective struggle against Western oppression. In that context, poets strove to highlight that death was not an end but a new beginning which could, by strengthening their individual and collective selves, open a world of possibilities. Decline was interpreted as a necessary stage to construct something new. Ruins could act as new foundations. As Iqbal strikingly said in *K̲h̲iẓr-e Rāh* (1921),

guft Rūmī 'har banā-e kuhnah k'ābādāṇ kunand'
mī nadānī 'awwal āṇ bunyād-rā wīrāṇ kunand'

Rumi said that every old building that is to be rebuilt
Did you not know that the building is first demolished?[142]

Indian Muslim leaders, who mobilised around the Kanpur mosque or Khilafat issues, put religion at the centre of their communal reconstruction at the same time as they encouraged Hindu–Muslim cooperation. In 1909, Iqbal recited *Shikwah* ('The Complaint'), which was certainly inspired by Hali's *Shikwah-e Hind*, and continued the tradition of the *qaumī marṡiyah*.[143] The poem was, however, strongly criticised by Hindus who disliked its communal tone – the melody of the poem also drew much from Arabic and Persian vocabulary.[144]

140 *The Comrade*, 4 November 1911, vol. 2, 19, p. 380. 141 Ibid.
142 '*K̲h̲iẓr-e Rāh*', in *The Call of the Marching Bell*, p. 353. I modified the translation of the second line to better reflect the past negative tense of *mī nadānī*. I am grateful to Hamid Moein for reading the Persian with me.
143 Iqbal's *Shikwah* not only had the same subject matter (and title) as Hali's *Shikwah-e Hind*, but was also set in the same metre. See also D. J. Matthews, 'Iqbal and His Urdu Poetry', p. 105 and A. Ahmad, 'Muhammad Iqbal', p. 25.
144 See, for instance, G. C. Narang, 'The Sound Structure of Iqbal's Urdu Poetry', pp. 202–206. About the overall formal aspect of Iqbal's poetry see M. Sadiq, *A History of Urdu Literature*, pp. 372–88.

The poem came as a 'big disappointment to his Hindu admirers',[145] who had previously praised his nationalist poems *Tarānah-e Hindī* and *Nayā Shivālā*. Hindu Urdu authors such as Kashmiri Pandit Chamupati Rai and Pandit Anand Narain Mulla (1901–1997) even wrote counter-poems in which Iqbal's communal sentiments were openly reproved.[146] In 1929, twenty years after the poem was first recited and a few years after the fall of pan-Islamic dreams, Anand Narain Mulla complained:

Jis ko īmān kahtā hai tū, pardah hai tirī nādānī kā
Allah tirā kyā hai? ik nām faqat̲ jahl-e-insānī kā
apnī ruswā'ī kā bā'iṡ, ta'līm yeh 'maiṇ' aur 'tū' kī hai
insāṇ kī taraqqī kī dushman tafrīq yeh rang-o bū kī hai
merā bas ho to har masjid se rū-e zamīṇ ko pāk karūṇ
har mandir ko mismār karūn, har ek kalīsā k̲h̲āk karūṇ

What you call your faith is the veil of your innocence
What is your Allah? It is merely the name of man's foolishness.
The cause of your disgrace is the teaching of 'you' and 'me'
The enemy to humanity's progress is the colour and scent of differentiation
If it were in my power, I would clear off the earth of mosques,
I would demolish every temple, destroy every church.[147]

Āshob poetry, which remained popular among Hindu and Muslim Urdu-speaking elites alike, possessed the particularity of being able to complain about perceived ruin and satirise contemporary politics. *Āshob*s were written on capitalism and budget cuts, on poverty, on the India Act of 1935, and so on.[148] In 1922, for instance, Kaifi composed an *'alam āshob* and explained that what induced him to write the poem was the presentation of the decreased Budget of the Governement of India to the Council of State and Legislative Assembly in Delhi on

[145] K. N. Sud, *Iqbal and His Poems (A Reappraisal)*, p. 19.
[146] See, for instance, Pandit Chamupati Rai's *Gang Tarang*: 'His [Iqbal's] parched lips burn at the sight of a stream, and to quench his thirst he repairs to the sands of Arabia!' quoted by K. N. Sud, *Iqbal and His Poems*, p. 19.
[147] Pandit Anand Narain Mulla, '*Shikwah az Iqbāl*', in *Zamānah*, February 1929, pp. 118–9.
[148] For partial repertoires of twentieth-century *āshobs*, see S. M. H. Rizwi, '*shahr āshob*', *Nuqoosh* 102, 1965, pp. 5–45; A. Arifi, *Shahr āshob: ek tajziyah*, p. 255 ff.; R. Kumar Parti, *Āshob*.

1 March 1922, with the imposition of new taxes.[149] Safi Lakhnawi (1862–1950) and Umr Ansari are also known to have written *dahr āshobs* in 1928 and 1937, respectively.[150] *Shi'r āshobs* ('the ruin of poetry'), such as the *musaddas* by Zarif Lakhnawi (1870–1937) in 1934, lamented the state of Urdu poetry with sarcasm.[151] Throughout the first half of the twentieth century, *āshob* poetry continued to be meaningful, as it was constantly re-adapted by Urdu poets who mourned decline, denounced oppression, and strove to construct a hopeful future.

[149] A. Arifi, *Shahr āshob*, p. 256.

[150] S. M. H. Rizwi, '*shahr āshob*', p. 259 ff. Umr Ansari's *dahr āshob musaddas* on the India Act of 1935 was published in the *Akhbār-e Taraqqī Lakhna'ū* on 1 July 1937.

[151] See Zarif Lakhnawi, *Intikhāb-e Kalām-e Zarīf*, ed. 2004, Lucknow, p. 51.

5 Nostalgia in Delhi

Local Memory and Identity, c. 1910–1940

> Besides, a new Delhi would mean new people, new ways, and a new world altogether. That may be nothing strange for the newcomers: for the old residents it would mean an intrusion. As it is, strange people had started coming into the city, people from other provinces of India, especially the Punjab. They brought with them new customs and new ways. The old culture, which had been preserved within the walls of the ancient town, was in danger of annihilation. Her language, on which Delhi had prided herself, would become adulterated and impure, and would lose its beauty and uniqueness of idiom. She would become the city of the dead.[1]

The construction of New Delhi prompted not only the rise of political discourse and mobilisations around the fate of Delhi monuments in Mohamed Ali's press but also the blooming of local narratives about the Mughal city. In this chapter, I analyse some of the city memoirs that appeared from the beginning of the twentieth century, and more frequently from the 1930s, particularly Hakim Khwajah Nasir Naziruddin Firaq Dehlawi's *A Glimpse of the Red Fort* (c. 1900), Rashid ul Khairi's *Delhi's Last Spring* (1911 to 1937), Mirza Farhatullah Beg's *The Last musha'irah of Delhi* (1928) and *Bahadur Shah and the Festival of Flower-sellers* (1932), Sayyid Wazir Hasan Dehlawi's *The Last Sight of Delhi* (1932), and Arsh Taimuri's *Glimpses of the Exalted Fort* (1937).

In the fast-changing landscape of imperial Delhi, local writers expressed their experience of loss, and the disruption to their place of attachment through nostalgia. They looked back fondly at the sophistication and liveliness of the pre-colonial city, of its language and of its people. Rather than focusing on the built environment, they recalled the 'interactional past' of the urban landscape. Partly inspired by the

[1] A. Ali, *Twilight in Delhi*, p. 144.

late nineteenth-century book *Bazm-e āk͟hir* ('The Last Gathering', 1885) by Munshi Faizuddin, those new compositions adopted some of the stylistic devices of storytelling traditions to construct collective memory through multi-sensory stimulation. Nostalgia enabled them to maintain continuity with their former collective selves by recalling (idealised) qualities that made their present less daunting.[2] In those memoirs, sorrow only served to 'heighten the quality of recaptured joy or contentment'.[3]

The memory of Delhi's Mughal culture particularly crystallised around elements that resisted colonial and reformist critiques. The local authors revalorised aspects that were condemned by colonial officers and by late nineteenth-century Muslim reformers: local dialects, courtesans and performers, and the Mughal king Bahadur Shah Zafar. While dreaming of imaginary spaces where the figure of Bahadur Shah impersonated the lost *bazm* (feasting) of Delhi's life and acted as the organising force behind cultural production and Hindu–Muslim harmony, they articulated critiques about the present. Their fantasies of communal harmony, however, disclosed ideals of perfect governance, which reflected their construction of a collective Muslim identity at a time when communal violence was growing in the city.

1 Displacement and Loss in Early Twentieth-century Delhi

The announcement of the transfer of the colonial capital to Delhi, which had for a time galvanised Urdu-speaking elites longing to see Delhi regain some of its imperial glory, had soon turned sour. As we have seen in Chapter 3, the construction of New Delhi threatened to wash away memories of a Mughal past. The reconfiguration and modernisation of the city landscape and the arrival of new populations further accentuated the loss of local writers who longed for the pre-1857 city and wrote their memories of better times. On one hand, the local population was often displaced to make way for the new roads and buildings, disrupting previous places of social interactions. As Major Beadon explained in September 1912, there was no need to stop local fairs, since 'the petty ones will cease automatically with the removal of the populace and the

[2] F. Davis, *Yearning for Yesterday*, p. 36. [3] Ibid., p. 13.

demolition of the institutions'.[4] This took place at the same time as the last generation of Mughal aristocracy who had experienced life at the court was disappearing by the day, and their descendants fell into deep poverty.[5] On the other hand, the influx of people into Delhi that had started in the 1890s continued.[6] It led to an immediate rise in the cost of living and difficulties in securing accommodation.[7] The construction of the new capital quickly resulted in increased congestion in the old city, which gradually deteriorated into a slum.[8]

It is noteworthy that Delhi memoirs mainly originated from local Delhi writers. At the same time as *qaṣbah* (small town) authors were expressing longing for their locality,[9] Delhi-born writers expressed similar feelings for their city. Khwajah Nasir Naziruddin Firaq Dehlawi (1865–1933), Rashid ul Khairi (1868–1937), Farhatullah Beg Dehlawi (1883–1947), Sayyid Wazir Hasan Dehlawi, and Arsh Taimuri (b. 1921) all descended from families that had been associated with the Mughal court for generations, and most of them were related in one way or another to the famous Delhiite family of Deputy Nazir Ahmed.[10] Arsh Taimuri was directly related to Bahadur Shah Zafar.[11] They all came from a similar, influential, and close-knit milieu.[12] Further, they claimed

[4] Demi-official letter from Major H.C. Beadon, Home, Delhi, September 1912, Deposit 9, p. 1.

[5] D. Ferrell, 'Delhi, 1911–1922', pp. 128–9.

[6] N. Gupta, *Delhi between Two Empires*, p. 157. [7] Ibid., p. 195.

[8] R. Priya, 'Town Planning, Public Health and Delhi's Urban Poor', p. 226.

[9] See R. Rahman, 'Qasbas as Place'.

[10] While Sayyid Wazir Hasan Dehlawi was one of his grandsons (R. Safvi (ed.), *City of my heart*, p. 3), Rashid ul Khairi was his nephew (N. Akhtar, *Monogrāf*, p. 10–13), Farhatullah Beg his pupil (see Farhatullah Beg, *Dr Naẕīr Aḥmad kī kahānī kuchh merī aur kuchh unkī zubānī*), and Firaq Dehlawi a close friend to both Nazir Ahmed and Sayyid Ahmed Dehlawi, author of *Rusūm-e Dehlī* (See Firaq Dehlawi, *Chār Chānd*, preface by Shahid Ahmed Dehlawi, p. 3).

[11] Arsh Taimuri's grandfather was Mirza Shah Rukh Beg, one of Bahadur Shah Zafar's sons who died in 1847. Arsh Taimuri, *Qila'h-e Mu'allah kī jhalkiyāṇ*, p. 10.

[12] The authors of those city memoirs belonged to a same publishing network. Khairi published in *Tamaddun*, *'Iṣmat* (Rashid ul Khairi's own magazines), *Niẕām ul-Mashā'ikh* (edited by Khwajah Hasan Nizami), or *Banāt* (edited by Khairi's son Raziq). Beg's *Bahadur Shah and the festival of flower-sellers* (1932) was first published in the 'Zafar Number' of Niaz Fatehpuri's magazine *Nigār* along with Wazir Hasan's *The last sight of Delhi* (See preface by Shahid Hasan, in Hasan, *Dillī kā ākhrī dīdār*, p. 32). Firaq's work first appeared in Shahid Ahmad Dehlawi's journal *Sāqī*.

to put into writing the memories that had been passed on to them personally by elders. In *Lāl qilaʿh kī ek jhalak*, Firaq Dehlawi wrote the stories of the Mughal court that 'Nani Dulhan' (or Banni Khanum, who was employed in the royal kitchen) used to tell him when he was only six to seven years old, and, in *Dillī kā ujṛā hū'ā lāl qilaʿh*, he related one of Bahadur Shah's hunting ventures that had been narrated to him by his father-in-law Mir Zarif Sahib Qibla.[13] Rashid ul Khairi told the stories of elder princesses that he met;[14] Farhatullah Beg created his novels from stories that he had heard from elders;[15] Wazir Hasan Dehlawi committed to paper the words of 'Aghai Begum' (also popularly known as Nani Hajjan);[16] and Arsh Taimuri dedicated his work to his father Majid Hazrat Labib, who had related his memories.[17] Early twentieth-century city memoirs were prompted by the realisation that the local past would soon be definitely lost.

The emergence of city memoirs concurred with the mobilisations for the preservation of historic sites, which Mohamed Ali had orchestrated since 1911 – the year of Rashid ul Khairi's first essays in *Tamaddun*.[18] Urdu writers in particular testified to the fear that houses would no longer be found, tombs forgotten, and pilgrimage routes forever altered. Local people were described as refugees in their own land. As Farhatullah Beg illustrated in 1928, a few years before the inauguration of the new imperial capital:

> Once dispersed, most of the aristocratic families of Delhi never again had the good fortune to see the face of their beloved city. The remaining families were expected to leave. Many were uprooted and many were about to be uprooted and a time was to come when there would be not a soul to tell where the house of the late Momin stood, as now there is perhaps no one, except myself, to point out Momin's tomb.[19]

In those writings, the cold stones of once-glorious monuments certainly encapsulated the immensity of the loss, but it was yet again the

[13] Firaq, *Dillī kā ujṛā hū'ā lāl qilaʿh*, p. 6.
[14] See, for instance, the story entitled 'The Princess with the Squirrels', in Rashid ul Khairi, *Dillī kī ak̲h̲rī bahār*, pp. 43–4.
[15] See Beg, *Bahadur Shah and the Festival of Flower-sellers*, p. 43.
[16] Hasan, *Dillī kā āk̲h̲rī dīdār*, p. 49.
[17] Arsh Taimuri, *Qilaʿh-e Muʿallah kī jhalkiyāṉ*, p. 18.
[18] Khairi, '*Inqilāb-e Tamaddun*' and '*Shāhī Melā*', *Dillī kī ak̲h̲rī bahār*, pp. 78–82 and 96–8.
[19] Beg, *The Last mushaʿirah of Delhi*, trans. A. Qamber, p. 53.

people, rather than the buildings, that were mourned. The experience of the new Delhi was one of displacement and disruption not only of the built environment but most importantly of its 'interactional past', that threatened identity continuity. As sociologists have argued, places of attachment are a major source for identity. When the continuity of those places is compromised, the continuity of identities will most likely be disrupted too.[20] However, as Melinda Milligan noted, it is not the 'physical site' in itself that is socially meaningful (although it certainly impacts 'locational socialisation'), but its 'interactional past and potential', that is, the interactions associated with or expected at the site. People are not only attached to the site, but to 'the cultural patterns that the site ma[kes] possible'.[21] The loss of place is then not only the loss of past experiences but also of expectations.

Descriptions of the Red Fort or of Chandni Chowk in the memoirs were indeed meaningful as settings for collective activities – festivals, processions, rituals, dinner parties. Preserving the city's past implied recording its social life. Wazir Hasan typically argued at the beginning of *The Last Sight of Delhi* that the Delhi of the past had been lost since its people were now dead: 'Dilli was never a city of just bricks and stones. Although the Haveli [Red Fort], the Jama Masjid and many other buildings of Dilli are still standing, the life and the soul of the city are dead.'[22] He continued, 'when the Dilliwalas didn't remain, how could Dilli survive? All that's left now is the name of Allah' (*jab woh Dillīwāle hī nah rahe to Dillī kyā rahtī? Allah kā nām rah gayā*).[23] Rashid ul Khairi also explained in 1932 how the city had died and was buried under modern buildings, although he mourned the people more than anything else:

> Before me the canals of *Sādat Khan* and *Mursara* were inhumed. I have seen the same for the watermill. I can still see the (bygone) image of the rooms of *Zīnat Mahal*, the green shrubbery's trees dried out and the grand buildings of Paharganj crumbled before my eyes. Today, Delhi is composed of the Vice regal Lodge, of the High Court House, of Raisina's modern roads and beautiful gardens and when I hear that buildings have been constructed as far as the Qutub, I spontaneously ask: houses have been built but where are the inhabitants?[24]

[20] M. J. Milligan, 'Displacement and Identity Discontinuity', p. 382.
[21] M. J. Milligan, 'Interactional Past and Potential', p. 17.
[22] Hasan, *Dillī kā ākhrī dīdār*, p. 33, trans. R. Safvi (ed.), *City of My Heart*, p. 5.
[23] Hasan, *Dillī kā ākhrī dīdār*, p. 34, trans. R. Safvi (ed.), *City of My Heart*, p. 6.
[24] Khairi, '*Agle logoṇ kī waẓa'dārī*', in unknown paper, in *Dillī kī ākhrī bahār*, p. 58.

In consequence, writings like Arsh Taimuri's *Glimpses of the Red Fort*[25] tended to resemble genealogical trees more than true narratives. Farhatullah Beg and Wazir Hasan also gave close attention to the exact place that people occupied in *darbārs* or *mushāʿirahs*, and ancestors or princes were described in a *taẕkirah*-like fashion.[26] Rashid ul Khairi said that he still saw the Delhi of the past (and particularly its ruin) in the faces of once-prominent princesses, now seen begging in the street.[27] City memoirs increasingly developed the style of *k͟hākah* or *shak͟hṣiyat nigārī* in which the description of colourful characters was central, and which Ashraf Sabuhi Dehlawi's famous *Dillī kī chand ʿajīb hastiyāṉ* ('Some Extraordinary Lives of Delhi', 1943) would later admirably display.[28]

The importance of past interactions was conspicuous in the striking attention paid to the local language. This was already visible from the titles of the works themselves, which usually called Delhi *Dillī* (instead of *Dehlī*) as an act of local patriotism. In a striking passage, Wazir Hasan claimed 'the city is no longer Dilli; it is now Dehli, a city of foreigners (*ab shahr-e Dillī nahīṉ Dehlī hai; bāharwāloṉ kī bastī hai*).[29] This was rather new, and in fact, even *shahr āshob* poetry on 1857 only marginally used the term *Dillī*. In 1911, Rashid ul Khairi further noted:

> Those simple people who used to call salt '*nūn*' and knife '*chakwā*' were guests of a few days. How our ears long for their voices, our eyes for their appearance and our hearts for their words.[30]

The local speech, as well as the *begamātī zubān* (the ladies' speech), the Urdu dialect used by *pardah*-observing women of north Indian courts,[31] was particularly cherished. In *Bazm-e āk͟hir*, colloquial

25 The book was published in Delhi in 1937 by the al-Maṭabaʿ Barqi Press in the Jama Masjid market at 1,000 copies when Arsh Taimuri, then a citizen of Hyderabad, was only sixteen years old. See Arsh Taimuri, *Qilaʿh-e Muʿallah kī jhalkiyāṉ*, p. 9.

26 See, for instance, Hasan, *Dillī kā āk͟hrī dīdār*, p. 54. Beg even gave the seating plan of his imaginary *mushāʿirah*; see *The last mushaʿirah*, p. 50.

27 See, for instance, Khairi, *Dillī kī ak͟hrī bahār*, pp. 41, 57.

28 See Sabuhi, *Dillī kī chand ʿajīb hastiyāṉ*.

29 Hasan, *Dillī kā āk͟hrī dīdār*, p. 61.

30 Khairi, '*Inqilāb-e Tamaddun*', *Tamaddun*, 1911, in *Dillī kī ak͟hrī bahār*, p. 79.

31 See G. Minault, 'Begamati Zuban: Women's Language and Culture', pp. 155–70, online version, p. 20. For more bibliography on the topic, see M. Hasan, *Dillī kī Begamātī Zubān*; W. Nasim, *Urdū Zubān aur ʿAurat*; Sayyid Ahmad Dehlawi, *Luġhat un-Nisā*.

dialogues interspersed the long descriptive pieces, as was often the case in oral narratives when storytellers modulated their voice and adopted particular gestures to make the story come alive.[32] The everyday dialogues in the local language with colourful idioms and familiar interjections added a special touch of realism and humour to the texts. Such scenes were sometimes introduced by a 'Listen to their conversation and enjoy',[33] and footnotes or indexes of the words used indicated the mixed impressions of strangeness, curiosity, and amusement that such passages provoked amongst readers. Describing a scene in the women's quarter at Holi, Munshi Faizuddin humorously narrated the daily quarrels and gossips amongst the court's begums in their typical dialect, full of words of Indic origin:

> *lāl joṛā maṭkā'e kyā ṭhasse se beṭhī haiṇ. ailo! yeh aur qahar toṛā ke pople munh meṇ missī kī dhaṛī aur sūkhe sūkhe hāthoṇ meṇ mehndī bhī lagī hu'ī hai!*

> With what elegance does she sit flirtatiously in her red ensemble ... Look! She even grossly painted her toothless mouth with *missī* powder[34] and applied henna on her dry parched hands![35]

Rashid ul Khairi similarly, though with less humour and more pathos, illustrated daily dialogues between distressed Delhi begums exiled to Lucknow, presenting the plethora of interjections and typical idioms of the local language.[36] Firaq Dehlawi too was acknowledged as an authority for his fine knowledge of the Delhi patois.[37] With the singular relish that such language provoked (and still provokes)[38] in the

32 C. M. Naim, 'Transvestic Words: The *Rekhti* in Urdu', p. 21.

33 See, for instance, Khairi, '*Shāhjahānābād ke sadā bahār phūl*', *Tamaddun* (1913), in *Dillī kī ak͟hrī bahār*, p. 39.

34 *Missi* powder used to be applied on teeth and gums to blacken them, a common practice in Mughal India that disappeared with new canons of beauty that valorised white teeth instead. See T. J. Zumbroich, "The *missi*-Stained Finger-tip of the Fair".

35 Faizuddin, *Bazm-e āk͟hir*, p. 89.

36 Khairi, *Dillī kī ak͟hrī bahār*, p. 84. The use of expressions linked to the *chūlhā* (stove, fire) was quite common. See G. Minault, 'Begamati Zuban', online version, p. 6.

37 R. Parekh, 'Nasir Nazeer Firaq, His Prose and Delhi's Cultural History', dawn.com/news/1239539

38 See the reading of *begamātī zubān* passages from *Bazm-e āk͟hir* by Zia Mohyeddin at the Jashn-e Rekhta festival, 2015 youtube.com/watch?v=oYhay7_TLj0

audience, peculiar aesthetics were also conveyed: the uniqueness of the locality, the privacy of women-only palaces, and the luxury of a mode of life which was no longer sustainable.[39]

The enhancement of the colloquial women's language of Delhi contrasted with its fast disappearance with the rise of twentieth-century standardised Urdu. Although many Urdu reformist writers such as Nazir Ahmed and Altaf Husain Hali mastered the women's speech, which they particularly used in their didactic works directed towards female audiences,[40] it had developed a bad reputation. The idiom was generally used for entertainment because of its 'earthy, graphic, and colourful'[41] character, which was far from 'ladylike',[42] and the fact that it borrowed much from local dialects and used many words of Indic origin also meant that it only displayed 'a tenuous adherence to the Islamic great tradition',[43] something that late-nineteenth century Urdu reformers usually disapproved of. Its use was consequently discouraged by Urdu modernist writers who only put the dialect in the mouths of 'bad' women – good women speaking almost like men in a more standard form of Urdu, with Persian loanwords.[44] The deprecation of local dialects by reformers, the development of standardised Urdu with the rise of mass publishing and education, and the questioning of the social milieu of the *zanānah* and of the practices of *pardah* with which the *begamātī zubān* was associated put further strain on the women's speech, which started dwindling.[45] While the use of the idiom may be partly linked to the fact that the city memories that writers strove to put into writing were usually passed on to them by elder women, it may also be explained by the authors' profound attachment to locality.

Sociologists argue that threats to the continuity of local interactions and of places of attachment are threats to collective identity.

[39] D. Ferrell, 'Delhi, 1911–1922', p. 128.
[40] See, for instance, Nazir Ahmed's *Mirāt ul-'urūs*; Altaf Husain Hali's *Majālis un-nisā*.
[41] G. Minault, 'Begamati Zuban', online version, p. 4. [42] Ibid.
[43] Ibid., p. 10. In *Rusūm-e Dehlī*, Sayyid Ahmad Dehlawi 'warned' his readers that the traditional practices of Muslim women were more Indian than Islamic. See Sayyid Ahmad Dehlawi, *Rusūm-e Dehlī*, p. 1.
[44] C. M. Naim, 'Transvestic Words?' p. 19.
[45] G. Minault, 'Begamati Zuban', online version, p. 20. Paradoxically, however, as Gail Minault and Faisal Devji have noted, reformist authors who usually disapproved of such usages generally helped their very preservation. See Ibid., p. 11, and F. Devji, 'The Equivocal History of a Muslim Reformation', p. 23.

As Davis argued, it is precisely when identity is endangered that nostalgia occurs as a way to maintain or reconstruct a sense of identity continuity.[46] It serves to provide a positive sense of self in order to face challenging circumstances. Nostalgia is a yearning for continuity. Yet, it is not just memory, but 'memory with the pain removed'.[47] The past is endowed with positive qualities – even less positive dimensions are remembered with affection.[48] City writers indeed unequivocally praised the Mughal city, and even if some elements were humorously described,[49] they only increased softheartedness for the past. Some writers, particularly Rashid ul Khairi, who earned the nickname 'painter of sorrow' (*muṣawwir-e ġham*), depicted the plight of Mughal princes and princesses after 1857 in his stories,[50] but the adoration of the past always triumphed 'over lamentations for the present'.[51] The perfect past was unequivocally compared to an imperfect present, in which the world had been turned upside-down. Grief was less dwelled on per se, but was used as contrast to depict past happiness. Wazir Hasan, for instance, recalled that 'every day was Eid and every night Shab-e Barat' (*din ʿīd rāt Shab-e Barāt thī*),[52] and Rashid ul Khairi lamented the contemporary fall of values in a typical *shahr āshob* stance that 'the things that Muslims thought were defects (*ʿaib*) fifty years ago are today's accomplishments (*hunar*). And what we think of as defects today used to be accomplishments.'[53] Sharar also made use of such tropes in his *Guzashtah Lakhna'ū*.[54]

The prose narratives of the city memoirs thus resembled *shahr āshob* poetry in their tone. In fact, *shahr āshob* poems were sometimes quoted: Wazir Hasan's booklet opened with a poem by Zafar, Rashid ul Khairi's articles occasionally included a couple of nostalgic verses[55] – *Bazm-e*

[46] F. Davis, *Yearning for Yesterday*, p. 31, and M. J. Milligan, 'Displacement and Identity Discontinuity', p. 383.
[47] F. Davis, *Yearning for Yesterday*, p. 37.
[48] M. J. Milligan, 'Interactional Past and Potential', p. 11.
[49] For instance, Beg's or Wazir Hasan's narratives.
[50] He also wrote *Widāʿ-e Ẕafar* and *Naubat-e panj rozah*, which I have not analysed.
[51] F. Davis, *Yearning for Yesterday*, p. 16.
[52] Hasan, *Dillī kā āḵẖrī dīdār*, p. 34.
[53] Khairi, '*Agle logoṇ kī bāteṇ*', in *ʿIṣmat* (1932), in *Dillī kī āḵẖrī bahār*, p. 76.
[54] A. H. Sharar, *The Last Phase of an Oriental Culture*, p. 185.
[55] For instance, Khairi, *Dillī kī aḵẖrī bahār*, p. 127.

āk͟hir, the first city memoir of this kind also opened with a *shahr āshob* poem. Maritta Schleyer argued that the works of Khwajah Hasan Nizami used nostalgia to reform contemporary manners. They re-enacted the suffering of 1857 in the form of *ʿibrat* (warning) to bring the readers to moral reform as a way to negotiate colonial rule.[56] City memoirs were indeed sometimes characterised by present-day editors as tales of warning (*ʿibrat-nāmahs*),[57] and Rashid ul Khairi certainly bemoaned the loss of virtues such as kindness, generosity, humility, respect, and modesty to encourage the readers of his reformist magazines to practise those virtues. But, generally, it seems that the evocation of the past rather worked at rehabilitating and expressing a profound attachment to the local past, which, as Rashid ul Khairi titled one of his articles, was 'ever-blooming'.[58]

2 Constructing Multi-sensory Heritage: City Novels as *qiṣṣah*s

Generally, the prefaces of early twentieth-century city memoirs on Delhi mention Munshi Faizuddin's 1885 *Bazm-e āk͟hir* (or 'The Last Gathering') as the pioneering work that inspired later compositions.[59] The book was written by one of Mirza Ilahi Bakhsh's attendants and was published by the *Armuġhan-e Dehlī* press near Turkman Gate in Delhi.[60] It was indeed the first of a kind: it described the everyday life of the Delhi court and the yearly events celebrated by the last two Mughal kings with detailed precision, scrupulously recording whole lists of items (food, clothes, musical instruments, and the like).

[56] M. Schleyer, 'Ghadr-e Dehli ke Afsane', p. 35.

[57] For instance, in the preface of Hasan, *Dillī kā āk͟hrī dīdār*, by Shahid Ahmad Dehlawi, p. 32.

[58] Khairi, '*Shāhjahānābād ke sadā bahār phūl*', in *Tamaddun*, 1913, in *Dillī kī ak͟hrī bahār*, p. 35.

[59] See Aslam Parvez, in Arsh Taimuri, *Qilaʿh-e Muʿallah kī jhalkiyāṇ*, p. 11; Kamil Qureshi in Faizuddin, *Bazm-e āk͟hir*, p. 11; Sayyid Zamir Hasan in Hasan, *Dillī kā āk͟hrī dīdār*, p. 24.

[60] Kamil Qureshi in his preface to the work mentions that the original manuscript is in the Hardinge Municipal Library in Delhi and was re-edited in 1945. See the introduction to Faizuddin, *Bazm-e āk͟hir*, Delhi, 2009 [1885], pp. 9–11. See also M. Pernau, 'Nostalgia: Tears of Blood for a Lost World', p. 90, partly reproduced in M. Pernau, *Emotions and Modernity*, p. 207. For more on the different editions and manuscripts see A. Farouqui, *The Last Gathering*.

Organised into different short subtitled sections, the book began with general information on the Delhi court (the Fort's daily routine, names of popular dishes, etc.), and followed with an account of the regular activities of the nobility, punctuated by seasonal festivals and pilgrimages to local shrines. The 1885 preface by Munshi Agha Mirza (presumably the publisher) insisted that the work was commissioned by the publishing house and had required 'a lot of money and effort'.[61]

Bazm-e ākhir was the first of a series of city writings, often composed by former Mughal courtiers or their descendants, which apparently aimed at memorialising old Delhi and preserving the knowledge of Mughal times. It was followed in 1889 by Shahzadah Mirza Ahmad Akhtar Gorgani's *Sawāneḥ-e Dehlī* ('Story of Delhi') which contained precise reports of the history of Islamic dynasties and a quantity of tables indicating the dates of Muslim rulers and British residents, interspersed with a thorough list of Delhi monuments occasionally illustrated by paintings in the fashion of Syed Ahmed Khan's *Āṡār us-Sanādīd*; and, later, by the aforementioned 1910s–1930s memoirs. The 'plain' and matter-of-fact language and the meticulous inventories of entire categories of items that characterised *Bazm-e ākhir* led scholars to emphasise the similarity of that type of city literature with the anthropological accounts of local customs that started to be published by local informants during the late nineteenth and early twentieth centuries.[62] Faizuddin indeed listed in the first few pages of the book under the heading 'names of food' some twenty-four *pulā'os* and twenty-six types of bread: '*chapātiyāṇ, phulke, parāṭhe, roġhnī roṭī, birī roṭī, besnī roṭī, khamīrī roṭī, nān, shīrmāl, gā'odīdah, gā'ozubān, kulchah, bāqarkhānī* [...]'[63] As Margrit Pernau argued, Faizuddin's account, which displayed a 'writing style that was as precise as it was unemotional'[64] – in striking contrast to previous pathetic *shahr āshob* poetry – was similar in style and content to Sayyid Ahmad Dehlawi's anthropological account *Rusūm-e Dehlī* (c. 1900–1905).[65]

[61] Faizuddin, *Bazm-e ākhir* (edition 1885), p. 3, trans. Faizuddin, *The Last Gathering* (A. Farouqui), p. xxiii.
[62] M. Pernau, 'Nostalgia', pp. 90–2; M. Pernau, *Emotions and Modernity*, p. 208.
[63] See Faizuddin, *Bazm-e ākhir*, p. 40.
[64] M. Pernau, *Emotions and Modernity*, p. 207.
[65] While G. Minault mentions the date 1905 (see, for instance, G. Minault, 'Sayyid Ahmad Dehlavi and the "Delhi Renaissance"', p. 183), M. Pernau, following Khaliq Anjum's introduction to the re-edition by the Urdu Academy in 1984, dates it to 1900 (see M. Pernau, *Emotions and Modernity*, p. 209).

If *Rusūm-e Dehlī*, like Shahzadah Gorgani's *Sawāneḥ-e Dehlī* and, later, Mirza Herat Dehlawi's *Chirāġh-e Dehlī* (1930) were conscious scholarly works that aimed at cultural preservation,[66] *Bazm-e āḵẖir* (and most of the literary writings on Delhi that followed) also displayed remarkable sensory dimensions.

Faizuddin's book, I argue, incorporated elements that evoked the *qiṣṣah* (story, romance) tradition.[67] At that time, traditional *qiṣṣahs* were indeed being written down: they were recorded in costly volumes,[68] but also circulated in chapbook editions for the broader public, especially in urban areas.[69] This process occurred as the romance tradition declined with the rise of the novel (which still owed much to storytelling practices) and, more importantly, as Pasha Khan highlighted, with the devaluation of the *qiṣṣah* as an 'untruthful' genre.[70] Frances Pritchett noted that written *qiṣṣahs* still carried on oral storytelling techniques and were probably designed to be read aloud (at least to oneself),[71] but they were unlikely to reveal any actual performance nor, even, 'the author's desire for oral presentation'.[72] In many respects, *Bazm-e āḵẖir* and later 1930s city memoirs read like *qiṣṣahs*. They were often introduced as such, and their authors were sometimes even referred to as storytellers (*dāstāngos*).[73] Early twentieth-century writers sometimes claimed to reflect orality. Wazir Hasan's 1932 booklet in particular staged discussions with his 'informant', adding pauses and interruptions to the narrative as the old woman lamented or stopped to help herself to *paan*, after which she needed to be reminded by the audience where she had left the story.[74] But, aside

[66] G. Minault, 'Sayyid Ahmad Dehlavi', p. 183.

[67] W. Hanaway, 'Dastan-sarai'; F. W. Pritchett, *The Romance Tradition*; F. W. Pritchett, 'The Dastan Revival: An Overview'.

[68] The first volumes published from 1883 to 1890 related the famous story of *Ṯilism-e Hoshrubā* by Muhammad Husain Jah (see F. W. Pritchett, *The Romance Tradition*, pp. 21–8). Nawal Kishore hired three famous Lucknow *dāstāngos* for the publication of his forty-six volumes on Amir Hamzah: Muhammad Husain Jah, Ahmad Husain Qamar, and Tasadduq Husain. See P. M. Khan, 'The Broken Spell: The Romance Genre', p. 7.

[69] Pasha M. Khan, 'The Broken Spell: The Romance Genre', p. 8. See also C. Servan-Schreiber, 'Littératures orales de l'Inde du Nord', pp. 214–5.

[70] P. M. Khan, *The Broken Spell*, pp. 10–21.

[71] F. W. Pritchett, *Marvelous Encounters*, pp. 145–54. [72] Ibid., p. 155.

[73] See Intizar Mirza's introduction to Firaq, *Lāl qila'h kī ek jhalak*, p. 12; Kamil Qureshi's introduction to Faizuddin, *Bazm-e āḵẖir*, p. 9.

[74] Hasan, *Dillī kā āḵẖrī dīdār*, pp. 62–3: *bātoṇ bātoṇ meṇ maiṇ to kāṇ (kahāṇ) se kāṇ nikal ga'ī, jāne maiṇ kyā kah rahī thī?* [...] *hāṇ to...*

from the oral context of composition, stylistic elements of the city memoirs conspicuously recalled the methods used by traditional storytellers. Before exploring what the resort to such techniques actually *did* and the effect they produced on the memory of the Mughal past, let us first analyse what city memoirs had in common with *qiṣṣahs* by taking the first example of Faizuddin's 1885 book.

Bazm-e āḵẖir is what we can call a patchwork text or a heterogeneous narrative, a characteristic that has been associated with romances.[75] It opens with a poem recalling the days of the king-flower and the autumn that left the gardener in tears,[76] and then continues with interjections ('Look!' 'Oho!'), long descriptive pieces, lists of items, and colourful dialogues in *begamātī zubān* and the language of the court. The book displayed a particular rhythm to the narrative by skilfully alternating between fast and lively dialogues and slow, serene setting descriptions. The cadence recalled that of storytelling sittings where 'more dense and static passages occur like islands within a narrative stream that otherwise tends to be plain, colloquial, direct, and fast-flowing'.[77] In *Bazm-e āḵẖir*, long passages often described picturesque and romantic scenes taking place in and around the Red Fort, in which the recitation of catalogues 'to evoke all items of a certain class as exhaustively as possible'[78] appeared as a crucial device, which slowed down the narrative to widen into 'the realms of personal fantasy'[79] – a process which was usually facilitated by the consumption of opium during *dāstāngo'ī* sessions.

As Pasha Khan demonstrated in the case of Mir Baqir Ali (1850–1928), Delhi's last professional *dāstāngo*, those 'sumptuous lists' enabled *qiṣṣahs* to stand as a 'repository of other kinds of knowledge' that provided 'a better understanding of the culture' and could eventually gain value according to British colonial epistemologies.[80] In a way, this dimension of the *qiṣṣah* concurred with the style of anthropological accounts to which city memoirs are often compared in scholarship. Yet, if one looks attentively, the lists of *Bazm-e āḵẖir*, which resemble Baqir Ali's lists,[81] do not always produce valuable scholarly knowledge about the court: it is difficult to attribute much scientific

[75] P. M. Khan, *The Broken Spell*, p. 129; F. Orsini, *Print and Pleasure*, p. 106.
[76] Faizuddin, *Bazm-e āḵẖir*, p. 37.
[77] F. W. Pritchett, *The Romance Tradition*, p. 19.
[78] Ibid., p. 17. [79] Ibid.
[80] P. M. Khan, *The Broken Spell*, pp. 54 and 83.
[81] Ibid., p. 82 quotes Mir Baqir Ali, *T̤ilism-e Hoshafzā*, p. 264.

benefit to the referencing of the twenty-three different colours of fabric described at the beginning of the book, except of course for the 'language exemplarity' and refinement that such lists offered.[82] More essentially, besides providing information, such lists aimed at creating a pleasurable, multi-sensory effect.

In his story (1943) about Mir Baqir Ali, Ashraf Sabuhi explained that professional *dāstāngos* had to be knowledgeable to add intended flavour to their tales. 'In his old age' Sabuhi tells us '[Mir Baqir Ali] wanted to learn medicine and he went to attend lectures at Delhi's Tibiyya College. He did not want to become a doctor but he developed in his tales a medical flavour'.[83] Faizuddin's narrative methods were quite similar: through his catalogues, he built a particular atmosphere. The litany of items thus not just provided factual and linguistic knowledge – which certainly gave value to his tale – but also stimulated the imagination of the audience. Muhammad Husain Jah, who worked on the writing down of *T̤ilism-e Hoshrubā*, for instance, explained about that specific method:

> [E]veryone knows that even when children tell stories, as far as they are able, they say [not merely 'a garden' but] things like 'a garden of flowers, with lovers' bowers, with nightingales singing, with all kinds of fruit on the trees.' Truly, 'the only pleasure of a short story is in prolonging it.[84]

Faizuddin's description of the garden of the Red Fort's *zanānah* clearly used the same technique:

> In front of the king's Moti Mahal there is a big garden. Its name is Hayyat Bakhsh. In the middle of it, there is a tank of 60 *guz* on 60 *guz*, and in the tank there is a water palace. To the south and north, there are two pavilions called Sawan and Bhadon entirely made of marble in the middle of which there are small tanks. Water falls into the tanks like a curtain. On every side, water flows in four big canals made of red sandstone, and around the canals are intricate red sandstone flowerbeds. In those flowerbeds are blooming marigolds, garden balsams, *gul-e naurang*s, *shabbu*s, peacock flowers, lilies, sunflowers, etc. The scent of Arabic jasmine, royal jasmine, wild jasmine, Sambac jasmine, roses, dog roses, creepers and *maulsarī* flowers perfume the garden. Nightingales chirrup. The greenery is glowing. Look! Trees

[82] Ibid., pp. 49 and 88. [83] A. Sabuhi, *Dillī kī chand 'ajīb hastiyāṉ*, p. 52.
[84] Muhammad Husain Jah, *T̤ilism-e hoshrubā*, vol. 3, p. 920, quoted in F. W. Pritchett, *The Romance Tradition*, p. 25.

are swinging, laden with flowers and fruits like mangoes (*shehedkozahs*, *batāshahs*, *bādshāh pasands*, *Muḥammad Shāhī laḍḍūs*),[85] pomegranates, guavas, *jāmun*, oranges, tangerines, grapefruits, citron, lemon [...]. Mynah birds are warbling, peacocks are singing and crested cuckoos are chanting 'pīhū pīhū'.[86]

The effect of list writing served to evoke a sense of place, an 'architecture of the senses' as urban scholars could say,[87] not to reach scientific accuracy. While, of course, the description can enhance our knowledge about flora in Mughal Delhi, there is a magical feel to the description that portrays trees laden with fruit and flowers at the same time, without evoking seasonality. Lists brought the garden to life thanks to the sheer abundance of details, which carried a multi-sensorial sense of place.

Bazm-e āk͟hir and many of the Delhi memoirs that were written in the early twentieth century did display factual knowledge about the Mughal court at a time when that knowledge was slowly threatening to disappear, and recorded a sophisticated vocabulary, sometimes providing footnotes or translations of unusual terms, as in Baqir Ali's oral tales.[88] They did produce historical knowledge at a time when it was highly valued; yet, they also transported the past into realms of imagination. It is indubitable that the authors of city memoirs were aware of Western methods and interest in local history and ethnography, and thus incorporated modern historiographical practices into their traditional understandings and modes of description of the past.[89] The past, however, was also always imbued with enchantment. Of course, no princess fairies, dangerous sorcerers, and magical adventures are to be found in Delhi accounts as they were in *qiṣṣahs*, but the historical and wondrous were closely intertwined.[90] *Bazm-e āk͟hir* emphasised a past of amazement, refinement, and fantasy. Through their narratives, the writers made the Mughal past enter into the realm of imagination where it could be endlessly consumed and remembered. After all, in

[85] Those are all different types of mangoes. [86] Faizuddin, *Bazm-e āk͟hir*, p. 87.
[87] M. Adams and S. Guy, 'Editorial: Senses and the City', p. 133.
[88] P. M. Khan, *The Broken Spell*, p. 50.
[89] M. Schleyer, 'Ghadr-e Dehli ke Afsane', p. 39.
[90] While *qiṣṣahs* traditionally situated their plots in some distant and wondrous past, they were sometimes supported by records and ancient chronicles. See F. W. Pritchett, *The Romance Tradition*, p. 12; *qiṣṣah* and *tārīk͟hs* were treated 'as close cousins with porous limits' in Indo-Persian tradition; see P. M. Khan, *The Broken Spell*, p. 134.

late nineteenth- and still more in early twentieth-century Delhi, the Mughal past was starting to feel almost as faraway and mysterious as the mythical past of the *Ḥamzah-nāmah*. In his story on the flower-seller fair in Delhi, Farhatullah Beg indeed concluded 'after reading, everyone would question in their hearts whether these are true events or some make-believe tale (*ko'ī man-ghaṛat qiṣṣah*)'.[91]

3 'Open your inner eyes': Remembering and Re-presencing the Past

Now, what did the use of storytelling devices do to memories of pre-1857 times in the early twentieth century? Besides preserving local knowledge, I argue that they were part of the process of recovering and internalising the lost sites of Mughal Delhi. They constructed an idealistic collective memory and induced pleasure and pride in their readers, as a form of escapism almost, to confront a frightening present. Besides implementing a 'texture of place',[92] scholars have since long emphasised the role of the senses in triggering memory.[93] As Low argued, 'memories are vivified by sensory dimensions' and, consequently, the construction of memory generally occurs through sensory re-creation.[94] In the preface to *Bazm-e ākhir*, Agha Mirza had indeed emphasised that 'the best aspect (*sab se baṛī khūbī*) of this book is that it is written in such a way that the reader can picture himself in that place and see the whole story with his own eyes (*ek aisī pur asar taṣwir khīnchdī hai keh jis se har ek paṛhnewālā goyā usī jagah beṭhā hū'ā ma'lūm hotā aur ek ek bāt ko apnī ānkh se dekh rahā hai*).'[95]

Farhatullah Beg was perhaps one of the most gifted in doing so. Taking as an example Muhammad Husain Azad's *Nairang-e khayāl* and inspired by Maulvi Karimuddin's *tażkirah Ṯabaqāt-e shu'arā-e Hind*, he skilfully staged an imaginary *mushā'irah* in 1846 Delhi. With the help of portraits and photographs of Bahadur Shah Zafar, Ghalib, and Momin to render his narrative more realistic,[96] Farhatullah Beg

[91] Beg, *Bahādur Shāh aur Phūlwāloṇ kī sair*, p. 51.
[92] See R. Khan, 'Local Pasts', p. 719.
[93] See, for instance, S. Lahiri, 'Remembering the City'.
[94] K. Low, 'Summoning the Senses', p. 106.
[95] Faizuddin, *Bazm-e ākhir*, p. 3, trans. *The Last Gathering* (A. Farouqui), p. xxiii.
[96] D. Bredi, 'Nostalgia in the Re-construction of Muslim Identity', p. 150; Beg, *The last musha'irah*, pp. 8 and 51.

drew a vivid picture of Mughal Delhi as a city of light and velvety elegance. Consciously describing the preparation of the venue before the *mushāʿirah* as the scene of an enchanting fairy tale, Beg wrote:

> The entire house had been whitewashed with a mixture of lime and mica which caused the walls to glimmer. [...] There was such a profusion of chandeliers, candelabra, wall lamps, hanging lamps, Chinese lanterns and other lights that the house was converted into a veritable dome of light (*baqaʿh-e nūr*). Everything was elegant, in good taste and in its appointed place. In the dead centre of the middle row stood a small embroidered canopy of green velvet, supported on gold- and silver-coloured posts fastened with green silk tent-cords. In this pavilion was placed the green velvet embroidered seat with embroidered green cushions [Farhatullah Beg noted that green was the colour of Delhi royalty]. On each of the four tent-posts were hung eight small silver lanterns. [...] From the centre of the roof were hung rows upon rows of jasmine garlands and streamers and these were fastened all round the walls of the canopy and created an umbrella of flowers. [...] In short, the whole scene was like a strange, rare spectacle (*ʿajīb tamāshā*). I moved like the enchanted Abul-Hassan, a character of *Alif Laila*, and wherever my eyes roved there they stayed! While I stood still, entranced and fascinated (*mahw*) by the scene, the guests began to arrive.[97]

Twentieth-century novelists remembered Mughal places while giving them an air of timelessness, insouciance, and playfulness with images of kites of every colour flying in a cloudless sky, of the golden sunlight spreading at dusk over a city resounding with the calls of *āżān* during Ramzan, of cheeky egg fights at Nauroz, and of other paradisiac scenes spreading over whole pages.

Through a shared sensory memory of the locality, city memoirs constructed collective identity. Mughal 'sensescapes' could be transported into collective imagination. Often, descriptions would emphasise many if not all the senses at once: the experience of the court carried the gustatory and olfactory feel of foods and garden scents, the aural memory of singing birds and musical performances, but also the visual and kinaesthetic experience of garden strolls. The movability and peripatetic nature of the court were often highlighted – despite the fact that during the reigns of the last two Mughal kings, the court's outings were limited and controlled by the British resident.

[97] Beg, *Dehlī kī āḵẖrī shamaʿ*, New Delhi, 1992, pp. 50–2, trans. Beg, *The last mushaʿirah*, pp. 82–4.

Wazir Hasan, for instance, described in the typical style of late nineteenth-century *Bazm-e ākẖir*:

The light carriage first stopped at *Sulṯānjī* and then at the Tomb of the Emperor Humayun. Everyone reads the *fātihah* and disperses flowers. From there, the spring breeze [the court] travels straight to the madrasah. There one, two, five poles pavilions (*rā'oṭī*) have been brought and tents (*kẖaimah*) erected. On one side a big *shāmyānah* has been put up, in the middle of which a platform and, on the platform, the King's throne is placed. Behind, two *zanānah* tents have been erected. On all sides big green tent walls have been attached. Outside the tomb too tent walls are attached. There, about twenty ovens are heated. There are sounds of pans clanging together. Big cauldrons make noise. In them, *gīlānī*, *īrānī*, *nūr mahalī*, *zamurradī*, *nargisī*, *motī pulā'os* are being steamed and there *muġhla'ī dopyāzah*, *chāshnī dār* fish, *kẖāṣe ke karele*, *shāh pasand* lentils, *kundan qaliyah*, *kofte*, *parsande* [sic], every type of *dulmah*, *doġh*, *burānī rā'itā*, *lauzātī*, *husainī kebabs*, *shāmī kebabs*, *shikampur kebabs*, *murġh musāllam*, and *samosas* are being prepared. Look on one side thin *chapātis* and *parāṭhas* are piled up and on the other side rich *bāqarkẖānīs* and *pazdī nāns, tang nāns* and *gulzār nāns* are taken out of the oven![98]

City novelists certainly responded to the urge for finding their own cultural spaces within colonial modernity, even if those spaces were only imagined ones. As Hannah Segal argued about Proust's literary masterpiece, artistic creativity such as fiction has the power to integrate emotional recollections and to make them permanent.[99] The fact that Farhatullah Beg wrote some of his novels in the first person singular and gave them a particular atmosphere of intimacy further showed how he aimed to recover the lost past in his own self and for the public to share, just as Wazir Hasan Dehlawi and other writers enabled his readers to become the eternal witnesses of their elders' storytelling sessions by using the present tense. Through descriptions of picturesque scenes, direct language and interjections, and litanies of items, memories of the Mughal past were fixed as fiction by Urdu writers and turned into works of art, commodities, and spectacles that could be consumed daily and forever. By bringing the past back to life, writers gave it an eternal life.[100] Wazir Hasan indeed ended his narrative with an interesting reflection:

[98] Hasan, *Dillī kā ākẖrī dīdār*, p. 59.
[99] H. Segal, 'A Psychoanalytical Approach to Aesthetics', p. 207.
[100] Ibid., p. 208.

Is our imagination (*takhayyul*) taking us on a sightseeing tour (*sairbīn*) of the past to show us new miracles (*na'e karishme dikhātī hai*) from that era, or did they ever really take place? Individuals can decide this as per their capacity and ability. However, whenever I hear the sweet songs of my beloved Dilli, images embedded in my subconscious mind come to the fore (*yād-e ayyām kī aisī gharhiyān jāg jatīṇ thīṇ*) and run in my veins like an elixir. [...] The past, present and future fuse into one entity in my mind.[101]

That such texts worked at re-presencing the past also appears sporadically through injunctions by city novelists to forget about contemporary Delhi and to 'close one's eyes and look'.[102] It was not unusual, especially in Rashid ul Khairi's essays, to refer to specific sites where the 'interactional past' could be made alive again, in one's memory and heart. In 1936, for instance, he exhorted his readers: 'Go to the flat ground on the old '*īdgāh*'s eastern side, and close your "outward" eyes (*zāhirī ānkhen*); open your heart's eyes (*dil kī ānkhen*) and you will see their faces'.[103]

In one of Firaq Dehlawi's short stories, *Jinn-o Parī* ('Jinns and Fairies', undated), the people of the past still inhabited the sites of Old Delhi as *jinns* (good spirits).[104] He recounted that on the night of Ashura, Maulvi Tasli Sahib, a famous *marsiyahkhwān*, was walking alone. Passing before Agrasen ki Baoli – Firaq explained that the place had been haunted since 1857 – he finally reached an animated Chandni Chowk. There, he encountered mace-bearers (*chobdārs*) who saluted him and informed him that the king was waiting for him to recite the *fātihah* for Imam Husain. Maulvi Tasli Sahib went through the gate, and was bewildered (*hairān*) by what he found: a beautiful (*dilfareb*) blooming fruit orchard and a garden whose flowers perfumed the mind (*phūlon kī khushbū ne dimāġh mu'attar kar diyā*). In the middle was a courtyard in which thousands of men, dressed in black, were seated silently. One of them wore a crown and rose when he entered, kissed his hand, and asked him to recite the *fātihah*.

---

[101] Hasan, *Dillī kā ākhrī dīdār*, pp. 73–4, trans. R. Safvi (ed.), *City of My Heart*, pp. 61–2. Sharar also described about the past that 'everything was fantasy and illusion' (A. H. Sharar, *Lucknow, The Last Phase of an Oriental Culture*, p. 75).

[102] Khairi, *Dillī kī akhrī bahār*, p. 36: 'My dear! Close your eyes for a few moments. Forget the present-day Delhi. [...] Look! With a full heart, look!'

[103] Khairi, '*sohbat-e shab kī akhrī ghariyān*', in *Niẓām ul-mashā'ikh* (1936), in *Dillī kī akhrī bahār*, pp. 62–3.

[104] Firaq, '*Jinn-o parī*', in *Maẓāmīn-e Firāq*, pp. 75–80. See A. V. Taneja, *Jinnealogy*.

Maulvi Tasli Sahib did as requested, after which the king gave him forty kilograms of sweets as *tabarruk* (sacred offering). Maulvi Tasli Sahib was surprised by the quantity and said that he would not be able to carry it all by himself, so a ten-year-old boy was appointed to escort him out with the sweets. As soon as they arrived in the street animated with the processions, the boy vanished. The maulvi was left with the forty-kilo *tabarruk* in his arms, so he called for help and people ran to assist him. Those sweets, Firaq Dehlawi concluded, were the tastiest and sweetest. In the story, the world of Mughal *jinns* was described as beautiful, natural, and serene, and was only another dimension of the present, which followed the same calendar, the same celebrations, as contemporary times. Delhi sites still preserved the (invisible) presence of those exceptional people of the past.

The past described in Firaq's *jinn* story and in city memoirs was presented as still accessible in one's heart. Thereby, the memory of power was re-created and internalised to provide continuity with a past that was disappearing by the day. By fictionalising their memories, Urdu writers gained popular success – articles appeared as series, books were re-edited several times – and offered their readers both a form of escapism and an imaginary space of pre-colonial life that contrasted with contemporary grief and from which they could articulate critiques of the present. Fantasising about a power that was lost, city memoirs showed an effort to accommodate, but also at times to resist,[105] colonial rule and the rising communal tensions of the late 1920s and 1930s.

4 Praising the Past, Criticising the Present

If we now turn to the content of the city memoirs in more detail, it appears striking that, besides Mughal courtiers and princesses, the characters that were commonly represented in city novels were cultural performers such as famous musicians, poets, festivalgoers, and courtesans (*ṯawā'if*). While Rashid ul Khairi and Farhatullah Beg usually focussed on poetic gatherings and figures such as Ghalib, Momin, or Zauq, Arsh Taimuri recalled famous musicians – especially Tanras Khan[106] – and

[105] M. Pernau, 'Nostalgia: Tears of Blood'.

[106] Arsh Taimuri consecrated a whole chapter to Tanras Khan, who worked at Bahadur Shah's court and settled in Hyderabad a few years after 1857. Arsh Taimuri, *Qilaʿh-e Muʿallah kī jhalkiyāṇ*, p. 58.

Wazir Hasan and Abdul Halim Sharar more generally wrote on poets, *qawwāls*, musicians, and dancing girls. Since at least Mirza Muhammad Hadi Ruswa's novel *Umrā'o Jān Ādā* (1899),[107] courtesans had become a preferred subject of longing and romance, and their character often encompassed a whole world of culture and tradition. Their decline in the modern world echoed the fate of the elite culture that they used to perform. Until 1857, they had been a very powerful group: 'they dictated the law of fashion, etiquette, music, dance; they enjoyed the regard of the court'.[108] As Veena Oldenburg noted, 'they were not only recognised as preservers and performers of the high culture of the court, but they actively shaped the developments in Hindustani music and Kathak dance styles. [...] They commanded great respect in the court and in society, and association with them bestowed prestige on those who were invited to their salons for cultural soirées'.[109] In one emblematic passage, Wazir Hasan described one of the delightful dance performances of Bahadur Shah's times with the famous Tanras Khan on one side, striking tunes from a *sarānchah* accompanied by *sārangī* students, and dancing girls on the other side. Focussing on the dancing girls, he continued,

> They were such dolls of etiquette and culture, what can I say of their respectable garments? On seeing them the soul delights. [...] In those times they were not like [today's] prostitutes. Their conversation, singing, fondling and expertise were such that they were recognisable among lakhs of women. [...] People would bring them their children to learn manners.[110]

Courtesans were more than cultural performers; they were educators and transmitters of knowledge. They taught etiquette and proper *savoir-vivre*. Farhatullah Beg, for instance, remembered in his biography of Nazir Ahmed that one of his fellow students who was unacquainted with poetry was sent 'to Kali Jan's place when she gives music lessons in the evenings' to train his ears.[111] Sharar also remembered how, only forty years before he wrote his *Guzashtah Lakhna'ū*, courtesans still displayed great skill and left the educated and refined crowds of Matiya Burj completely spellbound.[112]

107 Ruswa, *Umrao Jan Ada: Courtesan of Lucknow*; Ruswa, *Umrā'o Jān Ādā*.
108 D. Bredi, 'Fallen Women: A Comparison of Rusva and Manto', p. 112, quoted in A. Safadi, 'The "Fallen" Woman in Two Colonial Novels', p. 22.
109 V. Oldenburg, 'Lifestyle as Resistance', p. 260.
110 Hasan, *Dillī kā āk͟hrī dīdār*, pp. 65–6.
111 Beg, *Nazir Ahmad in His Own Words and Mine*, p. 32.
112 A. H. Sharar, *Lucknow: The Last Phase*, p. 145.

The fate of *ṯawā'if*s usually followed that of their patrons. After the Uprising, the instability of former elite households meant that it was difficult for them to earn a living, and British policies in sanitisation and health as well as puritanical Victorian morals targeted them 'as repositories of disease'.[113] As Erica Wald argued, from the early nineteenth century, British morality and medical knowledge from the East India Company army's surgeons and officers forced courtesans into the 'prostitute' category, which dramatically transformed their status within Indian society.[114] As prominent but declining cultural performers, courtesans and dancing girls still inspired Indian photographers, like Daroghah Haji Abbas Ali,[115] from Lucknow, who wished to immortalise 'the most celebrated and popular living historic singers, dancing girls and actresses of the Oudh Court and of Lucknow' in 1874.[116] While the *Indar Sabhā* theatre production was often looked upon with contempt by British officials who saw it as proof of the king's weakness and inefficiency,[117] the photographs of the 'beauties' of Lucknow in their *Indar Sabhā* outfits that were most probably destined to the local gentry were intended to constitute glimpses into 'the Oriental magnificence of the entertainment'[118] of Indo-Islamic courts (Figure 5.1).

In 1898, restrictions were introduced for courtesans in Benares and Lucknow, and in 1917 propositions to remove them from city centres were put forward by the Hindu middle classes influenced by the Arya Samaj.[119] In the 1920s, their situation had become critical. A number of Urdu novels started denouncing their precarious condition in northern India, amongst which was Premchand's *Bāzār-e Ḥusn* (1924),[120] which discussed the proposed banishment of prostitutes outside the city. In his work, they were elevated as preservers of tradition, with a nationalist twist.[121] In his story *Na'ī Dehlī* about modern change in

[113] V. Oldenburg, *The Making of Colonial Lucknow*, pp. 132–42, quoted in A. Safadi, 'The "Fallen" Woman', p. 23.
[114] E. Wald, 'From *begums* and *bibis* to Abandoned Females and Idle Women', p. 6.
[115] For more on Daroghah Haji Abbas Ali's photographs and comparisons with other photographers, see S. Gordon, 'Monumental Visions: Architectural Photography in India'.
[116] This is the subtitle given to his album *The Beauties of Lucknow*.
[117] S. Gordon, 'Monumental Visions', p. 195.
[118] Abbas Ali, *The Beauties of Lucknow*, preface quoted by Ibid.
[119] See A. Safavi, 'The "Fallen" Woman', p. 25.
[120] See also the short story by Ghulam Abbas in the 1940s, 'Anandi' (*The City of Bliss*) trans. G. A. Chaussée, pp. 324–49.
[121] Munshi Premchand, *Courtesans' Quarter*, trans. A. Azfar, p. 135.

Figure 5.1 *Juddan dancing girl* from ʿAbbās ʿAlī, *Beauties of Lucknow*, Albumen print, 1874

the city, Farhatullah Beg similarly staged a dialogue with an Old Delhi citizen who lamented the fall of values among the population and particularly among courtesans, strikingly claiming against his interlocutor's indifference: '*Sir,* prostitutes (*ranḍiyāṇ*) were a model of Dilli's culture (*tahẕīb*)'.[122]

In fact, courtesans had been vehemently criticised by British authorities since before 1857, and the depravity that they represented served to justify the British takeover in Awadh in 1856.[123] Sharar himself, while explaining the fall of the kingdom of Oudh, blamed the bad influence of courtesans.[124] Understandably, late nineteenth-century modernist Muslim reformers, who were anxious to respond to colonial critiques,

[122] Beg, *Mirzā Farḥatullah Beg ke maẓāmīn: Intik̲h̲āb*, p. 267.
[123] V. Oldenburg, 'Lifestyle as Resistance', p. 262.
[124] A. H. Sharar, *Lucknow: The Last Phase*, p. 63.

usually repudiated different figures of the Mughal court (and courtesans in particular).[125] In the process of uplifting the community from perceived degeneration, women were thus specifically targeted 'as the primary upholders of indigenous traditions, religion and culture'.[126] They were concerned with modernising the Muslims' 'backward' homes through the construction of model and virtuous women.[127]

From the turn of the twentieth century, the position of women in society more urgently came to the forefront of such discourses but they were still idealised as the defenders of the honour of their culture, religion, and traditions. In that respect, courtesans were a particularly sensitive matter: they had been linked to Mughal culture and to the very essence of the Urdu language. In the late nineteenth and early twentieth centuries, they notably personified in the anti-Urdu propaganda the deceitfulness and 'immorality' of the Urdu language and script.[128] As the Hindi supporter Bharatendu Harishchandra claimed before the Hunter Commission (1882),

> There is a secret motive which induces the worshippers of Urdu to devote themselves to its cause. It is the language of dancing-girls and prostitutes. The depraved sons of wealthy Hindus and youths of substance and loose character, when in the society of harlots, concubines, and pimps, speak Urdu, as it is the language of their mistresses and beloved ones.'[129]

The re-appropriation of the figure of the courtesan as an object of longing by Urdu city novelists thus denoted a particular stand vis-à-vis established colonial discourses on Indo-Muslim culture that diverged from late nineteenth-century Indian apologetic works.

While the description of *nautch* girls and the laments that authors sometimes expressed towards their contemporary decline into prostitution certainly crystallised their apprehensions and critiques towards their own community at large and left them with an enduring yearning for the jolly gatherings of Mughal times, they also encapsulated an

125 See K. A. Ali, 'Courtesans in the Living Room', p. 277.
126 See K. A. Deutsch, 'Muslim Women in Colonial North India', p. 35.
127 See Ibid., p. 6. See the didactic works of Ashraf Ali Thanawi, Nazir Ahmed, and Altaf Husain Hali. About the development of women's literature and journals, see G. Minault, *Secluded Scholars*; G. Minault, 'Sayyid Mumtaz 'Ali and *Tahzib un-Niswan*'.
128 See C. R. King, 'The Images of Virtue and Vice'.
129 Quoted in Ibid., p. 139.

attitude of resistance to colonial rule. As the Urdu and the culture of performance of the Exalted Fort was progressively washed away by the influx of Punjabi migrants and the rise of lower classes which had their own language and idioms, aristocratic Urdu writers most concretely felt that colonial authorities no longer sustained Delhi's particular Mughal urbanity. Through invocations of former cultural performers (and speakers of the Delhi dialect), early twentieth-century city writers aimed at reconstructing lost cultural performance in the new imaginary spaces that they had opened within their own minds. They sought to re-appropriate a world untouched by colonial rule and by Muslim reform, by re-asserting the cultural refinement of Mughal courts that had been discredited. They aimed at writing an alternative narrative to previous late nineteenth-century reformist agendas in which women, courtesans, and traditional poets were erected as fundamental, and patriotic, figures.

Another central figure around which all city narratives revolved – and to whom they were sometimes dedicated, in the case of Taimuri's book – was Bahadur Shah Zafar. He was the one who organised banquets, patronised the arts, and decided on the right time to break the fast during the month of Ramzan. He was described as the organising force behind the refined cultural performance of a world that was both virtuous and harmonious. This idealised description, however, was of course linked to a political context of defiance that had started to emerge before, but more deeply after, the transfer of the colonial capital to Delhi. As we have seen, in the early twentieth century, Delhi's Muslim population increasingly expressed anxiety over the fair treatment of the last Mughal king and his descendants. In the alternative narratives that Urdu writers constructed at the beginning of the twentieth century, as Margrit Pernau noticed, Bahadur Shah Zafar was presented as the perfect Sufi king whose rule 'transformed the ethical character of his subjects'.[130] Each with their own sensibility, city writers illustrated the close bonds between Mughal kings and their subjects, and their benevolence towards them – the divine justice of the Mughal court being sometimes blatantly opposed to British courts of justice. For instance, Farhatullah Beg, while re-creating the atmosphere of Delhi's festival of the flower-sellers (*phūlwāloṇ kī sair*) in 1848, wrote this emblematic passage:

[130] M. Pernau, *Emotions and Modernity*, p. 206.

Owing to the Mutiny, Delhi was ruined and Bahadur Shah was deported to Rangoon. It was like a tie that had broken loose (*bandhan ṭūṭ gayā*). What was once bound now lay scattered. The tie that was, was of love; now there is a tie – but it is that of law (*magar woh muḥabbat kā bandhan thā aur yeh qānūn kā bandhan hai*). Now every petty affair is taken to the law courts. The flower-sellers' festival was the manifestation of faith (*ʿaqīdat*) of the subjects in the King and of the love (*muḥabbat*) of the King for his subjects.[131]

Bahadur Shah's rule was described as natural, organic, based on reciprocated relationships of trust and devotion, while British rule was represented as cold and distant, performed only through the rigid system of judicial courts. Farhatullah Beg associated British rule and courts of law with the severing of harmonious relationships. As Mana Kia argued, Persianate and Mughal political ethics indeed valued and cultivated love and friendship as governing practices.[132] One important aspect of Bahadur Shah's rule in those texts was indeed the representation of the Hindu–Muslim harmony under Mughal rule. The description of the king's yearly activities always portrayed Hindu festivals, such as Dussehra, Diwali, or Holi, with the same excitement and lavishness as Muslim feasts (both Sunni and Shia) or as the king's birthdays. The fireworks of Shab-e Barat were narrated with the same buoyancy and wonder as Nauroz's egg fights and Holi's flirtatious games. The vitality and harmony of Mughal times, which was most visibly praised through the local festival of the *phūlwāloṇ kī sair*, was always described as having disappeared along with the Mughal king, the only one who could sustain them.

Urdu writers undoubtedly responded to the contemporary local and national contexts, which, especially after the collapse of the Khilafat movement in 1924, saw the increase of communal violence in north India and in Delhi in particular. Since at least the 1910s, the firm establishment of the Arya Samaj in Delhi and the conversion of Muslims to Hinduism by the Shuddhi movement as well as the arrival of Muslim communal organisations (such as the corresponding

131 Beg, *Bahādur Shāh aur Phūlwāloṇ kī sair*, p. 51, trans. Beg, *Bahadur Shah and the Festival of Flower-sellers*, p. 41. Margrit Pernau argued that the reciprocity between the king and his subjects in Farhatullah Beg's work denotes the author's 'democratic awareness' in comparison with previous authors like Rashid ul Khairi. See M. Pernau, *Emotions and Modernity*, p. 214.

132 M. Kia, 'Companionship as Political Ethic'.

Tabligh movement and in 1909 the implementation of a Delhi branch by the All India Muslim League) led to great tensions in the city, notably on regular orthodox Hindu–Muslim issues like language and cow slaughter.[133] Although World War I and the nationalist agitation, with Gandhi's non-violent campaigns and the early Khilafat movement, had buried communal conflicts for a time, the years from 1923 to 1928 saw a resurgence of Hindu–Muslim violence in north India.[134] In September 1924, a violent riot around the establishment of new slaughterhouses broke out in Delhi between orthodox Hindus and Muslims, particularly between the Jats of Sadar Bazaar, influenced by the Arya Samaj, and the Muslim butchers of Pahari Dhiraj.[135] In 1925, the establishment of the Hindu Mahasabha office in the city further intensified 'political rivalry between Hindu, Muslim, and secular nationalist groups'.[136] In December 1926, the murder of Swami Shraddhanand by a Muslim and the subsequent retaliatory actions further demonstrated the high level of communal tension that had spread in the city and as far as the municipal board.[137] As Gupta argued, in the 1930s, the political polarisation was complete:[138] Lala Sri Ram, for instance, condemned 'the "exhibition of strong communal feelings" in the administration of the city'.[139]

At about that time, Mirza Farhatullah Beg's *The Last musha'irah of Delhi* and *Bahadur Shah and the Festival of Flower-sellers* as well as Sayyid Wazir Hasan Dehlawi's *The Last Sight of Delhi* were published. Both Wazir Hasan Dehlawi and Farhatullah Beg gave lengthy descriptions of Delhi's festival of the flower-sellers,[140] a festival that had been founded in Delhi by Akbar Shah II when his son Jahangir came back from his forced exile to Allahabad, thus realising his mother Mumtaz Begum's wish to the Mehrauli Sufi saint Khwajah

[133] See K. W. Jones, 'Organized Hinduism in Delhi and New Delhi', pp. 212–4.
[134] Ibid., p. 214.
[135] See N. Gupta, *Delhi between Two Empires*, p. 219 and M. Pernau, 'Riots, Masculinity, and the Desire for Passion'.
[136] K. W. Jones, 'Organized Hinduism', p. 215. [137] Ibid.
[138] N. Gupta, *Delhi between Two Empires*, p. 220.
[139] Lala Sri Ram, *Municipal Problems in Delhi*, Delhi, 1932, p. 18, quoted by N. Gupta, *Delhi between Two Empires*, p. 220.
[140] The festival was a favourite topic in this type of literature. Being a Delhiite tradition, the festival was celebrated annually until 1942, when it was banned for security purposes before being revived in 1962 by the then prime minister Jawaharlal Nehru. See the introduction to Beg, *Bahadur Shah*, p. xii.

Qutubuddin Bakhtiyar Kaki.[141] Both authors described the festival as an example of Delhi's composite culture that brought together Hindus and Muslims in joyful harmony. Wazir Hasan's Aghai Begum, after having described the *pankhā* (fan) procession in Mehrauli during the festival, lamented:

> This was the city and the fair of my youth. Hindus and Muslims lived and celebrated together, and there was bonhomie between them. [...] Now the tide has turned (*ulṭā ho gayā*) [...] Enmity has seeped into our bones and the hostility between the two communities seems to never end.[142]

In *Bahadur Shah and the Festival of Flower-sellers*, published in 1932, Farhatullah Beg pointed at the degradation of communal harmony in the colonial world by intimately linking it to the figure of the Mughal king.[143] Once again, with the glorification of Bahadur Shah's pacifying role, Farhatullah Beg resisted the colonial reading of communal violence as a 'primordial religious conflict' that necessitated the benevolent presence of the British colonial state.[144] On the contrary, the lack of 'emotional integration' from British authorities was pointed out as the reason behind the rise of Hindu–Muslim tensions that were said to be absent from earlier times. In city memoirs, Urdu writers usually underscored the intimate link between the ruler and his kingdom. As a just and virtuous king produced thriving and peaceful citizens, bad governance would result, as was felt to be the case in the colonial world, in recession and strife. Farhatullah Beg pointed to the British imbalance towards Hindu and Muslim communities. Bahadur Shah, on the other hand, was shown as ably negotiating and appeasing the religious feelings of both communities, refusing to show any bias.[145]

Despite dreaming of lost social harmony, however, Urdu writers nonetheless had difficulties representing a past that was truly and uniformly multi-religious. If, as Perkins has noted, Sharar – like most city novelists – 'went about creating this past world to foster the creation of an alternative public characterized not by religious animosities and divisions but by a shared cultural world',[146] this composite world

[141] Faizuddin, *Bazm-e āḵẖir*, p. 23.
[142] Hasan, *Dillī kā āḵẖrī dīdār*, p.72, trans. R. Safvi (ed.), *City of My Heart*, p. 60.
[143] Beg, *Bahadur Shah*, pp. 37–42.
[144] W. Fusfeld, 'Communal Conflict in Delhi: 1803–1930'.
[145] Beg, *Bahādur Shāh aur Phūlwāloṇ kī sair*, p. 47, trans. Beg, *Bahadur Shah*, p. 39.
[146] C. R. Perkins, 'Partitioning History', p. 30.

struggled to materialise outside of their imagination. On the contrary, as other scholars have shown, Sharar rather expressed concerns about Hindu–Muslim relations in his magazine *Dil Gudāz*: he regularly encouraged contributions from Hindus 'to make their history, religion and culture known to Muslims',[147] but was forced to recognise as early as 1887 that '[*Dil Gudāz*] is becoming more and more engrossed in the affairs of Islam to the exclusion of other points of view'.[148]

In fact, although Urdu writers remembered the joy of Hindu festivals, the mixed dialect of Urdu court women, and the so-called harmonious relations of the past, they nevertheless asserted a collective Muslim identity. In the novels, Muslims were individualised but Hindus were usually exclusively treated as masses. Muslim saints, princes and princesses, courtesans, musicians, and even cooks[149] were precisely named and commemorated whereas Hindu lives were usually consigned to oblivion. Muslims' deaths were repeatedly recounted and grieved; Hindus' were not. Dipesh Chakrabarty remarked on a similar process in post-Partition Bengal, where the Hindus' selective memory of religious harmony served to assert the group's cultural superiority.[150] It seems that the depiction of peaceful cohabitation during Mughal times in Delhi memoirs too rather fed a yearning for Muslim power.

5 Conclusion

The nostalgic prose narratives about Delhi that grew at the turn of the twentieth century are interesting sources to study how the collective memory of the local past was constructed over the course of a couple of decades. Written by Muslim *ashrāf* descended from families associated with Mughal courts since before 1857, they were particularly sensitive to the need for memorialising their locality after the transfer of the colonial capital in 1911, when the death or financial ruin of the Mughal aristocracy and the simultaneous influx of outsiders from Bengal and the Punjab metamorphosed the living landscape of the city. Through typical methods usually associated with storytelling traditions, Delhi authors strove to remember and to re-presence the interactional past of their place of attachment through the senses.

[147] F. Hussain 'A Note', in A. H. Sharar, *Lucknow Last Phase*, p. 23.
[148] Quoted by Ibid. [149] Ibid., p. 156.
[150] D. Chakrabarty, 'Remembered Villages: Representations of Hindu-Bengali Memories'.

The nostalgic memoirs, however, engaged less with contemporary *ġham* than with past happiness. The contrast between past and present served to provide continuity in the experience of loss and displacement, but also to criticise colonial Delhi. The memory of the Mughal past hence crystallised on specific elements (the local dialect, courtesans, Bahadur Shah Zafar) that had been discredited by colonial discourses and late nineteenth-century reformers. The memory of the festival of the flower-sellers and the idealised depiction of religious harmony in Mughal times in particular responded to the increase in communal violence in the city in the late 1920s. Nostalgia marked a generation of Delhi authors who constructed a shared multi-sensory heritage of their locality, and aimed at sustaining a local Muslim collective identity through the memory of past power.

Epilogue

At about 2 a.m. I woke up and did not find Sir Syed in his bed. When I went out of the room in his search, I saw him pacing up and down the veranda. His eyes were filled with tears (*barāmdeh meṇ ṭahal rahe haiṇ aur zār-o qaṯār rote jāte haiṇ*). I got worried and asked him whether he had received some bad news (*afsosnāk k͟habar*). He retorted (*yeh sun kar aur zyādah rone lage*): 'what greater catastrophe can be there? The Muslims are ruined and still they are following the path of destruction.' [...] After witnessing the condition (*hālāt*) of Sir Syed, I felt so much worried that I cannot describe it (*jo kaifiyat mere dil par guzrī usko bayān nahīṇ kar saktā*), and for me, admiration for that man became boundless.[1]

Thus Nawab Mohsin ul-Mulk described to Hali the night that he spent with Syed Ahmed Khan in Benares before a meeting discussing the progress of education amongst Indian Muslims in 1872. This anecdote about Syed Ahmed Khan's manifestation of grief at the miserable Muslim present is representative of what emotions can do. Through his bitter weeping, his anxious pacing up and down, and his laments, Aligarh's founder embodied and communicated his dedication to a Muslim community that was far from being well defined or homogeneous. His emotional state impacted his friend so much that it elicited a profound admiration, and grief and worry overwhelmed the latter too to the point that it validated Syed Ahmed Khan's concerns and interests, and convinced Mohsin ul-Mulk to support him. Mohsin ul-Mulk became one of the strongest supporters of the Aligarh movement, and one of the founders of the All-India Muslim League in 1906. The emotions of Syed Ahmed Khan, but also of the poets writing on the Kanpur mosque and the Khilafat movement, were contagious and became the drive behind many collective endeavours. As William

[1] Hali, *Ḥayāt-e Jāwed*, part I, pp. 152–3 trans. Hali, *Hayat-e Jawed* (R. A. Alavi), pp. 97–8.

Reddy and Barbara Rosenwein emphasised, emotional expressions have a performative quality that enables them to become agents of change, 'engines of conversion'.[2]

Ġham created bonding, but also prompted claims of public acknowledgment and political action. Often, emotion and memory were linked to a search for continuity and, at the same time, their expression provided the basis for a shared sense of belonging. They actively shaped community identity, delineating its boundaries and, by the same process, estranging other groups. Emotional registers were cultivated in colonial north India, and they were usually developed and publicised in the periodical press, whose ability to construct imagined communities has been well studied in scholarship. This, I have shown, did not occur in a linear process: communities sometimes clashed over their emotional styles (Chapter 2), while others were specific to a particular moment (Chapter 1) or locality (Chapter 5). I have argued for a diversity of emotional expressions and a diversity of *ġham*s.

Indeed, if the communities created by *ġham* were not uniform, their *ġham* was not either. I have illustrated through a close attention to the pasts summoned and to the emotional vocabulary deployed in the sources that actors activated different semantic nets according to their preferences and aims. *Ġham* was an umbrella term that covered different meanings according to whether it was associated with physical suffering; complaint; regret and repentance; oppression and injustice; or love, devotion, and pleasure. From Aligarh partisans to Khilafat supporters, *ġham* was central, but its meaning was not the same. As I emphasised, there were diverse indigenous perceptions of what grief is and does: classical *ġhazal* poetic conventions about amorous separation, melancholy as a disease in ethical treatises, Sufi understandings of *ġham* as devotion. But grief was also influenced in colonial north India by official British validation of collective (especially religious) feelings (Chapter 3). Likewise, the past that was recalled was varied: it ranged from the time of the Prophet, of Andalusian kingdoms, and of Muslim rule in Delhi, to the rule of the very last Mughal king. Nevertheless, the past to which *ġham* was usually linked was always one of secular power. It was described in close relation to feelings of loss, powerlessness, and sometimes humiliation during colonial rule. It anchored most visibly in the city, even beyond strict *shahr āshob* aesthetics.

[2] B. Rosenwein, *Emotional Communities*, p. 19.

The study of the transformation of the *shahr āshob* genre from 1857 to the 1930s was particularly fruitful. Although the codes of the genre certainly shaped the expression of emotions in very stereotypical images such as autumn or the blowing of a candle, they also enabled creative change. I have highlighted that *shahr āshob* was truly a protean genre: besides pure nostalgia it also carried a significant potentiality for political satire. From mourning, it easily transformed into complaint – a process that was further enabled by its association with the secular *marṡiyah*. The fact that some communities favoured the *shahr āshob* and *marṡiyah* genres supports the idea that those were indeed the most compatible with their styles.[3]

This book ends in late 1930s Delhi. It does not delve into the 1940s and the way grief and the imaginations of an Islamic past developed during the Pakistan movement, or after the Partition of 1947. *Shahr āshob* poetry and the *qaumī marṡiyah* nonetheless continued to resonate and to serve a variety of purposes. During World War II, Simab Akbarabadi composed a book of 400 pages of month-by-month *ʿālam āshobs* from May 1940 to December 1943.[4] On 13 December 1948, Jamal Mian Farangi Mahall, writing under the *takhalluṣ* Sharir Banbasi, lamented the state of post-Partition Lucknow in a *shahr āshob* published in *Hamdam*.[5] In 1950–1951, Josh Mahilabadi expressed his delusion and his longing for pre-partitioned India in his *Mātam-e Āzādī* that was recited at the Red Fort of Delhi.[6] In Pakistan, Faiz Ahmad Faiz composed a *shahr āshob* in February 1966 after the Indo-Pakistan war and the contested Pakistani presidential elections of 1965;[7] Jaun Eliya composed one on Zia ul-Haq's oppressive rule (1978–1988);[8] Mohsin Bhopali and Gulnar Afrin wrote *shahr āshobs* to oppose 'Operation Clean-up' in Karachi that was launched

3 B. Rosenwein, *Emotional Communities*, p. 27.
4 Simab Akbarabadi, *ʿālam āshob*.
5 Sharir Banbasi, 'Shahr āshob', in *Hamdam*, 13 December 1948. I am grateful to Francis Robinson for providing the poem in translation by Mahmood Jamal. For an extract of the original in Urdu see S. M. H. Rizwi, 'shahr āshob', *Nuqoosh* 102, pp. 43–5.
6 For other post-1947 *shahr āshob* poems see A. Arifi, *Shahr āshob*, pp. 255–85.
7 Faiz Ahmad Faiz, '*Ek shahr āshob kā āġhāz*', in *Nuskhahā-e wafā*, p. 417. I am grateful to Julien Columeau for discussing the context of the poem with me.
8 Jaun Eliya, '*Shahr āshob*' in *Shāyad*, pp. 46–9. I thank Anne Castaing for bringing this poem to my attention.

by Nawaz Sharif in 1992.[9] More recently, the coronavirus outbreak generated mournful yet satirical poems criticising the UP government's handling of the crisis.[10] At the time of writing this book, translations of the Delhi memoirs of Chapter 5 were published – *The Last Gathering* by Ather Farouqui and *City of My Heart* by Rana Safvi – showing that nostalgia for pre-colonial Delhi still resounds in contemporary Indian politics, where local populations and minorities are anxious to maintain collective identity.

Of course, the present book calls for further studies. I have mainly focused on textual printed sources, although the orality and bodily gestures that accompanied those materials were whenever possible specified. Further, the sources I used were produced by elite Urdu-speaking *ashrāf* who usually navigated colonial rule successfully and were acquainted with Western culture. They did not always share the same ideas and interests, but they came from similar backgrounds, and usually had links with Delhi and the former Mughal aristocracy, even if, at times, their practices and discourses spilled over class boundaries. Occasionally, I have been able to point to counterpoints, usually from the newspaper archive. The longing for an extra-Indian past, for instance, aroused many critiques from the cosmopolitan milieu of the *Awadh Punch*, but also from Hindu Urdu poets contributing to *Zamānah*.

I have not noticed significant difference in emotional expressions between Hindu and Muslim Urdu-speaking actors, but, as historians have increasingly highlighted, histories of colonial north India need to address multiple languages and multilingual practices. Finally, to go further, *ġham* would gain from being put in closer relation with a set of other emotions – especially shame,[11] sympathy (*hamdardī*), anger, and happiness – to refine our understanding of emotional styles and communities in British India.[12] Hopefully, this book constitutes a first step in that direction.

[9] M. Bhopali and G. Afrin, *Shahr āshob-e Karāchī*.
[10] See, for instance, Parul Khakkar's famous Gujarati poem *Shav-vāhinī Gangā* (2021).
[11] See, for instance, A. Zaidi, *Making a Muslim*.
[12] See, for instance, B. Rosenwein, 'Problems of Method', p. 11.

Glossary

akhlāq	Islamic ethics
ashrāf	sg. sharīf, "noble", a South Asian Muslim elite group that claims foreign origin and is subdivided into Sayyids (descendants of the Prophet), Shaikhs (descendants of the Prophet's companions), Pathans (from Afghanistan), and Mughals (from Iran and Central Asia)
āżān	Muslim call for prayer
Ashura	tenth day of the month of Muharram, which commemorates the martyrdom of Imam Husain
begum	woman of high rank
begamātī zubān	High-ranking women's speech
chārbāġh	Indo-Persian-style quadrilateral garden
chaukīdār	watchman
dālān	vestibule, hall
dargāh	shrine
dāstān	tale (traditionally oral); dāstāngo: storyteller
dīwān	collection of poems by a single author
darbār/Durbar	court or public audience held by a ruler
Eid	Islamic festival
fatwa	formal authoritative legal ruling
fatiḥah	short first surah of the Qur'an; prayer for the dead
ġhazal	lyric poem
ġham	generic term for grief
hadith	tradition; record of the sayings and doings of the Prophet
hajw	satire; poem of humorous insult
hakīm	practitioner of Islamic medicine

Haramain Sharifain	Islamic holy places, i.e. Mecca and Medina
haveli	large house; mansion with inner courtyards
Holi	Hindu spring festival
ʿibrat	warning, especially the lesser signs announcing Doomsday
ʿīdgāh	open ground devoted to Eid prayers at the outskirts of a city
Iram	legendary garden city whose king bid to rival God and was eventually destroyed
jihad	holy war against non-Muslims; personal struggle against one's baser instincts
jinn	supernatural entity (usually good)
kalimah	Islamic declaration of faith
Karbala	ground in modern-day Iraq where Imam Husain was martyred (680 A.D.)
Kayasth	Hindu caste of north India traditionally associated with scribal occupations
Khatri	Predominantly Hindu caste of north India traditionally associated with commercial and clerical professions
Khilafat	successorship of the Prophet Muhammad as leader of the Muslim community
Mahdi	Messiah
maqt̠aʿ	closing verse of a ġhazal
marṡiyah	elegy, often to commemorate someone's death; Shia marṡiyahs are devoted to Karbala martyrs and especially Imam Husain; marṡiyahk̲h̲wān: elegist
maṡnawī	(usually long) narrative poem
millat	Muslim religious community
Muharram	first month of the Islamic year in which the martyrdom of Imam Husain is commemorated
muḥallah	city neighbourhood
mujāhidīn	those who wage jihad
muk̲h̲ammas	cinquain; poem composed of stanzas of five lines
musaddas	sextain; poem composed of stanzas of six lines
mutawallī	administrator of a *waqf*
mushāʿirah	poetic gathering

Naḥdah	'Arab renaissance'; late nineteenth- to twentieth-century cultural movement that developed in the Arabic-speaking regions of the Ottoman Empire
namāz	Islamic ritual prayer
nauḥah	poetic lament; requiem
Nauroz	first day of the Iranian calendar year; celebration of the spring equinox
pardah	lit. curtain; practice of female seclusion
pīr	Sufi master
qaṣbah	small fortified market town
qaṣidah	'ode'; panegyric poem
qaum	community; nation
qiṯaʿ	section of a ġhazal which sometimes evolves into an independent poem
qiṣṣah	tale; romance
Ramzan	ninth month of the Islamic year during which Muslims observe fasting
satyagraha	political movement of nonviolent resistance initiated by Gandhi
Shab-e Barat	fifteenth night of the Islamic month of Sha'ban during which Muslims pray for the forgiveness of sins
shahr āshob	poetic genre on the devastation of cities, also of the world (*dunyā āshob*), of the age (*zamānah, dahr āshob*), or of the community and Islam (*qaum āshob, islām āshob*)
shams ul ʿulamāʾ	lit. the sun among scholars; official title given to renowned scholars in British India
sharīʿah	Islamic law
shajrah	genealogical tree
shikwah	complaint; petition
shuddhī	Hindu religious proselytist movement in north India
sīrat (literature)	literature on the life of the Prophet Muhammad
surah	chapter of the Qur'an
Swadeshi	nationalist movement which promoted the use of domestic goods and boycotted foreign imports and institutions

tabarruk	sacred offering (often made of food items) distributed after a religious celebration, especially as part of Muharram rituals
tak̲h̲alluṣ	pen name
tārīk̲h̲	chronogram
tażkirah	collective biography
tanẕīm	Muslim religious proselytist movement in north India
tauḥīd	unity of God; essential tenet of the Islamic faith
t̤awā'if	courtesan
Timur	Timur Lang (Tamerlane), Turko-Mongol conqueror (1370–1405)
ulama	sg. alim; religious scholar
ummah	Islamic community created by Prophet Muhammad at Medina
ustād	master, often of poetry or music
waqf	pl. *awqāf*; Islamic endowment
zamīndār	landowner
zanānah	women's quarters in a household
żikr	lit. remembrance, prayer, or litany for recalling God

Bibliography

Periodicals

Al-Hilāl (Calcutta), Lucknow: Uttar Pradesh Urdu Academy, ed. 2010 (6 vols): from July 1912 to April 1914

Aligarh Institute Gazette (Aligarh) AMU: volumes 1866–1869, 1871–1888

Awadh Punch (Lucknow) SJM & JMI: volumes 1877–1879, 1888 to February 1889, 1891–1892, 1902–1904, 1930, October 1935, June 1937, December 1937, September 1938

Hamdard (Delhi) NMML & JMI: from May 1913 to April 1915 and 3 May 1926 to 15 May 1927

Kayastha Samachar and Hindustan Review (Allahabad) SOAS & NMML: from January 1901 (vol. 3, no. 1) to June 1911 (vol. 23, no. 142)

Tahżīb ul-Ak̲h̲lāq (Aligarh) AMU: volumes 1881, 1878–1880, 1893–1894, 1874, 1873, 1870–1876, 1880, 1897

The Comrade (Calcutta, Delhi) NMML & JMI: from January 1911 (vol. 1, no. 1) to November 1925 (vol. 3, no. 18)

Zamānah (Lahore) NAI and EAP566 BL: volumes 1908–1914, 1929

Private Papers

Mohamed Ali Papers, JMI

Mohamed Ali Papers, NMML

Jawaharlal Nehru Papers, NMML

Government Records

CC, Home, 27/1914 B: Question of the payment of compensation for mosques and tombs [DSA]

CC, Revenue and Agriculture, 39/1915 B: Demolition and restoration of Maulana Abdul Haq's mosque near Okhla [DSA]

CC, Education, File no. 77/1915 B: Mohammadan graveyards in Delhi [DSA]

CC, Education, 24/1918 B: Protection of monuments in Delhi Province [DSA]
CC, Education, 1(6), 1930 (B): Petition from Muhammad Abdul Ghafar regarding exemption of his property at Qutab from the Ancient Monuments Act of 1904 [DSA]
Commissioner Officc, 68/1894: Defacement of tombs of British officers on the Ridge [DSA]
Confidential Records, Home, 1914, B, 8: Pamphlet entitled Ahkam ul-masajid regarding the demolition of mosques [DSA]
Confidential, Education, 3/1915 (B) Enquiry regarding a book entitled 'Ghadr Delhi ke Afsane' by Hassan Nizami [DSA]
First Report of the Curator of Ancient Monuments in India for the year 1881–82, Simla, 1882
Foreign, External, May 1907, Proceedings no. 764–796 [DSA]
Hansard (1803–2005) online, Commons Sitting, Orders of the Day, 'Government of Scotland Bill', House of Commons, 30 May 1913, vol. 53, pp. 471–551
Home Department, Public, 14th May 1858, no. 97 [NAI]
Home, Political B, November 1912, Proceedings 82–86: weekly reports of the director of criminal intelligence on the political situation for the month of October 1912 [NAI]
Home, Delhi, A Proceedings, April 1912, 103–39: Acquisition of land at Delhi and the planning and building of the new city of Delhi [NAI]
Home, Delhi, September 1912, Deposit no. 9: Question of the treatment of mosques, temples and tombs in connection with land acquisition proceedings at Delhi [NAI]
Home, Public, Deposit no. 36, August 1913: Question of the treatment of mosques, temples, and tombs in connection with land acquisition proceedings in Delhi [NAI]
Home, Political, A, October 1913, Proceedings 100–18: Riot at Cawnpore in connection with the demolition of a mosque in Machli Bazar. State of Muhammadan feeling in India [NAI]
Home, Political A, October 1913, Proceedings 142–9: Demand of security under section 3 of the Indian Press Act, 1910 from the keepers of the Comrade and Hamdard press and the Baitul Sharaf Press Delhi [NAI]
Home, Public, B, December 1913, 170: Questions and answers in the Imperial legislative council regarding the acquisition of Muslim mosques etc. and regarding the preservation of religious edifices [NAI]
Imperial Gazetteer of India, vol. 3: Economic, Oxford: Clarendon Press, 1908
Indian Penal Code (Act XLV of 1860): with Notes, ed. W. Morgan and A. G. Macpherson, Calcutta: Hay and Co, 1863
Justice for Islam and Turkey. Speeches delivered at a meeting held at Kingsway Hall, on Thursday, the 22nd April 1920 to demand justice for Islam and Turkey, London: Indian Khilafat Deputation, 1920

Native Newspapers Reports for the North-Western Provinces and Oudh: volumes 1864 to 1937 [NAI, BL]

Primary Sources and Translations

Abbas, Ghulam, ‘Anandi’, translated by G. A. Chaussée, *Annual of Urdu Studies*, 18, 2 (2003), pp. 324–9

Abu al-Baqa al-Rundi, ‘Lament for the Fall of Seville’, translated by J. T. Monroe, in O. R. Constable (ed.), *Medieval Iberia: Readings from Christian, Muslim and Jewish Sources* (Philadelphia: University of Pennsylvania Press, 2012), pp. 220–2

Abul Fazl, *The Ain-i Akbari*, vol. 1, translated by H. Blochmann (Calcutta: Bibliotheca Indica, 1873)

Ahmed, Nazir, *The Bride’s Mirror: A Tale of Life in Delhi a Hundred Years Ago*, translated by G. E. Ward with an afterword by F. W. Pritchett (New Delhi: Permanent Black, 2004)

Ahmed, Nazir, *Mirāt ul-‘urūs* (Lahore: Sang-e Meel Publications, 1998)

Ahmad Dehlawi, Sayyid, *Farhang-e āsafiyah*, vol. 3 (Lahore: Urdu Science Board, 2010 [1898])

Ahmad Dehlawi, Sayyid, *Luġhat un-Nisā* (Lahore: Kashi Ram Press, 1917)

Ahmad Dehlawi, Sayyid, *Rusūm-e Dehlī* (Delhi: Urdu Academy, 1975 [1900–1905])

Akbar Allahabadi, *Kulliyāt-e Akbar Allahābādī*, vol. 3 (Badaun: Naqeeb Press, 1921)

al-Khafaji, Ahmad ibn Muhammad, *Rayḥānat al-alibbā fī zahrat al-ḥayāt al-dunyā* (Misr: unknown, 1888, reprint)

Ali, Abbas, *The Beauties of Lucknow: Consisting of Twenty-four Selected Photographed Portraits, Cabinet Size, of the Most Celebrated and Popular Living Historic Singers, Dancing Girls and Actresses of the Oudh Court and of Lucknow* (Calcutta: Calcutta Central Press, 1874)

Ali, Sayyid Amir, *Memoirs and Other Writings of Syed Ameer Ali*, edited by S. R. Wasti (Lahore: People’s Publishing House, 1968)

Ali, Ahmed, *Twilight in Delhi* (New York: New Directions, 1994 [1940])

Ali, Mohamed, *Intik͟hāb-e Hamdard*, edited by S. Umar (Lucknow: UP Urdu Academy, 1988)

Ali, Mohamed, Jauhar, *Kalām-e Jauhar* (Delhi: Maktaba Jamia Limited, 1936)

Ali, Mohamed, Khilafat Conference Presidential Address by Muhammad Ali (Calcutta, December 1928)

Ali, Mohamed, *My Life a Fragment: An Autobiographical Sketch of Maulana Mohamed Ali* (New Delhi: Manohar Publications, 1999 [1942])
Ali, Mohamed, *Unpublished Letters of the Ali Brothers*, edited by M. Shan (Delhi: Idarah-e Adabiyat-e Dilli, 1979)
Andrews, C. F., *Zaka Ullah of Delhi* (Cambridge: Heffer and Sons, 1929)
Awadh Punch, *Intikẖāb-e Awadh Punch*, edited by R. Kazmi (Lucknow: Kitabi Dunya, 1964)
Azad, Muhammad Husain, *Āb-e Ḥayāt* (Lahore: Nawal Kishore Gas Printing Works, 1907 [1883])
Azad, Muhammad Husain, *Ab-e Hayat: Shaping the Canon of Urdu Poetry*, translated and edited by F. W. Pritchett and S. R. Faruqi (New Delhi: Oxford University Press, 2003)
Babur, Zahir uddin Muhammad, *Babur Nama: Journal of Emperor Babur*, translated by A. S. Beveridge (New Delhi: Penguin Books, 2006)
Barq, Mirza Raza, *Intikẖāb-e ġhazaliyāt-e Barq* (Lucknow: UP Urdu Academy, 1983)
Beg, Farhatullah, *Bahadur Shah and the Festival of Flower-sellers*, translated by M. Zakir (Hyderabad: Orient Blackswan, 2012)
Beg, Farhatullah, *Bahādur Shāh aur Phulwāloṇ kī sair* (Delhi: Mahboob ul-Mataba, 1943 [1932])
Beg, Farhatullah, *Dehlī kā ek yādgār ākẖrī mushāʿirah, 1261 hijrī muṯābiq 1846 ʿiswī meṇ* (Aligarh: Educational Book House, n.d. [1928])
Beg, Farhatullah, *Dr Nażīr Aḥmad kī kahānī kuchh merī aur kuchh unkī zubānī* (Delhi: Anjuman-e Taraqqi-e Urdu, 2009)
Beg, Farhatullah, *The Last mushaʿirah of Delhi*, translated by A. Qamber (New Delhi: Orient Blackswan, 1979 [1928])
Beg, Farhatullah, *Nazir Ahmad: In His Own Words and Mine*, translated by M. Zakir (New Delhi: Orient Blackswan, 2009 [1927])
Beg, Farhatullah, *Maẓāmīn-e Farḥat*, vol. 2 (Hyderabad: Matbua Dakan La Report, n. d.)
Beg, Farhatullah, *Mirzā Farḥatullah Beg ke Maẓāmīn: Intikẖāb*, edited by A. Parvez (Delhi: Urdu Academy, 2009)
Constable, Archibald, *A Selection from the Illustrations Which Have Appeared in the Oudh Punch from 1877 to 1881* (Lucknow: Oudh Punch Office, 1881)
Dawani, Ibn Asad Jalal Al-din Muhammad, *Practical Philosophy of the Muhammadan People, Being a Translation of the Akhlak-i-Jalaly*, translated by W.F. Thompson (London: W.H. Allen and Co, 1839)
Faiz, Faiz Ahmad, *Nuskẖahā-e wafā* (Delhi: Educational Publishing House, 1986)
Faizuddin, Munshi, *Bazm-e ākẖir* (Delhi: Urdu Academy, 2009 [1885])
Faizuddin, Munshi, *The last gathering: a vivid portrait of life in the Red Fort*, translated by A. Farouqui (New Delhi: Roli Books, 2021)

Firaq Dehlawi, Hakim Khwajah Nasir Naziruddin, *Chār Chānd* (Delhi, Dilli Printing Works, n.d.)
Firaq Dehlawi, Hakim Khwajah Nasir Naziruddin, *Dillī kā ujṛā hū'ā lāl qilaʿh* (Delhi, Shahjahan Book Agency, n. d.)
Firaq Dehlawi, Hakim Khwajah Nasir Naziruddin, *Lāl qilaʿh kī ek jhalak* (Delhi: Urdu Academy, 2006 [c. 1900])
Firaq Dehlawi, Hakim Khwajah Nasir Naziruddin, *Maẓāmīn-e Firāq* (Delhi: Anjuman-e Taraqqi-e Urdu, n.d.)
Ghalib, Mirza Asadullah Khan, *Ghalib. 1797–1869, vol. 1: Life and Letters*, edited by R. Russell and K. Islam (London: Allen and Unwin, 1969)
Ghalib, Mirza Asadullah Khan, *K͟hut̤ūt̤-e Ġhālib*, 2 vols (Lahore: Punjab University Press, 1969)
Gorgani, Mirza Ahmad Akhtar, *Sawāneḥ-e Dehlī* (Delhi: Urdu Academy, 2009)
Hali, Altaf Husain, *Hali's Musaddas: A Story in Verse of the Ebb and Tide of Islam*, translated by S. S. Hameed (New Delhi: Harper Collins, 2003)
Hali, Altaf Husain, *Hayat-e Javed. A Biographical Account of Sir Sayyid*, translated by K. H. Qadiri and D. J. Matthews (Delhi: Idarah-e Adabiyat-e Dilli, 2009)
Hali, Altaf Husain, *Ḥayāt-e Jāwed* (Lahore: Anjuman-e Taraqqi-e Urdu, 1939)
Hali, Altaf Husain, *Hayat-e Jawed: A Biographical Account of Sir Syed Ahmad Khan, Part I–II*, translated by R. A. Alavi (Aligarh: Sir Syed Academy, 2008 [1901])
Hali, Altaf Husain, *Madd-o Jazr-e Islām: al-maʿrūf bah Musaddas-e Ḥālī* (Delhi: unknown, 1884 [1879])
Hali, Altaf Husain, *Majālis un-nisā* (New Delhi: Qaumi Council Bara-e Farogh-e Urdu Zaban, 2012)
Hali, Altaf Husain, *Makātīb-e Ḥālī*, edited by M. I. Panipati (Lahore: Urdu Markaz, 1950)
Hali, Altaf Husain, *Muqaddamah-e shiʿr-o shāʿirī* (Aligarh: Muslim University Press, 1928)
Hali, Altaf Husain, *Tarkīb band mausum bah Shikwah-e Hind* (Lahore: Sahafi Press, 1888)
Hali, Altaf Husain, C. Shackle, and J. Majeed, *Hali's Musaddas: The Flow and Ebb of Islam* (Oxford: Oxford University Press, 1997)
Hasan Dehlawi, Wazir, *Dillī kā āk͟hrī dīdār* (Delhi: Urdu Academy, 2013 [1932])
Herat Dehlawi, Mirza, *Chirāġh-e Dehlī* (Delhi: Urdu Academy, 2009 [1931])
Hunter, W., *Indian Musalmans* (London: Trübner and Co, 1876, 3rd ed.)
Iqbal, Sir Muhammad, *Asrār-o Rumūz* (Delhi: Kutubkhana Naziriya, 1962)
Iqbal, Sir Muhammad, *Bang-e Darā* (Delhi: Jamia Hamdard, 1991 [1924])

Iqbal, Sir Muhammad, *The Call of the Marching Bell, English Translation and Commentary of Bang-i Dara*, translated by M. A. K. Khalil (Lahore: M. A. Khalil, 1997)

Iqbal, Sir Muhammad, *Gabriel's Wing*, translated by D. J. Matthews, N. Siddiqui, and S. A. A. Shah (Lahore: Iqbal Academy Pakistan, 2014)

Iqbal, Sir Muhammad, *The Mysteries of Selflessness: A Philosophical Poem*, translated by A. J. Arberry (London: Dar al-Islamiya, 2001 [1918])

Iqbal, Sir Muhammad, 'Political Thought in Islam', *Kayastha Samachar*, 23, 136 (December 1910), pp. 527–33

Iqbal, Sir Muhammad, *Presidential Address by Dr. Sir Muhammad Iqbal, Barrister-at-Law, Lahore*, All India Muslim League, Allahabad Session (December 1930)

Iqbal, Sir Muhammad, *The Reconstruction of Religious Thought in Islam* (London: Oxford University Press, 1934)

Iqbal, Sir Muhammad, *The Secrets of the Self: Asrar-i Khudi*, translated by R. A. Nicholson (Lahore: M. Ashraf, 1960)

Iqbal, Sir Muhammad, *Shikwah* (Lahore: Kapoor Art Printing Works, n.d. [1909])

Iqbal, Sir Muhammad *Shikwa and Jawab-i Shikwa. Complaint and Answer. Iqbal's Dialogue with Allah*, translated from the Urdu with an introduction by Khushwant Singh (Oxford: Oxford University Press, 1990)

Iqbal, Sir Muhammad, www.allamaiqbal.com/

Jaun Eliya, *Shāyad* (Karachi: Ibn Husain Printing Press, 1991)

Jur'at, Shaikh Qalandar Bakhsh, 'In the Presence of the Nightingale: A shahr ashob', translated by S. R. Faruqi, and F. W. Pritchett, *Annual of Urdu Studies*, 3 (1983), pp. 1–9

Kaifi, Brij Mohan Dattatreya, *Bhārat Darpan yā Musaddas-e Kaifī* (Lahore: Matba Mufeed-e Aam, 1905)

Kanda, K. C., *Masterpieces of Patriotic Urdu Poetry: Text, Translation, and Transliteration* (New Delhi: Sterling Publishers, 2005)

Kaukab, Tafazzul Husain, *Fuġhān-e Dehlī* (Delhi: Akmal ul-Maṯābe', 1863); (Lahore: Academy Punjab Trust, 1954); (Lahore: Naurang Kitab Ghar, 2007)

Khan, Syed Ahmed, *Āṡār uṣ-Ṣanādīd* (Delhi: Qaumi Council Bara-e Farogh-e Urdu Zuban, 2011 [1852])

Khan, Syed Ahmed, *K̲h̲uṯūṯ-e Sir Sayyid* (Badaun: Nizami Press, 1924)

Khan, Syed Ahmed, *The Present State of Indian Politics: Consisting of Speeches and Letters, Reprinted from the 'Pioneer'* (Allahabad: The Pioneer Press, 1888)

Khan, Syed Ahmed, *Selected Letters of Sir Syed Ahmad*, edited by M. A. Mannan (Aligarh: Sir Syed Academy, 2007)

Khairi, Rashid ul, *Dillī kī ak̲h̲rī bahār* (Delhi: Urdu Academy, 2010 [1937])

Mir, Mir Taqi, *Zikr-e Mir, The Autobiography of the Eighteenth Century Mughal Poet: Mir Muhammad Taqi 'Mir'*, translated, introduced and commented by C. M. Naim (New Delhi: Oxford University Press, 2002)

Muhsin, Bhopali, and Gulnar Afrin, *Shahr āshob-e Karāchī: naẕmeṇ, ġhazleṇ aur adabī k͟hut̤ūt̤* (Karachi: Aiwan-e Adab, 1997)

Mulla, Pandit Anand Narain, 'Shikwah az Iqbal', *Zamānah* (February 1929), pp. 118–19

Nazim, Muhammad Abdullah Tonki, *Musaddas-e Nāẕim* (Lahore: Matba Nami Garami, 1900)

Nazir, Akbarabadi, 'The Vile World Carnival: A *shahr-ashob* by Nazir Akbarabadi (1740–1830)', translated by F. W. Pritchett and S. R. Faruqi, *Annual of Urdu Studies*, 4 (1984), pp. 25–35

Nizami, Badayuni, *Faryād-e Dehlī* (Badaun: Nizami Press, 1931)

Nizami, Khwajah Hasan, *Ġhadar-e Dehlī ke afsāne. Ḥiṣṣah Awwal* (Delhi: unknown 1918)

Nizami, Khwajah Hasan, *Kānpūr kī k͟hūnī dāstān* (Meerut: Hamidia Press, 1913)

Premchand, Munshi, *Courtesans' Quarter: A Translation of Bazaar-e Husn*, translated by A. Azfar (Oxford: Oxford University Press, 2003 [1924])

Premchand, Munshi, *Karbalā* (Delhi: Lajpat Rai and Sons, 1974 [1924])

Proceedings of the Muslim Educational Conference (Aligarh: Muhammadan Anglo-Oriental College, 1887)

Ruswa, Mirza Muhammad Hadi, *Umrā'o Jān Ādā* (Islamabad, 2000 [1899])

Ruswa, Mirza Muhammad Hadi, *Umrao Jan Ada: Courtesan of Lucknow*, translated by Khushwant Singh, Delhi: Orient Blackswan, 2008

Sabuhi Dehlawi, Ashraf, *Dillī kī chand 'ajīb hastiyāṇ* (Delhi: Qaumi Council Bara-e Farogh-e Urdu Zuban, 2011 [1943])

Shan, M., *The Indian Muslims: A Documentary Record*, vol. 2: The Tripoli and Balkan Wars (Meerut: Meenakshi Prakashan, 1980)

Shan, M., *The Indian Muslims: A Documentary Record*, vol. 4: Mosque Incident, Kanpur and Communal Harmony (Meerut: Meenakshi Prakashan, 1981)

Sharar, Abdul Halim, *Guẕashtah Lukhna'ū: Hindustān meṇ mashriqī tamaddun kā āk͟hrī namūnah* (New Delhi: Maktabah Jamia Limited, 2011)

Sharar, Abdul Halim, *Lucknow: The Last Phase of an Oriental Culture*, translated by E. S. Harcourt and F. Hussain (London: Elek, 1975)

Shauq Qidwai, Munshi Ahmad Ali, *Lail-o Nahār* (Agra: Matba' Mufīd-e 'ām, 1892)

Shibli, Numani, *Kulliyāt-e Shiblī* (Azamgarh: Shibli Academy, 2007)

Shibli, Numani, *Maqālāt-e Shiblī*, vol. 1 (Azamgarh: Shibli Academy, 1954)

Shibli, Numani, *Ṣubḥ-e Ummīd ma' Musaddas-e Qaumī* (Lucknow: Qaumi Press, 1889)

Shirazi, M. M. S., *Maʿrakah-e Chakbast-o Sharar yaʿnī mubāhisah-e Gulzār-e Nasīm* (Lucknow: Naseem Book Depot, 1966)
Simab, Akbarabadi, *ʿālam āshob* (Agra: Maktaba Qasrul Adab, 1943)
Tabatabai, Ali Hyder, *Nazm-e Ṯabāṯabā'ī* (Hyderabad: unknown, n.d.)
Taimuri, Arsh, *Qilaʿh-e muʿallah kī jhalkiyāṇ* (Delhi: Urdu Academy, 2009 [1937])
Tusi, Nasiruddin, *Akhlāq-e Nāṣirī* (Lucknow: Nawal Kishore Press, 1924)
Tusi, Nasiruddin, *The Nasirean Ethics*, translated by G. M. Wickens (London: G. H. Allen and Unwin, 1964)
United Indian Patriotic Association, *Pamphlets Issued by the United Indian Patriotic Association, no. 2: Showing the Seditious Character of the Indian National Congress and the Opinions Held by Eminent Natives of India Who Are OPPOSED to the Movement* (Allahabad: The Pioneer Press, 1888)
Zahir, Dehlawi, *Dastan-e ghadar: The Tale of the Mutiny*, translated by R. Safvi (Gurgaon: Penguin Books, 2017)
Zahir, Dehlawi, *Dastān-e ġhadar, yaʿnī hangāmah-e 1857 ke chashamdīd ḥālāt* (Lahore: Academy Punjab Trust, 1955)
Zarif Lakhnawi, *Intikhāb-e Kalām-e Zarīf* (Lucknow: UP Urdu Academy, 2004)

Secondary Literature

Abbasi, Z., 'The Classical Islamic Law of Waqf: A Concise Introduction', in *Arab Law Quarterly*, 26, 2 (2012), pp. 121–53
Abdel-Sattar, I., 'Saudi Arabia', in D. B. Baker (ed.), *The Oxford Handbook of the History of Psychology: Global Perspectives* (New York: Oxford University Press, 2012)
Adams, M., and Guy, S., 'Editorial: Senses and the City', *The Senses and Society*, 2, 2 (2007), pp. 133–6
Aghamohammadi, M., 'An Apology for Flowers', *International Journal of Comparative Literature and Translation Studies*, 5, 1 (2017), pp. 31–9
Ahmad, A., *Islamic Modernism in India and Pakistan, 1857–1964* (Oxford: Oxford University Press, 1967)
Ahmad, A., *Muslim Self-statement in India and Pakistan, 1857–1947* (Wiesbaden: Harrassowitz, 1970)
Ahmad, A., 'Hali', in H. A. R. Gibb (ed.), *The Encyclopaedia of Islam* (Leiden: Brill, 1999, 1st ed. 1965)
Ahmad, A., 'Muhammad Iqbal', in M. I. Chaghatai (ed.), *Iqbal: New Dimensions. A Collection of Unpublished and Rare Iqbalian Studies* (Lahore: Sang-e Meel Publications, 2003), pp. 24–7

Ahmad, Mirza Bashiruddin M., *Remembrance of Allah: Zikr-i Ilahi* (Tilford: Islam International Publications, 2003)

Ahmad, N., *Shahr āshob* (New Delhi: Maktaba Jamia Limited, 1947)

Ahmad, N., *Shahr āshob kā taḥqīqī muṯāla'h* (Aligarh: Adabi Academy, 1979)

Ahmad, S., *Urdū Ṣaḥāfat aur Taḥrīk-e Āzādī* (New Delhi: Modern Publishing House, 2009)

Ahmad, S. F., 'Sir Syed Ahmad Khan, Beck and the Indian National Congress', unpublished MPhil dissertation, Aligarh Muslim University (1989)

Ahmed, A. A., 'Specters of Macaulay: Blasphemy, the Indian Penal Code, and Pakistan's Postcolonial Predicament', in R. Kaur and W. Mazzarella(eds.), *Censorship in South Asia: Cultural Regulation from Sedition to Seduction* (Bloomington: Indiana University Press, 2009), pp. 172–205

Ahmed, H., *Muslim Political Discourse in Postcolonial India: Monuments, Memory, Contestation* (New Delhi: Routledge, 2014)

Akhtar, N., *Monogrāf: Allāmah Rāshidul K͟hairī* (Delhi: Urdu Academy, 2012)

Alavi, S., 'Rethinking Religion and Politics: Ulema Histories and the Appropriation of 1857', in K. Narain and M. C. Das (eds.), *1857 Revisited: Myth and Reality* (Mumbai: Himalaya Publishing House, 2008), pp. 147–63

Al-Azmeh, A., 'Rhetoric of the Senses: A Consideration of Muslim Paradise Narratives', *Journal of Arabic Literature*, 26, 3 (1995), pp. 215–31

Alemi, M., 'Princely Safavid Gardens: Stage for Rituals of Imperial Display and Political Legitimacy', in M. Conan and D. Oaks (eds.), *Middle East Garden Traditions: Unity and Diversity, Questions, Methods and Resources in a Multicultural Perspective* (Washington: Harvard University Press, 2007), pp. 113–38

Alexander, J. C., *Cultural Trauma and Collective Identity* (Berkeley: University of California Press, 2004)

Ali Engineer, A., 'A Critical Appraisal of Iqbal's "Reconstruction of Religious Thought in Islam"', in A. Sardar Jafri and K. S. Duggal (eds.), *Iqbal: Commemorative Volume* (Lahore: Iqbal Academy Pakistan, 2004), pp. 122–3

Ali, D., and Flatt, E. (eds.), *Friendship in Pre-Modern South Asia, Special issue of Studies in History*, 33, 1 (2017)

Ali, K. A., 'Courtesans in the Living Room', *Annual of Urdu Studies*, 20 (2005), pp. 274–9

Alwan, M. B., 'The History and Publications of al-Jawā'ib Press', in *MELA Notes*, 11 (May 1977), pp. 4–7

Anderson, B., *Imagined Communities: Reflections on the Origins and Spread of Nationalism* (London: Verso, 2006 [1983])

Andrews, P. A., 'The Generous Heart or the Mass of Clouds: The Court Tents of Shah Jahan', *Muqarnas: An Annual on Islamic Art and Architecture*, 4 (1987), pp. 149–65
Andrews, P. A., *Felt Tents and Pavilions: The Nomadic Tradition and Its Interaction with Princely Tentage*, 2 vols (London: Melisende, 1999)
Anjum, S., *Monogrāf Khwājah Alṯāf Ḥusain Ḥālī* (Delhi: Urdu Academy, 2007)
anon., 'Shahr āshob', in Shafi, Mohammad (ed.), *Urdū Dā'irah-e Ma'ā rīf-e islāmiyah*, 11 (Lahore: Punjab University, 1975), pp. 824–6
anon., 'Sketch-writing and Ashraf Suboohi', *Dawn* (15 April 2008) dawn.com/news/938530/sketch-writing-and-ashraf-suboohi
Ansarullah, M., *Jāma'-e tażkirah*, vol. 3 (Delhi: unknown 2007)
Appadurai, A., *Modernity at Large: Cultural Dimensions of Globalization* (Minneapolis: University of Minnesota Press, 1996)
Ardalan, N., and Bakhtiar, L., *The Sense of Unity: The Sufi tradition in Persian Architecture* (Chicago: University of Chicago Press, 1973)
Arifi, A., *Shahr āshob: Ek tajziyah* (New Delhi: Delhi University, 1994)
Asher, C. B., 'Babur and the Timurid Char Bagh: Use and Meaning', in *Environmental Design*, 1–2 (1991), pp. 46–55
Assmann, A., *Memory and Political Change* (Basingstoke: Palgrave Macmillan, 2012)
Aziz, K. K. (ed.), *The Indian Khilafat Movement, 1915–1933: A Documentary Record* (Karachi: Sang-e Meel Publications, 1972)
Aziz, K. K., *The Murder of History: A Critique of History Textbooks Used in Pakistan* (Lahore: Sang-e Meel Publications, 1993)
Bagheri, M., 'Conceptualizations of Sadness in Persian', in A. Korangy and F. Sharifian (eds.), *Persian Linguistics in Cultural Contexts* (London: Routledge, 2020), pp. 127–40
Bailey, T. G., *A History of Urdu Literature* (Karachi: Oxford University Press, 2008)
Bard, A., 'Value and Vitality in a Literary Tradition: Female Poets and the Urdu Marsiya', *Annual of Urdu Studies*, 15 (2000), pp. 323–35
Bard, A., '"No Power of Speech Remains": Tears and Transformation in South Asian Majlis Poetry', in K. C. Patton and J. S. Hawley (eds.), *Holy Tears: Weeping in the Religious Imagination* (Princeton: Princeton University Press, 2005), pp. 145–64
Barrier, N. G., 'The Punjab Disturbances of 1907: The Response of the British Government in India to Agrarian Unrest', *Modern Asian Studies*, 1, 4 (1967), pp. 353–83
Basu, A., 'Mohamed Ali in Delhi: The Comrade Phase, 1912–1915', in M. Hasan (ed.), *Communal and Pan-Islamic Trends in Colonial India* (New Delhi: Manohar Publications, 1981), pp. 109–25

Bausani, A., 'The Concept of Time in the Religious Philosophy of Muhammad Iqbal', in *Die Welt des Islams, New Series*, 3, 3 (1954), pp. 158–86

Bayly, C. A., 'Delhi and Other Cities of North India during the "Twilight"', in R. E. Frykenberg (ed.), *Delhi through the Ages: Selected Essays in Urban History, Culture and Society* (Delhi: Oxford University Press, 1993), pp. 121–36

Bayly, C. A., *The Local Roots of Indian Politics: Allahabad, 1880–1920* (Oxford: Clarendon Press, 1975)

Bayly, C. A., *Empire and Information: Intelligence Gathering and Social Communication in India, 1780–1870* (Cambridge: Cambridge University Press, 1997)

Bhandari, V., 'Print and the Emergence of Multiple Publics in Nineteenth-Century Punjab', in S. Alcorn Baron, E. N. Lindquist, and E. F. Shevlin, *Agent of Change: Print Culture Studies after Elizabeth L. Eisenstein* (Amherst: University of Massachusetts Press, 2007), pp. 268–86

Bhabha, H., 'Of Mimicry and Man: The Ambivalence of the Colonial Discourse', *October*, 28 (1984), pp. 125–33

Birchok, D. A., 'Sojourning on Mecca's Verandah: Place, Temporality, and Islam in an Indonesian Province', unpublished PhD dissertation, University of Michigan (2013)

Blachère R., and Bausani, A., 'Ghazal', *Encyclopaedia of Islam*, 2nd ed. online

Blake, S. P., *Shahjahanabad: The Sovereign City in Mughal India, 1639–1739* (Cambridge: Cambridge University Press, 1991)

Blamberger G., and Nutton V., 'Melancholy', in H. Cancik, H. Schneider, and M. Landfester (eds.), *Brill's New Pauly* online (2006)

Blom, A., 'Emotions and the Micro-foundations of Religious Activism: The Bitter-sweet Experiences of "Born-again" Muslims in Pakistan', *The Indian Economic & Social History Review*, 54, 1 (2017), pp. 123–45

Blom, A., and Jaoul, N. (eds.), *The Moral and Affectual Dimension of Collective Action in South Asia*, Special Issue of the *South Asia Multidisciplinary Academic Journal*, 2 (2008)

Blom, A., Jaoul, N., and Tawa Lama-Rewal, S. (eds.), *Emotions, Mobilisations and South Asian Politics* (London: Routledge, 2019)

Böwering, G., 'The Concept of Time in Islam', *Proceedings of the American Philosophical Society*, 141, 1 (1997), pp. 55–66

Bonanno, G. A., Goorin, L., and Coifman, K. C., 'Sadness and Grief', in M. Lewis, J. M. Haviland-Jones, and L. Feldman Barrett (eds.), *Handbook of Emotions*, 3rd ed. (New York: The Guilford Press, 2008), pp. 797–810

Bonnett, A., *Left in the Past: Radicalism and the Politics of Nostalgia* (London: Bloomsbury, 2010)

Boquet D., and Nagy, P., *Le Sujet des émotions au Moyen Âge* (Paris: Beauchesne, 2008)

Boquet D., and Nagy, P., *Politiques des émotions au Moyen Âge* (Florence: Ed. del Galluzzo, 2010)

Boquet D., and Nagy, P., *La Chair des émotions: Pratiques et représentations corporelles de l'affectivité au Moyen-Age*, Médiévales 61 (St Denis: Presses Universitaires de Vincennes, 2011)

Boym, S., *The Future of Nostalgia* (New York: Basic Books, 2001)

Brass, P., *Language, Religion and Politics in North India* (Cambridge: Cambridge University Press, 1974)

Bredi, D., 'Nostalgia in the Re-construction of Muslim Identity in the Aftermath of 1857 and the Myth of Delhi', in A. Kuczkiewicz-Fras (ed.), *Islamicate Traditions in South Asia: Themes from Culture and History* (New Delhi: Manohar Publishers, 2013), pp. 25–43

Bredi, D., 'Nostalgia "restauratrice" all'opera: 'Sicilia' e 'La Moschea di Cordova' di Muhammad Iqbal', *Rivista degli studi orientali*, 83, 1–4 (2010), pp. 317–32

Brennan, L., 'The Illusion of Security: The Background to Muslim Separatism in the United Provinces', *Modern Asian Studies*, 18, 2 (1984), pp. 237–72

Bricteux, A., 'Pasquinade sur la ville de Tébriz, par maître Lissani de Chiraz', in Istas, M. Institut supérieur d'histoire et de littératures orientales (Liège) *Mélanges de philologie orientale publiés à l'occasion du Xe anniversaire de la création de l'Institut supérieur d'Histoire et de Littératures Orientales de l'université de Liège* (Louvain: Institut supérieur d'histoire et de littératures orientales, 1932), pp. 1–56

Briggs, J., *Never in Anger: Portrait of an Eskimo Family* (Cambridge, MA: Harvard University Press, 1981)

Bruijn, J. T. P., de, Halman, T. S., and Rahman, M., 'Shahrangiz' in P. Bearman, Th. Bianquis, C. E. Bosworth, et al. (eds.), *Encyclopaedia of Islam*, 2nd ed. online (Leiden: Brill, first published online 2012)

Buehler, A. F., 'Trends of ashrāfization in India', in K. Morimoto (ed.), *Sayyids and Sharifs in Muslim Societies* (New York: Routledge, 2012), pp. 231–46

Burton, C. G., 'A Validation of Metrics for Community Resilience to Natural Hazards and Disasters Using the Recovery from Hurricane Katrina as a Case Study', *Annals of the Association of American Geographers*, 105, 1 (2015), pp. 67–86

Calder, N., 'History and Nostalgia: Reflections on John Wansbrough's "The Sectarian Milieu"', in M. Siddiqui (ed.), *Islam*, vol. 1 (London: Sage, 2010), pp. 243–66

Carroll, L., 'Origins of the Kayastha Temperance Movement', in *Indian Economics Social History Review*, 11, 4 (1974), pp. 432–47

Carroll, L., 'Life Interests and Inter-Generational Transfer of Property: Avoiding the Law of Succession', *Islamic Law and Society* 8, 2 (2001), pp. 245–86

Case, Margaret H., 'The Social and Political Satire of Akbar Allahabadi, (1846–1921)', *Mahfil*, 1, 4 (1964), pp. 11–20

Chakrabarty, D., 'The Public Life of History: An Argument out of India', *Postcolonial Studies*, 11, 2 (2008), pp. 169–90

Chakrabarty, D., 'Remembered Villages: Representations of Hindu-Bengali Memories', *Economic and Political Weekly*, 31, 32 (1996), pp. 2143–51

Chakravarty, G., *The Indian Mutiny and the British Imagination* (Cambridge: Cambridge University Press, 2005)

Chaghatai, M. I. (ed.), *Iqbal: New Dimensions. A Collection of Unpublished and Rare Iqbalian Studies* (Lahore: Sang-e Meel Publications, 2003)

Chaliand, G., *Revolution in the Third World: Myths and Prospects* (Hassocks: Penguin Books, 1977)

Chandra, A., *Building Community Resilience to Disasters: A Way Forward to Enhance National Health Security* (Santa Monica: Rand, 2011)

Chandra, S., *The Oppressive Present: Literature and Social Consciousness in Colonial India* (Delhi: Oxford University Press, 1992)

Chatterjee, P., *The Nation and Its Fragments: Colonial and Postcolonial histories* (Princeton: Princeton University Press, 1994)

Chatterjee, P., *Nationalist Thought and the Colonial World: A Derivative Discourse* (Minneapolis: University of Minnesota Press, 1993)

Chatterjee, E., Krishnan, S., and Robb, M. 'Feeling Modern: The History of Emotions in Urban South Asia', *Journal of the Royal Asiatic Society*, 27, 4 (2017), pp. 539–57

Chattopadhyay, S., 'Cities of Power and Protest: Spatial Legibility and the Colonial State in Early Twentieth-century India', *International Journal of Urban Sciences*, 19, 1 (2015), pp. 1–13

Chaudhary, V. C. P., *Secularism versus Communalism: An Anatomy of the National Debate on Five Controversial History Books* (Patna: Navdhara Samiti, 1977)

Christensen, E. A., 'Government Architecture and British Imperialism: Patronage and Imperial Policy in London, Pretoria, and New Delhi (1900–1931)', unpublished PhD dissertation, Northwestern University (1995)

Cohen, B., 'Modernising the Urban Environment: The Musi River Flood of 1908 in Hyderabad, India', *Environment and History*, 17, 3 (2011), pp. 409–32

Cohn, B., 'Representing Authority in Victorian India', in E. Hobsbawm and T. Ranger (eds.), *The Invention of Tradition* (Cambridge: Cambridge University Press, 1992), pp. 165–210

Congino, A., 'Collective Memory and Cultural History: Problems of Method', *The American Historical Review*, 102, 5 (1997), pp. 1386–1403
Connerton, P., *How Modernity Forgets* (Cambridge: Cambridge University Press, 2009)
Cook, D., *Martyrdom in Islam* (New York: Cambridge University Press, 2007)
Crane, S., 'Writing the Individual Back into Collective Memory', *The American Historical Review*, 102, 5 (1997), pp. 1372–85
Daechsel, M., *The Politics of Self-expression: The Urdu Middle-class Milieu In Mid-twentieth-century India and Pakistan* (Abingdon: Routledge, 2006)
Dalmia, V., *The Nationalization of Hindu Traditions: Bharatendu Harischandra and Nineteenth-century Benares* (New Delhi: Oxford University Press, 1997)
Dalrymple, W., *The Last Mughal: The Fall of a Dynasty: Delhi, 1857* (London: Bloomsbury, 2006)
Damousi, J., *Living with the Aftermath: Trauma, Nostalgia and Grief in Post-war Australia* (Cambridge: Cambridge University Press, 2001)
Das, S. K., *History of Indian Literature: 1911–1956: Struggle for Freedom. Triumph and Tragedy* (New Delhi: Sahitya Akademi, 1995)
Davis, F., *Yearning for Yesterday: A Sociology of Nostalgia* (New York: Macmillan, 1979)
Delvecchio Good, M. J., and Good, B. J., 'Ritual, the State, and the Transformation of Emotional Discourse in Iranian Society', *Culture, Medicine and Psychiatry*, 12, 1 (March 1988), pp. 43–63
Deutsch, K. A., 'Muslim Women in Colonial North India circa 1920–1947: Politics, Law and Community Identity', unpublished PhD dissertation, University of Cambridge (1998)
Devji, F., 'Muslim Nationalism: Founding Identity in Colonial India', unpublished Ph.D. dissertation, University of Chicago (1993)
Devji, F., 'India in the Muslim Imagination: Cartography and Landscape in 19th Century Urdu Literature', *South Asian Multidisciplinary Academic Journal*, 10 (2014) journals.openedition.org/samaj/3751
Devji, F., 'A Shadow Nation: The Making of Muslim India', in K. Grant, P. Levine, and F. Trentmann(eds.), *Beyond Sovereignty: Britain, Empire and Transnationalism, c. 1880–1950* (London: Palgrave Macmillan, 2007), pp. 126–45
Devji, F., 'The Equivocal History of a Muslim Reformation', in F. Osella and C. Osella (eds.), *Islamic Reform in South Asia* (Cambridge: Cambridge University Press, 2013), pp. 3–25
Dey, A., *The Image of the Prophet in Bengali Muslim Piety, 1850–1947* (Kolkata: Readers Service, 2005)

Diagne, S. B., 'Bergson in the Colony: Intuition and Duration in the Thought of Senghor and Iqbal', *Qui parle*, 17, 1 (2008), pp. 125–45

Dubrow, J., *Cosmopolitan Dreams: The Making of Modern Urdu Literary Culture in Colonial South Asia* (Honolulu: Hawaii University Press, 2018)

Dudney, A., 'Literary Decadence and Imagining the Late Mughal City', *Journal for Early Modern Cultural Studies*, 18, 3 (2018), pp. 187–211

Duerr, H. P., *Nudité et Pudeur: Le mythe du processus de civilisation* (Paris: Maison des Sciences de l'Homme, 1998)

Dugassa, B., 'Colonial Trauma, Community Resiliency and Community Health Development: The Case of the Oromo People in Ethiopia', *Journal of Health Development*, 4, 1–4 (2008), pp. 43–63

Ebied R. Y., and Young, M. J. L., 'Abū'l-Baqā' al-Rundi and His Elegy on Muslim Spain', *The Muslim World*, 66, 1 (1976), pp. 29–34

El Gharbi, J., 'Thrène de Séville', *Cahiers de la Méditerranée*, 79 (2009), pp. 26–30

Elinson, A. E., *Looking Back at al-Andalus: The Poetics of Loss and Nostalgia in Medieval Arabic and Hebrew Literature* (Leiden: Brill Studies in Middle Eastern Literatures 34, 2009)

Ernst, C., 'India as a Sacred Islamic Land', in S. Lopez Donald (ed.), *Religions of India in Practice* (Princeton: Princeton University Press, 2021), pp. 556–63

Fairchild-Ruggles, D., *Islamic Gardens and Landscapes* (Philadelphia: University of Pennsylvania Press, 2007)

Farahani, L. M., Motamed, B., and Jamei, E., 'Persian Gardens: Meanings, Symbolism, and Design', *Landscape Online*, 46 (2016), pp. 1–19

Farooqi, M. A., 'The Secret of Letters: Chronograms in Urdu Literary Culture', *Edebiyât*, 13, 2 (2003), pp. 147–58

Faruqi, S. R., 'Jur'at's shahr ashob: an afterword', *Annual of Urdu Studies*, 3 (1983), pp. 11–6

Faruqi, S. R., 'How to Read Iqbal', *Annual of Urdu Studies*, 20 (2005), pp. 1–33

Faruqi, S. R., 'Burning Rage, Icy Scorn: The Poetry of Ja'far Zatalli', paper presented at the Hindi-Urdu Flagship Program, University of Texas (2008) columbia.edu/itc/mealac/pritchett/00fwp/srf/srf_zatalli_2008.pdf

Faruqi, S. R., 'The Power Politics of Culture: Akbar Ilahabadi and the Changing Order of Things', paper presented at Zakir Husain College, New Delhi (2002) columbia.akadns.net/itc/mealac/pritchett/00fwp/srf/srf_akbar_ilahabadi.pdf

Faruqi, S. R., 'Sādgī, aṣliyat aur josh', in *Andāz-e guftagū kyā hai* (New Delhi: Maktaba Jamia Limited, 1993)

Faruqi, S. R., and Pritchett, F. W., 'A Vile World Carnival', *Annual of Urdu Studies*, 4 (1984), pp. 24–35

Febvre, L., 'La sensibilité et l'histoire: comment reconstituer la vie affective d'autrefois?', *Annales d'histoire sociale*, 3, 1/2 (1941), pp. 5–20

Ferrell, D. W., 'Delhi, 1911–1922: Society and Politics in the New Imperial Capital of India', unpublished PhD dissertation, Australian National University, Canberra (1969)

Fleischer, C., 'Royal Authority, Dynastic Cyclism, and Ibn Khaldunism in Sixteenth-century Ottoman Letters', *Journal of Asian and African Studies*, 18, 3 (1983), pp. 198–220

Freitag, S., 'The Roots of Muslim Separatism in South Asia: Personal Practice and Public Structures in Kanpur and Bombay', in E. Burke and I. Lapidus (eds.), *Islam, Politics and Social Movements* (Berkeley: University of California Press, 1988), pp. 115–45

Freud, S., 'Mourning and Melancholia', in *Collected Papers*, IV (London: Hogarth Press, 1971), pp. 152–70

Fromkin, D., *A Peace to End All Peace: The Fall of the Ottoman Empire and the Creation of the Modern Middle East* (New York: H. Holt, 2001)

Fuchs, M. M., 'Islamic Modernism in Colonial Punjab: The Anjuman-i Himayat-i Islam, 1884–1923', unpublished PhD dissertation, Princeton University (2019)

Fusfeld, W., 'Communal Conflict in Delhi, 1803–1930', *The Indian Economic and Social History Review*, 19, 2 (1982), pp. 181–200

Gardet, L. 'Dhikr', in P. Bearman, Th. Bianquis, C. E. Bosworth, et al. (eds.), The Encyclopaedia of Islam, 2nd ed. online (Leiden: Brill, first published online 2012)

Gill, D. E., *Melancholic Modalities: Affect, Islam, and Turkish Classical Musicians* (New York: Oxford University Press, 2017)

Gooptu, N., *The Politics of the Urban Poor in Early Twentieth-century India* (Cambridge: Cambridge University Press, 2001)

Gordon, S., 'Monumental Visions: Architectural Photography in India, 1840–1901', unpublished PhD dissertation, School of Oriental and African Studies (SOAS), University of London (2011)

Goswami, M., '"Englishness" on the Imperial Circuit: Mutiny Tours in Colonial South Asia', *Journal of Historical Sociology*, 9, 1 (1996), pp. 54–84

Green, N., *Making Space: Sufis and Settlers in Early Modern India* (New Delhi: Oxford University Press, 2012)

Gregg, G. S., *The Middle East: A Cultural Psychology* (Oxford: Oxford University Press, 2005)

Grima, B., *The Performance of Emotions among Paxtun Women: 'the misfortunes which have befallen me'* (Oxford: Oxford University Press, 2004)

Guichard, S., *The Construction of History and Nationalism in India: Textbooks, Controversies and Politics* (London: Routledge, 2010)

Günther, S., and Lawson, T. (eds.), *Roads to Paradise: Eschatology and Concepts of the Hereafter in Islam, Islamic History and Civilization: Studies and Texts*, Collection Islamic History and Civilization, vol. 136 (Leiden: Brill, 2017)

Gupta, C., 'The Icon of the Mother in Late Colonial India: "Bharat Mata", "Matri Bhasha" and "Gau Mata"', *Economic and Political Weekly*, 36, 45 (2001), pp. 4291–9

Gupta, N., *Delhi between Two Empires, 1803–1931: Society, Government, and Urban Growth* (Delhi: Oxford University Press, 1981)

Habermas, J., *The Structural Transformation of the Public Sphere: An Inquiry into a Category of Bourgeois Society*, translated by Th. Burger (Cambridge, MA: Massachusetts Institute of Technology, 1989)

Habibullah, A. B. M., 'Historical Writing in Urdu: A Survey of Tendencies', in C. H. Philips (ed.), *Historians of India, Pakistan and Ceylon* (London: SOAS, 1961), pp. 481–96

Halbwachs, M., *La mémoire collective* (Paris: Presses Universitaires de France, 1968 [1950])

Hämeen-Anttila, J., 'Paradise and Nature in the Quran and Pre-Islamic Poetry', in S. Günther and T. Lawson (eds.), *Roads to Paradise: Eschatology and Concepts of the Hereafter in Islam, Islamic History and Civilization: Studies and Texts*, vol. 136 (Leiden: Brill, 2017), pp. 136–61

Hanaway, W., 'Paradise on Earth: The Terrestial Garden in Persian Literature', in E. B. MacDougall and R. Ettinghausen (eds.), *The Islamic Garden* (Washington, DC: Dumbarton Oaks, 1976), pp. 43–67

Hanaway, W., 'Dastan-sarai', in *Encyclopaedia Iranica Online* (New York: Brill, 1996)

Harder, H., and Mittler, B. (eds.), *Asian Punches: A Transcultural Affair* (Heidelberg: Springer, 2013)

Hardy, P., 'Modern Muslim Historical Writing on Medieval Muslim India', in C. H. Philips (ed.), *Historians of India, Pakistan and Ceylon* (London: SOAS, 1961), pp. 294–309

Hardy, P., *The Muslims of British India* (Cambridge: Cambridge University Press, 1972)

Harré, R. (ed.) *The Social Construction of Emotions* (Oxford: Blackwell, 1988)

Hasan, I., 'Later Mughals as Represented in Urdu Poetry: A Study in the Light of Shahr Ashobs from Hatim, Sauda and Nazir', *Annali dell'Instituto Universitario Orientale di Napoli*, Nuova Series 9 (1959), pp. 131–53

Hasan, I., 'Later Mughals as Represented in Urdu Poetry: A Study of Qa'im's shahr ashob', *Annali dell'Instituto Universitario Orientale di Napoli*, 12 (1962–1963), pp. 129–52

Hasan, M., *Nationalism and Communal Politics, 1885–1930* (New Delhi: Manohar Publications, 1991)

Hasan, I., 'The Legacies of 1857 among the Muslim Intelligentsia of North India', in C. Bates et al. (eds.), *Mutiny at the Margins: New Perspectives on the Indian Uprising of 1857*, vol. 5: Muslim, Dalit and Subaltern Narratives (New Delhi: Sage Publications, 2014), pp. 103–16

Hasan, I., *Wit and Humour in Colonial North India* (New Delhi: Niyogi Books, 2007)

Hasan, I., *From Pluralism to Separatism. Qasbas in Colonial Awadh* (New Delhi: Oxford University Press, 2012)

Hassan, M., *Dillī kī Begamātī Zubān* (New Delhi: Nayi Awaz, 1976)

Hassen, M., 'Recherches sur les poèmes inspirés par la perte ou la destruction des villes dans la littérature arabe du IIIe/IXe siècle à la prise de Grenade en 897/1492', vol. 1, unpublished PhD dissertation, Sorbonne (1977)

Hashmi, A., 'Three Poems of Iqbal: A Psychological Interpretation', *Annual of Urdu Studies*, 25 (2010), pp. 108–21

Hautemanière, N., 'Mohamed Iqbal, penseur d'un autre Islam', *Les clés du Moyen-Orient* (2014) lesclesdumoyenorient.com/Mohamed-Iqbal-penseur-d-un-autre.html

Helmreich, P., *From Paris to Sèvres. The Partition of the Ottoman Empire at the Peace Conference of 1919–1920* (Columbus: The Ohio State University Press, 1974)

Hendrich, G., 'Identitätskonstruktion und Geschichtsbilder im arabo-islamischen Modernediskurs', in A. Hartmann (ed.), *Geschichte und Erinnerung im Islam* (Göttingen: Vandenhoeck and Ruprecht, 2004), pp. 31–49

Hermansen, M. K., and Lawrence, B. B., 'Indo-Persian Tazkiras as Memorative Communications', in D. Gilmartin and B. Lawrence (eds.), *Beyond Turk and Hindu: Rethinking Religious Identities in Islamicate South Asia* (New Delhi: India Research Press, 2002), pp. 149–71

Hermansen, M., 'Imagining Space and Siting Collective Memory in South Asian Muslim Bibliographical Literature (Tazkirahs)', *Studies in Contemporary Islam*, 4, 2 (2002), pp. 1–21

Hjortshoj, K., *Urban Structures and Transformations in Lucknow, India* (Ithaca: Cornell University Progam in Urban and Regional Studies, 1979)

Hobsbawm, E., and Ranger, T. (eds.), *The Invention of Tradition* (Cambridge: Cambridge University Press, 2003)

Horne, V., 'The Politicisation of Muslim Delhi in the 1910s: Mohamed Ali, Comrade and the Public Sphere', *South Asia Chronicle*, 11 (2021), pp. 217–49

Hosagrahar, J., *Indigenous Modernities: Negotiating Architecture and Urbanism* (London: Routledge, 2005)

Howard, D., *Being Human in Islam: The Impact of the Evolutionary Worldview* (London: Routledge, 2011)
Husain, A. A., *Scent in the Islamic Garden: A Study of Deccani Urdu Literary Sources* (Karachi: Oxford University Press, 2000)
Husain, S. A., *Yādgār-e Ḥālī* (New Delhi: Anjuman-e Taraqqi-e Urdu, 2001)
Hyder, S. A., 'Recasting Karbala in the Genre of Urdu Marsiya', *South Asia Graduate Research Journal*, 2, 1 (1995), www.columbia.edu/itc/mealac/pritchett/00urdu/anis/txt_hyder_marsiya.html
Hyder, S. A., *Reliving Karbala: Martyrdom in South Asian Memory* (Oxford: Oxford University Press, 2006)
Ikramullah, S. S., *A Critical Survey of the Development of the Urdu Novel and Short Story* (London: Longmans Green, 1945)
Irving, R. G., *Indian Summer: Lutyens, Baker, and Imperial Delhi* (London: Yale University Press, 1981)
Islam, M., 'The Conscious Poet of Nationalism: Chakbast', in *Indian History Congress Proceedings*, 49th session, Dharwad (1988)
Jain, M. S., *The Aligarh Movement* (New Delhi: Icon Publications, 2006)
Jalal, A., and Bose, S. (eds.), *Nationalism, Democracy and Development: State and Politics in India* (Delhi: Oxford University Press, 1997)
Jalal, A., *Self and Sovereignty: Individual and Community in South Asian Islam since 1850* (London: Routledge, 2000)
Jalal, A., 'Exploding Communalism: The Politics of Muslim Identity in South Asia', in S. Bose and A. Jalal (eds.), *Nationalism, Democracy and Development: State and Politics in India* (New Delhi: Oxford University Press, 2009), tcd.ie/iiis/documents/archive/pdf/communalismayesha.pdf
Jalibi, J. (ed.), *Urdū Luġhat Tārīk̲h̲ī Uṣūl par*, vol. 8 (Karachi: Taraqqī Urdū Borḍ, 1987)
Jalil, R., 'Reflections of 1857 in Contemporary Urdu Literature', in C. Bates, A. Major, M. Carter, and G. Rand (eds.), *Mutiny at the Margins: New Perspectives on the Indian Uprising of 1857*, vol. 1: Anticipations and Experiences in the Locality (New Delhi: Sage Publications, 2013), pp. 120–31
Jayyusi-Lehn, Gh., 'The Epistle of Yaʿkub ibn Ishaq al-Kindi', *British Journal of Middle Eastern Studies*, 29, 2 (2002), pp. 121–35
Jones, J., 'Shiʿism, Humanity and Revolution in Twentieth-century India: Selfhood and Politics in the Husainology of ʿAli Naqi Naqvi', *Journal of the Royal Asiatic Society*, 24, 3 (2014), pp. 415–34
Jones, K. W., 'Organized Hinduism in Delhi and New Delhi', in R. E. Frykenberg (ed.), *Delhi through the Ages* (Delhi: Oxford University Press, 1992), pp. 212–4
Kaif, S. S., *Chakbast: Makers of Indian Literature* (New Delhi: Sahitya Akademi, 1986)

Kansteiner, W., 'Finding Meaning in Memory: A Methodological Critique of Collective Memory Studies', *History and Theory*, 41, 2 (2002), pp. 179–97

Katz, M. H., *The Birth of the Prophet Muhammad. Devotional Piety in Sunni Islam* (London: Routledge, 2007)

Kaviraj, S., 'A Strange Love of the Land: Identity, Poetry and Politics in the (Un)Making of South Asia', *South Asia Multidisciplinary Academic Journal*, 10 (2014), https://journals.openedition.org/samaj/3756

Kaviraj, S., *The Unhappy Consciousness: Bankimchandra Chattopadhyay and the Nationalist Discourse in India* (Delhi: Oxford University Press, 1995)

Kavuri-Bauer, S., *Monumental Matters: The Power, Subjectivity, and Space of India's Mughal Architecture* (Durham: Duke University Press, 2011)

Khan, J. A., *Muhammad Shibli Nomani* (Azamgarh: Shibli Academy, 2004)

Khan, N. A., *Hindustānī Pres (1556 tā 1900)* (Lucknow: UP Urdu Academy, 1990)

Khan, P. M., 'From *the Lament for Delhi*', translated and introduction to selected poems from Fughān-i Dihlī', in S. Nijhawan (ed.), *Nationalism in the Vernacular: Hindi, Urdu, and the Literature of Indian Freedom* (Delhi: Ranikhet Permanent Black, 2009), pp. 88–92

Khan, P. M., Draft paper, 'What Is a *Shahr-Ashob*?' workshop at Columbia University, 2009, columbia.edu/itc/mealac/pritchett/00urduhindilinks/workshop2009/txt_pasha_fughanintro.pdf

Khan, P. M., 'The Broken Spell: The Romance Genre in Late Mughal India', PhD dissertation, Columbia University (2013)

Khan, P. M., *The Broken Spell: Indian Storytelling and the Romance Genre in Persian and Urdu* (Detroit: Wayne State University Press, 2019)

Khan, R., 'The Social Production of Space and Emotions in South Asia', *Journal of the Economic and Social History of the Orient*, 58, 5 (2015), pp. 611–33

Khan, R., 'Local Pasts: Space, Emotions and Identities in Vernacular Histories of Princely Rampur', *Journal of the Economic and Social History of the Orient*, 58, 5 (2015), pp. 693–731

Khan Mahmudabad, A., *Poetry of Belonging: Muslim Imaginings of India, 1850–1950* (New Delhi: Oxford University Press, 2020)

Khanduri, R. G., *Caricaturing Culture in India: Cartoons and History in the Modern World* (Cambridge: Cambridge University Press, 2016)

Khanduri, R. G., '*Punch* in India: Another History of Colonial Politics?' in H. Harder and B. Mittler (eds.), *Asian Punches: A Transcultural Affair* (Heidelberg: Springer, 2013), pp. 165–84

Kia, M., 'Moral Refinement and Manhood in Persian', in M. Pernau et al. (eds.), *Civilizing Emotions: Concepts in Nineteenth Century Asia and Europe* (Oxford: Oxford University Press, 2015), pp. 146–66

Kia, M., 'Companionship as Political Ethic: Friendship, Intimacy, and Service in Late Mughal Visions of Just Rule', webinar *Islam After Colonialism*, 2021, youtube.com/watch?v=prOqrLEBbKA&list=WL&index=4&t=568s

Kidwai, M. S., 'Sir Sayyid's Contribution to Journalism with Special Reference to the *Aligarh Institute Gazette* and the *Tahzibul Akhlaq*', PhD dissertation, Aligarh Muslim University (2005)

King, A. D., *Colonial Urban Development: Culture, Social Power and Environment* (London: Routledge, 1976)

King, C. R., 'Forging a New Linguistic Identity: The Hindi Movement in Banaras, 1868–1914', in S. B. Freitag (ed.), *Culture and Power in Banaras: Community, Performance and Environment, 1800–1980* (Berkeley: University of California Press, 1989)

King, C. R., 'The Images of Virtue and Vice: The Hindi-Urdu Controversy in Two Nineteenth Century Hindi Plays', in K. Jones (ed.), *Religious Controversy in British India* (Albany: New York State University Press, 1992), pp. 123–48

King, C. R., *One Language, Two Scripts: The Hindi Movement in Nineteenth Century North India* (New Delhi: Oxford University Press, 1994)

Koch, E., 'Shah Jahan's Visits to Delhi prior to 1648: New Evidence of Ritual Movement in Urban Mughal India', *Environmental Design: Journal of the Islamic Environmental Design Research Centre*, 11, 1–2, Mughal Architecture: Pomp and Ceremonies (1991), pp. 18–29

Koch, E., 'My Garden Is Hindustan: The Mughal Padshah's Realization of a Political Metaphor', in M. Conan (ed.), *Middle East Garden Traditions: Unity and Diversity: Questions, Methods and Resources in a Multicultural Perspective* (Washington, DC: Dumbarton Oaks, 2007), pp. 159–75

Koch, E., 'Flowers in Mughal Architecture', *MARG*, 70, 2 (2018–2019), pp. 24–33

Kogan, I., *The Struggle against Mourning* (Lanham: J. Aronson, 2007)

Kozlowski, G. C., *Muslim Endowments and Society in British India* (Cambridge: Cambridge University Press, 1985)

Kumar Parti, R., *Āshob* (New Delhi: National Archives of India, 1993)

Kurin, R., 'Morality, Personhood, and the Exemplary Life: Popular Conceptions of Muslims in Paradise', in B. Metcalf (ed.), *Moral Conduct and Authority: The Place of adab in South Asian Islam* (Berkeley: University of California Press, 1984), pp. 196–220

Lahiri, S., 'Remembering the City: Translocality and the Senses', *Social and Cultural Geography*, 12, 8 (2011), pp. 855–69

Lane, E. W., *Arabic-English Lexicon, Book 1, Part 3* (London: Williams and Norgate, 1867)

Lange, C., 'The Discovery of Paradise in Islam: The Here and the Hereafter in Islamic Traditions', Oratie (Utrecht: University of Utrecht, 2012)

Lange, C., *Paradise and Hell in Islamic Traditions* (New York: Cambridge University Press, 2016)

Lapidus, I. M., 'The Golden Age: The Political Concepts of Islam', in M. Siddiqui (ed.), *Islam*, vol. 4 (London: Sage, 2012), pp. 229–41

Latif, R., 'Divergent Trajectories of "Masjid-e Qurtuba": Iqbal's Imaginings and the Historical Life of the Monument', *Annual of Urdu Studies*, 26 (2011), pp. 124–34

Lawlor, L., and Moulard Leonard, V., 'Henri Bergson', in Edward N. Zalta (ed.), *The Stanford Encyclopedia of Philosophy* (Stanford: Stanford University Press, 2016)

Le Goff, J., *Histoire et Mémoire* (Paris: Gallimard, 1988)

Lee, J., 'Disgust and Untouchability: Towards an Affective Theory of Caste', *South Asian History and Culture*, 12, 2–3 (2021), pp. 310–27

Lehmann, F., 'Urdu Literature and Mughal Decline', *Mahfil*, 6, 2/3 (1970), pp. 125–31

Lelyveld, D., *Aligarh's First Generation: Muslim Solidarity in British India* (New Delhi: Oxford University Press, 2010)

Levesque, J., and Gautier, L. (eds.), Historicizing Sayyid-ness: Social Status and Muslim Identity in South Asia, *Special Number of the Journal of the Royal Asiatic Society*, 30, 3 (2020)

Liddle, S., 'Azurdah: Scholar, Poet, and Judge', in M. Pernau (ed.), *The Delhi College: Traditional Elites, the Colonial State, and Education before 1857* (New Delhi: Oxford University Press, 2006), pp. 125–44

Lory, P., 'Elie', in M. A. Amir-Moezzi (ed.), *Dictionnaire du Coran* (Paris: Robert Laffont, 2007), p. 244–6

Low, K., 'Summoning the Senses in Memory and Heritage Making', in D. Kalekin-Fishman and K. E. Y. Low (eds.), *Everyday Life in Asia: Social Perspectives on the Senses* (Farnham: Ashgate, 2010)

Lutz, C. A., *Unnatural Emotions: Everyday Sentiments on a Micronesian Atoll and Their Challenge to Western Theory* (Chicago: University of Chicago Press, 1988)

Lynton, H. R., and Rajan, M., *The Days of the Beloved* (Berkeley: University of California Press, 1974)

Mahmood, S., *Politics of Piety: The Islamic Revival and the Feminist Subject* (Princeton: Princeton University Press, 2012)

Majeed, J., *Muhammad Iqbal: Islam, Aesthetics and Postcolonialism* (New Delhi: Routledge, 2009)

Majeed, J., 'Muhammad Iqbal: Rumuz-e Bekhudi [Mysteries of Selflessness]', in C. Gallien, P. K. Malreddy, D. Munos, M. Shamsie and N. Zaman(eds.), *The Literary Encyclopedia*, vol. 10.3.2: Pakistani and Bangladeshi Writing and Culture (Slough: The Literary Dictionary Company, July 2010), www.litencyc.com/php/sworks.php?rec=true&UID=30671

Majeed, J., 'Muhammad Iqbal: Islam, Aesthetics and Postcolonialism', in G. Nash, K. Kerr-Koch, and S. Hackett (eds.), *Postcolonialism and Islam: Theory, Literature, Culture, Society and Film* (Abingdon: Routledge 2013), pp. 35–47

Majeed, J., *Autobiography, Travel and Postnational Identity: Gandhi, Nehru and Iqbal* (New York: Primus Books, 2015)

Malik, H., *Iqbal: Poet-Philosopher of Pakistan* (New York: Books Abroad, 1971)

Malik, H., 'Iqbal, Muhammad', in J. Esposito (ed.), *The Oxford Encyclopedia of the Modern Islamic World online* (New York: Oxford University Press, 2001)

Masood, N., 'Discovery of Lost Glory', in S. Chandra and R. Taqui (eds.), *Conservation of Lucknow heritage: Preservation, Methodology and International Dimensions* (New Delhi: Tech Books International, 2006), pp. 1–6

Matthews, D. J., 'Iqbal and His Urdu Poetry', in M. I. Chaghatai (ed.), *Iqbal: New Dimensions. A Collection of Unpublished and Rare Iqbalian Studies* (Lahore: Sang-e Meel Publications, 2003), pp. 101–110

Meisami, J. S., 'Allegorical Gardens in the Persian Poetic Tradition: Nezami, Rumi, Hafez', *International Journal of Middle East Studies*, 17, 2 (1985), pp. 229–60

Meisami, J. S., *Medieval Persian Court Poetry* (Princeton: Princeton University Press, 1987)

Meisami, J. S., 'Ghaznavid Panegyrics: Some Political Implications', *Iran*, 28 (1990), pp. 31–44

Meisami, J. S., 'Poetic Microcosms: The Persian Qasida to the End of the Twelfth Century', in S. Sperl and C. Shackle (eds.), *Qasida Poetry in Islamic Asia and Africa: vol. 1: Classical Traditions and Modern Meanings* (Leiden: Brill, 1996), pp. 173–82

Meisami, J. S., and Starkey, P. (eds.), *Encyclopedia of Arabic Literature* (London: Routledge, 1998)

Mélikoff, I., 'La fleur de la souffrance: recherche sur le sens symbolique de lale dans la poésie mystique turco-iranienne', *Journal asiatique*, 255, 5 (1967), pp. 341–60

Metcalf, B., 'Reflections on Iqbal's mosque', in M. I. Chaghatai (ed.), *Iqbal: New Dimensions. A Collection of Unpublished and Rare Iqbalian Studies* (Lahore: Sang-e Meel Publications, 2003), pp. 165–70

Metcalf, B., *Moral Conduct and Authority: The Place of Adab in South Asian Islam* (Berkeley: University of California Press, 1984)

Milligan, M. J., 'Displacement and Identity Discontinuity: The Role of Nostalgia in Establishing New Identity Categories', *Symbolic Interaction*, 26, 3 (2003), pp. 381–403

Milligan, M. J., 'Interactional Past and Potential: The Social Construction of Place Attachment', *Symbolic Interaction*, 21, 1 (1998), pp. 1–33

Minault, G., 'Urdu Political Poetry during the Khilafat Movement', *Modern Asian Studies*, 8, 4 (1974), pp. 459–71

Minault, G., 'Khilafat Movement', in U. Daniel, P. Gatrell, O. Janz et al. (eds.), *1914–1918: International Encyclopedia of the First World War online* (Berlin: Freie Universität Berlin, 2015)

Minault, G., *The Khilafat Movement: Religious Symbolism and Political Mobilization in India* (New York: Columbia University Press, 1982)

Minault, G., 'Begamati Zuban: Women's Language and Culture in Nineteenth-Century Delhi', *India International Centre Quarterly*, 11, 2 (1984), pp. 155–70

Minault, G., 'Sayyid Ahmad Dehlavi and the "Delhi Renaissance"', in R. E. Frykenberg (ed.), *Delhi through the Ages* (Delhi: Oxford University Press, 1992), pp. 174–85

Minault, G., 'Sayyid Mumtaz 'Ali and Tahzib un-Niswan: Women's Rights in Islam and Women's journalism in Urdu', in K. W. Jones (ed.), *Religious Controversy in British India: Dialogues in South Asian languages* (Albany: New York State University Press, 1992), pp. 179–99

Minault, G., *Secluded Scholars: Women's Education and Muslim Social Reform in Colonial India* (Delhi: Oxford University Press, 1998)

Mitchell, L., 'Whose Emotions? Boundaries and Boundary Markers in the Study of Emotions, *South Asian History and Culture*, 12, 2–3 (2021), pp. 345–55

Mitra, S., *Periodicals, Readers and the Making of Modern Literary Culture: Bengal at the Turn of the Twentieth Century, Indological Library Collection, vol. 52* (Leiden: Brill, 2020)

Moynihan, E. B., *Paradise as a Garden in Persia and Mughal India* (New York: G. Braziller, 1979)

Murad, M. A., *Intellectual Modernism of Shibli Nu'mani: An Exposition of his Religious and Political Ideas* (New Delhi: Kitab Bhavan, 1996)

Mustansir, M., *Tulip in the Desert: A Selection of the Poetry of Muhammad Iqbal* (London: C. Hurst, 2000)

Naim, C. M., 'The Art of the Urdu Marsiya', in M. Israel and N. K. Wagle (eds.), *Islamic Society and Culture: Essays in Honour of Professor Aziz Ahmad* (New Delhi: Manohar Publications, 1983), pp. 101–116

Naim, C. M., 'A Note on Shahr Ashob', *Annual of Urdu Studies*, 4 (1984), p. 42

Naim, C. M., 'Prize-Winning Adab: A Study of Five Urdu Books Written in Response to the Allahabad Government Gazette Notification', in B. D. Metcalf (ed.), *Moral Conduct and Authority: The Place of Adab in South Asian Islam* (Berkeley: University of California Press, 1984), pp. 290–314

Naim, C. M., 'Mughal and English Patronage of Urdu Poetry: A Comparison', in B. S. Miller (ed.), *The Powers of Art: Patronage in Indian Culture* (New Delhi: Oxford University Press, 1992), pp. 259–76

Naim, C. M., 'Transvestic Words: The *Rekhti* in Urdu', *Annual of Urdu Studies*, 16 (2001), pp. 3–26

Naim, C. M., *Urdu Texts and Contexts: The Selected Essays* (Delhi: Permanent Black, 2004)

Naim, C. M., 'Interrogating "the East", "Culture", and "Loss" in Abdul Halim Sharar's Guzashta Lakhnau', in A. Patel and K. Leonard (eds.), *Indo-Muslim Cultures in Transition* (Leiden: Brill, 2012), pp. 189–204

Naeem, S., *Shināsan-e Sir Syed*, vol. 2 (Aligarh: Sir Syed Academy, 2011)

Nanda, B. R., *Gandhi: Pan-Islamism, Imperialism and Nationalism in India* (New Delhi: Oxford University Press, 2002)

Nanda, R., and Gupta, N., *Delhi: The Built Heritage. A Listing* (New Delhi: INTACH, 1999)

Naqvi, N., 'The Nostalgic Subject: A Genealogy of the "Critique" of Nostalgia', Università degli studi di Messina, working paper 23 (2007)

Narang, G. C., 'The Sound Structure of Iqbal's Urdu Poetry', in A. Sardar Jafri and K. S. Duggal (eds.), *Iqbal: Commemorative Volume* (Lahore: Iqbal Academy Pakistan, 2004), pp. 202–206

Nasim, W., *Urdū zubān aur ʿaurat* (Delhi: Taj Publishing House, 1964)

Nath, D., *Dehlī aur Āzādī: Dehlī kī jang-e āzādī kī kahānī 1857 tā 1947* (Delhi: Urdu Academy, 2011)

Noorani, Y., 'The Lost Garden of Al-Andalus: Islamic Spain and the Poetic Inversion of Colonialism', *International Journal of Middle East Studies*, 31, 2 (May 1999), pp. 237–54

Oesterheld, C., 'Campaigning for a Community: Urdu Literature of Mobilisation and Identity', *The Indian Economic and Social History Review*, 54, 1 (2017), pp. 43–66

Oesterheld, C., 'Changing Landscapes of Love and Passion in the Urdu Novel', *Contributions to the History of Concepts*, 11, 1 (2016), pp. 58–80

O'Hanlon, R., 'Kingdom, Household and Body History, Gender and Imperial Service under Akbar', *Modern Asian Studies*, 41, 5 (2007), pp. 889–923

Oldenburg, V., *The Making of Colonial Lucknow* (Princeton: Princeton University Press, 1984)

Oldenburg, V., 'Lifestyle as Resistance: The Case of the Courtesans of Lucknow', *Feminist Studies*, 16, 2 (1990), pp. 259–87

Orsini, F., *The Hindi Public Sphere, 1920–1940: Language and Literature in the Age of Nationalism* (New Delhi: Oxford University Press, 2009)

Orsini, F., *Print and Pleasure: Popular Literature and Entertaining Fictions in Colonial North India* (Ranikhet: Permanent Black, 2009)

Orsini, F. (ed.), *Love in South Asia: A Cultural History* (Cambridge: Cambridge University Press, 2007)

Özcan, A., *Indian Muslims, the Ottomans and Britain (1877–1924)* (Leiden: Brill, 1997)

Pamuk, O., *Istanbul: Memories and the City* (London: Faber and Faber, 2006)

Pant, K., *The Kashmiri Pandit: Story of a Community in Exile in the Nineteenth and Twentieth Centuries* (New Delhi: Allied Publishers, 1987)

Parekh, R., 'Nasir Nazeer Firaq: His Prose and Delhi's Cultural History', *Dawn* (15 February 2016), dawn.com/news/1239539

Pegors, M., 'A Shahr Ashob of Sauda', *Journal of South Asian Literature*, 25, 1 (1990), pp. 89–97

Pellat, Ch., Hanaway, W. L., Flemming, B., Haywood, J. A., and Knappert, J., 'Marthiya', in P. Bearman, Th. Bianquis, C. E. Bosworth, et al. (eds.), *Encyclopaedia of Islam*, 2nd ed. online (Leiden: Brill, first published online 2012)

Perkins, C. R., 'Partitioning History: The Creation of an Islami Pablik in Late Colonial India, c. 1880–1920', unpublished PhD dissertation, University of Pennsylvania (2011)

Perkins, C. R., 'From the Mehfil to the Printed Word: Public Debate and Discourse in Late Colonial India', *Indian Economic Social History Review*, 50, 1 (2013), pp. 47–76

Pernau, M., *Ashraf into Middle Classes: Muslims in Nineteenth Century Delhi* (New Delhi: Oxford University Press, 2013)

Pernau, M., and Jaffery, Y., *Information and the Public Sphere: Persian Newsletters from Mughal Delhi* (New Delhi: Oxford University Press, 2009)

Pernau, M., 'Mapping Emotions, Constructing Feelings: Delhi in the 1840s', *Journal of the Economic and Social History of the Orient*, 58, 5 (2015), pp. 634–67

Pernau, M., 'Nostalgia: Tears of Blood for a Lost World', *SAGAR*, 23 (2015), pp. 74–109

Pernau, M., Jordheim, H., Saada, E., et al. (eds.), *Civilizing Emotions: Concepts in Nineteenth-century Asia and Europe* (Oxford: Oxford University Press, 2015)

Pernau, M., 'Feeling Communities: Introduction', *Indian Economic and Social History Review*, 54, 1 (2017), pp. 1–20.

Pernau, M., 'Introduction', *Contributions to the History of Concepts*, 11, 1 (2016), pp. 24–37

Pernau, M., 'From Morality to Psychology', *Contributions to the History of Concepts*, 11, 1 (2016), pp. 38–57

Pernau, M., 'Fluid Temporalities: Saiyid Ahmad Khan and the Concept of Modernity', *History and Theory*, 58, 4, Islamic Pasts: Histories, Concepts, Interventions (2019), pp. 107–31

Pernau, M., *Emotions and Modernity in Colonial India: From Balance to Fervor* (New Delhi: Oxford University Press, 2020)

Pernau, M., 'Riots, Masculinity, and the Desire for Passions: North India, 1917–1946', *South Asian History and Culture*, 12, 2–3 (2021), pp. 244–60

Pernau, M., 'The Time of the Prophet and the Future of the Community: Temporalities in Nineteenth and Twentieth Century Muslim India', *Time and Society*, 30, 4 (2021), pp. 477–93

Petievich, C., 'Poetry of the Declining Mughals: The *shahr ashob*', *Journal of South Asian Literature*, 25, 1 (1990), pp. 99–110

Petievich, C., 'From Court to Public Sphere: How Urdu Poetry's Language of Romance Shaped the Language of Protest', in A. Blom and S. Tawa Lama-Rewal (eds.), *Emotions, Mobilisations and South Asian Politics* (London: Routledge, 2019)

Petievich, C., and Stille, M., 'Emotions in Performance: Poetry and Preaching', *The Indian Economic and Social History Review*, 54, 1 (2017), pp. 67–102.

Platts, J. T., *A Dictionary of Urdu, Classical Hindi, and English* (London: W. H. Allen and Co., 1884)

Plamper, J., 'The History of Emotions: An Interview with William Reddy, Barbara Rosenwein and Peter Stearns', *History and Theory*, 49, 2 (2010), pp. 237–65

Powell, A., 'History Textbooks and the Transmission of the Pre-colonial Past in NW India in the 1860s and 1870s', in D. Ali (ed.), *Invoking the Past: The Uses of History in South Asia* (Delhi: Oxford University Press, 1999), pp. 91–133

Powell, A., 'Old Books in New Bindings: Ethics and Education in Colonial India', in I. Sengupta and D. Ali (eds.), *Knowledge Production, Pedagogy, and Institutions in Colonial India* (Basingstoke: Palgrave Macmillan, 2011), pp. 199–225

Powell, A., 'Questionable Loyalties: Muslim Government Servants and Rebellion', in C. Bates et al. (eds.), *Mutiny at the Margins: New Perspectives on the Indian Uprising of 1857*, vol. 5: Muslim, Dalit and Subaltern Narratives (New Delhi: Thousand Oaks, 2013), pp. 82–102

Power, D. S., 'Orientalism, Colonialism and Legal History, the Attack on Muslim Family Endowments in Algeria and India', *Comparative Studies in Society and History*, 31, 3 (1989), pp. 535–71

Pritchett, F. W., 'Convention in the Classical Urdu *Ghazal*: The Case of Mir', *Journal of South Asian and Middle Eastern Studies*, 3, 1 (1979), pp. 60–77

Pritchett, F. W., 'The World Upside Down: *shahr ashob* as a Genre', *Annual of Urdu Studies*, 4 (1984), pp. 37–41

Pritchett, F. W., *Marvelous Encounters: Folk Romance in Urdu and Hindi* (New Delhi: Manohar Publications, 1985)

Pritchett, F. W., 'The Dastan Revival: An Overview', *Annual of Urdu Studies*, 7 (1990), pp. 76–82

Pritchett, F. W., *The Romance Tradition in Urdu: Adventures from the Dastan of Amir Hamzah* (New York: University of Columbia Press, 1991)

Pritchett, F. W., *Nets of Awareness: Urdu Poetry and Its Critics* (Berkeley, University of California Press, 1994)

Pritchett, F. W., 'On Ralph Russell's Reading of the Classical Ghazal', *Annual of Urdu Studies*, 11 (1996), pp. 197–201

Priya, R., 'Town Planning, Public Health and Delhi's Urban Poor: A Historical View', in S. Patel and K. Deb (eds.), *Urban Studies* (New Delhi: Oxford University Press, 2006), pp. 223–45

Qadir, A., *The New School of Urdu literature* (Lahore: Punjab Observer, 1898)

Qadir, A., *Famous Urdu Poets and Writers* (Lahore: New Books Society, 1947)

Qureshi, N., *Pan-Islam in British Indian Politics: A Study of the Khilafat movement, 1918–1924* (Leiden: Brill, 1999)

Qureshi, R. B., 'The Urdu Ghazal in Performance', in R. Russell and C. Shackle (eds.), *Urdu and Muslim South Asia: Studies in Honour of Ralph Russell* (London: Oxford University Press, 1989), pp. 175–89

Rahim, A. A., and Rahim, Anita Abdul, 'A Study on Muhammad Iqbal's Framework of Ijtihad', *Islamiyyat: International Journal of Islamic Studies*, 36, 2 (2014), pp. 5–13

Rahman, R., 'Qasbas as Place: A Sense of Belonging and Nostalgia in Colonial India', *Journal of the Economic and Social History of the Orient*, 58, 5 (2015), pp. 668–92

Rahman, R., '"We Can Leave Neither": Mohamed Ali, Islam and Nationalism in Colonial India', in T. Fazal (ed.), *Minority Nationalisms in South Asia* (London: Routledge, 2013), p. 254–68

Ra'is, Q., *Premchand* (New Delhi: Qaumi Council Bara-e Farogh-e Urdu Zuban, 1985)

Raja, M. A., *Constructing Pakistan: Foundational Texts and the Rise of Muslim National Identity, 1857–1947* (Karachi: Oxford University Press, 2010)

Rajagopalan, M., *Building Histories: The Archival and Affective Lives of Five Monuments in Modern Delhi* (Chicago: University of Chicago Press, 2016)

Rajagopalan, M., 'Loss and Longing at the Qila Mu'alla: Āṣār us-Ṣanādīd and the Early Sayyid Ahmad Khan', in R. Rahman and Y. Saikia (eds.), *The Cambridge Companion to Sayyid Ahmad Khan* (Cambridge: Cambridge University Press, 2019), pp. 233–54

Ram, M., *Hali, Makers of Indian Literature* (New Delhi: Sahitya Akademi, 1982)

Ram, M., *Talāmīżah-e Ghālib* (New Delhi: Maktabah Jamia Limited, 1984)

Ramaswamy, S., *The Goddess and the Nation: Mapping Mother India* (Durham: Duke University Press, 2009)

Reddy, W., 'Against Constructionism: The Historical Ethnography of Emotions', *Current Anthropology*, 38, 3 (1997), pp. 327–51

Reddy, W., *The Navigation of Feeling: a Framework for the History of Emotions* (Cambridge: Cambridge University Press, 2001)

Ricoeur, P., *La mémoire, l'histoire, l'oubli* (Paris: Seuil, 2000)

Rizwi, S. M. H., 'shahr āshob', *Nuqoosh*, 102 (1965), pp. 5–45

Robinson, F., *Separatism among Indian Muslims: The Politics of the United Provinces' Muslims, 1860–1923* (London: Cambridge University Press, 1974)

Robinson, F., 'The British Empire and Muslim Identity in South Asia', *Transactions of the Royal Historical Society*, 8 (1998), pp. 271–89

Robinson, F., 'Municipal Government and Muslim Separatism in the United Provinces, 1883 to 1916', *Modern Asian Studies*, 7, 3 (1973), pp. 389–441

Robinson, F., 'Islam and the Impact of Print in South Asia', in F. Robinson (ed.), *Islam and Muslim History in South Asia* (Oxford: Oxford University Press, 2000), pp. 66–104

Robinson, F., 'The Memory of Power, Muslim "Political Importance" and the Muslim League', in F. Robinson (ed.), *The Muslim World in Modern South Asia: Power, Authority, Knowledge* (Albany: Ann Arbor Publishers, 2020), pp. 280–99

Robinson, F., *The Mughal Emperors and the Islamic Dynasties of India, Iran and Central Asia* (London: Thames and Hudson, 2007)

Robinson, F., 'Strategies of Authority in Muslim South Asia in the Nineteenth and Twentieth Centuries', in F. Robinson (ed.), *The Muslim World in Modern South Asia: Power, Authority, Knowledge* (Albany: Ann Arbor Publishers, 2020), pp. 180–203

Robb, M., *Print and the Urdu Public: Muslims, Newspapers, and Urban Life in Colonial India* (New York: Oxford University Press, 2020)

Robreau, Y., *L'honneur et la honte: leur expression dans les romans en prose du Lancelot-Graal (XIIe-XIIIe siècles)* (Genève: Droz, 1981)

Roper, G., 'Aḥmad Fāris al-Shidyāq and the Libraries of Europe and the Ottoman Empire', *Libraries & Culture*, 33, 3 (1998), pp. 233–48

Rosen, G., 'Nostalgia: A "Forgotten" Psychological Disorder', *Psychological Medicine*, 5, 4 (1975), pp. 340–54

Rosenthal, F., *A History of Muslim Historiography* (Leiden: Brill, 1952)

Rosenwein, B., *Emotional Communities in the Early Middle Ages* (Ithaca: Cornell University Press, 2006)

Rosenwein, B., 'Problems and Methods in the History of Emotions', *Passions in Context*, 1, 1 (2010), pp. 1–33
Rosenwein, B., 'Worrying about Emotions in History', *The American Historical Review*, 107, 3 (2002), pp. 821–45
Russell, R., and Islam K., *Three Mughal Poets: Mir, Sauda, Mir Hasan* (London: Allen and Unwin, 1969)
Rustomji, Nerina, *The Garden and the Fire: Heaven and Hell in Islamic Culture* (New York: Columbia University Press, 2009)
Sadiq, M., *A History of Urdu literature* (Delhi: Oxford University Press, 1995)
Safadi, A., 'The "Fallen" Woman in Two Colonial Novels: *Umra'o Jan Ada* and *Bazaar-e Husn/Sevasadan*', *Annual of Urdu Studies*, 24 (2009), pp. 16–53
Safvi, R., *City of My Heart: Four Accounts of Love, Loss and Betrayal in Nineteenth-Century Delhi* (New Delhi: Hachette, 2018)
Santesso, A., *A Careful Longing: The Poetics and Problems of Nostalgia* (Newark: University of Delaware Press, 2006)
Saul, J., *Collective Trauma, Collective Healing: Promoting Community Resilience in the Aftermath of Disaster* (New York: Routledge, 2014)
Scheer, M., 'Are Emotions a Kind of Practice (and Is That What Makes Them Have a History)? A Bourdieuian Approach to Understanding Emotion', *History and Theory*, 51, 2 (2012), pp. 193–220
Schimmel, A., *Classical Urdu Literature from the Beginning to Iqbal* (Wiesbaden: Harrassowitz, 1975)
Schimmel, A., 'The Celestial Garden in Islam', in E. B. MacDougall and R. Ettinghausen (eds.), *The Islamic Garden* (Washington, DC: Dumbarton Oaks, 1976), pp. 13–39
Schimmel, A., *And Muhammad Is His Messenger: The Veneration of the Prophet in Islamic Piety* (Chapel Hill: University of North Carolina Press, 1985)
Schimmel, A., *As through a Veil: Mystical Poetry in Islam* (New York: Columbia University Press, 1982)
Schimmel, A., *Gabriel's Wing: A Study into the Religious Ideas of Sir Muhammad Iqbal* (Lahore: Iqbal Academy Pakistan, 1989)
Schimmel, A., *The Secrets of Creative Love. The Work of Muhammad Iqbal*, Al Furqan Islamic Heritage Foundation, 5th Public lecture, Royal V&A Museum (1998)
Schimmel, A., *The Empire of the Great Mughals: History, Art and Culture* (London: Reaktion, 2004)
Schleyer, M., 'Ghadr-e Dehli ke Afsane', *Annual of Urdu Studies*, 27 (2012), pp. 34–56

Schneider, S., and Weinberg, H., *The Large Group Re-visited: The Herd, Primal Horde, Crowds and Masses* (London: Jessica Kingsley, 2003)

Schoeler, G., and Rahman, M., 'Musammat', in P. Bearman, Th. Bianquis, C. E. Bosworth, et al. (eds.), *Encyclopaedia of Islam* online (Leiden: Brill, first published online 2012)

Segal, H. 'A Psychoanalytical Approach to Aesthetics', in L. Stonebridge and J. Phillips (eds.), *Reading Melanie Klein* (London: Routledge, 1998), pp. 203–22

Sells, M. A., 'Memory', in *Encyclopaedia of the Qur'an online* (Leiden: Brill, 2005)

Sender, H. M., 'The Kashmiri Brahmins (Pandits) up to 1930: Cultural Change in the Cities of North India', unpublished PhD dissertation, University of Wisconsin–Madison (1981)

Sender, H. M., 'Kashmiri Pandits and their Changing Role in the Culture of Delhi', in R. E. Frykenberg (ed.), *Delhi through the Ages: Essays in Urban History, Culture and Society* (Delhi: Oxford University Press, 1986), pp. 316–31

Sengupta, I. (ed.) *Memory, History, and Colonialism: Engaging with Pierre Nora in Colonial and Costcolonial contexts* (London: German Historical Institute, 2009)

Servan-Schreiber, C., 'Littératures orales de l'Inde du Nord. La transmission du répertoire bhojpuri en Inde du Nord: formes orales et livrets de colportage', *Annuaire de l'Ecole pratique des hautes études*, 13 (1999), pp. 214–5

Seth, S., 'Constituting the "Backward but Proud Muslim": Pedagogy, Governmentality and Identity in Colonial India', in M. Hasan and N. Nakazato (eds.), *The Unfinished Agenda: Nation-building in South Asia* (New Delhi: Manohar Publications, 2001), pp. 129–50

Sevea, I. S., *The Political Philosophy of Muhammad Iqbal: Islam and Nationalism in Late Colonial India* (Cambridge: Cambridge University Press, 2012)

Shackle, C., 'Brij Mohan Dattatreya "Kaifi" (1866–1955): A Mirror for India, Translated from the Urdu and Introduced by Christopher Shackle', in S. Nijhawan (ed.), *Nationalism in the Vernacular: Hindi, Urdu, and the Literature of Indian freedom* (Ranikhet: Permanent Black, 2010), pp. 101–11

Shaikh, F., *Community and Consensus: Muslim Representation in Colonial India, 1860–1947* (Cambridge: Cambridge University Press, 1989)

Shaikh, F., *Making Sense of Pakistan* (London: Oxford University Press, 2009)

Sharma, S., 'The City of Beauties in Indo-Persia Poetic Landscape', *Comparative Studies in South Asia, Africa and the Middle East*, 24, 2 (2004), pp. 73–81

Sharma, S., '"The Errant Eye" and Mughal Pastoral Poetry', paper given at the CSAS seminar, SOAS (14 March 2013)

Siddique, S., 'Remembering the Revolt of 1857: Contrapuntal Formations in Indian Literature and History', unpublished PhD thesis, SOAS (2012)

Siddiqui, I. H., 'Sir Syed Ahmad Khan's Approach to History and History Writing', in *Sir Syed Centenary Papers: In Commemoration of the 100th Death Anniversary of Sir Syed Ahmad Khan* (Karachi: Sir Syed University Press, 1998), pp. 113–24

Siddiqui, M. A., *Yādgār-e Amjad* (Hyderabad: Matba Ibrahimiya, 1961)

Singh, G., *Deportation of Lala Lajpat Rai and Sardar Ajit Singh: History of the Freedom Movement in Punjab*, vol. 4 (Patiala: Punjab University, 1978)

Singh, N. G., 'Dehliviyat: The Making and Un-making of Delhi's Indo-Muslim Urban Culture, c. 1750–1900', unpublished PhD dissertation, Princeton University (2014)

Singh, S., *Freedom Movement in Delhi (1859–1919)* (New Delhi: Associated Publishing House, 1972)

Smith, J., and Haddad, Y., *Islamic Understanding of Death and Resurrection* (Oxford: Oxford University Press, 2002)

Sohal, S. S., 'Patterns of Political Mobilization in the Colonial Punjab (1901–1907)', *Proceedings of the Indian History Congress*, 50 (1989), pp. 462–73

Stark, U., *An Empire of Books: The Naval Kishore Press and the Diffusion of the Printed Word in Colonial India, 1858–1895* (Ranikhet: Permanent Black, 2007)

Stearns, P., *American Cool: Constructing a Twentieth-Century Emotional Style* (New York: New York University Press, 1994)

Steele, L., 'Hali and His Muqaddamah: The Creation of a Literary Attitude in Nineteenth Century India', *Annual of Urdu Studies*, 1 (1981), pp. 1–45

Stephens, J., 'The Politics of Muslim Rage: Secular Law and Religious Sentiment in Late Colonial India', *History Workshop Journal*, 77, 1 (2014), pp. 45–64

Stille, M., 'Between the Numinous and the Melodramatic: Poetics of Heightened Feelings in Bengali Islamic Sermons', in S. Dorpmüller et al. (eds.), *Religion and Aesthetic Experience: Drama – Sermons – Literature* (Heidelberg: Heidelberg University Publishing, 2018), pp. 125–48

Stout, L. C., 'The Hindustani Kayasthas: The Kayastha Pathshala, and the Kayastha Conference, 1873–1914', unpublished PhD dissertation, University of California (1975)

Stronach, D., 'The Garden as a Political Statement: Some Case Studies from the Near East in the First Millenium BC', *Bulletin of the Asia Institute, 4*, in honor of Richard Nelson Frye: Aspects of Iranian Culture (1990), pp. 171–80

Subtelny, M., *Le monde est un jardin: aspects de l'histoire culturelle de l'Iran médiéval, Studia Iranica 28* (Paris: Association pour l'avancement des études iraniennes, 2002)

Subtelny, M., 'A Late Medieval Persian *Summa* on Ethics: Kashifi's *Akhlaq-i Muhsini*', *Iranian Studies*, 36, 4 (2003), pp. 601–14
Sud, K. N., *Iqbal and His Poems (A Reappraisal)* (Delhi: Sterling Publishers, 1969)
Surdykowska, S., 'The Idea of Sadness: The Richness of Persian Experiences and Expressions', *Rocznik Orientalistyczny*, 67, 2 (2014), pp. 68–80
Taneja, A. V., *Jinnealogy: Time, Islam, and Ecological Thought in the Medieval Ruins of Delhi* (Stanford: Stanford University Press, 2017)
Thapar, R., 'Somnatha: Narratives of History', in R. Thapar, *Narratives and the Making of History: Two Lectures* (Delhi: Oxford University Press, 2000)
Tignol, E., 'A Note on the Origins of Hali's *Musaddas-e Madd-o Jazr-e Islam*', *Journal of the Royal Asiatic Society*, 26, 4 (2016), pp. 585–9
Tignol, E., 'Nostalgia and the City: Urdu *shahr āshob* Poetry in the Aftermath of 1857', *Journal of the Royal Asiatic Society*, 27, 4 (2017), pp. 559–73
Tignol, E., 'Genealogy, Authority and Muslim Political Representation in British India' *Journal of the Royal Asiatic Society*, 30, 3 (2020), pp. 449–65.
Tignol, E., 'The Language of Shame: A Study of Emotion in an Early-Twentieth Century Urdu Children's Periodical (*Phūl*)', *South Asian History and Culture*, 12, 2–3 (2021), pp. 222–43
Traïni, C., 'Des sentiments aux émotions (et vice-versa). Comment devient-on militant de la cause animale?', *Revue française de science politique*, 60, 2 (2010), pp. 335–58
Trivedi, M., 'A Genre of Composite Creativity: Marsiya and Its Performance in Awadh', in M. Hasan and A. Roy (eds.), *Living Together Separately: Cultural India in History and Politics* (New Delhi: Oxford University Press, 2005), pp. 195–221
Turki, M., 'Erinnerung und Identität. Ansätze zum Verstehen der gegenwärtigen Krise im arabish-islamischen Denken', in A. L. Hartmann (ed.), *Geschichte und Erinnerung im Islam* (Göttingen: Vandenhoeck and Ruprecht, 2004), pp. 31–49
Uçan, C., 'Breaking the News: A Case Study on Nineteenth Century Journalism and Selim Faris', *Middle Eastern Studies*, 57, 4 (2021), pp. 657–67
Umar, M., *National Movement in India: The Role of Hasrat Mohani* (Jaipur: Shree Niwas Publication, 2005)
Umer, Z., 'Maulana Shibli Numani: A Study of Islamic Modernism and Romanticism in India, 1882–1914', unpublished PhD dissertation, University of Oxford (1969)
Vahid, S. A., 'Iqbal and His Critics', *Iqbal Review*, 5, 1 (1964), pp. 4–24
Vanelli, N., 'Al-Jawaib: Exploring an Arabic Newspaper in Nineteenth-Century Istanbul', undergraduate dissertation, Brown University (2017)
Von Scheve, C., 'Collective Emotions in Rituals: Elicitation, Transmission and a "Matthew-effect"', in A. Michaels and C. Wulf (eds.), *Emotions in Rituals and Performances* (New Delhi: Routledge, 2012), pp. 55–77

Volkan, V. D., 'The Next Chapter: Consequences of Societal Trauma', in P. Gobodo-Madikizela and C. van der Merve (eds.), *Memory, Narrative and Forgiveness: Perspectives of the Unfinished Journeys of the Past* (Cambridge: Cambridge Scholars Publishers, 2009), pp. 1–26

Volkan, V. D., 'Not Letting Go: From Individual Perennial Mourners to Societies with Entitlement Ideologies', in L. Fiorini, T. Bokanowski, S. Lewkowicz, and E. Person (eds.), *On Freud's 'mourning and melancholia'* (London: Karnac Books, 2009), pp. 90–109

Wald, E., 'From *Begums* and *Bibis* to Abandoned Females and Idle Women: Sexual Relationships, Venereal Disease and the Redefinition of Prostitution in Early Nineteenth-century India', *The Indian Economic and Social History Review*, 46, 1 (2009), pp. 5–25

Walder, D., *Postcolonial Nostalgias: Writing, Representation, and Memory* (New York: Routledge, 2011)

Wansbrough, J., *The Sectarian Milieu: Content and Composition of Islamic Salvation History* (New York: Prometheus Books, 2006)

Waraich, S., 'A City Besieged and a Love Lamented: Representations of Delhi's *Qila-i Mualla* ("Exalted Fortress") in the Eighteenth Century', *South Asian Studies*, 35, 1 (2019), pp. 145–64

Wasti, S. R., 'Dr Muhammad Iqbal from Nationalism to Universalism', *Iqbal Review*, 19, 1 (1978), pp. 35–45

White, H., 'New Historicism: A Comment', in H. A. Veeser, *The New Historicism* (London: Routledge, 1989)

Williams, R. D., 'Hindustani Music between Awadh and Bengal, c. 1758–1905', unpublished PhD thesis, King's College London (2014)

Wilson, G.A., 'Community Resilience and Social Memory', *Environmental Values*, 24, 2 (2015), pp. 227–57

Wright, T., 'The Changing Role of the *sādāt* in India and Pakistan', *Oriente Moderno*, 79, 2 (1999), pp. 649–59

Yamame, S., 'Lamentation Dedicated to the Declining Capital: Urdu Poetry on Delhi during the Late Mughal Period', *Journal of the Japanese Association for South Asian Studies*, 12 (2000), pp. 50–72

Zaidi, S. A., *Making a Muslim: Reading Publics and Contesting Identities in Nineteenth-Century North India* (Cambridge: Cambridge University Press, 2021)

Zaidi, S. M. A., *Muṯālaʿh-e Dāġh* (Lucknow: Kitab Nagar, 1974)

Zaman, F., 'Beyond Nostalgia: Time and place in Indian Muslim Politics', *Journal of the Royal Asiatic Society*, 27, 4 (2017), pp. 627–47

Zulfiqar, G. H., *Iqbāl: Ek muṯālaʿh* (Lahore: Bazm-e Iqbal, 1997)

Zumbroich, T. J., '"The *Missi*-stained Finger-tip of the Fair": A Cultural History of Teeth and Gum Blackening in South Asia', *eJournal of Indian Medicine*, 8, 1 (2015), pp. 1–32

Index